HAMMER

VOLUME 2

FIGHT FOR THE OCEAN KINGDOM

STORY AND ART BY *JEYODIN*

ROCKPORT

CONTENTS

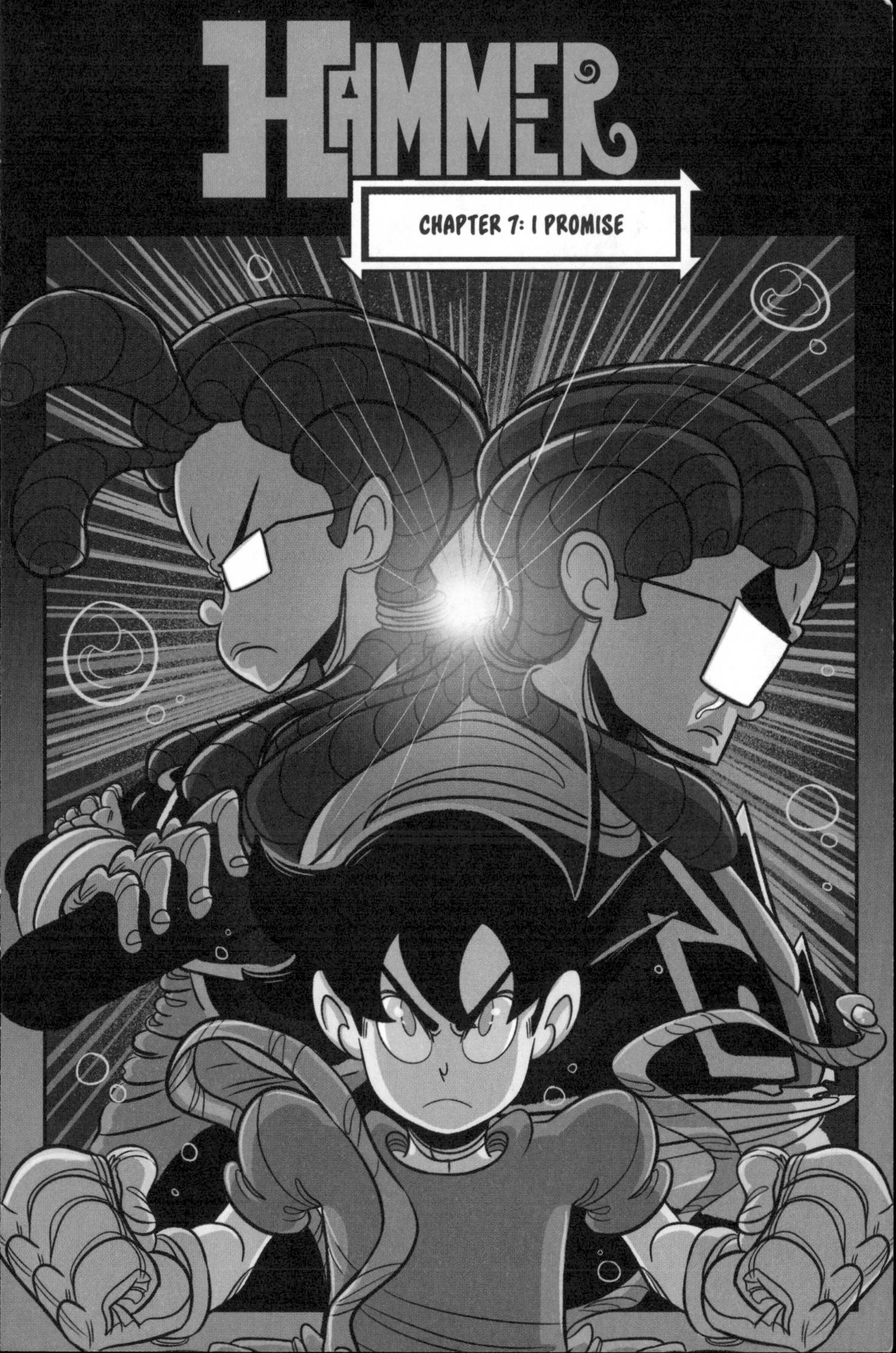
HAMMER
CHAPTER 7: I PROMISE

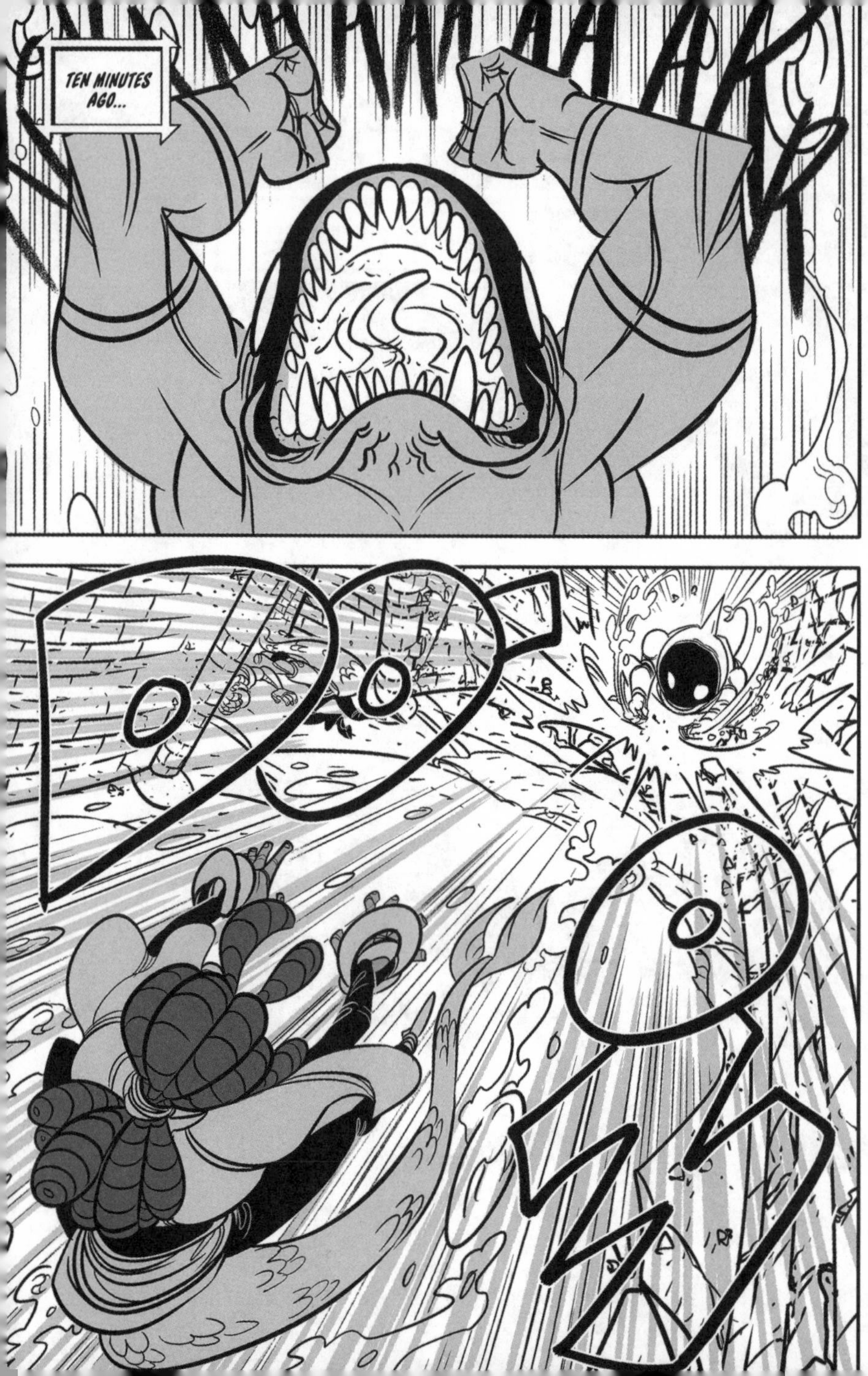
TEN MINUTES AGO...

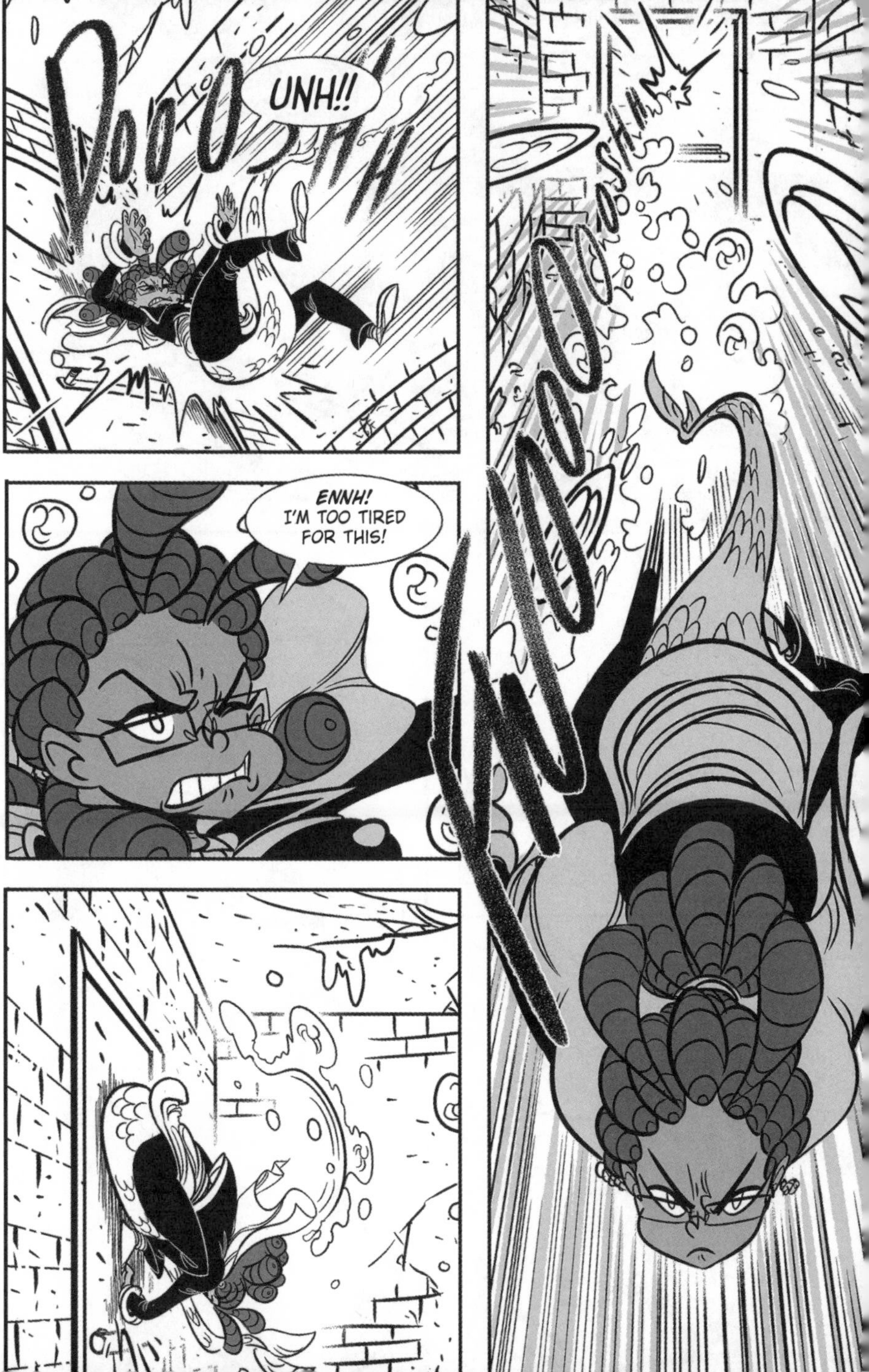
UNH!!
ENNH! I'M TOO TIRED FOR THIS!

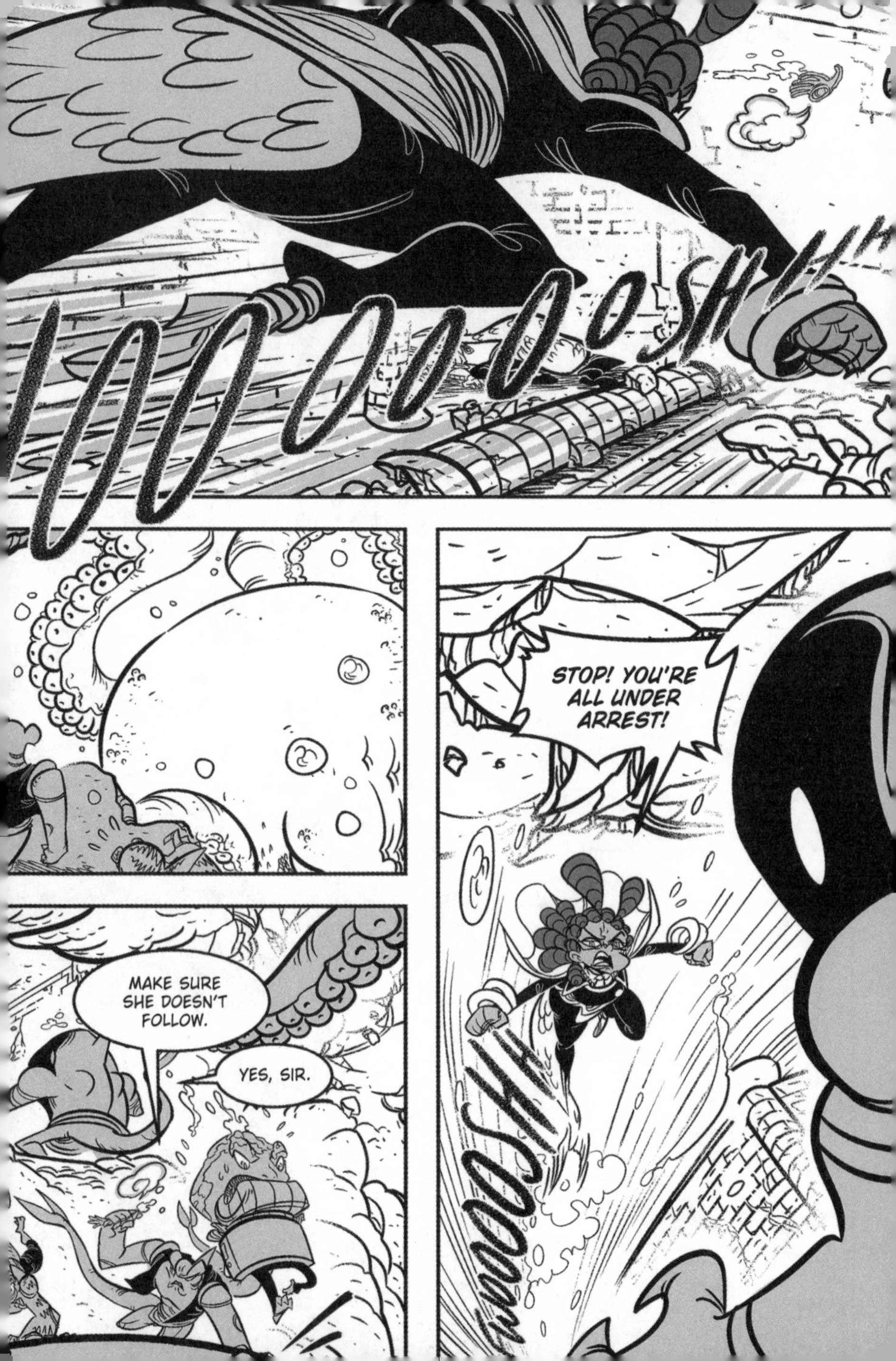
WHOOOOOOOSH!!
MAKE SURE SHE DOESN'T FOLLOW.
YES, SIR.
STOP! YOU'RE ALL UNDER ARREST!
WHOOOOOOSHH

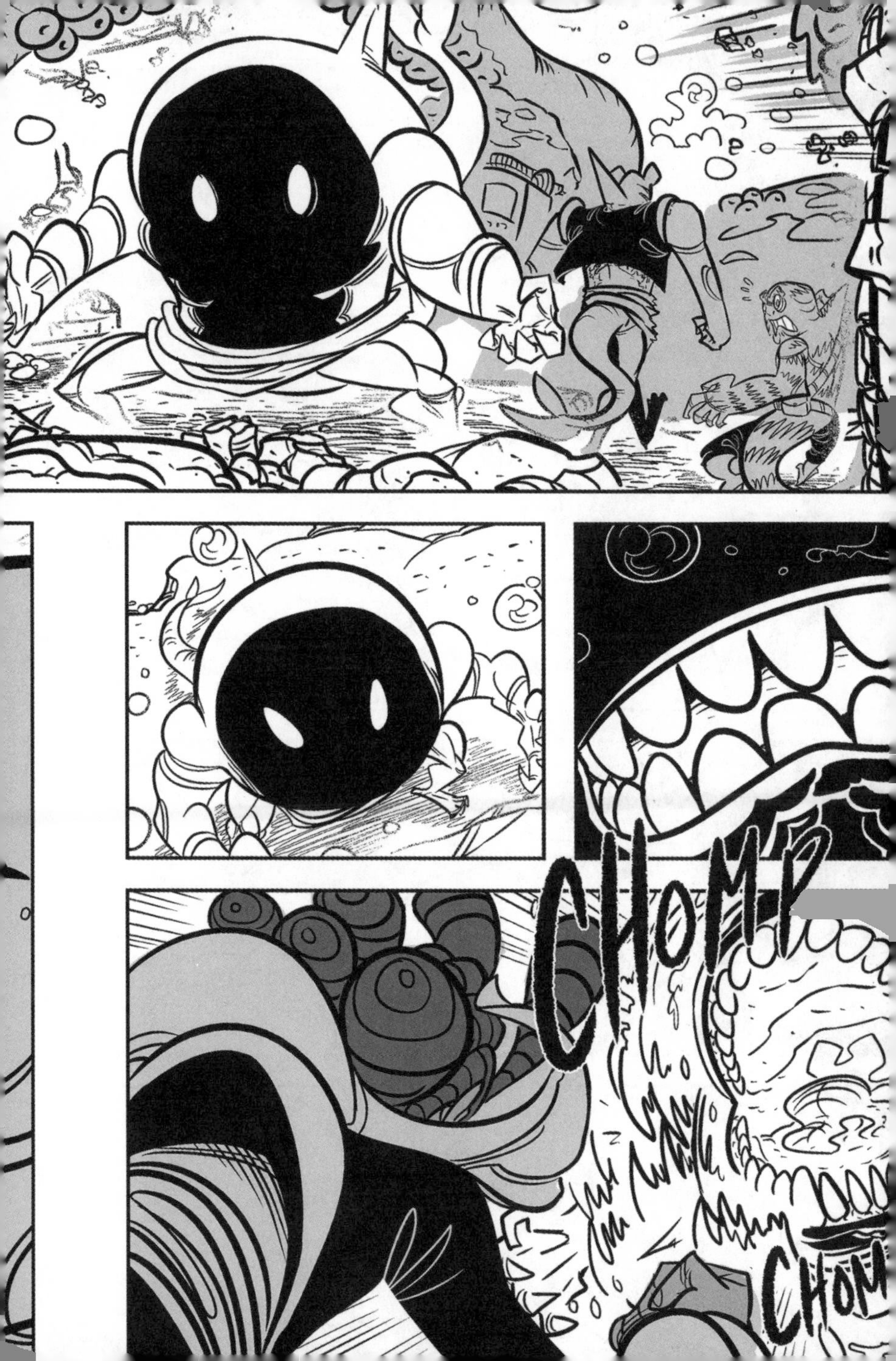

CHOMP
CHOM

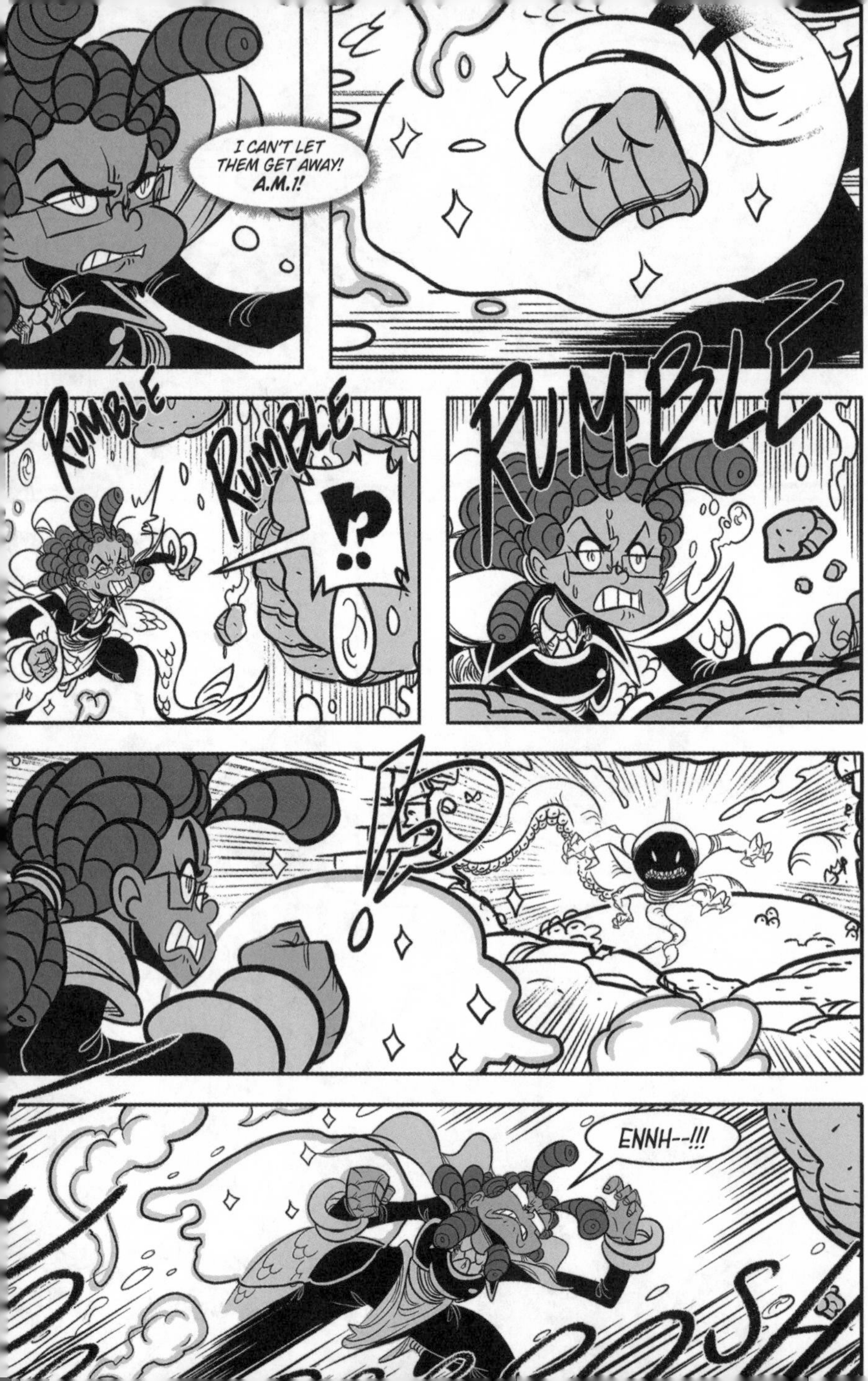
I CAN'T LET THEM GET AWAY! A.M.1!
RUMBLE
RUMBLE
!?
RUMBLE
ENNH--!!!

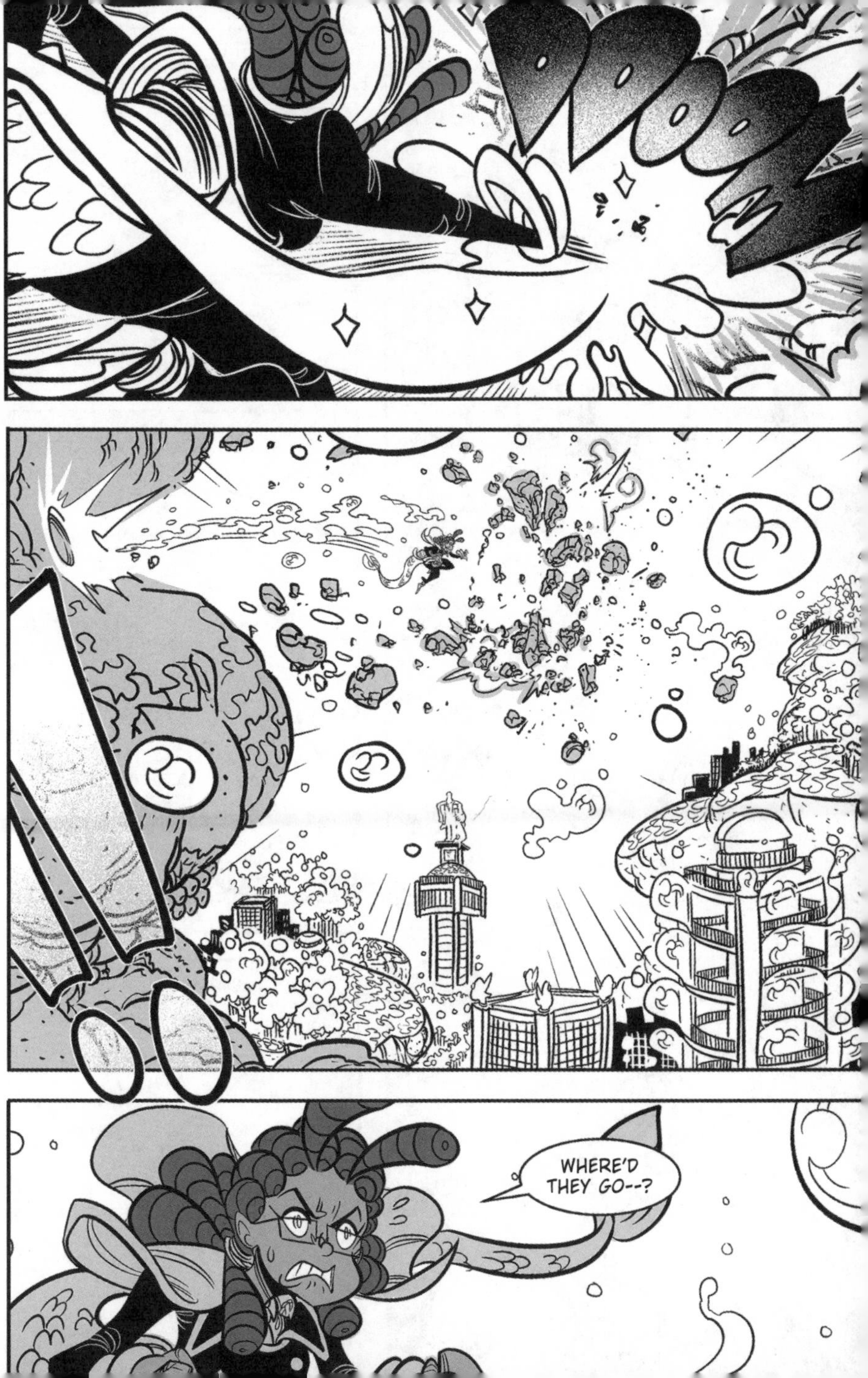
DOOOM
WHERE'D THEY GO--?

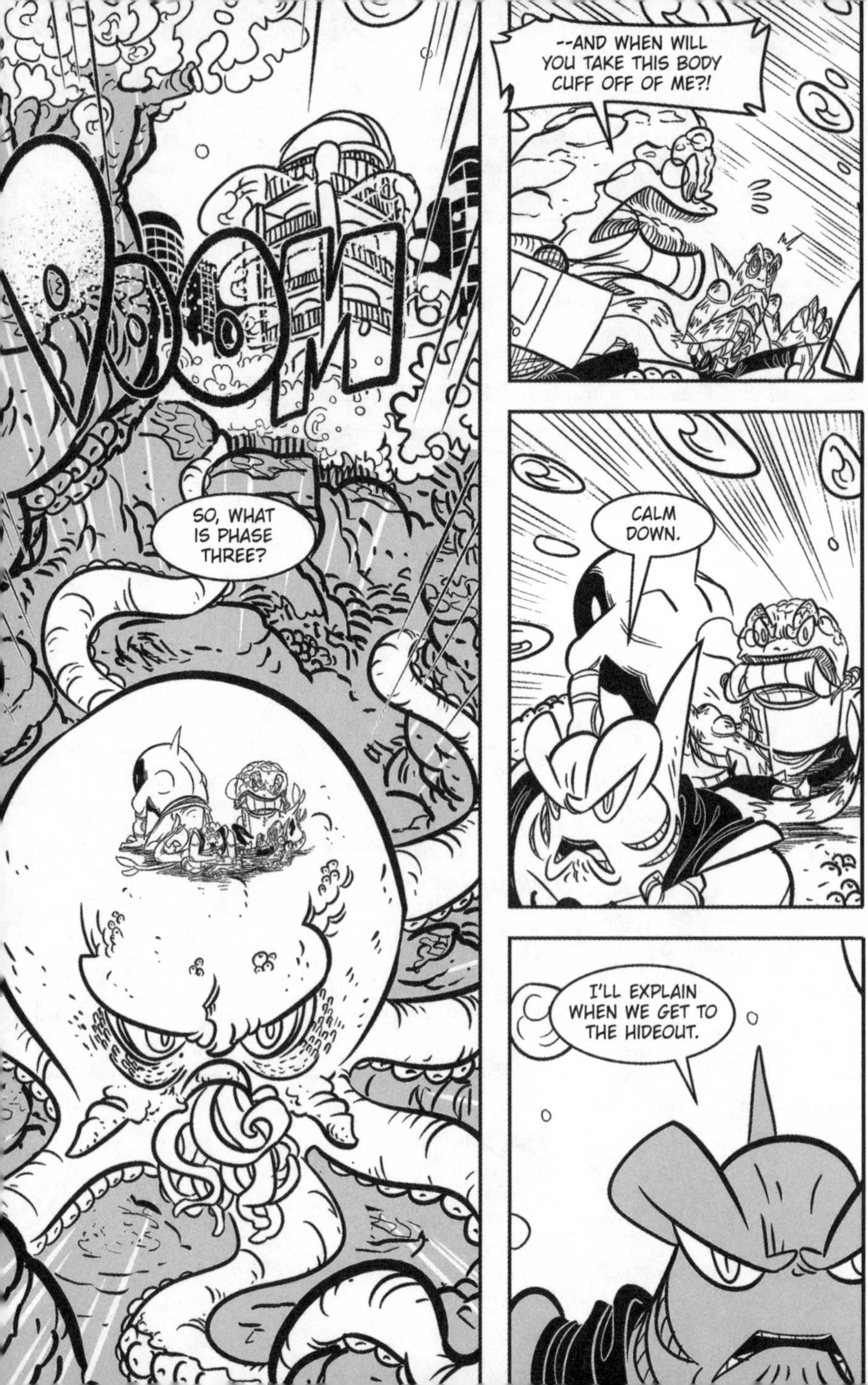
DOOOM
SO, WHAT IS PHASE THREE?
--AND WHEN WILL YOU TAKE THIS BODY CUFF OFF OF ME?!
CALM DOWN.
I'LL EXPLAIN WHEN WE GET TO THE HIDEOUT.

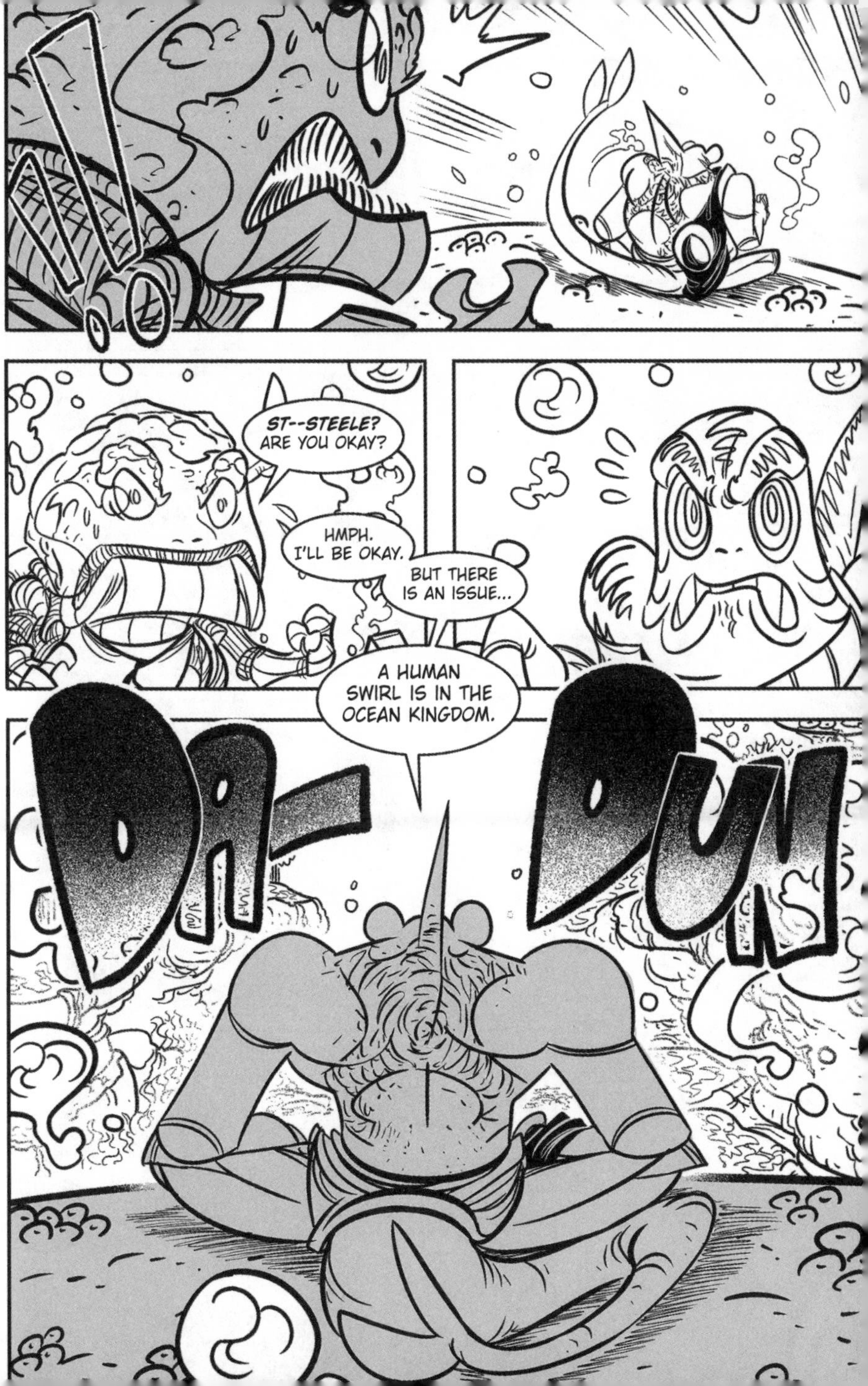
!
ST--STEELE? ARE YOU OKAY?
HMPH. I'LL BE OKAY.
BUT THERE IS AN ISSUE...
A HUMAN SWIRL IS IN THE OCEAN KINGDOM.
DA-
DUN

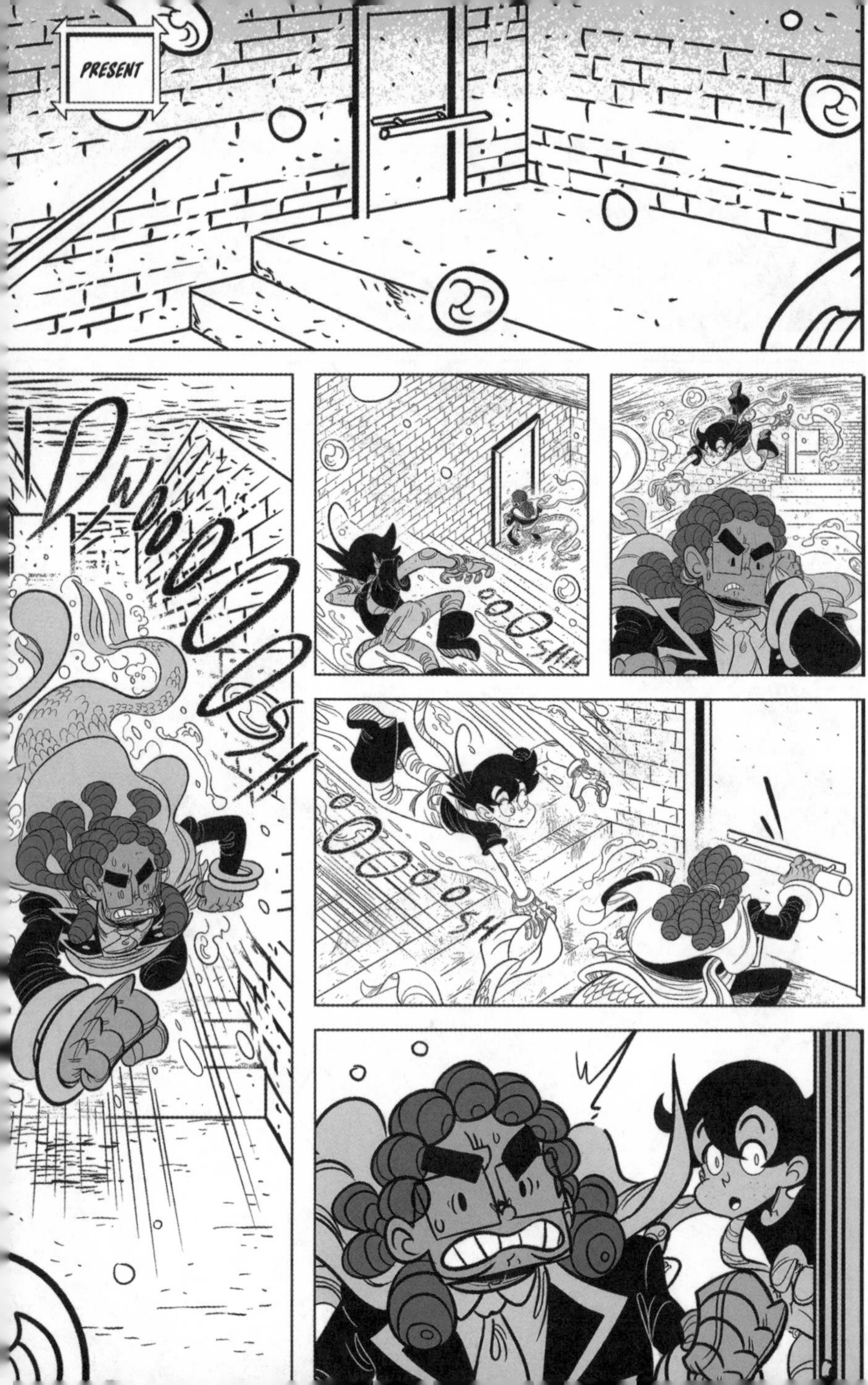

PRESENT
DWOOOOOOOSH
OOOOSHH
OOOOOOOOOSH

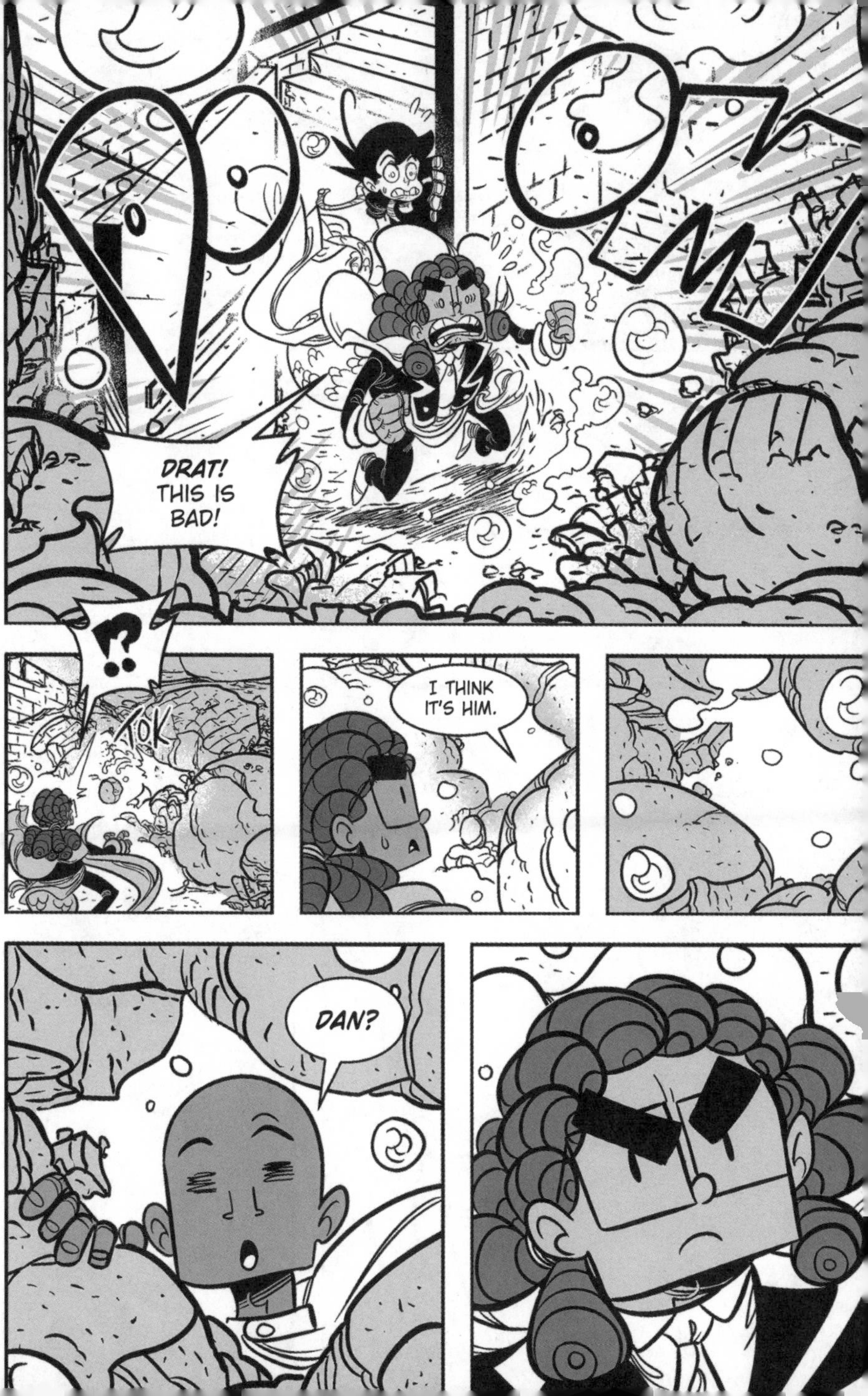
DRAT! THIS IS BAD!
!?
TOK
I THINK IT'S HIM.
DAN?

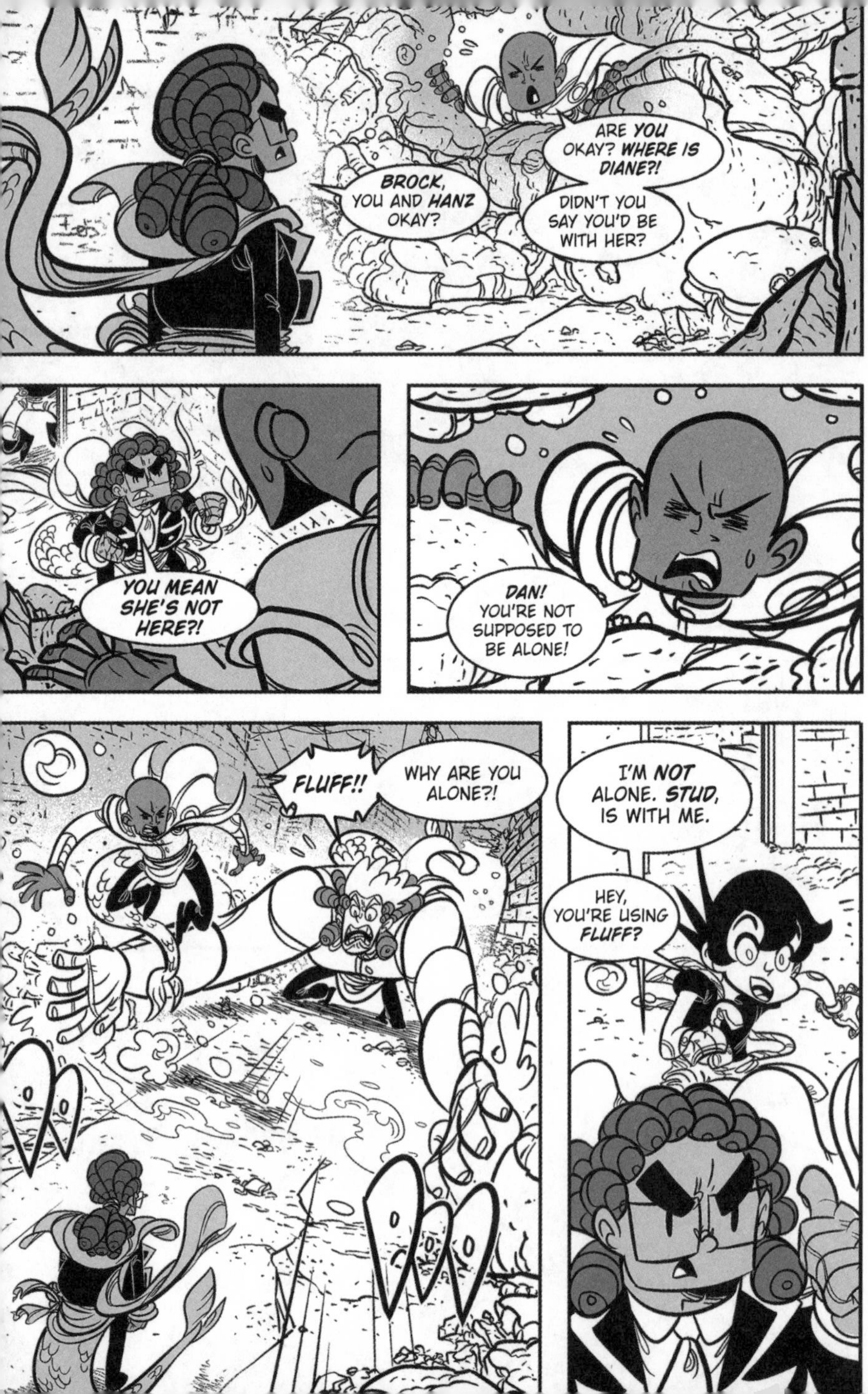
BROCK, YOU AND HANZ OKAY?
ARE YOU OKAY? WHERE IS DIANE?!
DIDN'T YOU SAY YOU'D BE WITH HER?
YOU MEAN SHE'S NOT HERE?!
DAN! YOU'RE NOT SUPPOSED TO BE ALONE!
FLUFF!!
WHY ARE YOU ALONE?!
I'M NOT ALONE. STUD, IS WITH ME.
HEY, YOU'RE USING FLUFF?

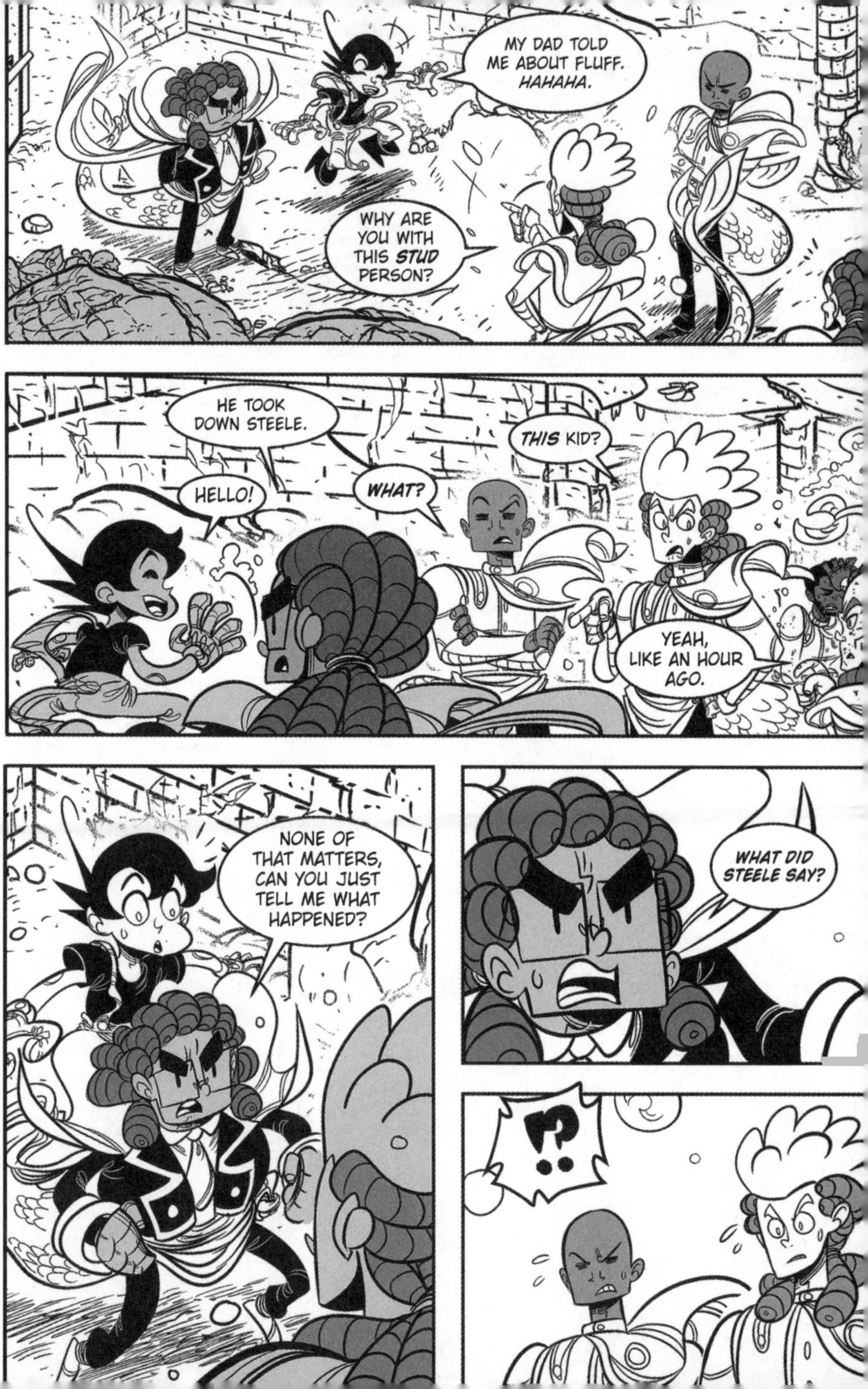
MY DAD TOLD ME ABOUT FLUFF. HAHAHA.
WHY ARE YOU WITH THIS STUD PERSON?
HE TOOK DOWN STEELE.
HELLO!
WHAT?
THIS KID?
YEAH, LIKE AN HOUR AGO.
NONE OF THAT MATTERS, CAN YOU JUST TELL ME WHAT HAPPENED?
WHAT DID STEELE SAY?
?!!

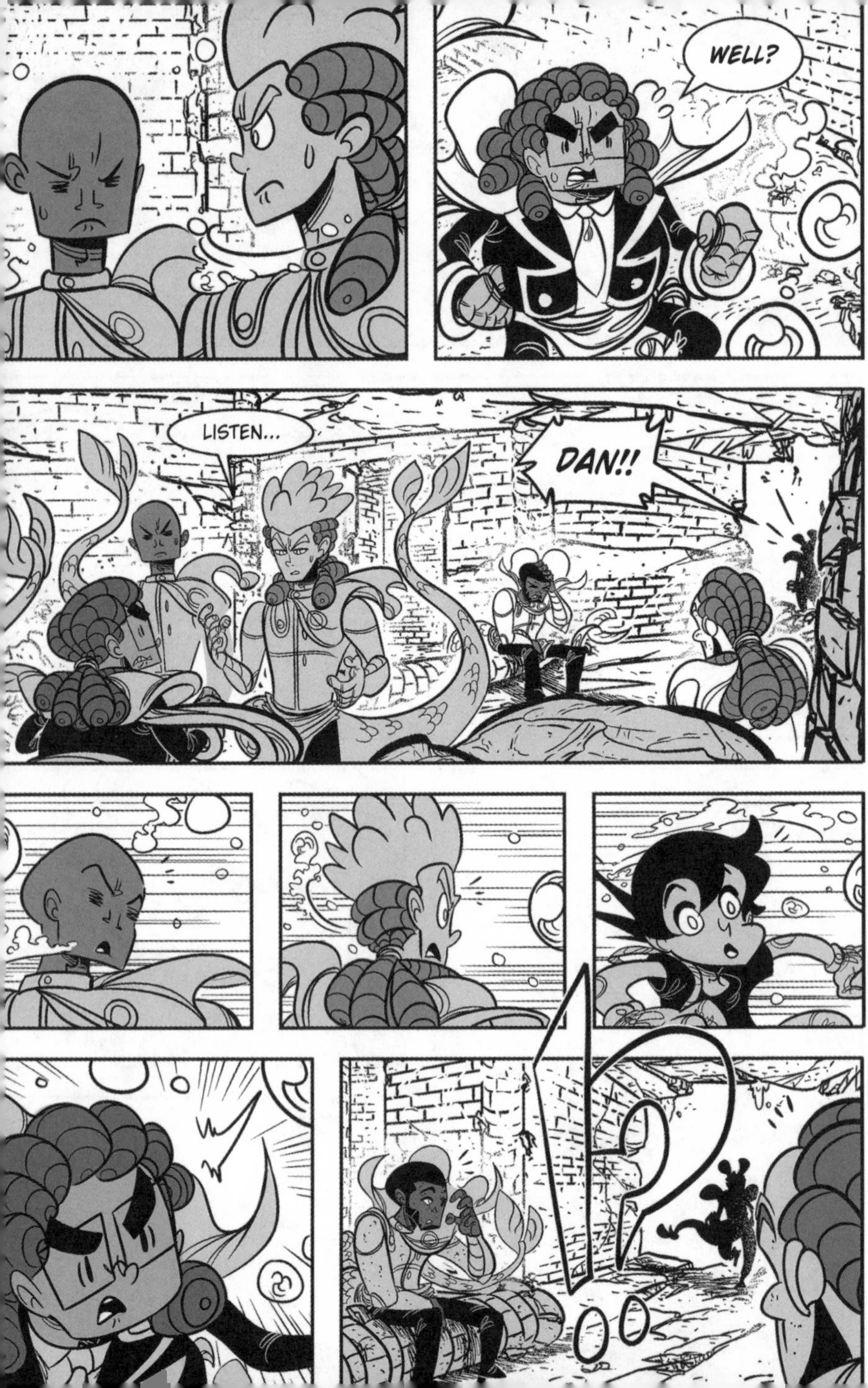
WELL?
LISTEN...
DAN!!

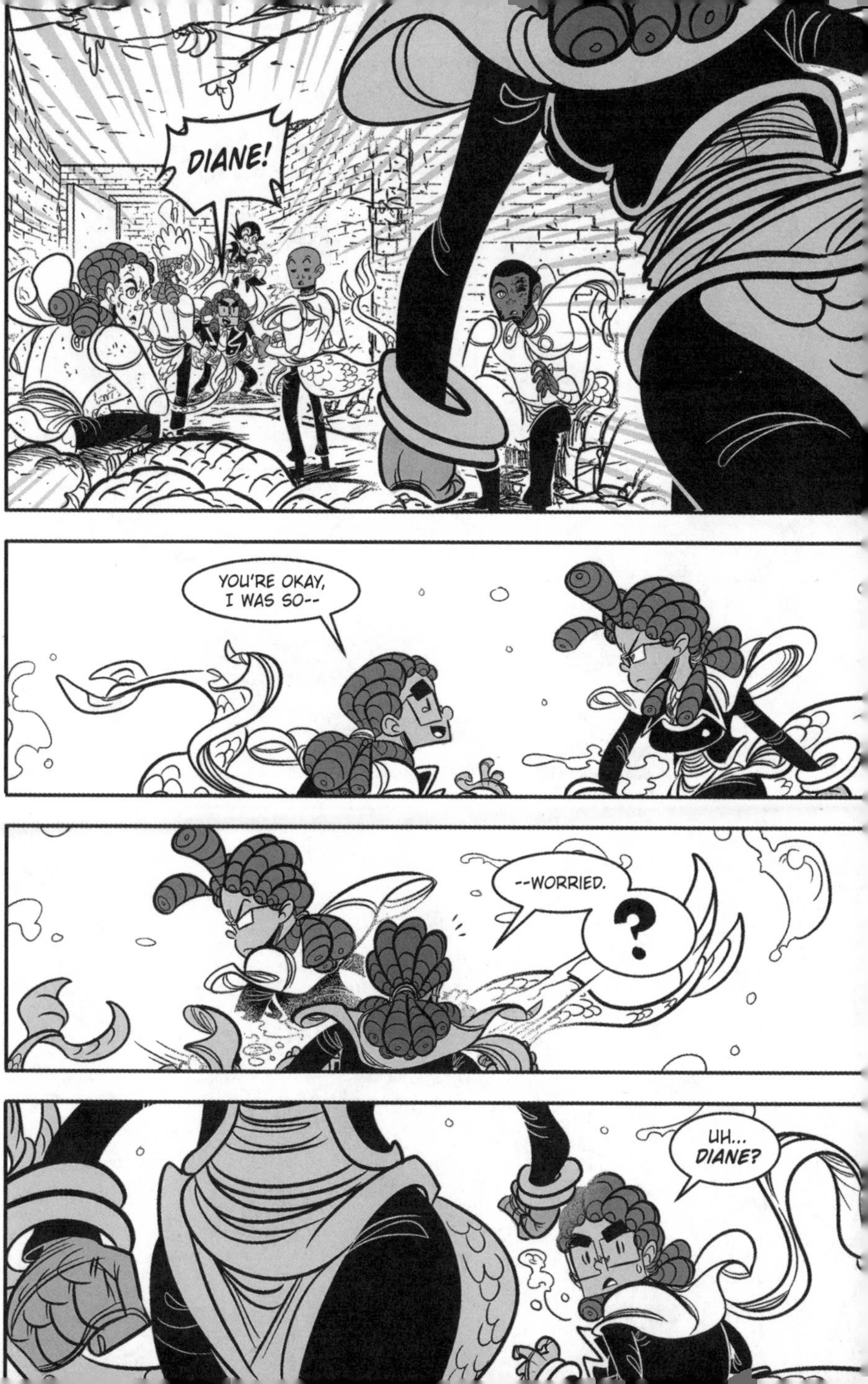
DIANE!
YOU'RE OKAY, I WAS SO--
--WORRIED.
?
UH... DIANE?

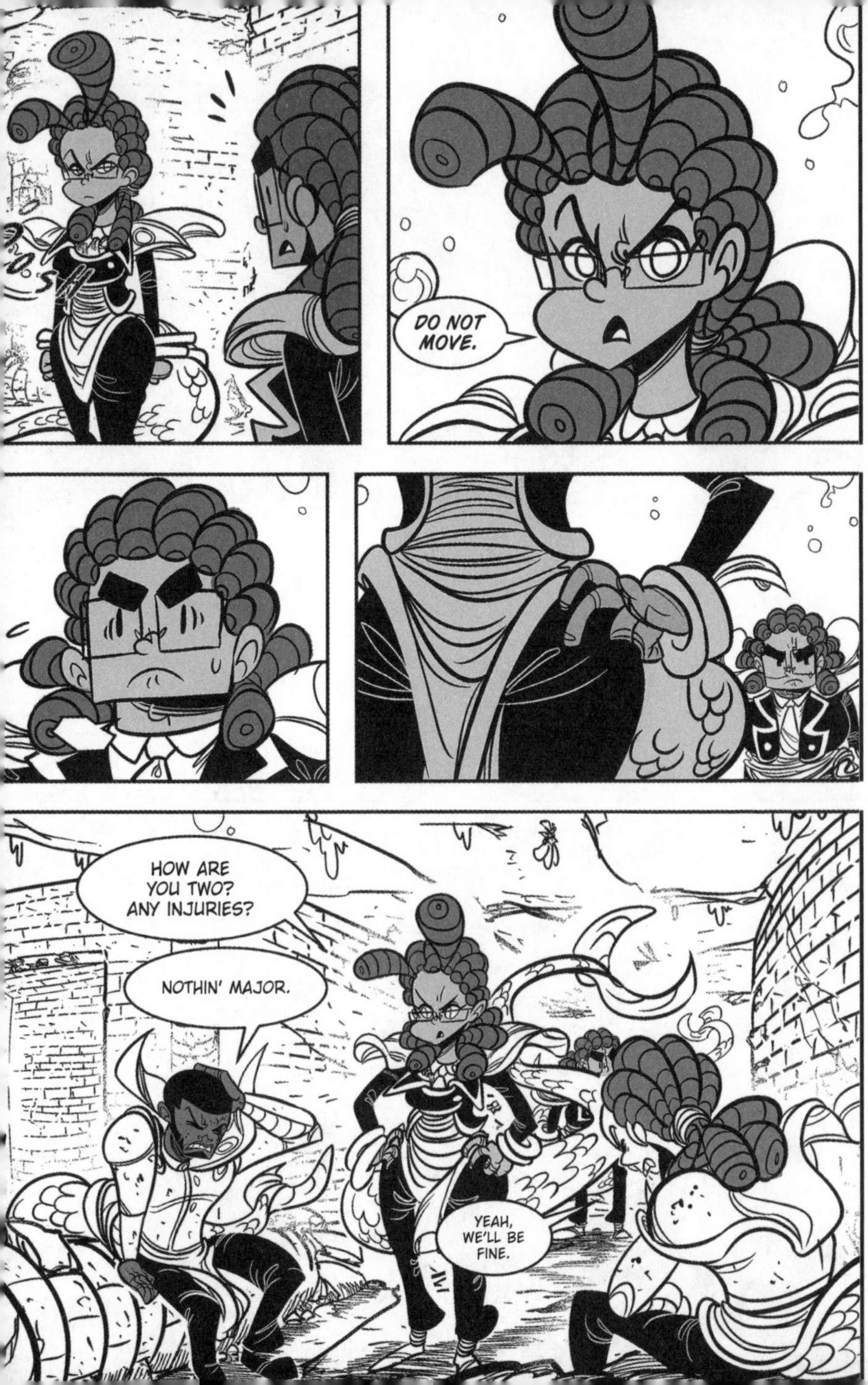
DO NOT MOVE.
HOW ARE YOU TWO? ANY INJURIES?
NOTHIN' MAJOR.
YEAH, WE'LL BE FINE.

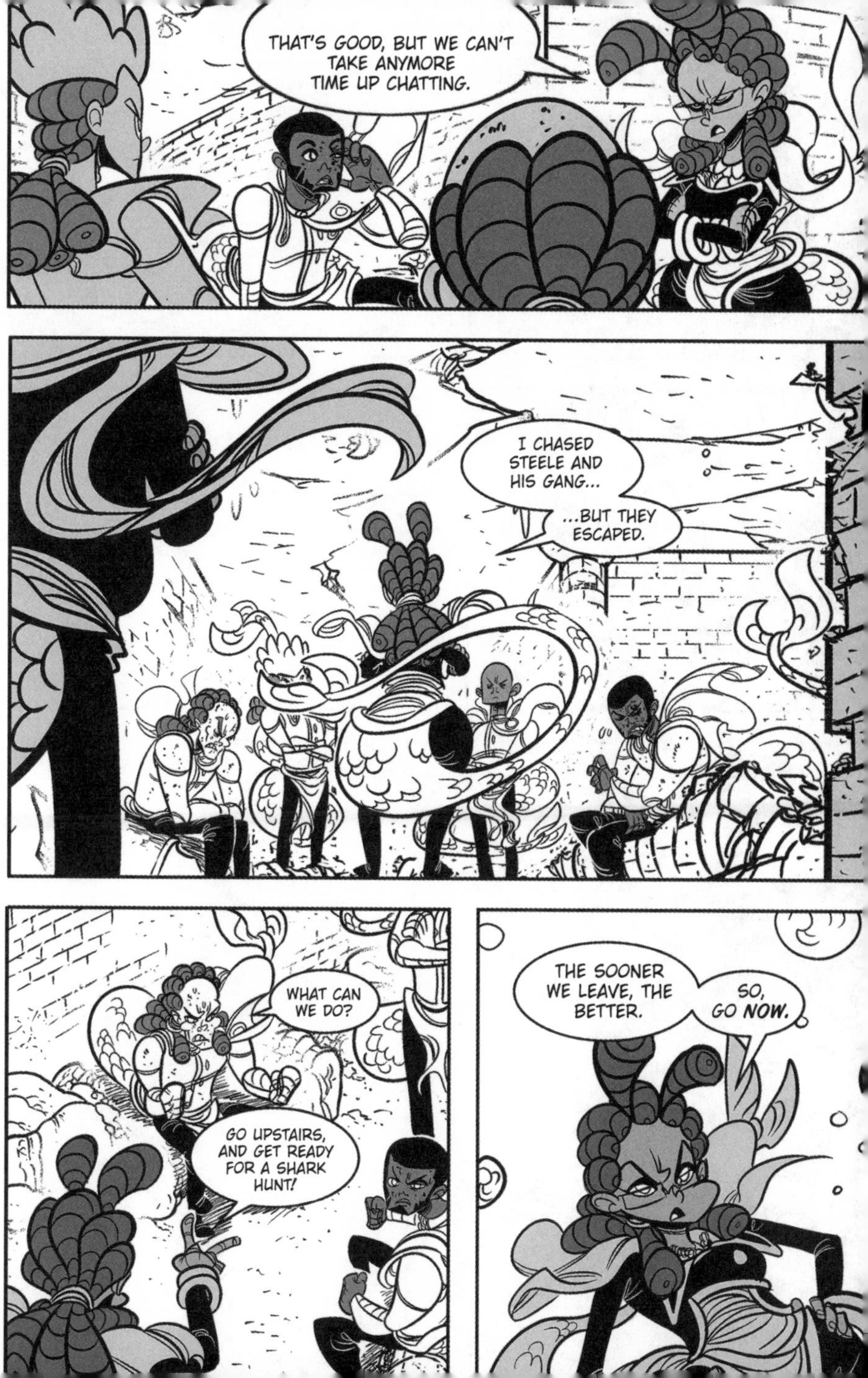
THAT'S GOOD, BUT WE CAN'T TAKE ANYMORE TIME UP CHATTING.
I CHASED STEELE AND HIS GANG...
...BUT THEY ESCAPED.
WHAT CAN WE DO?
GO UPSTAIRS, AND GET READY FOR A SHARK HUNT!
THE SOONER WE LEAVE, THE BETTER.
SO, GO **NOW.**

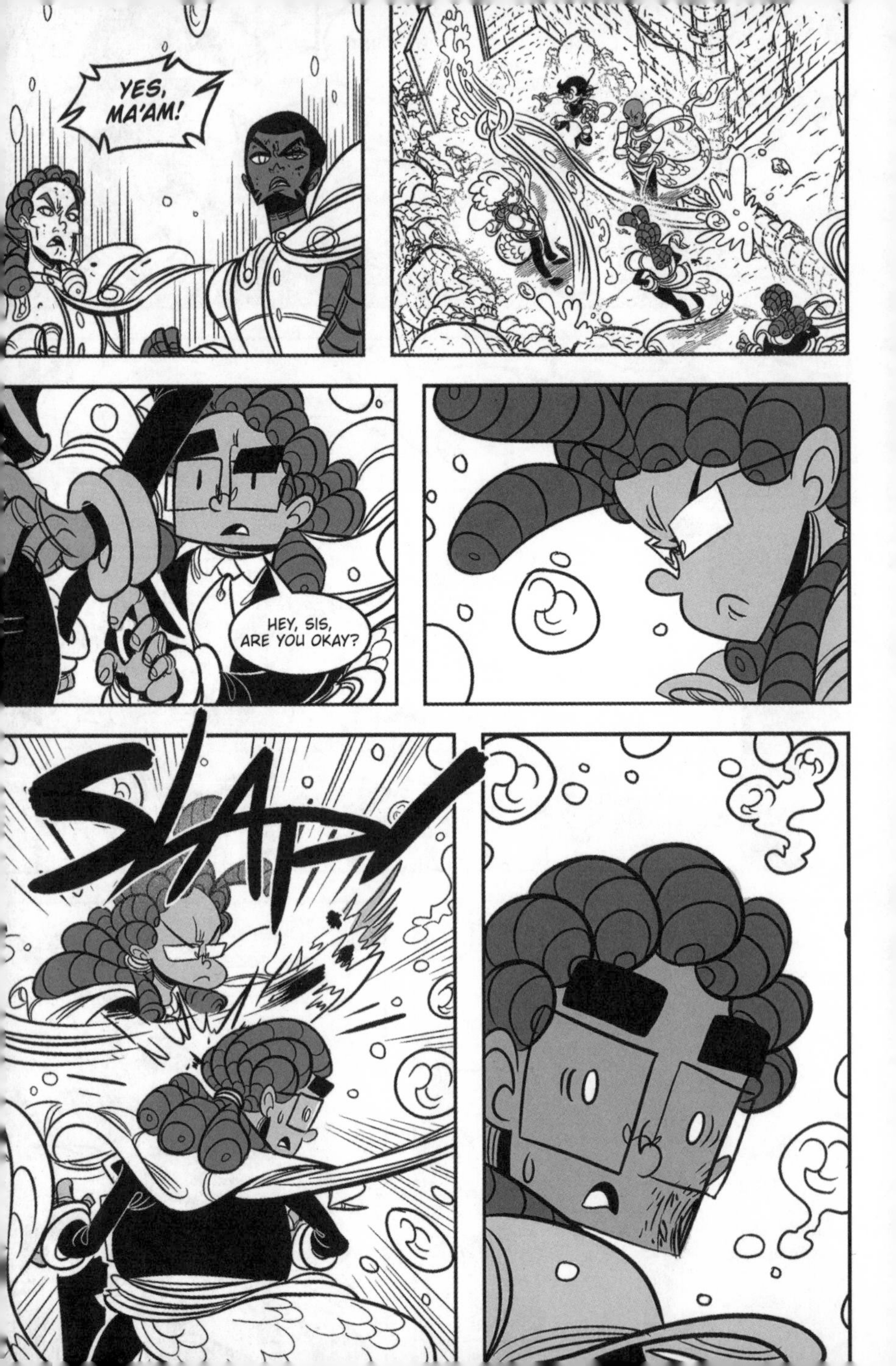
YES, MA'AM!
HEY, SIS, ARE YOU OKAY?
SLAP!

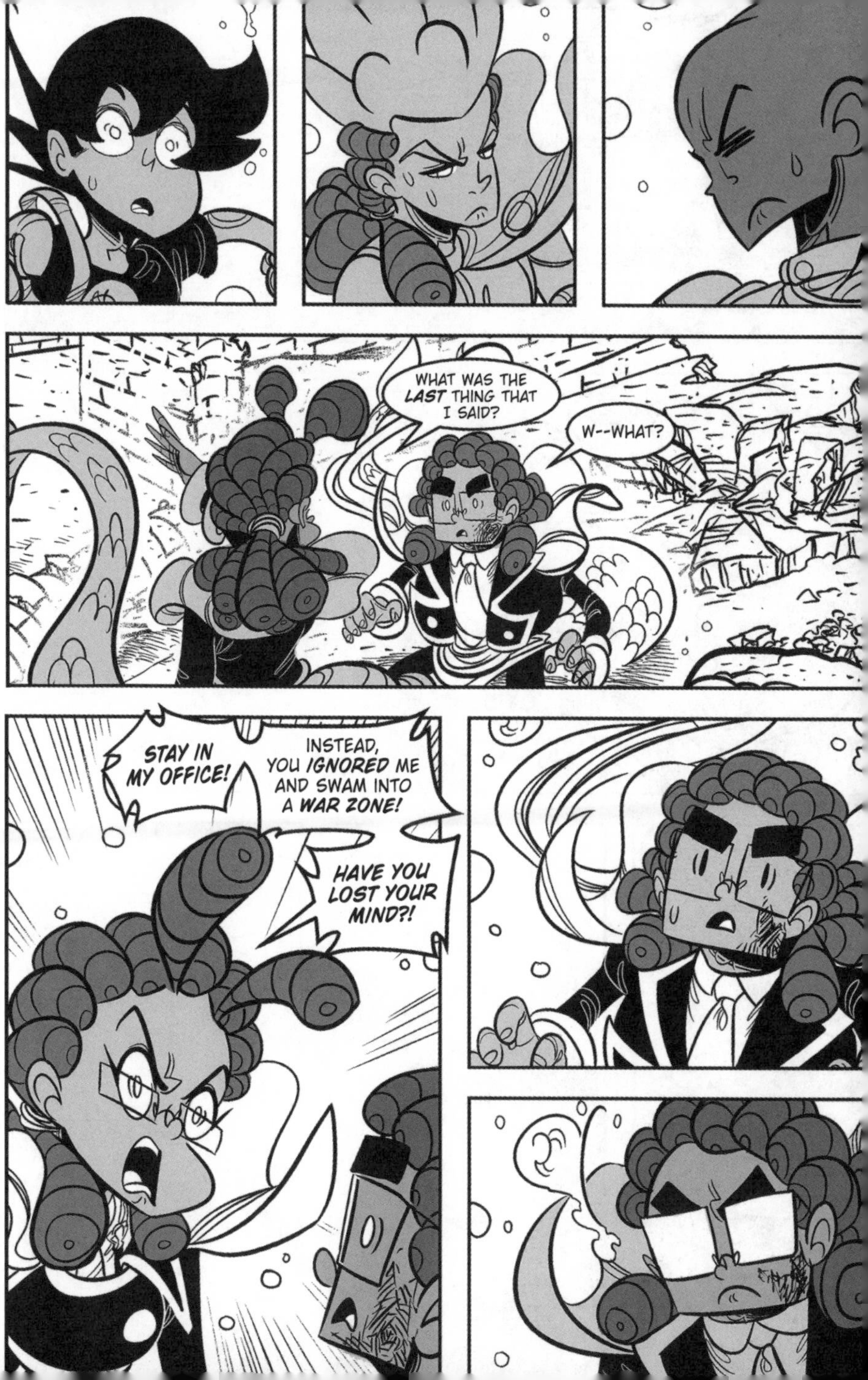
WHAT WAS THE LAST THING THAT I SAID?
W--WHAT?
STAY IN MY OFFICE!
INSTEAD, YOU IGNORED ME AND SWAM INTO A WAR ZONE!
HAVE YOU LOST YOUR MIND?!

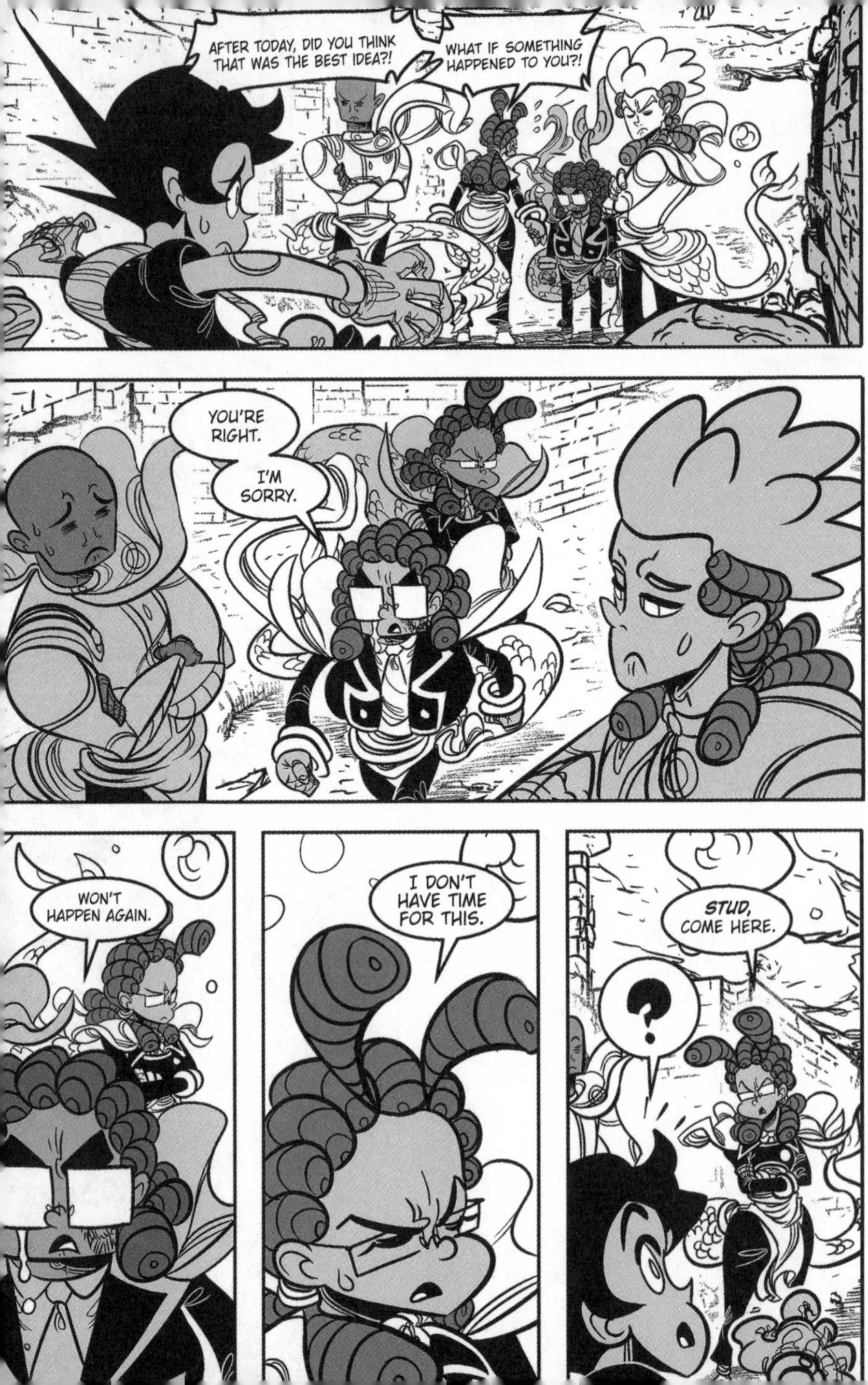
AFTER TODAY, DID YOU THINK THAT WAS THE BEST IDEA?!
WHAT IF SOMETHING HAPPENED TO YOU?!
YOU'RE RIGHT.
I'M SORRY.
WON'T HAPPEN AGAIN.
I DON'T HAVE TIME FOR THIS.
?
STUD, COME HERE.

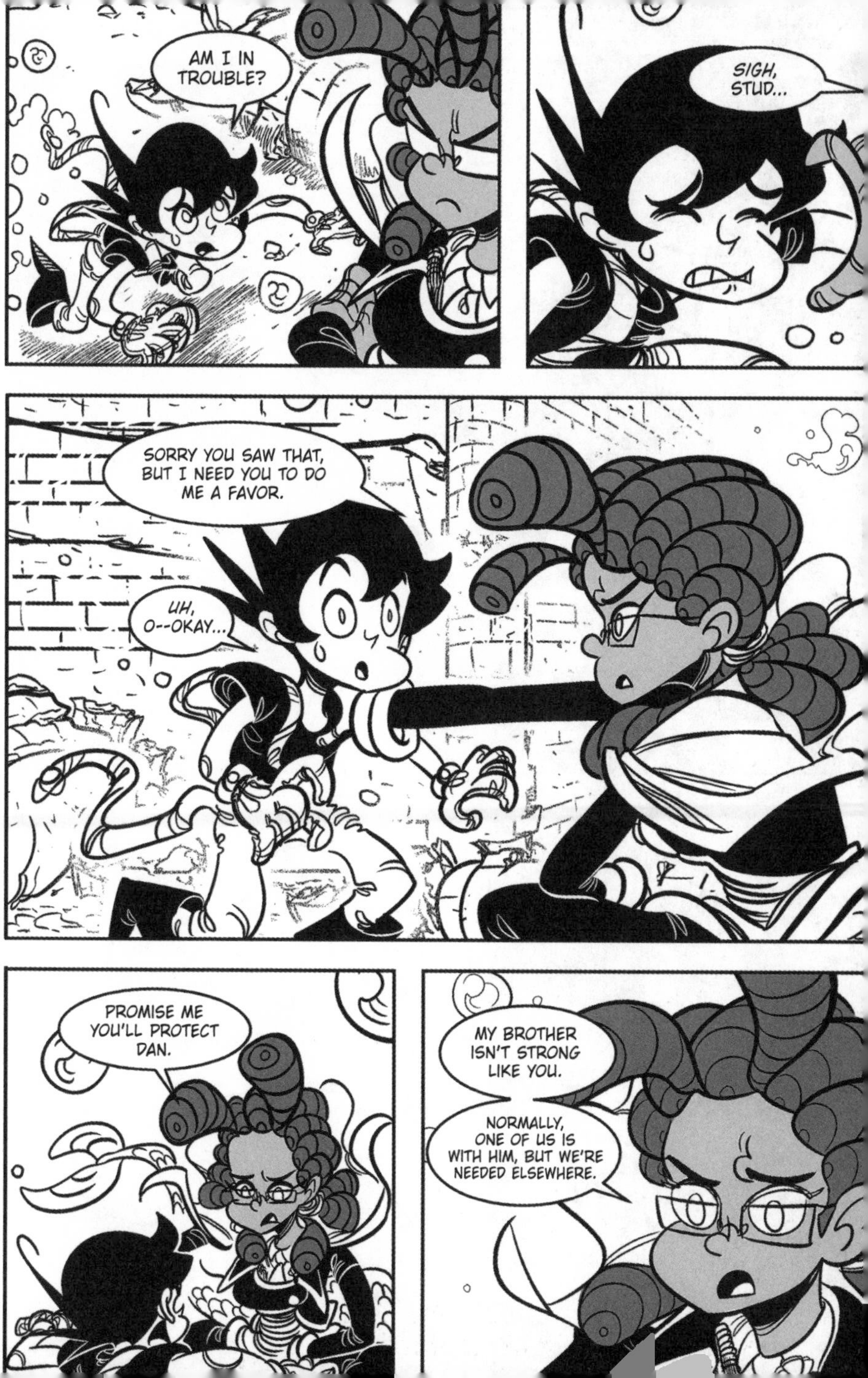
AM I IN TROUBLE?
SIGH, STUD...
SORRY YOU SAW THAT, BUT I NEED YOU TO DO ME A FAVOR.
UH, O--OKAY...
PROMISE ME YOU'LL PROTECT DAN.
MY BROTHER ISN'T STRONG LIKE YOU.
NORMALLY, ONE OF US IS WITH HIM, BUT WE'RE NEEDED ELSEWHERE.

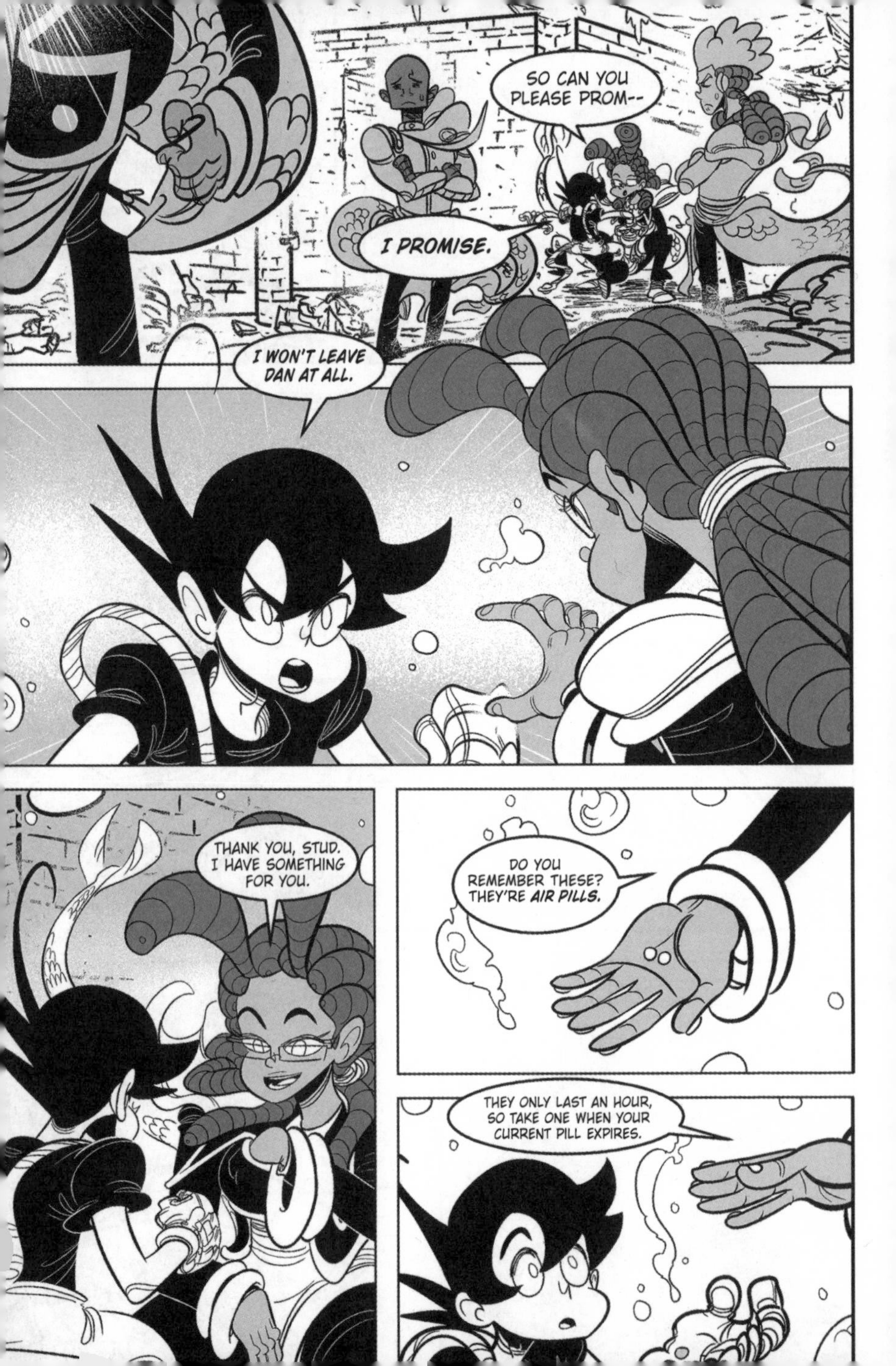
SO CAN YOU PLEASE PROM--
I PROMISE.
I WON'T LEAVE DAN AT ALL.
THANK YOU, STUD. I HAVE SOMETHING FOR YOU.
DO YOU REMEMBER THESE? THEY'RE AIR PILLS.
THEY ONLY LAST AN HOUR, SO TAKE ONE WHEN YOUR CURRENT PILL EXPIRES.

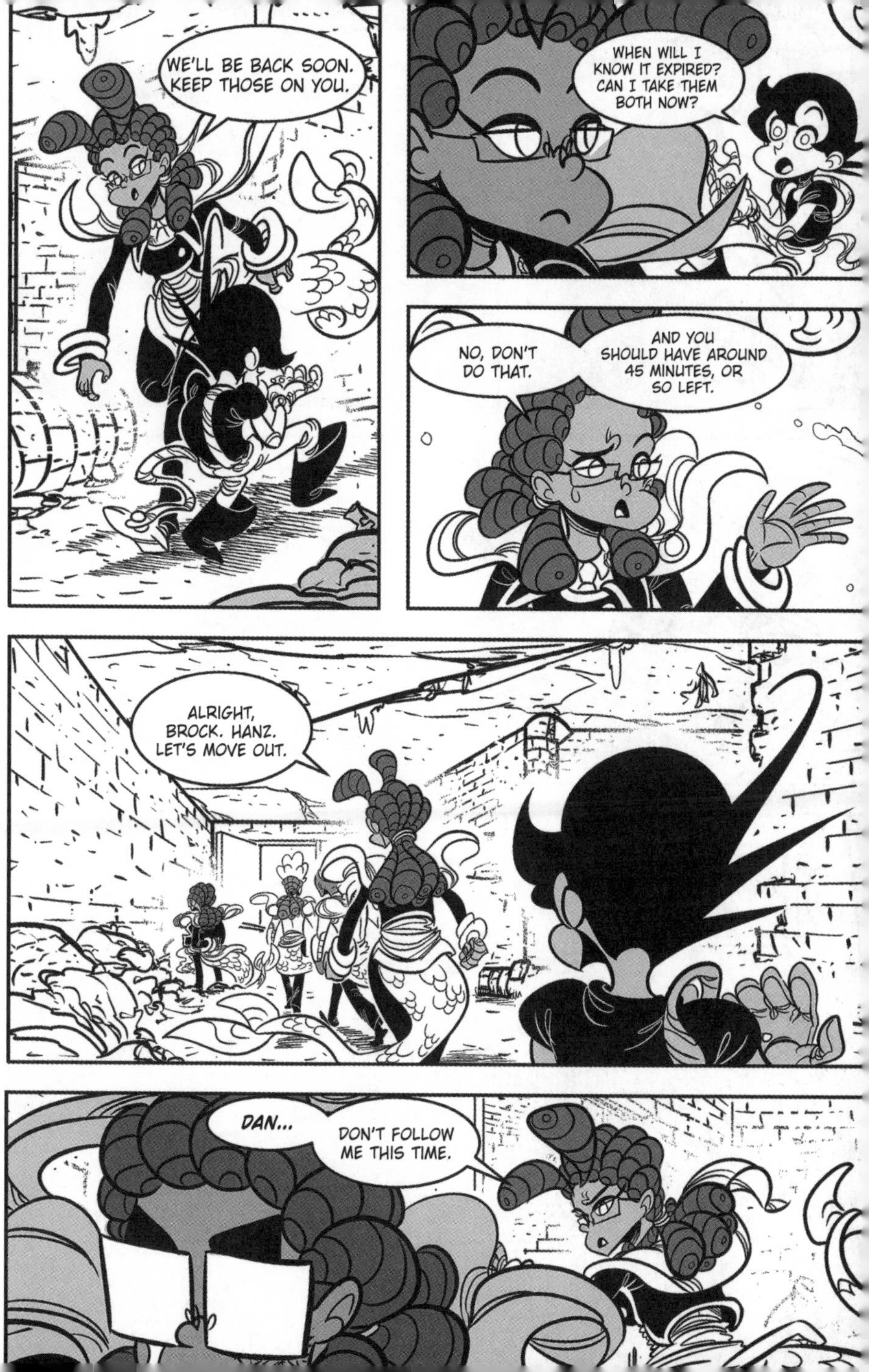

WE'LL BE BACK SOON. KEEP THOSE ON YOU.
WHEN WILL I KNOW IT EXPIRED? CAN I TAKE THEM BOTH NOW?
NO, DON'T DO THAT.
AND YOU SHOULD HAVE AROUND 45 MINUTES, OR SO LEFT.
ALRIGHT, BROCK. HANZ. LET'S MOVE OUT.
DAN...
DON'T FOLLOW ME THIS TIME.

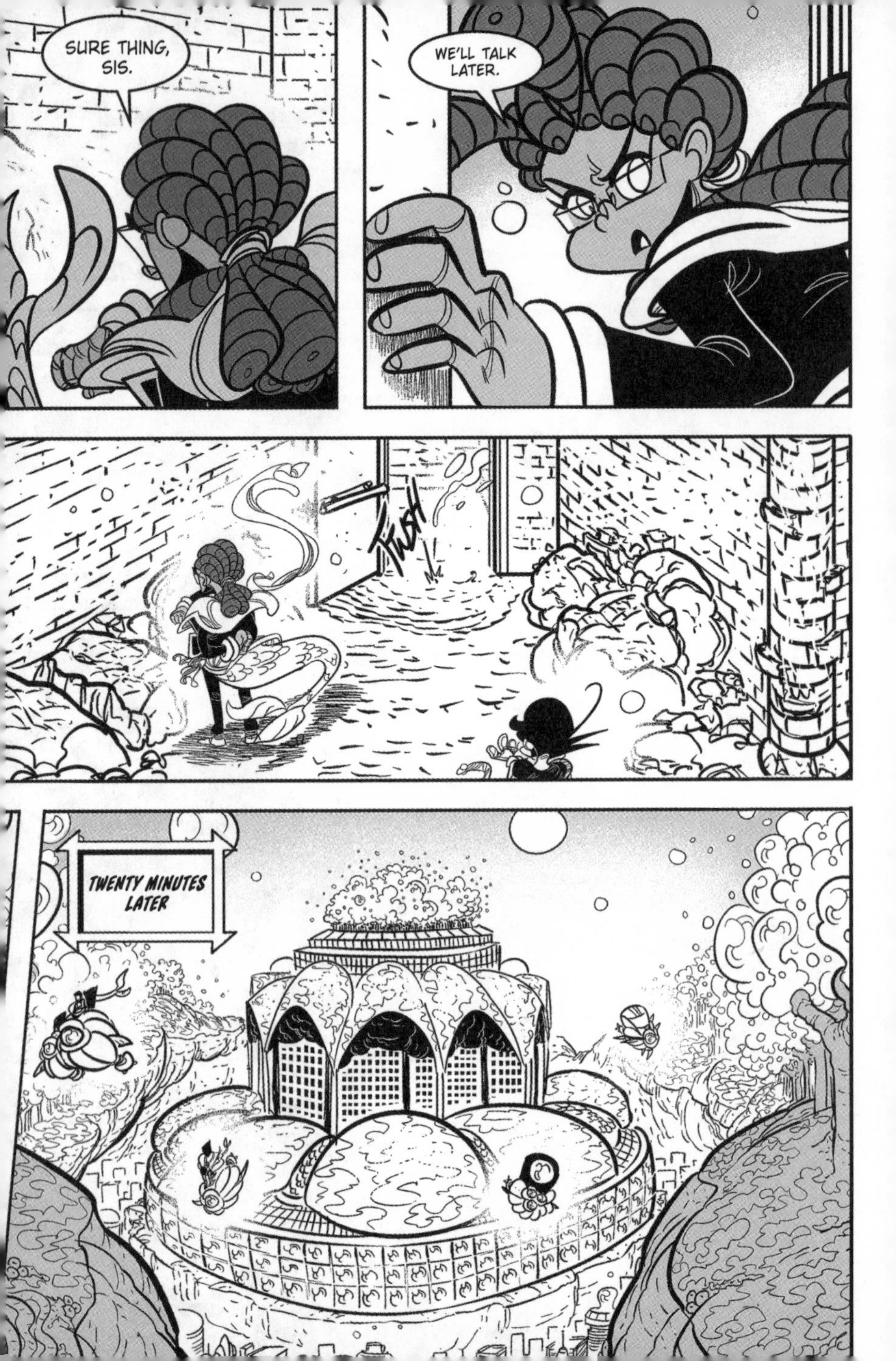
SURE THING, SIS.
WE'LL TALK LATER.
FWSH
TWENTY MINUTES LATER

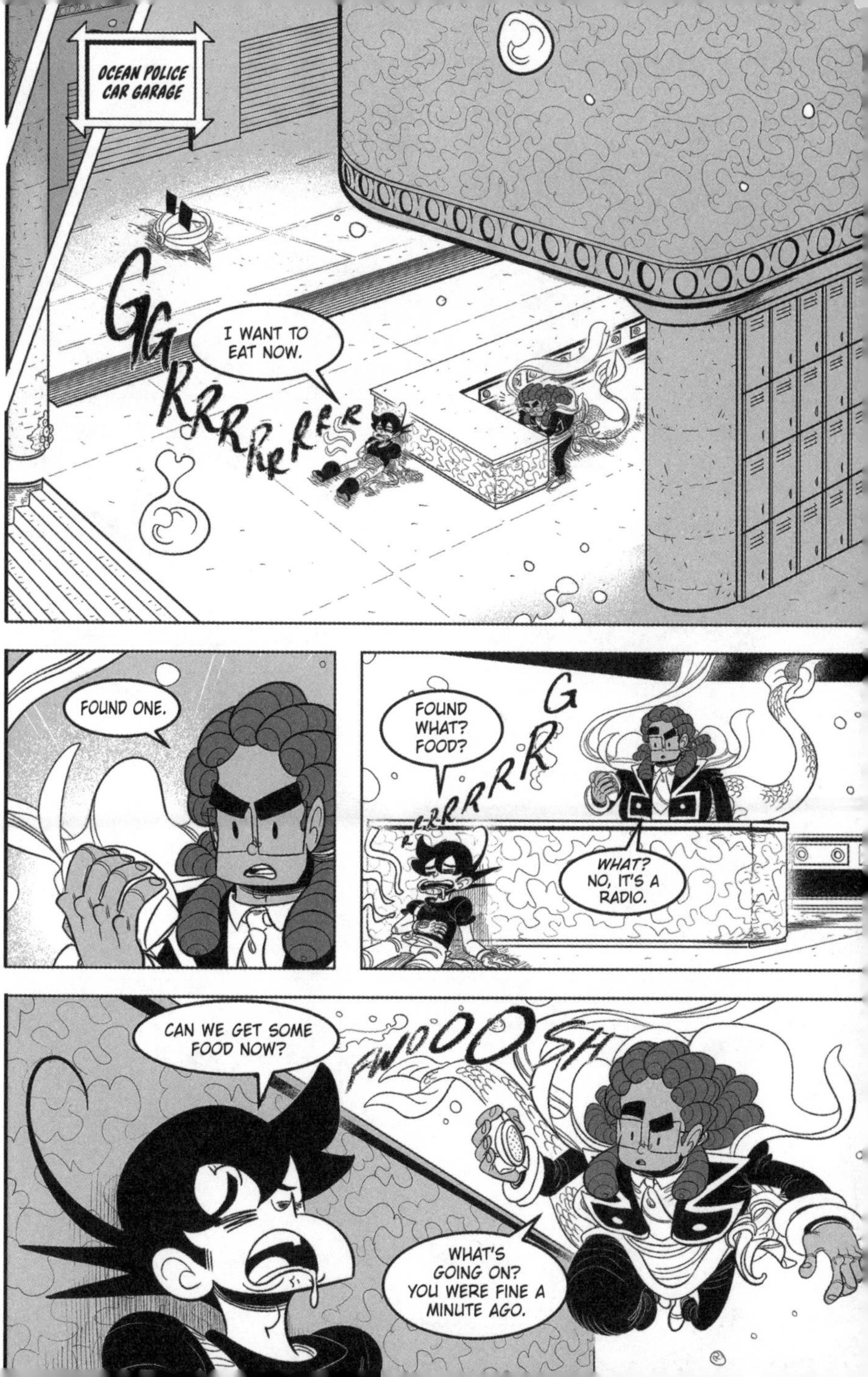
OCEAN POLICE
CAR GARAGE
GGRRRRRRRR
I WANT TO EAT NOW.
FOUND ONE.
FOUND WHAT? FOOD?
RRRRRRRRG
WHAT? NO, IT'S A RADIO.
CAN WE GET SOME FOOD NOW?
FWOOOOSH
WHAT'S GOING ON? YOU WERE FINE A MINUTE AGO.

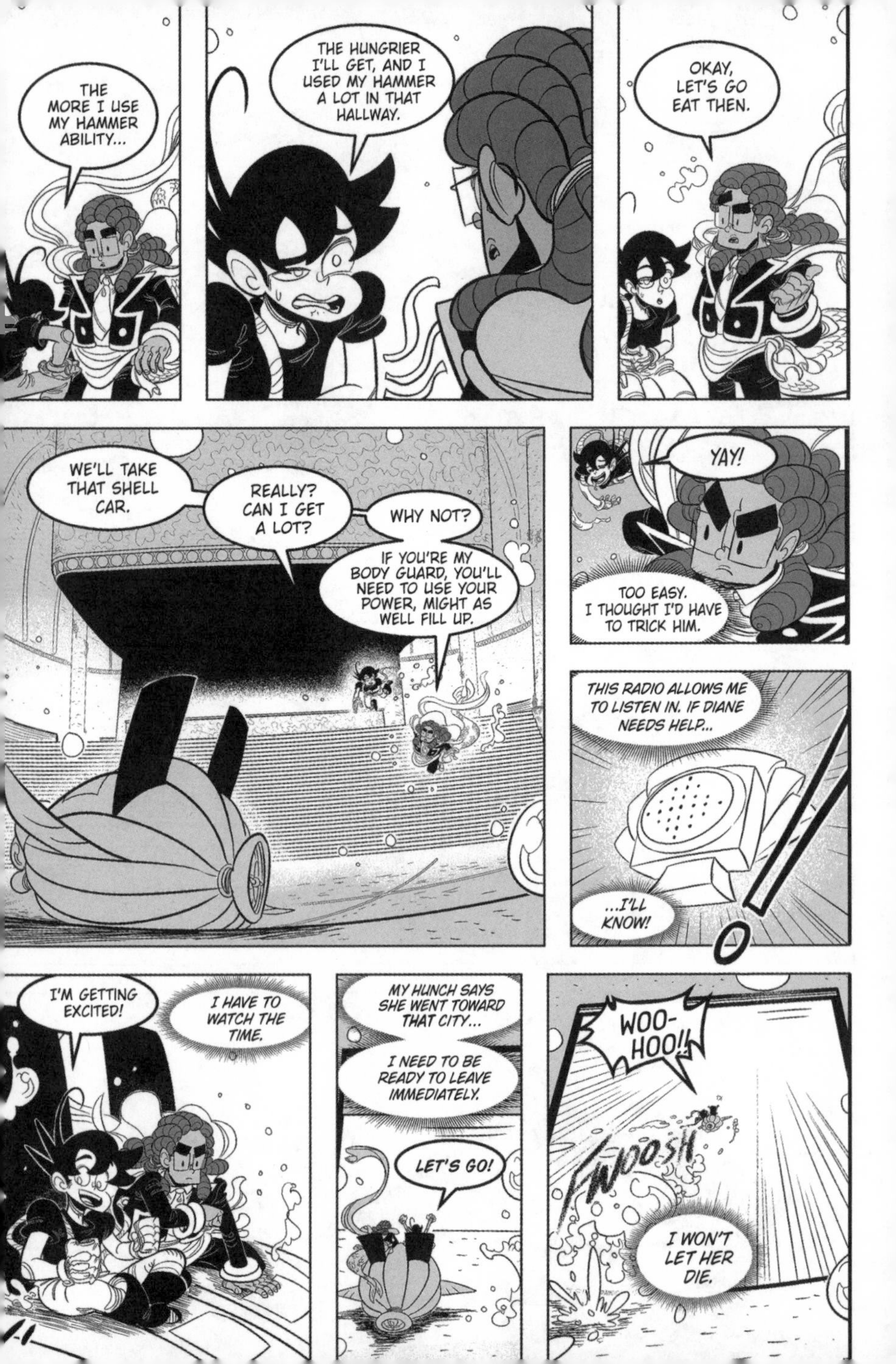
THE MORE I USE MY HAMMER ABILITY...
THE HUNGRIER I'LL GET, AND I USED MY HAMMER A LOT IN THAT HALLWAY.
OKAY, LET'S GO EAT THEN.
WE'LL TAKE THAT SHELL CAR.
REALLY? CAN I GET A LOT?
WHY NOT?
IF YOU'RE MY BODY GUARD, YOU'LL NEED TO USE YOUR POWER, MIGHT AS WELL FILL UP.
YAY!
TOO EASY. I THOUGHT I'D HAVE TO TRICK HIM.
THIS RADIO ALLOWS ME TO LISTEN IN. IF DIANE NEEDS HELP...
...I'LL KNOW!
I'M GETTING EXCITED!
I HAVE TO WATCH THE TIME.
MY HUNCH SAYS SHE WENT TOWARD THAT CITY...
I NEED TO BE READY TO LEAVE IMMEDIATELY.
LET'S GO!
WOO-HOO!!
FWOOSH
I WON'T LET HER DIE.

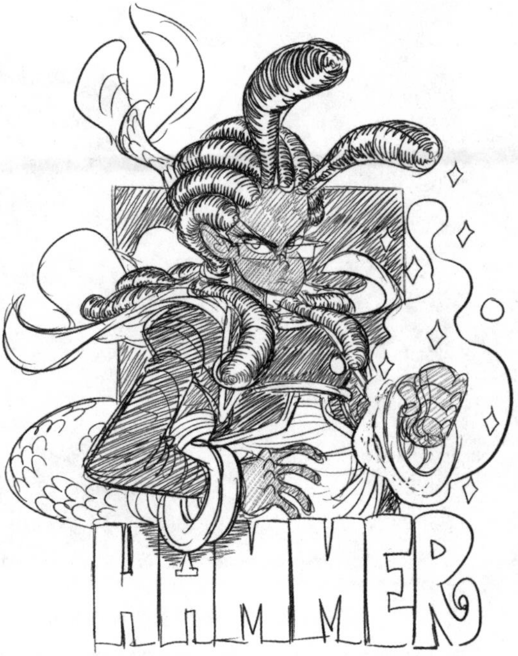
HAMMER

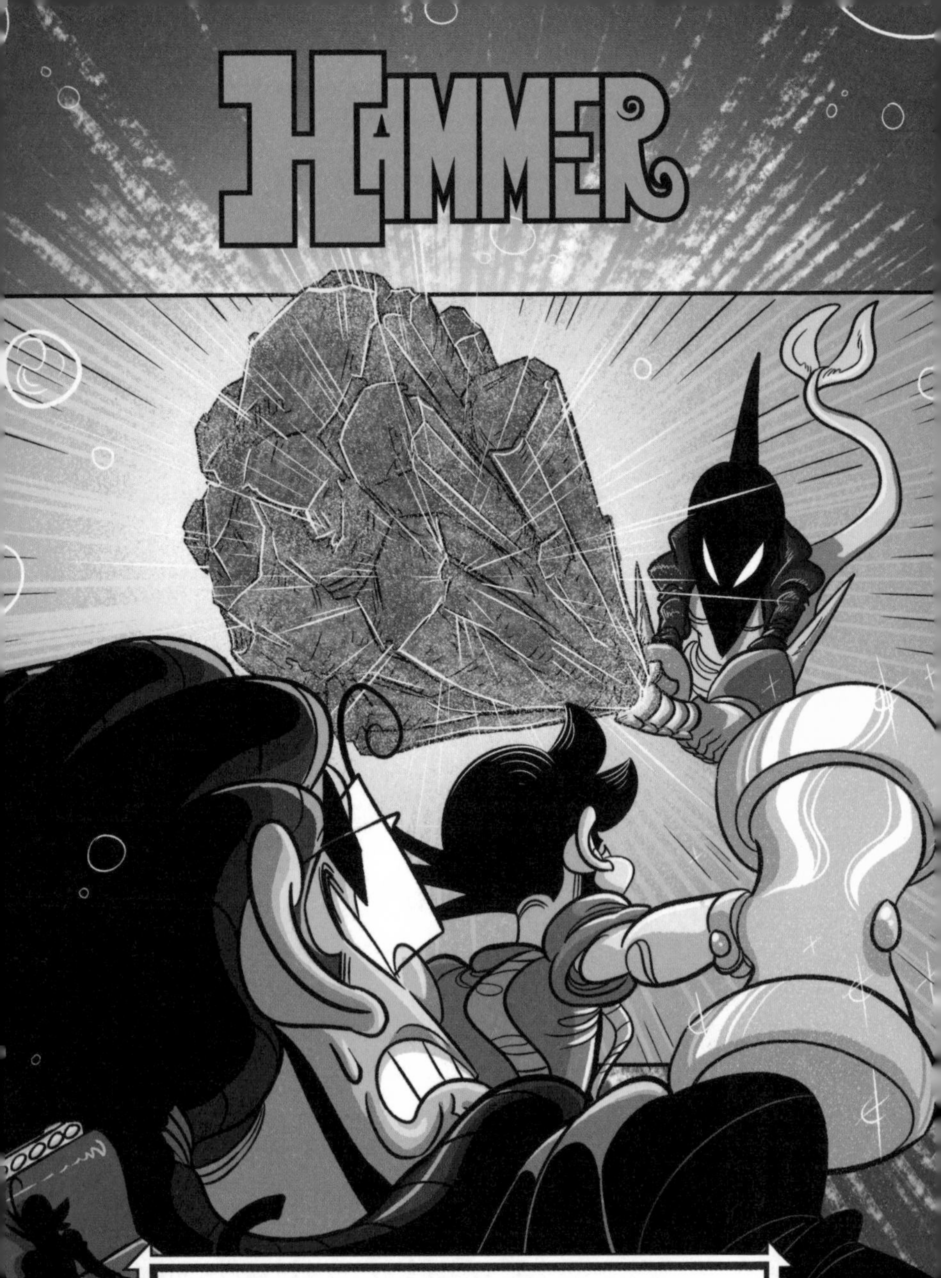
HAMMER
CHAPTER 8: MY HAMMER CAN BEAT ANYTHING

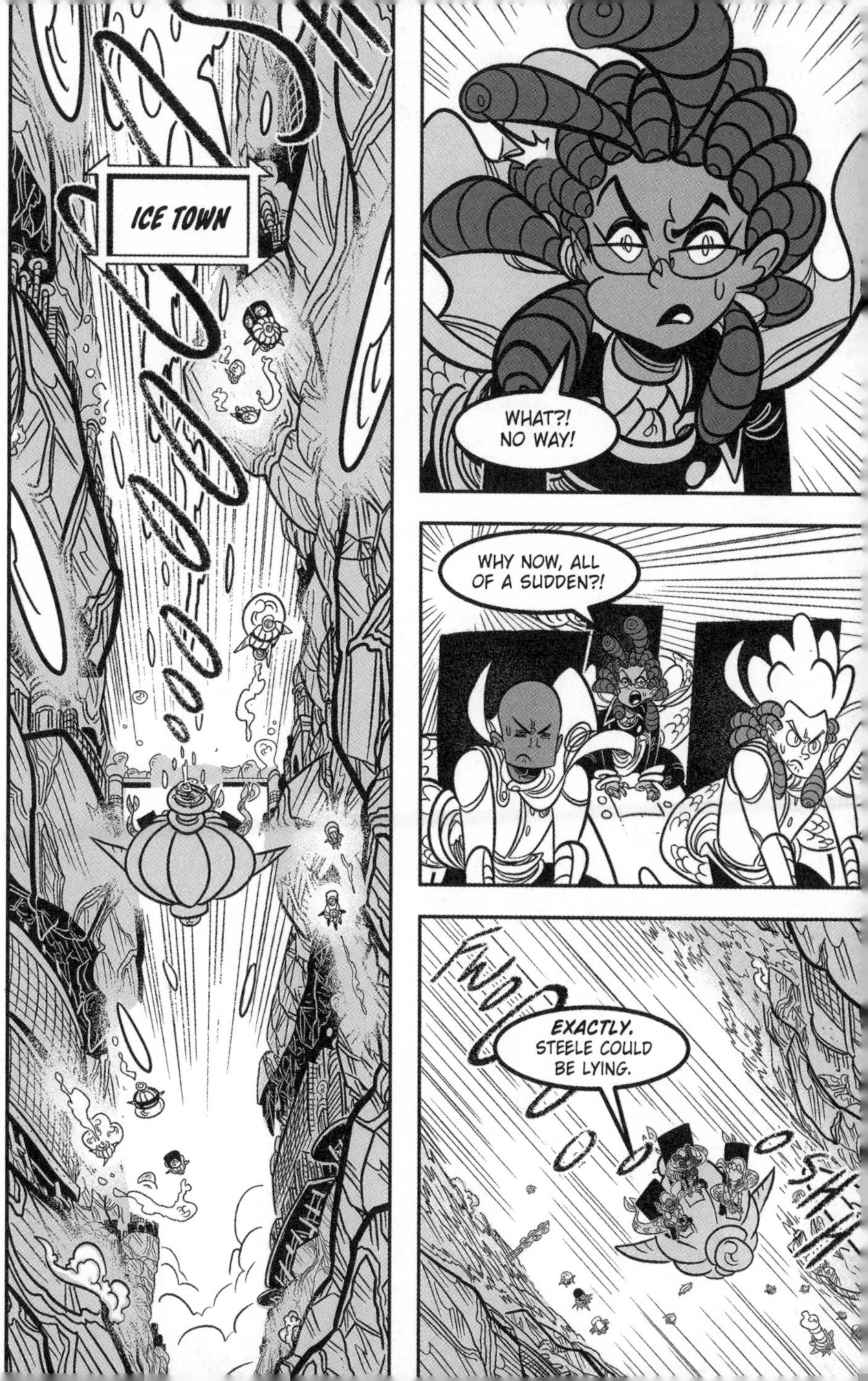
ICE TOWN
WHAT?! NO WAY!
WHY NOW, ALL OF A SUDDEN?!
EXACTLY. STEELE COULD BE LYING.

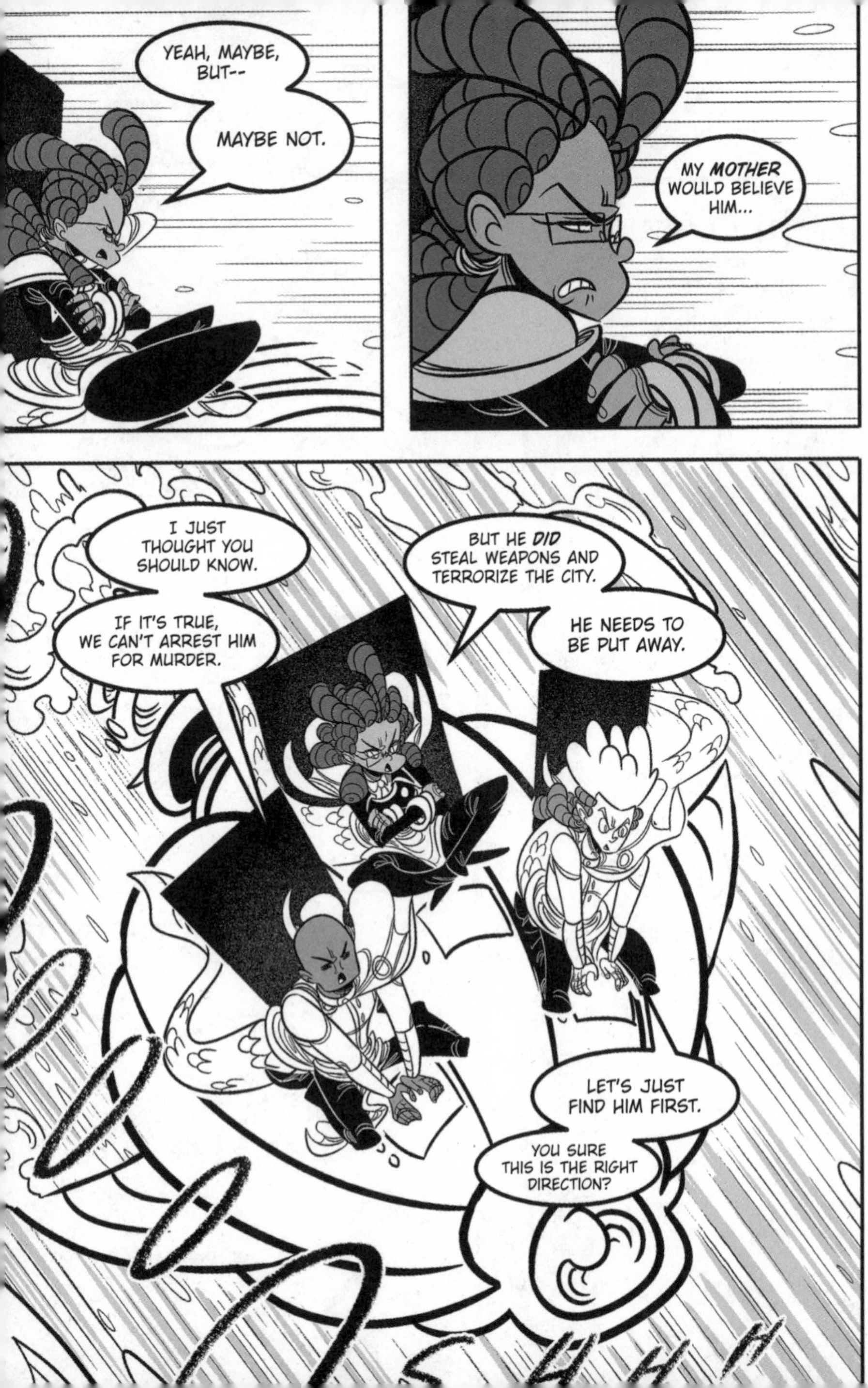
YEAH, MAYBE, BUT--
MAYBE NOT.
MY ***MOTHER*** WOULD BELIEVE HIM...
I JUST THOUGHT YOU SHOULD KNOW.
IF IT'S TRUE, WE CAN'T ARREST HIM FOR MURDER.
BUT HE ***DID*** STEAL WEAPONS AND TERRORIZE THE CITY.
HE NEEDS TO BE PUT AWAY.
LET'S JUST FIND HIM FIRST.
YOU SURE THIS IS THE RIGHT DIRECTION?

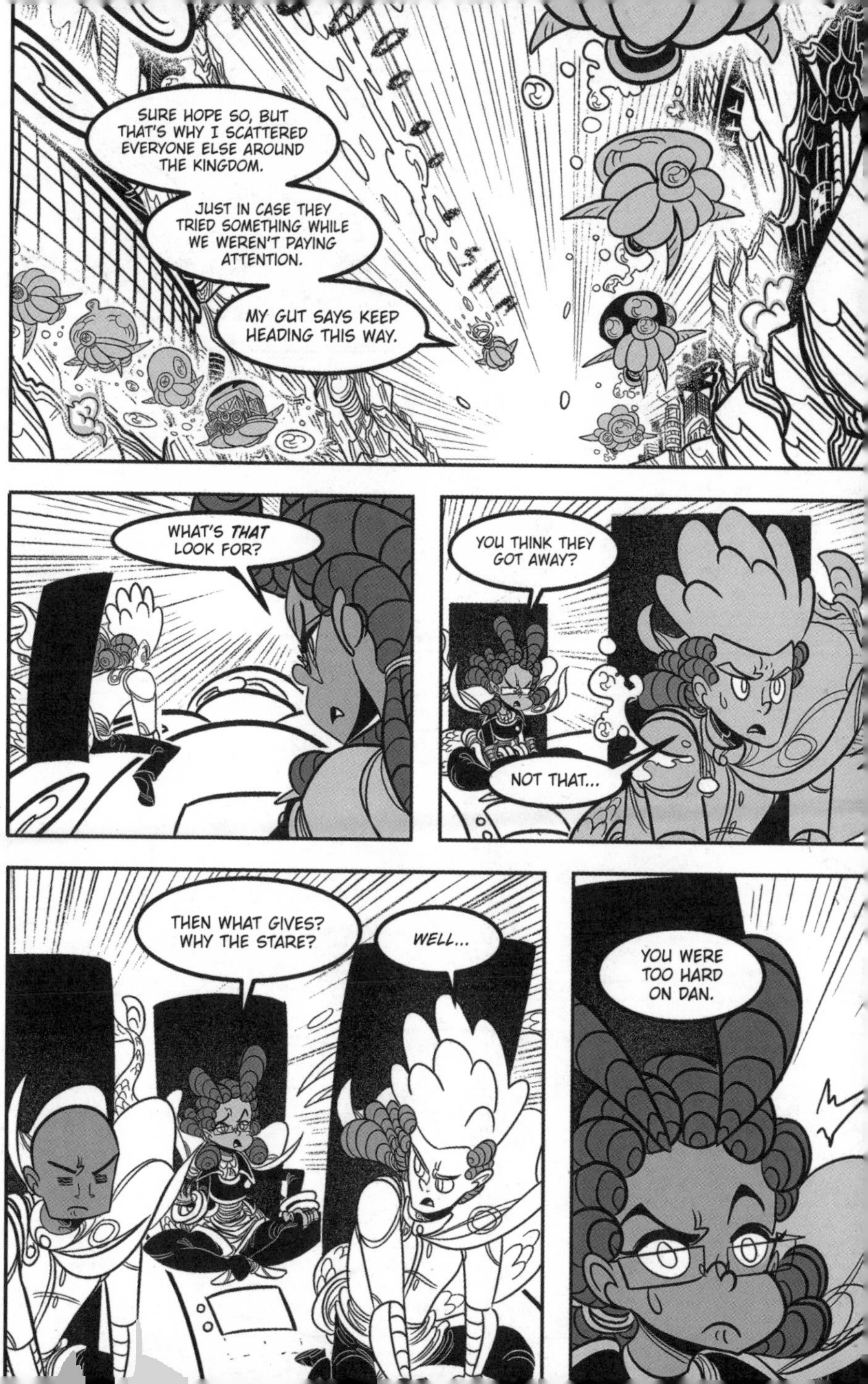

SURE HOPE SO, BUT THAT'S WHY I SCATTERED EVERYONE ELSE AROUND THE KINGDOM.
JUST IN CASE THEY TRIED SOMETHING WHILE WE WEREN'T PAYING ATTENTION.
MY GUT SAYS KEEP HEADING THIS WAY.
WHAT'S *THAT* LOOK FOR?
YOU THINK THEY GOT AWAY?
NOT THAT...
THEN WHAT GIVES? WHY THE STARE?
WELL...
YOU WERE TOO HARD ON DAN.

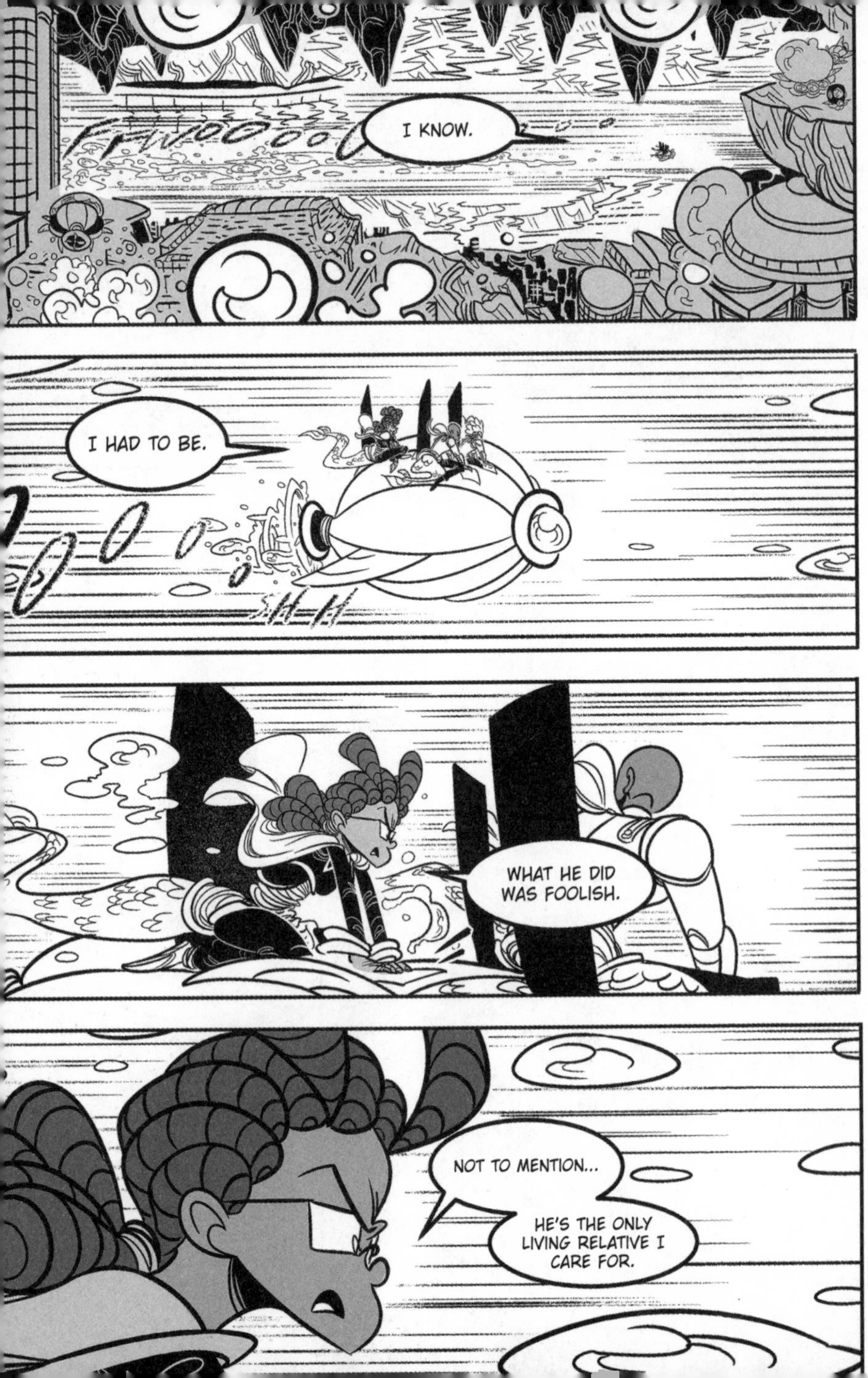
I KNOW.
I HAD TO BE.
WHAT HE DID WAS FOOLISH.
NOT TO MENTION...
HE'S THE ONLY LIVING RELATIVE I CARE FOR.

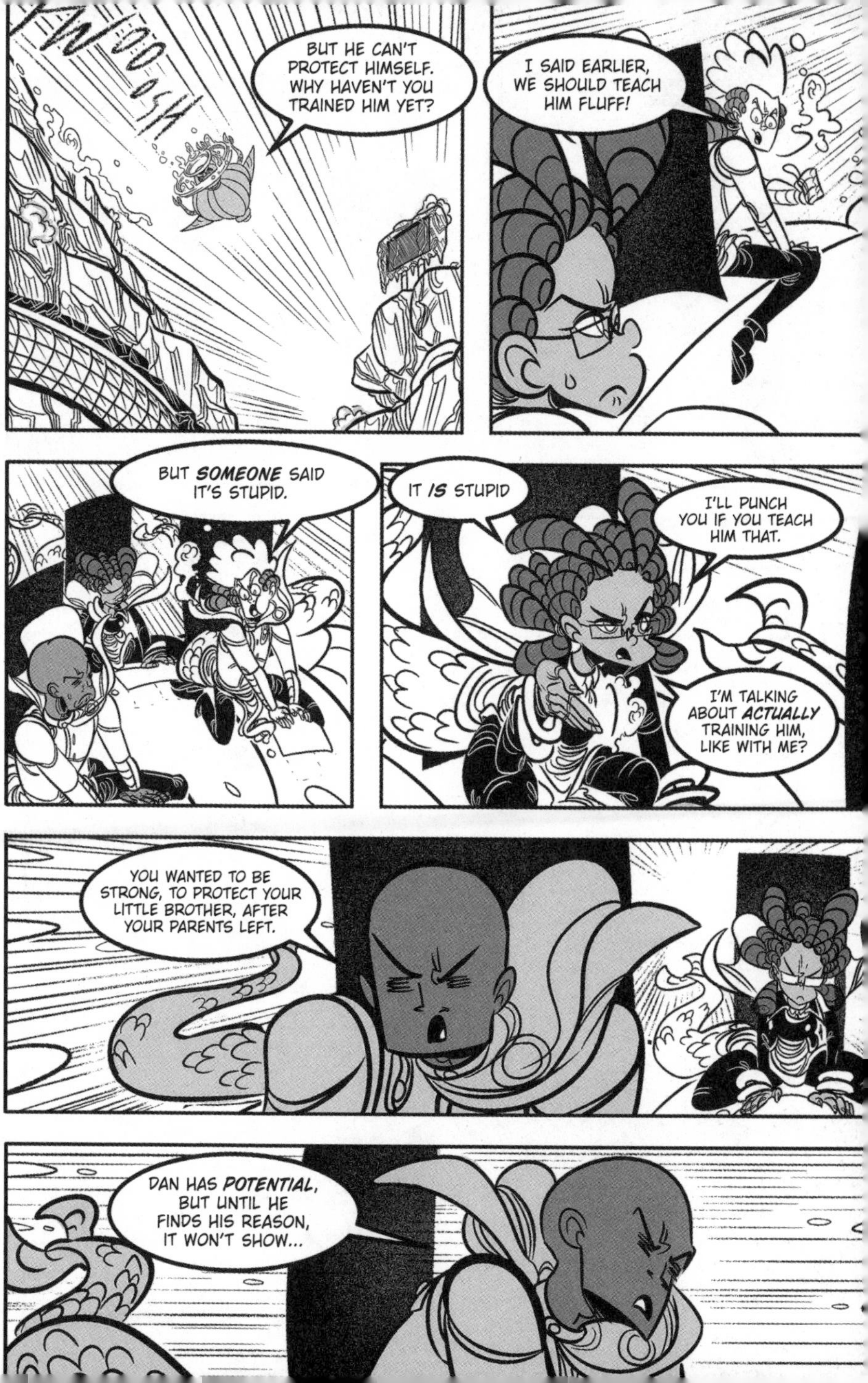
BUT HE CAN'T PROTECT HIMSELF. WHY HAVEN'T YOU TRAINED HIM YET?
I SAID EARLIER, WE SHOULD TEACH HIM FLUFF!
BUT **SOMEONE** SAID IT'S STUPID.
IT ***IS*** STUPID
I'LL PUNCH YOU IF YOU TEACH HIM THAT.
I'M TALKING ABOUT ***ACTUALLY*** TRAINING HIM, LIKE WITH ME?
YOU WANTED TO BE STRONG, TO PROTECT YOUR LITTLE BROTHER, AFTER YOUR PARENTS LEFT.
DAN HAS ***POTENTIAL***, BUT UNTIL HE FINDS HIS REASON, IT WON'T SHOW...

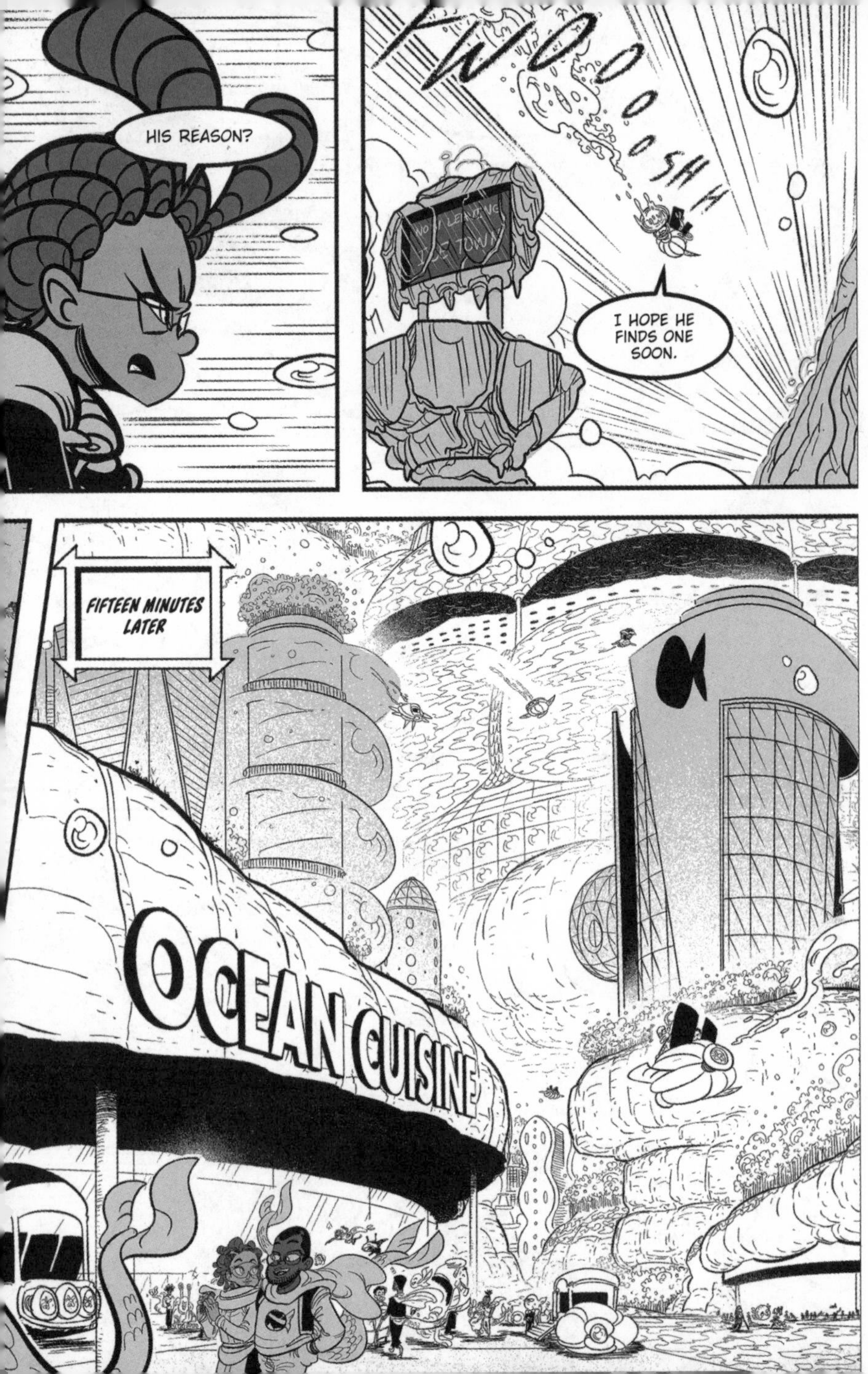
HIS REASON?
KWOOOOOSHH
I HOPE HE FINDS ONE SOON.
FIFTEEN MINUTES LATER
OCEAN CUISINE

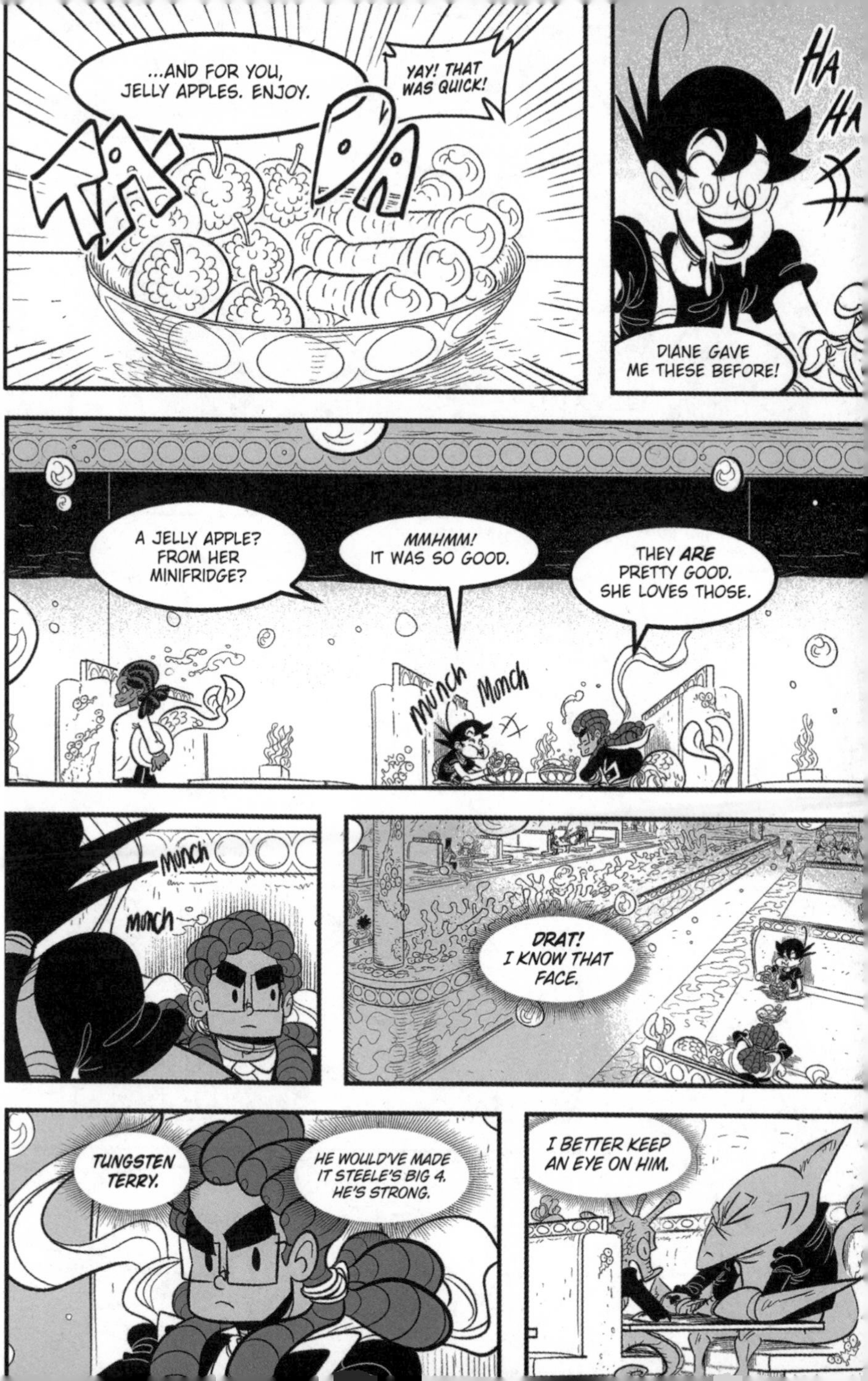
...AND FOR YOU, JELLY APPLES. ENJOY.
TA-DA
YAY! THAT WAS QUICK!
HA HA
DIANE GAVE ME THESE BEFORE!
A JELLY APPLE? FROM HER MINIFRIDGE?
MMHMM! IT WAS SO GOOD.
THEY ARE PRETTY GOOD. SHE LOVES THOSE.
MUNCH MUNCH
MUNCH
MUNCH
DRAT! I KNOW THAT FACE.
TUNGSTEN TERRY.
HE WOULD'VE MADE IT STEELE'S BIG 4. HE'S STRONG.
I BETTER KEEP AN EYE ON HIM.

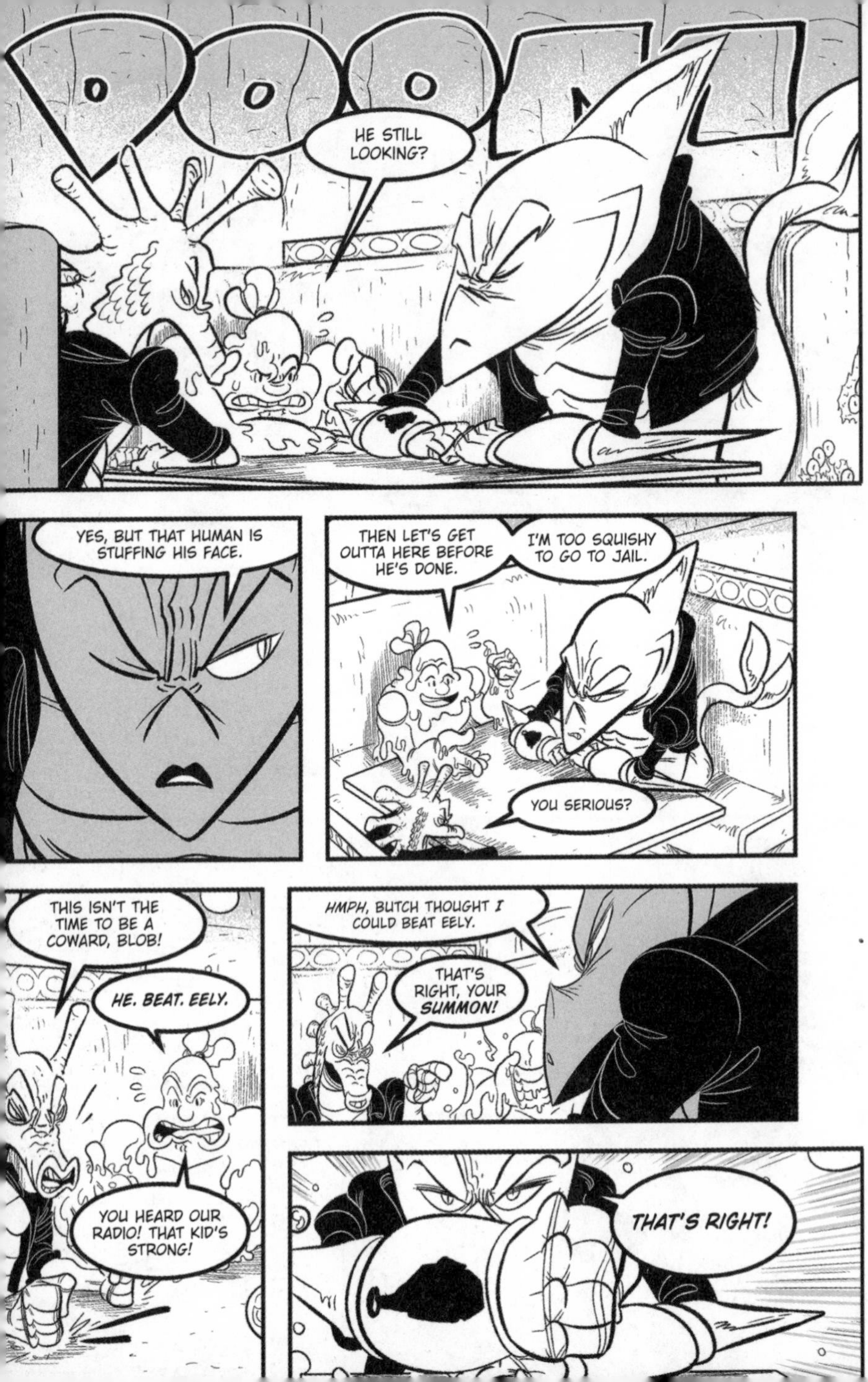
BOOM
HE STILL LOOKING?
YES, BUT THAT HUMAN IS STUFFING HIS FACE.
THEN LET'S GET OUTTA HERE BEFORE HE'S DONE.
I'M TOO SQUISHY TO GO TO JAIL.
YOU SERIOUS?
THIS ISN'T THE TIME TO BE A COWARD, BLOB!
HE. BEAT. EELY.
YOU HEARD OUR RADIO! THAT KID'S STRONG!
HMPH, BUTCH THOUGHT I COULD BEAT EELY.
THAT'S RIGHT, YOUR SUMMON!
THAT'S RIGHT!

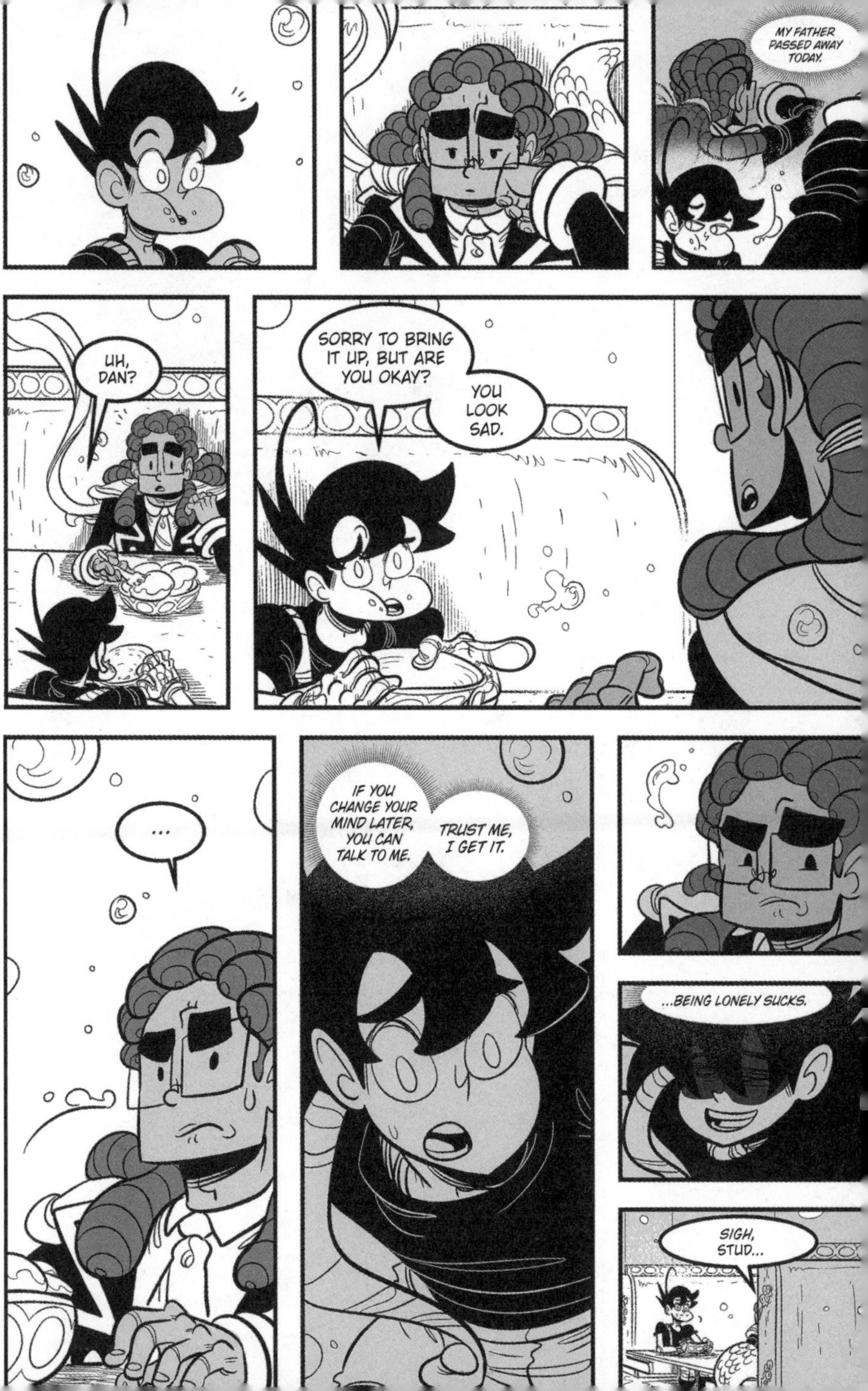
MY FATHER PASSED AWAY TODAY.
UH, DAN?
SORRY TO BRING IT UP, BUT ARE YOU OKAY?
YOU LOOK SAD.
...
IF YOU CHANGE YOUR MIND LATER, YOU CAN TALK TO ME.
TRUST ME, I GET IT.
...BEING LONELY SUCKS.
SIGH, STUD...

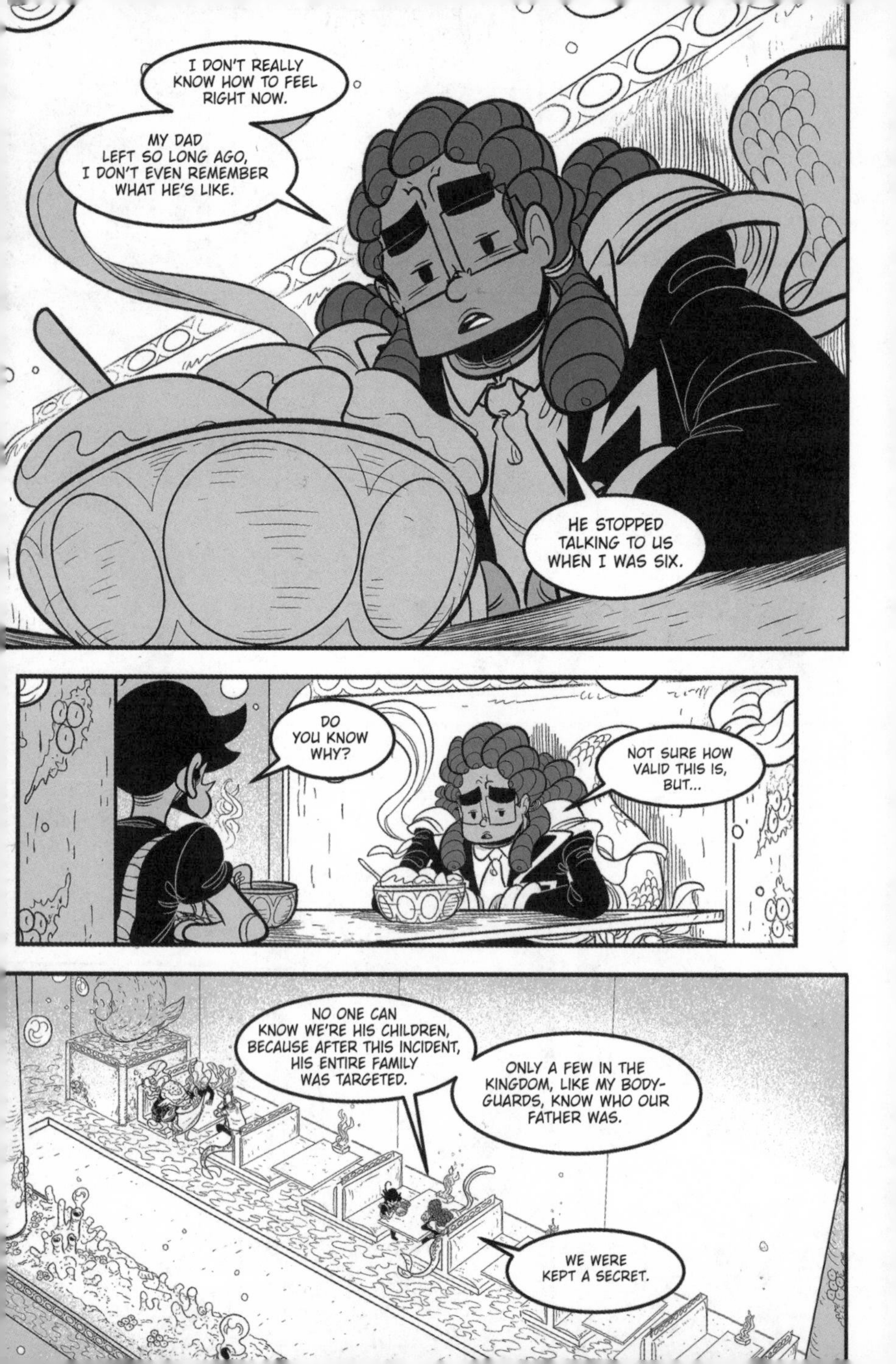
I DON'T REALLY KNOW HOW TO FEEL RIGHT NOW.
MY DAD LEFT SO LONG AGO, I DON'T EVEN REMEMBER WHAT HE'S LIKE.
HE STOPPED TALKING TO US WHEN I WAS SIX.
DO YOU KNOW WHY?
NOT SURE HOW VALID THIS IS, BUT...
NO ONE CAN KNOW WE'RE HIS CHILDREN, BECAUSE AFTER THIS INCIDENT, HIS ENTIRE FAMILY WAS TARGETED.
ONLY A FEW IN THE KINGDOM, LIKE MY BODY-GUARDS, KNOW WHO OUR FATHER WAS.
WE WERE KEPT A SECRET.

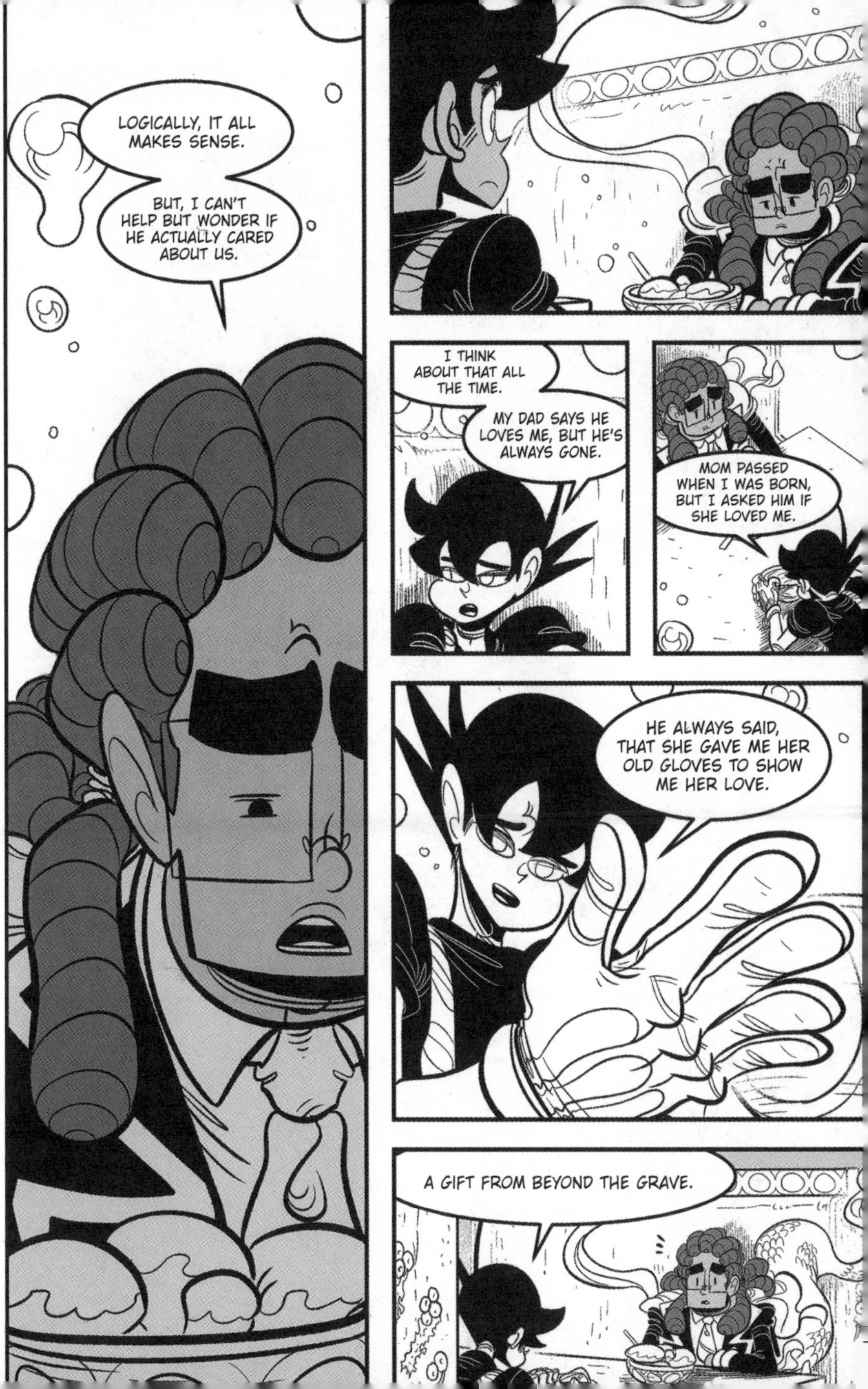
LOGICALLY, IT ALL MAKES SENSE.
BUT, I CAN'T HELP BUT WONDER IF HE ACTUALLY CARED ABOUT US.
I THINK ABOUT THAT ALL THE TIME.
MY DAD SAYS HE LOVES ME, BUT HE'S ALWAYS GONE.
MOM PASSED WHEN I WAS BORN, BUT I ASKED HIM IF SHE LOVED ME.
HE ALWAYS SAID, THAT SHE GAVE ME HER OLD GLOVES TO SHOW ME HER LOVE.
A GIFT FROM BEYOND THE GRAVE.

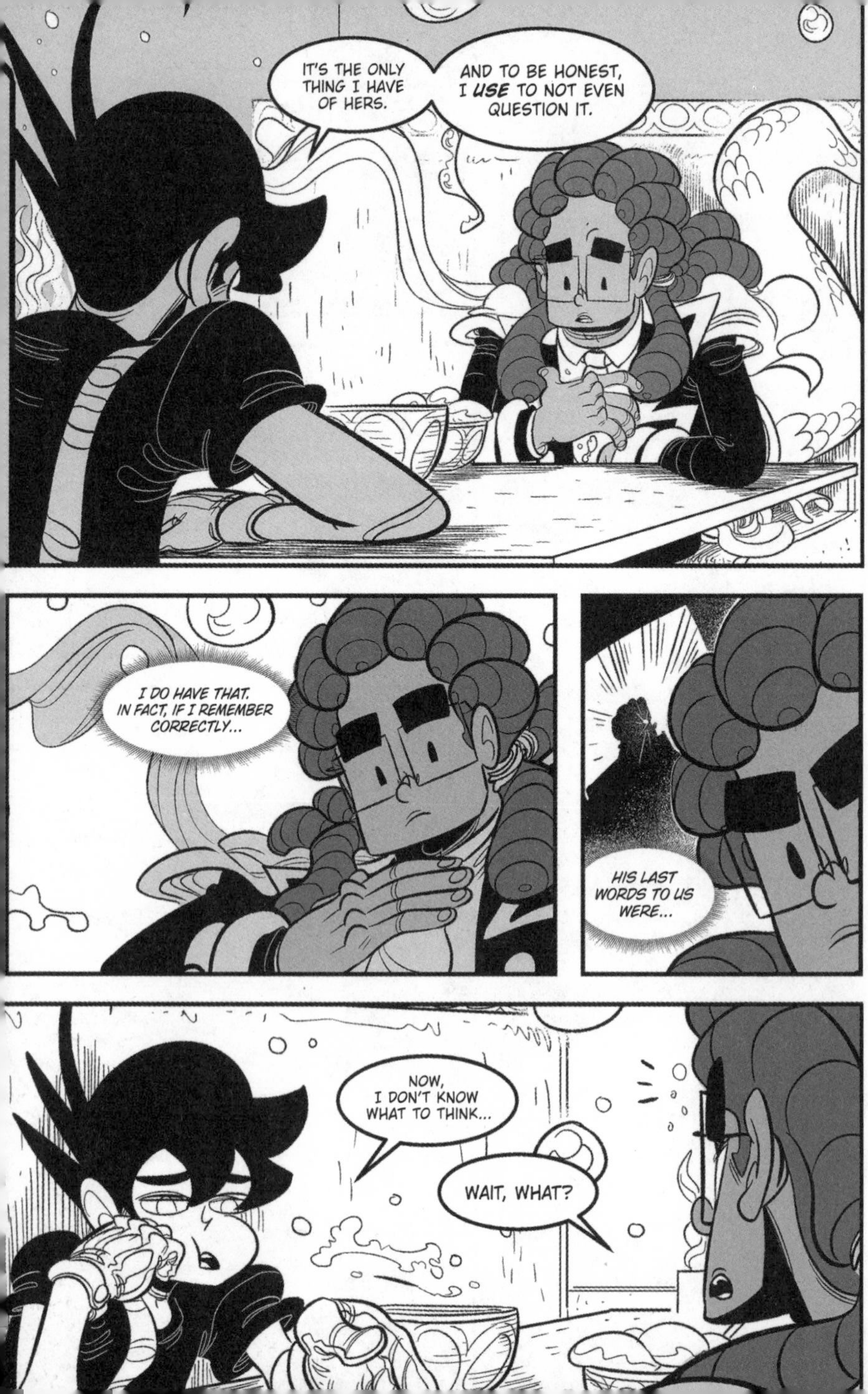
IT'S THE ONLY THING I HAVE OF HERS.
AND TO BE HONEST, I *USE* TO NOT EVEN QUESTION IT.
I DO HAVE THAT. IN FACT, IF I REMEMBER CORRECTLY...
HIS LAST WORDS TO US WERE...
NOW, I DON'T KNOW WHAT TO THINK...
WAIT, WHAT?

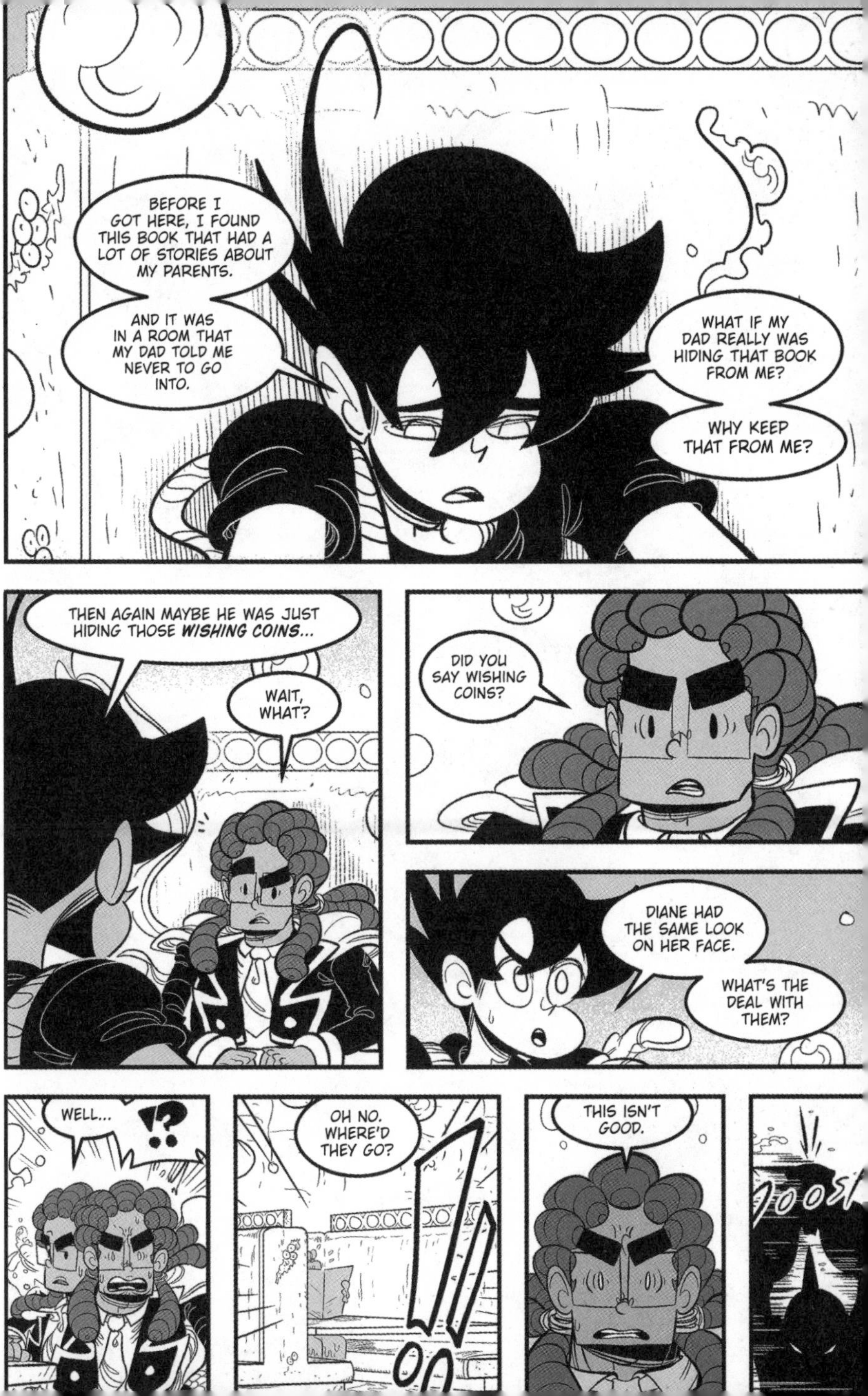
BEFORE I GOT HERE, I FOUND THIS BOOK THAT HAD A LOT OF STORIES ABOUT MY PARENTS.
AND IT WAS IN A ROOM THAT MY DAD TOLD ME NEVER TO GO INTO.
WHAT IF MY DAD REALLY WAS HIDING THAT BOOK FROM ME?
WHY KEEP THAT FROM ME?
THEN AGAIN MAYBE HE WAS JUST HIDING THOSE *WISHING COINS*...
WAIT, WHAT?
DID YOU SAY WISHING COINS?
DIANE HAD THE SAME LOOK ON HER FACE.
WHAT'S THE DEAL WITH THEM?
WELL...
!?
OH NO. WHERE'D THEY GO?
THIS ISN'T GOOD.

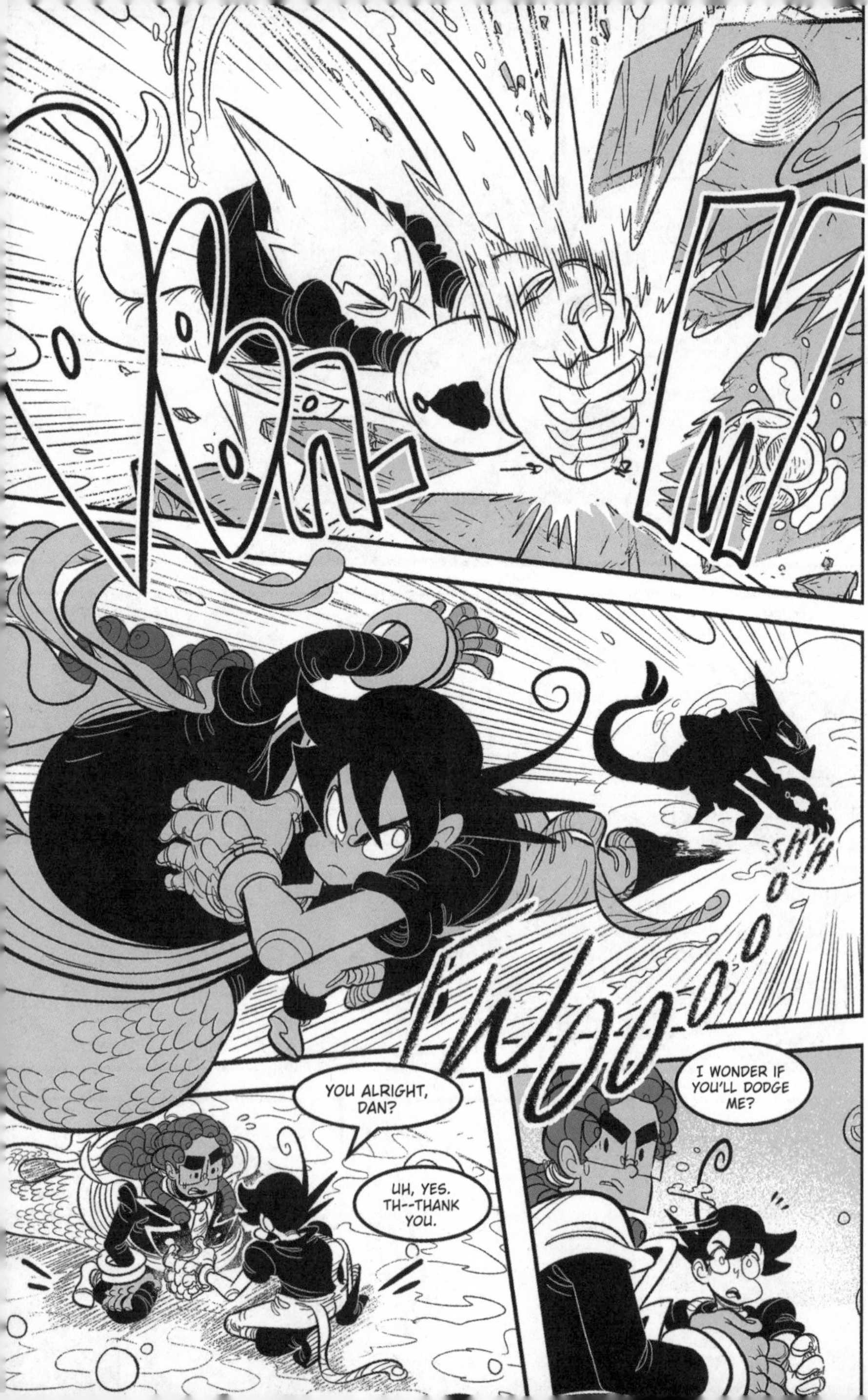
YOU ALRIGHT, DAN?
UH, YES. TH--THANK YOU.
I WONDER IF YOU'LL DODGE ME?

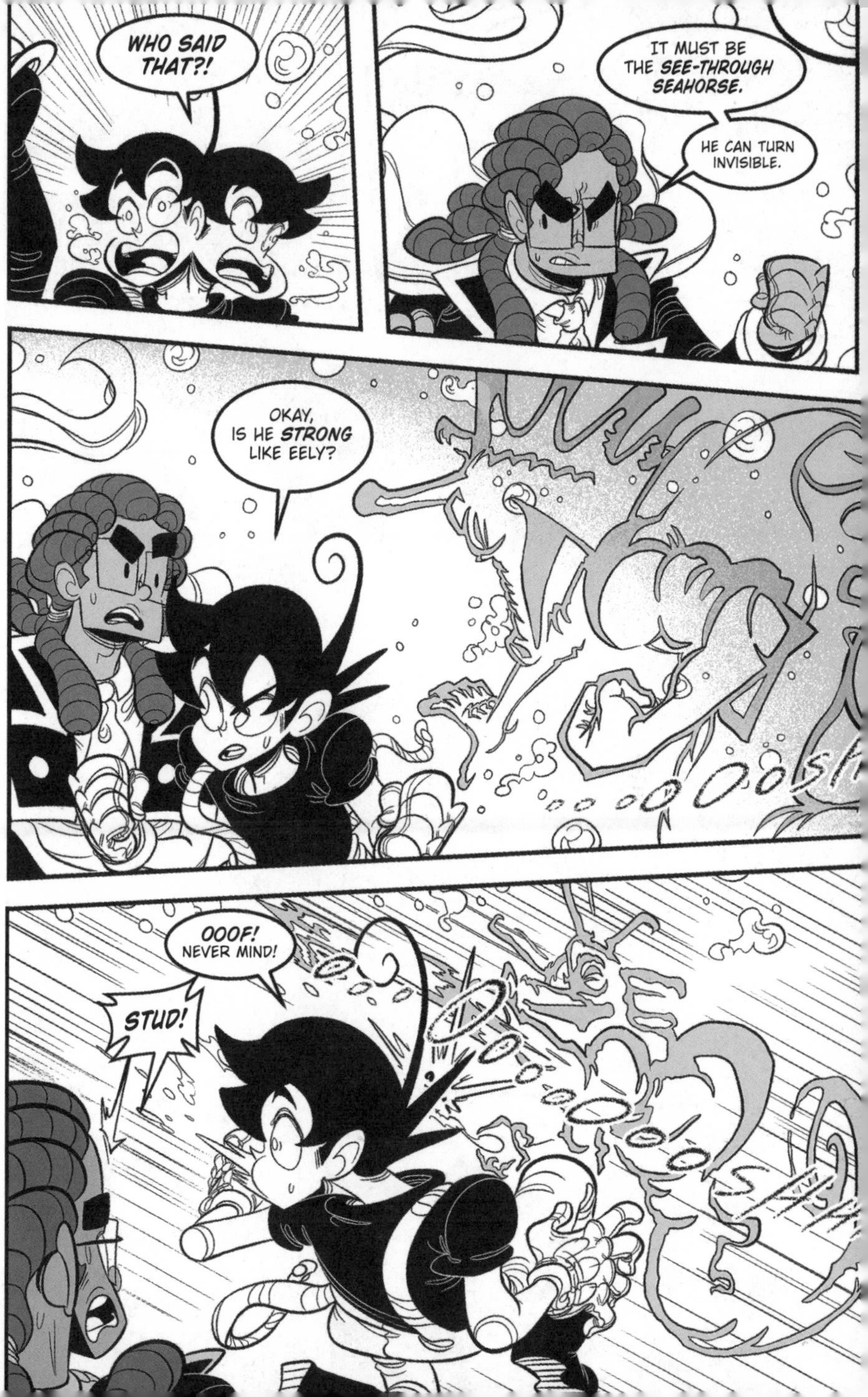
WHO SAID THAT?!
IT MUST BE THE SEE-THROUGH SEAHORSE.
HE CAN TURN INVISIBLE.
OKAY, IS HE STRONG LIKE EELY?
OOOF! NEVER MIND!
STUD!

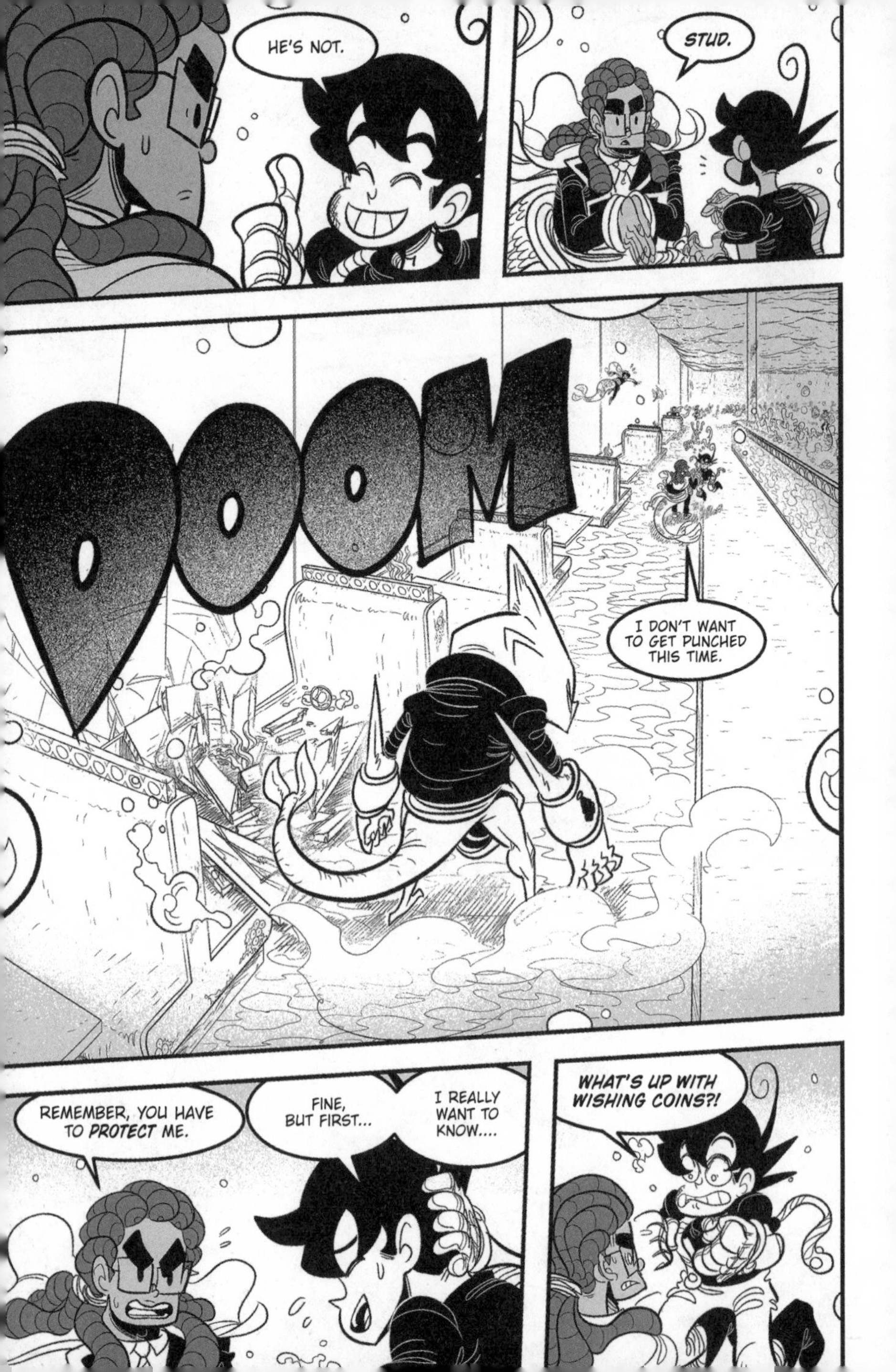

HE'S NOT.
STUD.
DOOM
I DON'T WANT TO GET PUNCHED THIS TIME.
REMEMBER, YOU HAVE TO *PROTECT* ME.
FINE, BUT FIRST...
I REALLY WANT TO KNOW....
WHAT'S UP WITH WISHING COINS?!

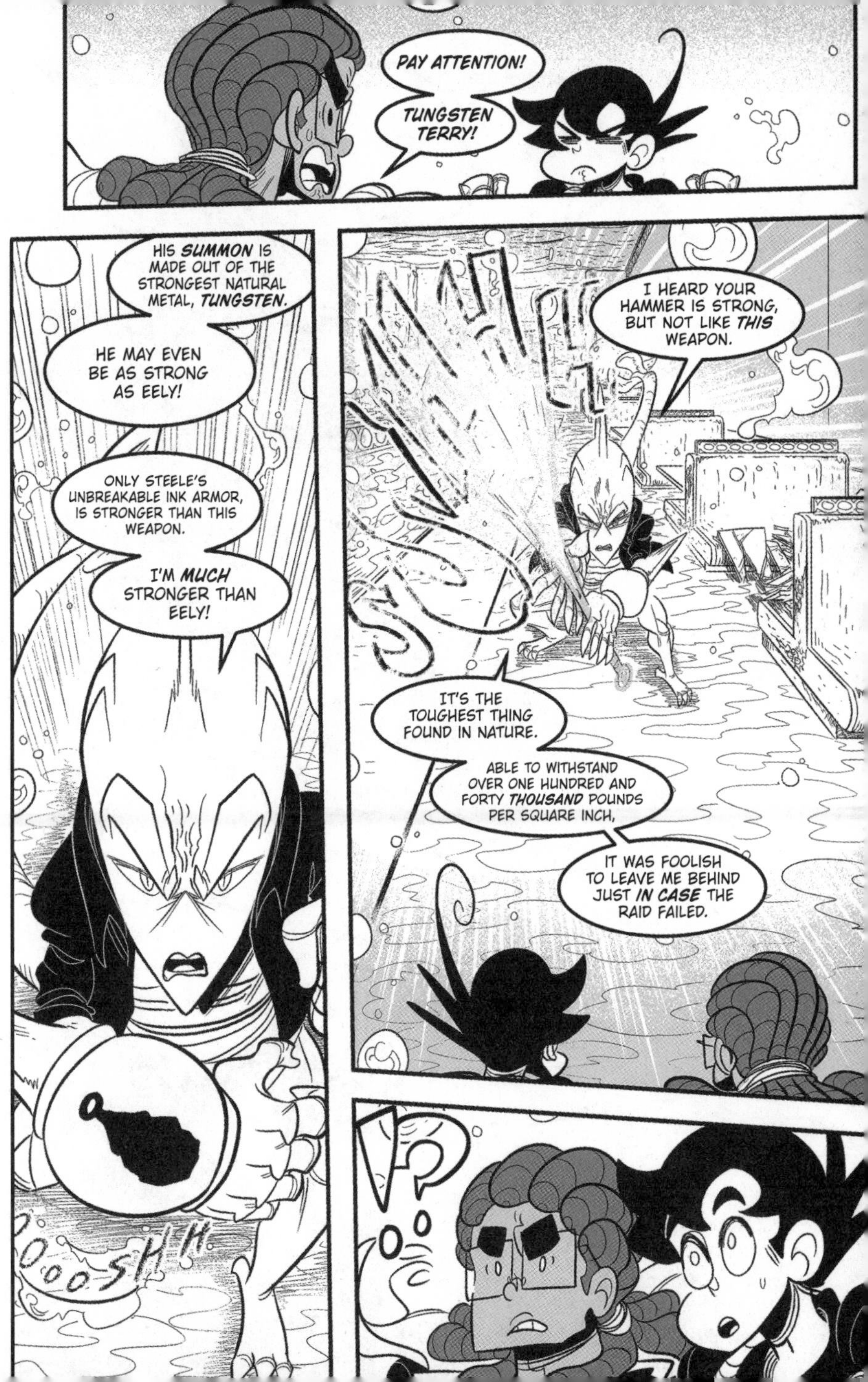
PAY ATTENTION!
TUNGSTEN TERRY!
HIS SUMMON IS MADE OUT OF THE STRONGEST NATURAL METAL, TUNGSTEN.
HE MAY EVEN BE AS STRONG AS EELY!
ONLY STEELE'S UNBREAKABLE INK ARMOR, IS STRONGER THAN THIS WEAPON.
I'M MUCH STRONGER THAN EELY!
WOOOSH!!
I HEARD YOUR HAMMER IS STRONG, BUT NOT LIKE THIS WEAPON.
IT'S THE TOUGHEST THING FOUND IN NATURE.
ABLE TO WITHSTAND OVER ONE HUNDRED AND FORTY THOUSAND POUNDS PER SQUARE INCH,
IT WAS FOOLISH TO LEAVE ME BEHIND JUST IN CASE THE RAID FAILED.

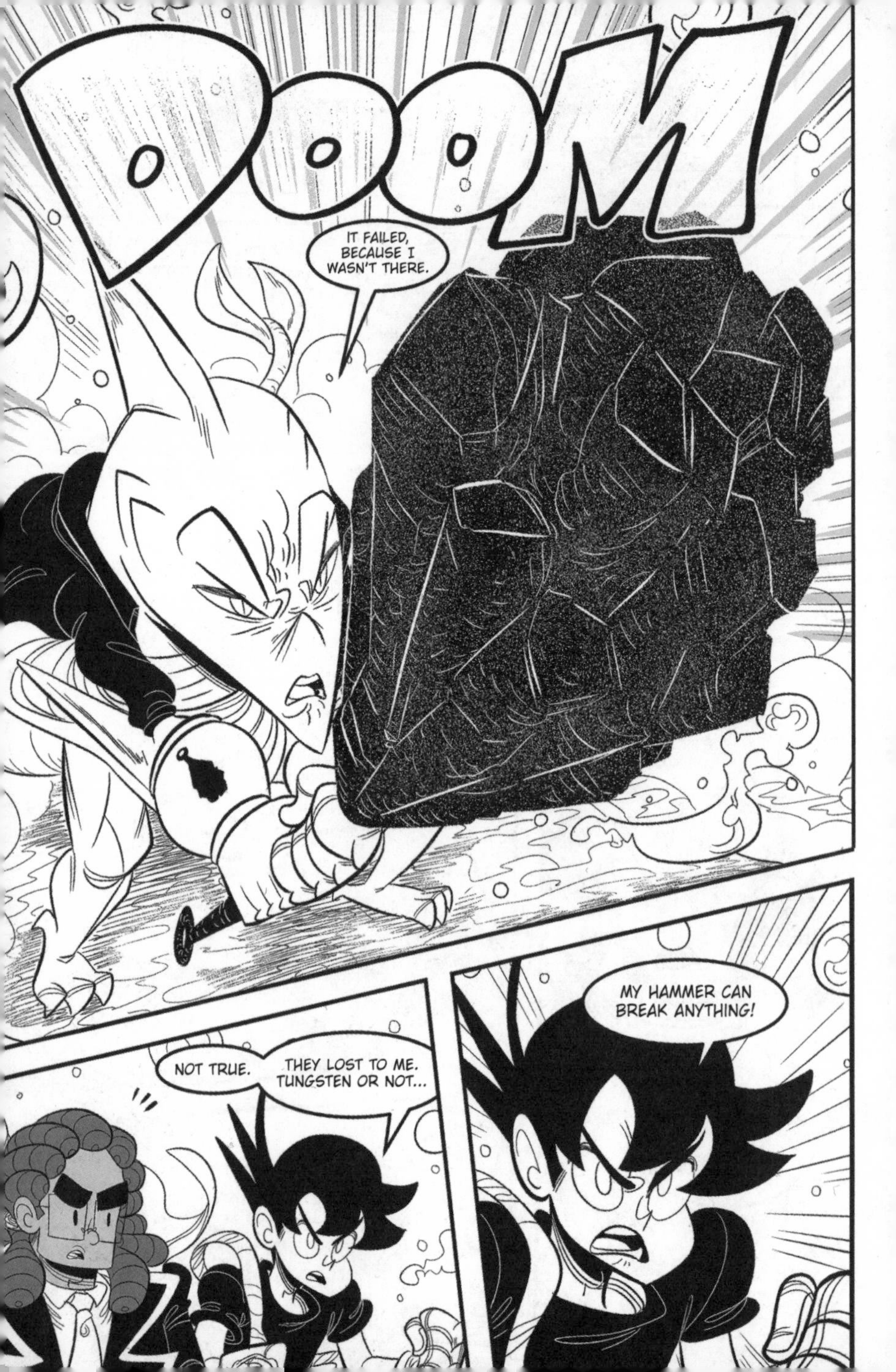
DOOM
IT FAILED, BECAUSE I WASN'T THERE.
NOT TRUE.
THEY LOST TO ME. TUNGSTEN OR NOT...
MY HAMMER CAN BREAK ANYTHING!

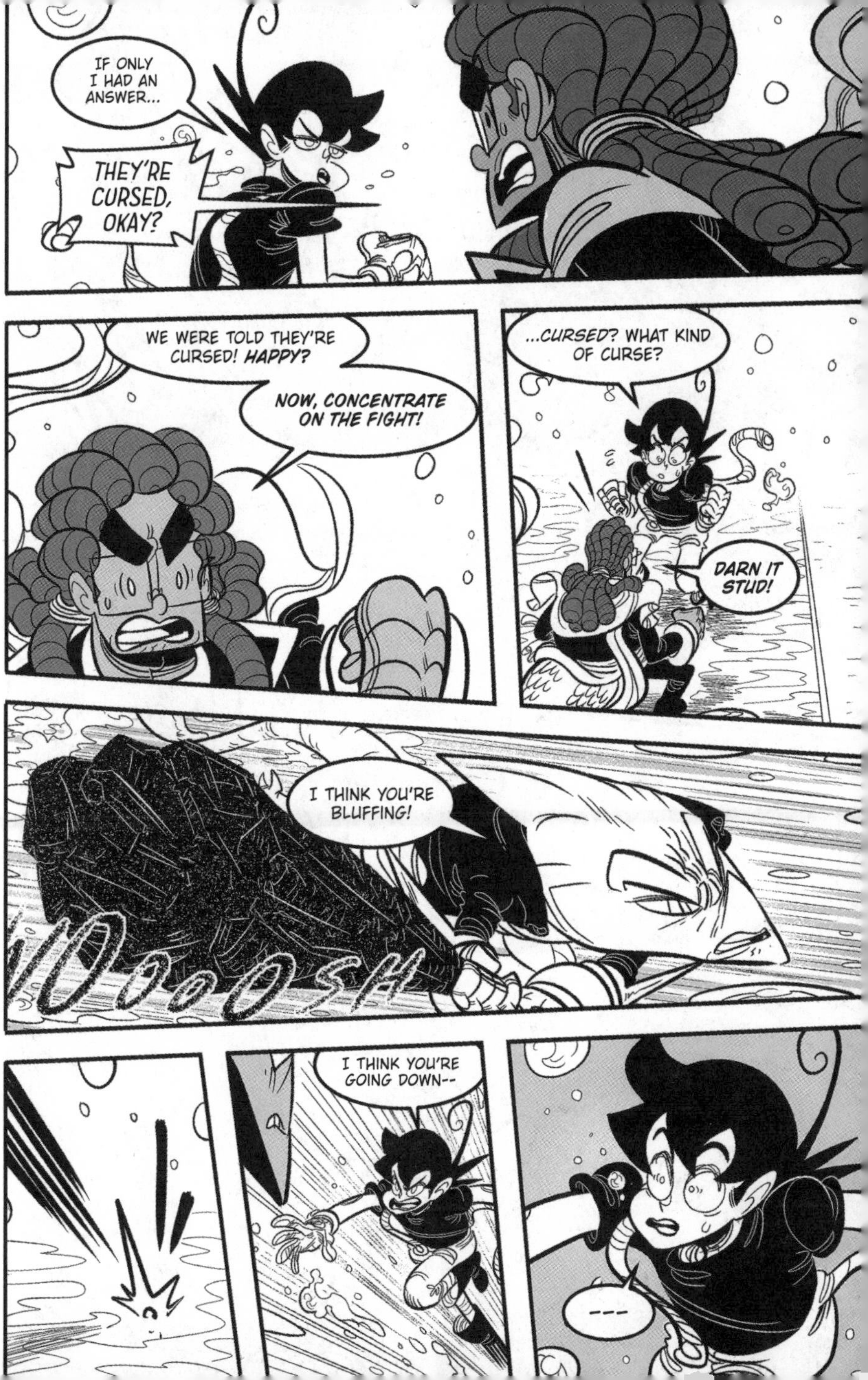
IF ONLY I HAD AN ANSWER...
THEY'RE CURSED, OKAY?
WE WERE TOLD THEY'RE CURSED! HAPPY?
NOW, CONCENTRATE ON THE FIGHT!
...CURSED? WHAT KIND OF CURSE?
DARN IT STUD!
I THINK YOU'RE BLUFFING!
WOOOoOOSH
I THINK YOU'RE GOING DOWN--

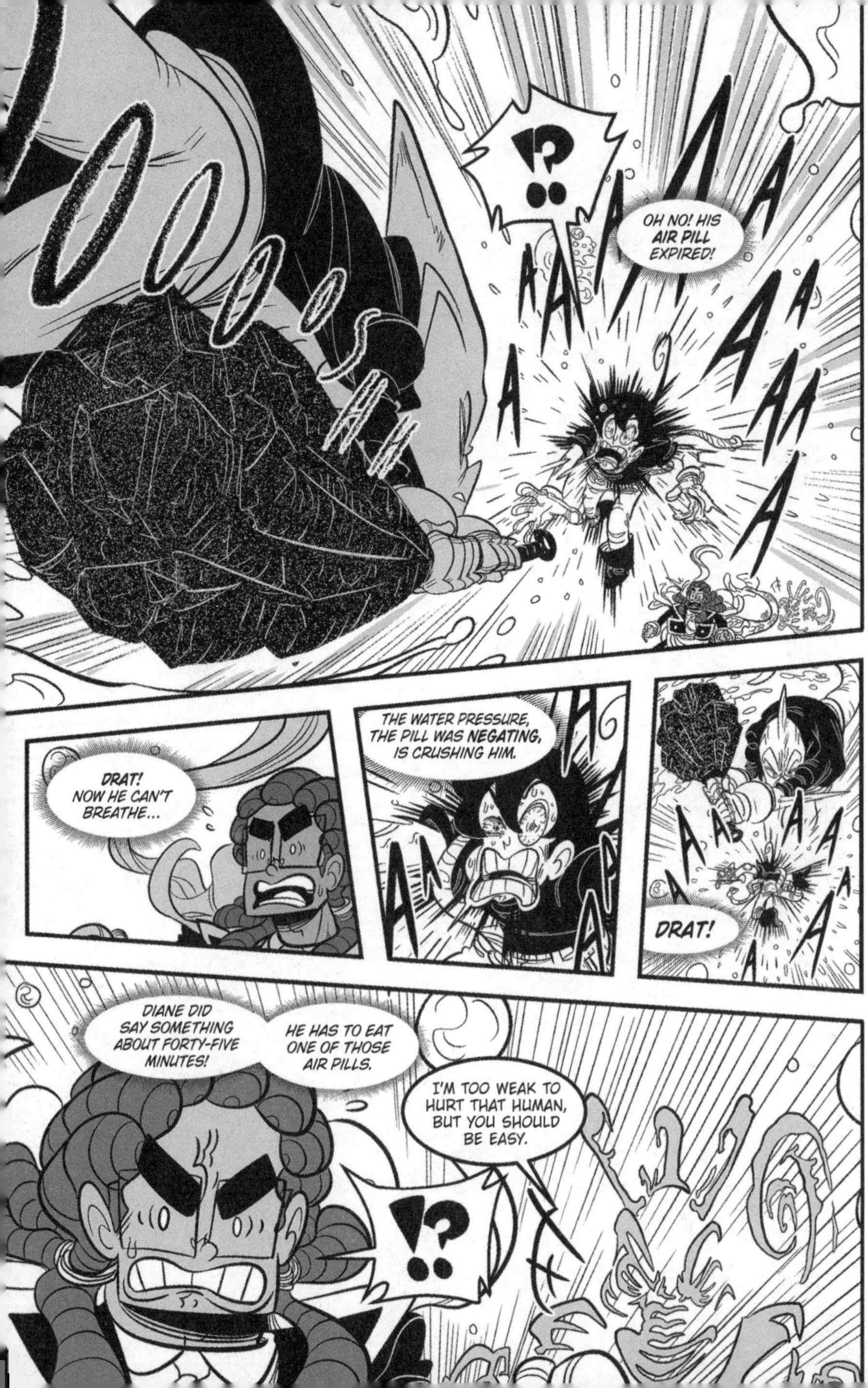
!?
OH NO! HIS AIR PILL EXPIRED!
DRAT! NOW HE CAN'T BREATHE...
THE WATER PRESSURE, THE PILL WAS NEGATING, IS CRUSHING HIM.
DRAT!
DIANE DID SAY SOMETHING ABOUT FORTY-FIVE MINUTES!
HE HAS TO EAT ONE OF THOSE AIR PILLS.
I'M TOO WEAK TO HURT THAT HUMAN, BUT YOU SHOULD BE EASY.
!?

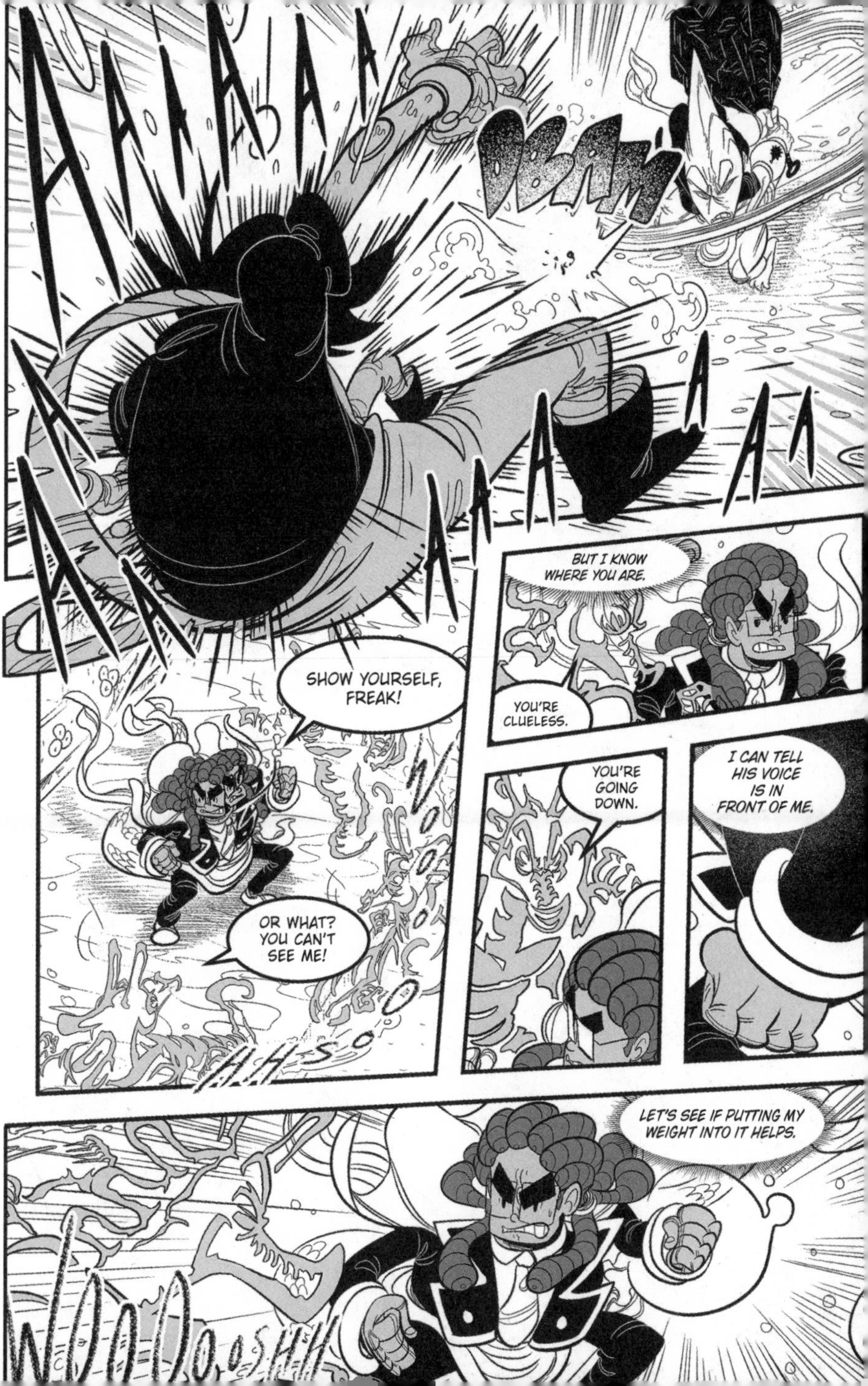
SHOW YOURSELF, FREAK!
OR WHAT? YOU CAN'T SEE ME!
BUT I KNOW WHERE YOU ARE.
YOU'RE CLUELESS.
YOU'RE GOING DOWN.
I CAN TELL HIS VOICE IS IN FRONT OF ME.
LET'S SEE IF PUTTING MY WEIGHT INTO IT HELPS.

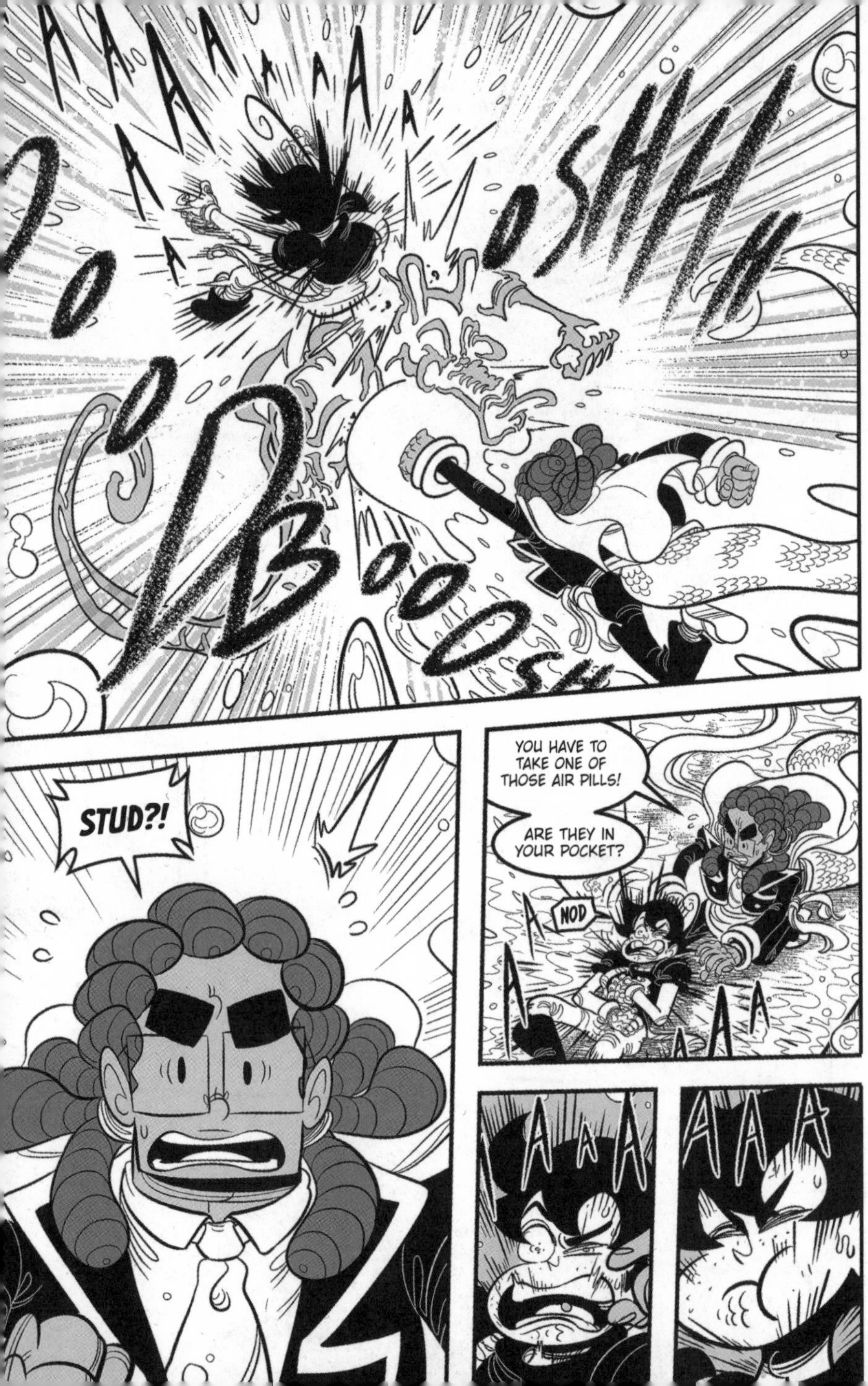
STUD?!
YOU HAVE TO TAKE ONE OF THOSE AIR PILLS!
ARE THEY IN YOUR POCKET?
NOD

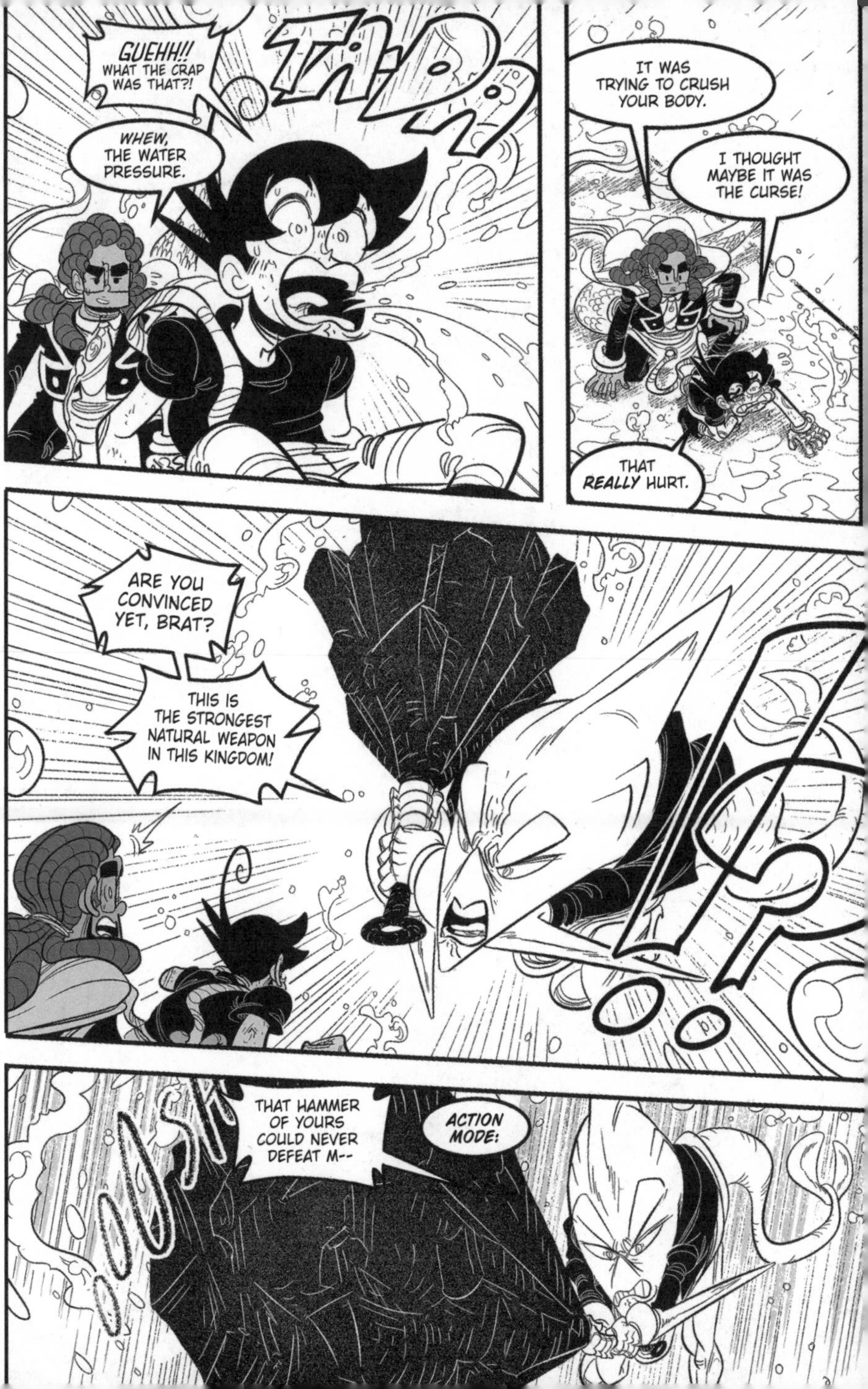
GUEHH!! WHAT THE CRAP WAS THAT?!
TAP
WHEW, THE WATER PRESSURE.
IT WAS TRYING TO CRUSH YOUR BODY.
I THOUGHT MAYBE IT WAS THE CURSE!
THAT REALLY HURT.
ARE YOU CONVINCED YET, BRAT?
THIS IS THE STRONGEST NATURAL WEAPON IN THIS KINGDOM!
THAT HAMMER OF YOURS COULD NEVER DEFEAT M--
ACTION MODE:

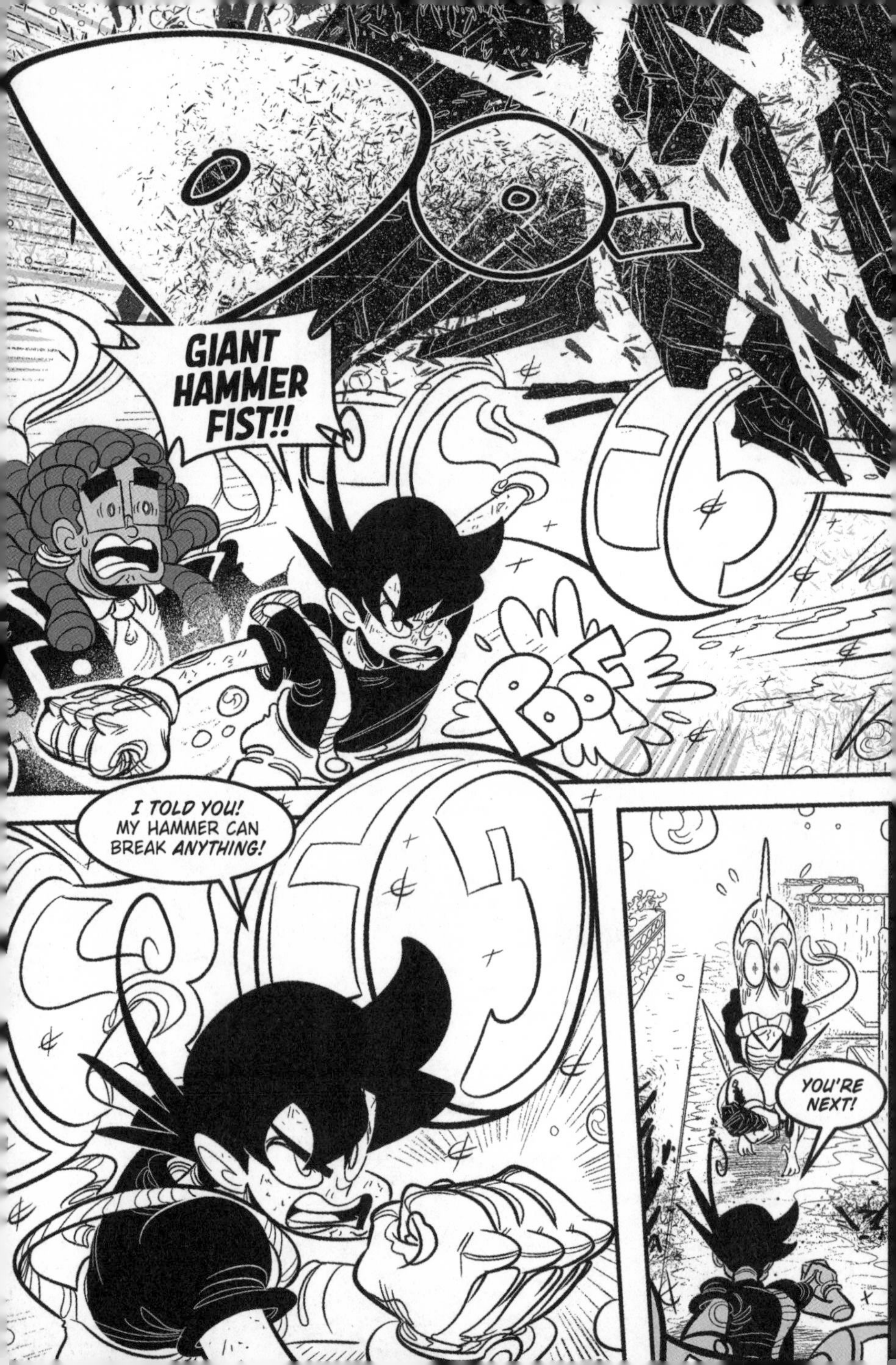
GIANT HAMMER FIST!!
POOF
I TOLD YOU! MY HAMMER CAN BREAK ANYTHING!
YOU'RE NEXT!

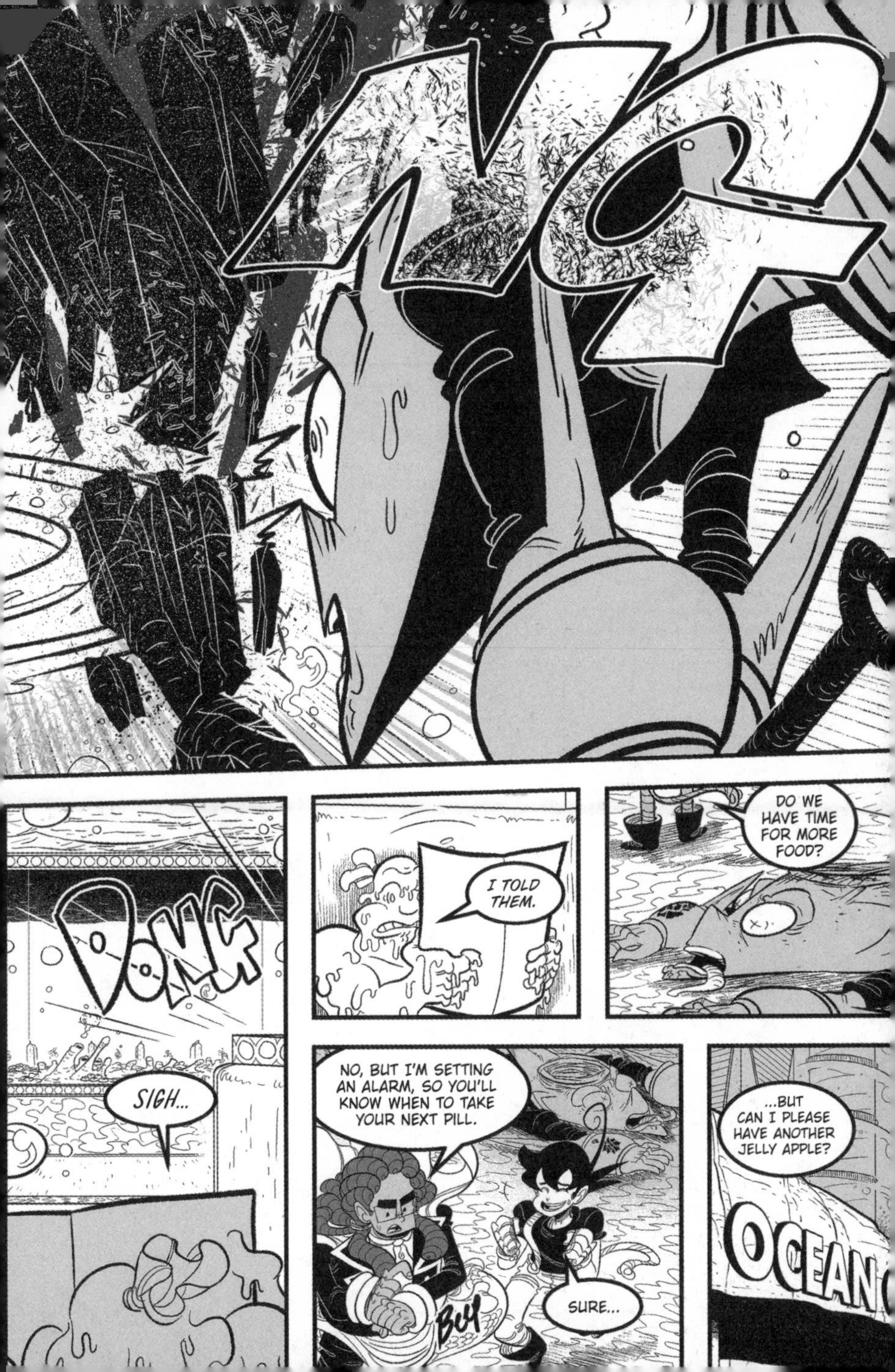
NG
DONG
SIGH...
I TOLD THEM.
DO WE HAVE TIME FOR MORE FOOD?
NO, BUT I'M SETTING AN ALARM, SO YOU'LL KNOW WHEN TO TAKE YOUR NEXT PILL.
SURE...
BUY
...BUT CAN I PLEASE HAVE ANOTHER JELLY APPLE?
OCEAN

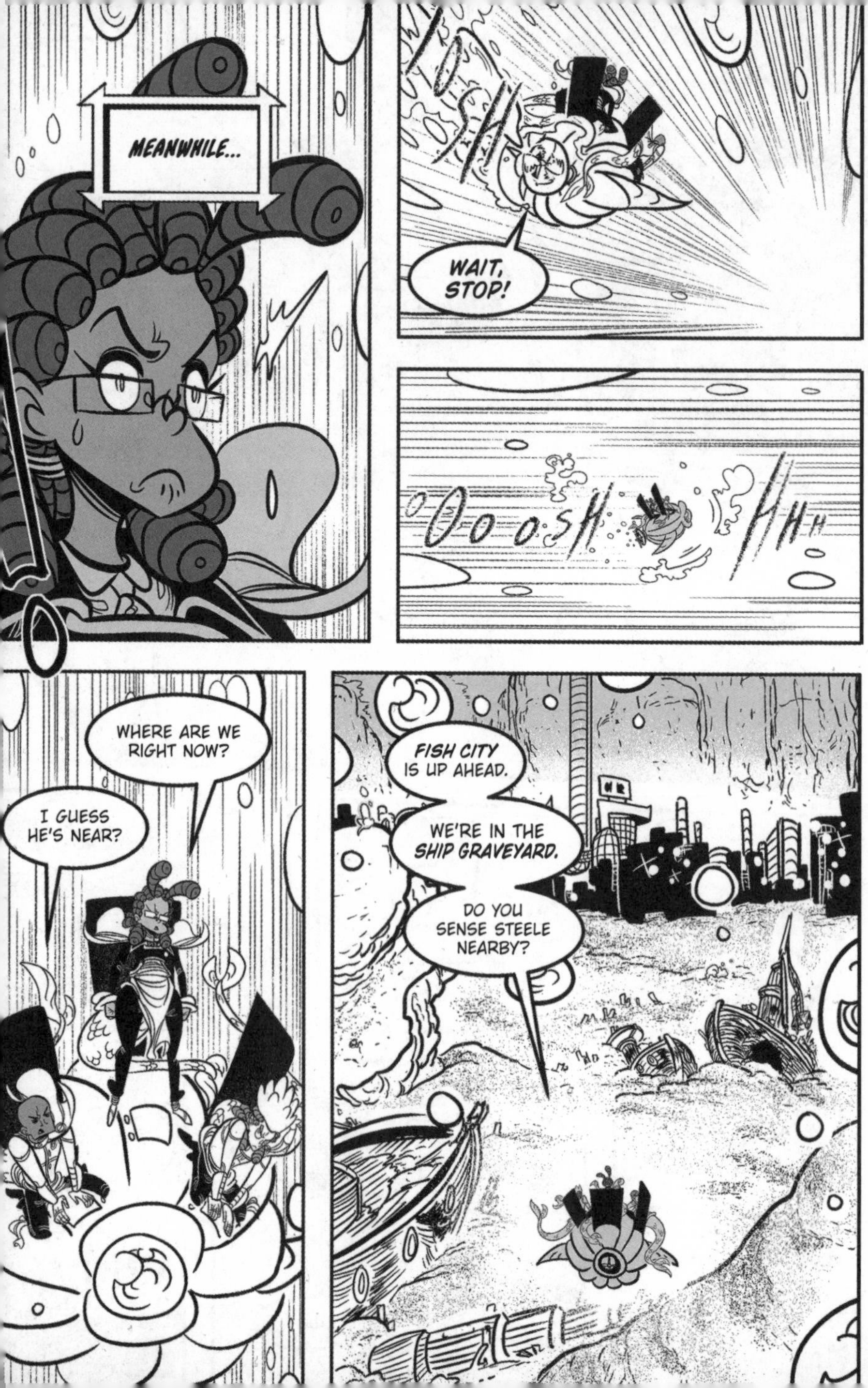
MEANWHILE...
WAIT, STOP!
WHERE ARE WE RIGHT NOW?
I GUESS HE'S NEAR?
FISH CITY IS UP AHEAD.
WE'RE IN THE SHIP GRAVEYARD.
DO YOU SENSE STEELE NEARBY?

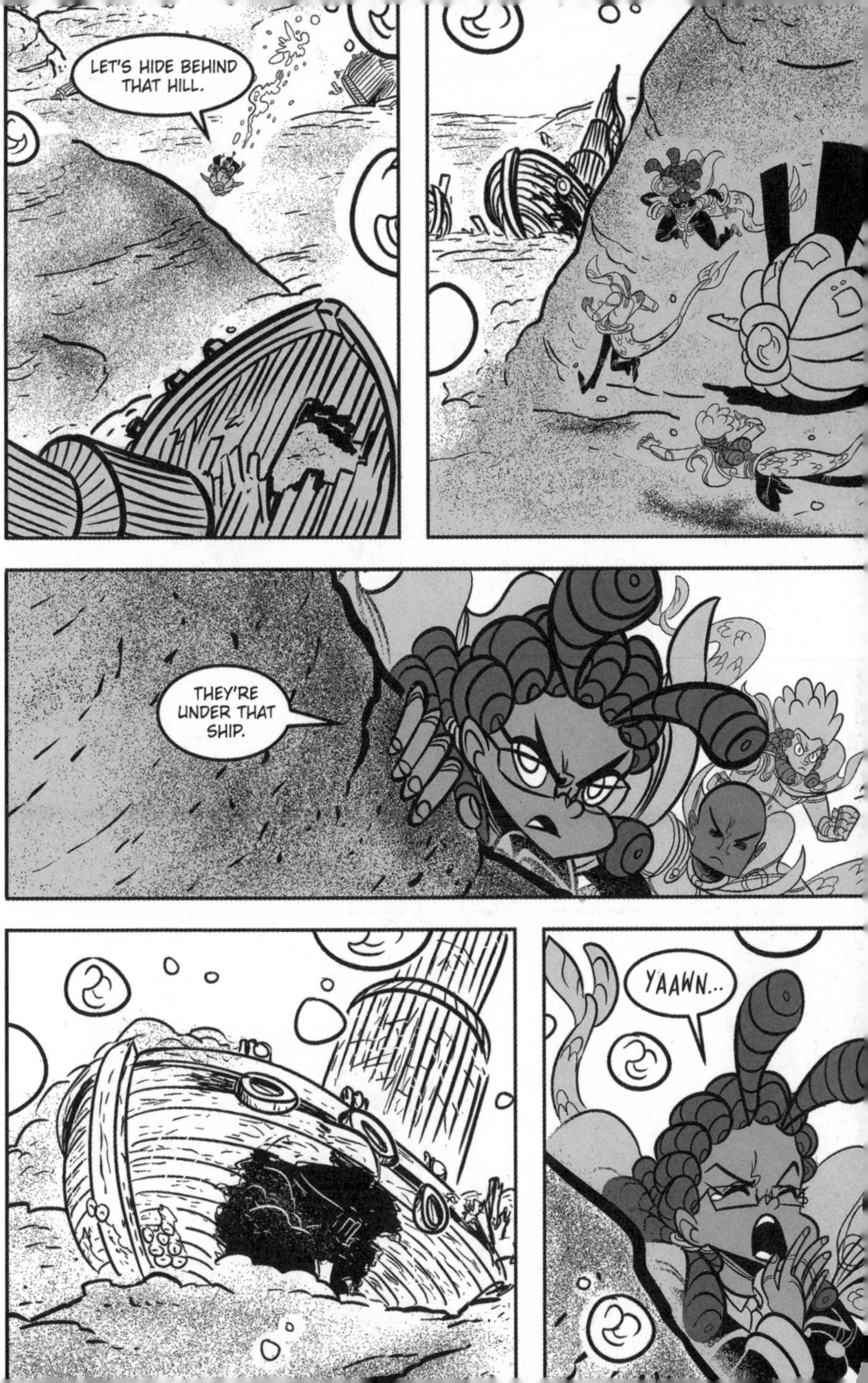
LET'S HIDE BEHIND THAT HILL.
THEY'RE UNDER THAT SHIP.
YAAWN...

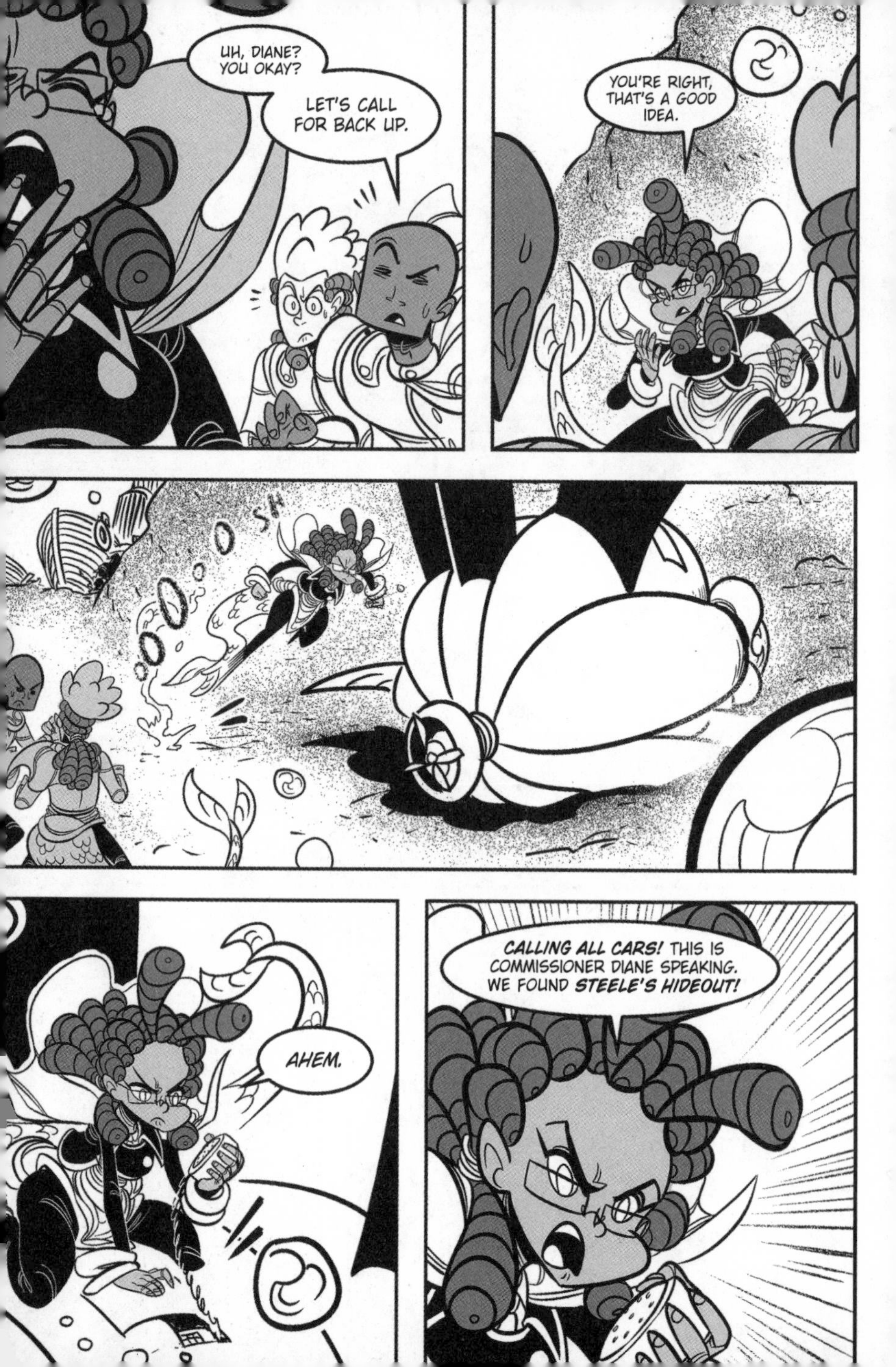
UH, DIANE? YOU OKAY?
LET'S CALL FOR BACK UP.
YOU'RE RIGHT, THAT'S A GOOD IDEA.
SH
AHEM.
CALLING ALL CARS! THIS IS COMMISSIONER DIANE SPEAKING. WE FOUND STEELE'S HIDEOUT!

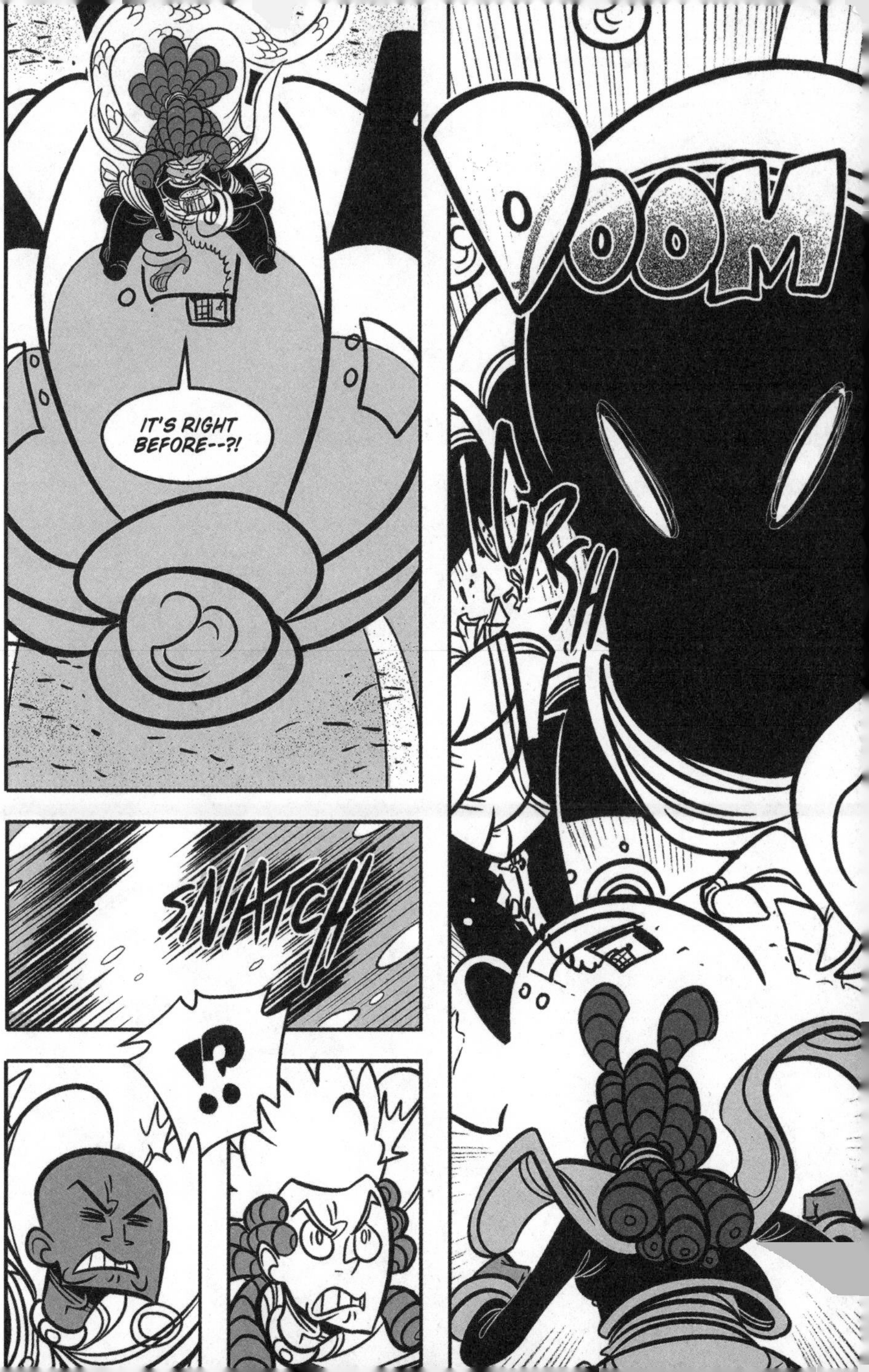
IT'S RIGHT BEFORE--?!
SNATCH
!?
VOOM
CRSH

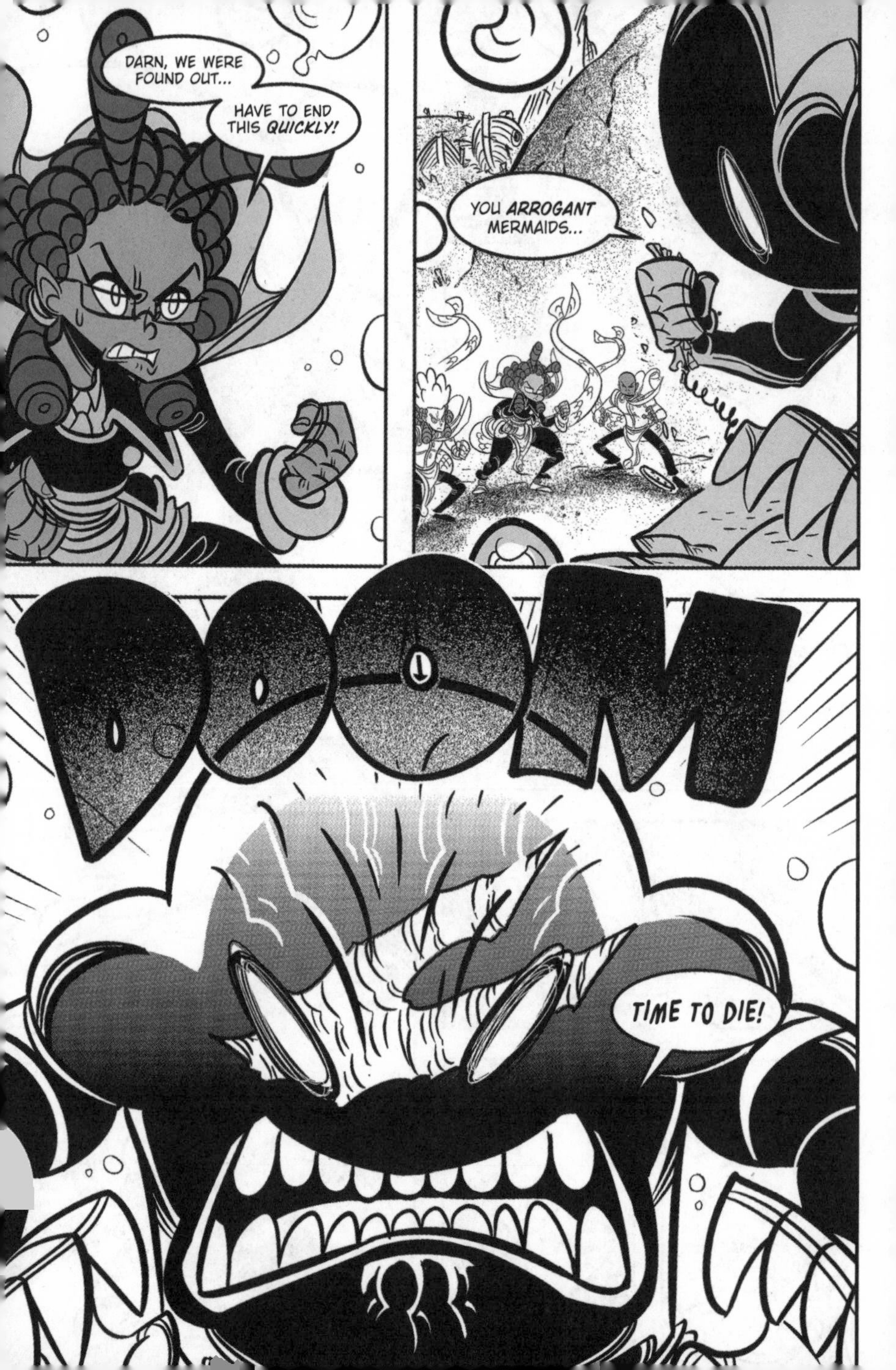
DARN, WE WERE FOUND OUT...
HAVE TO END THIS QUICKLY!
YOU ARROGANT MERMAIDS...
DOOM
TIME TO DIE!

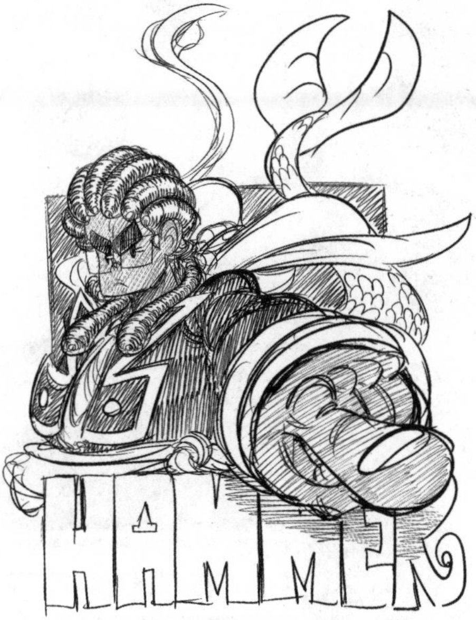
HAMMER

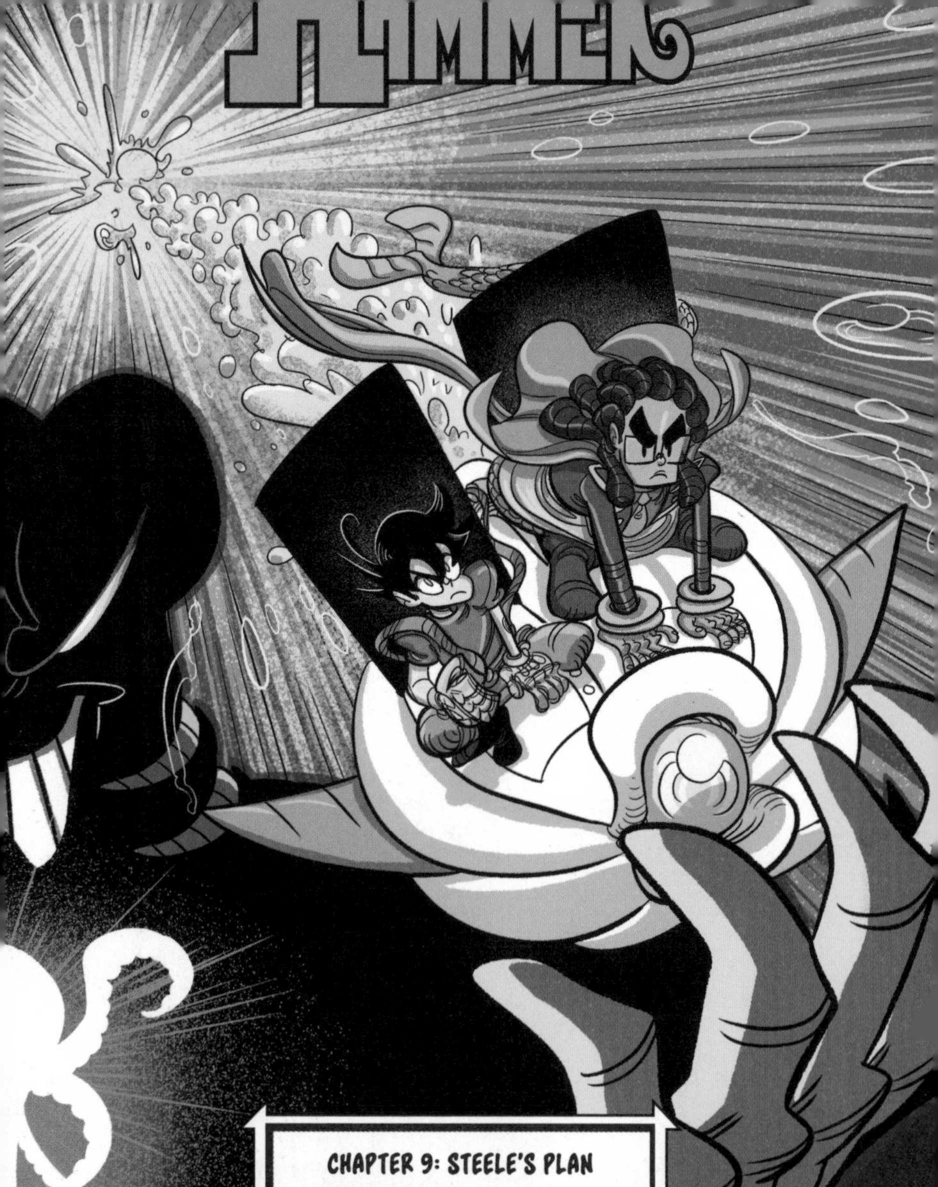
CHAPTER 9: STEELE'S PLAN

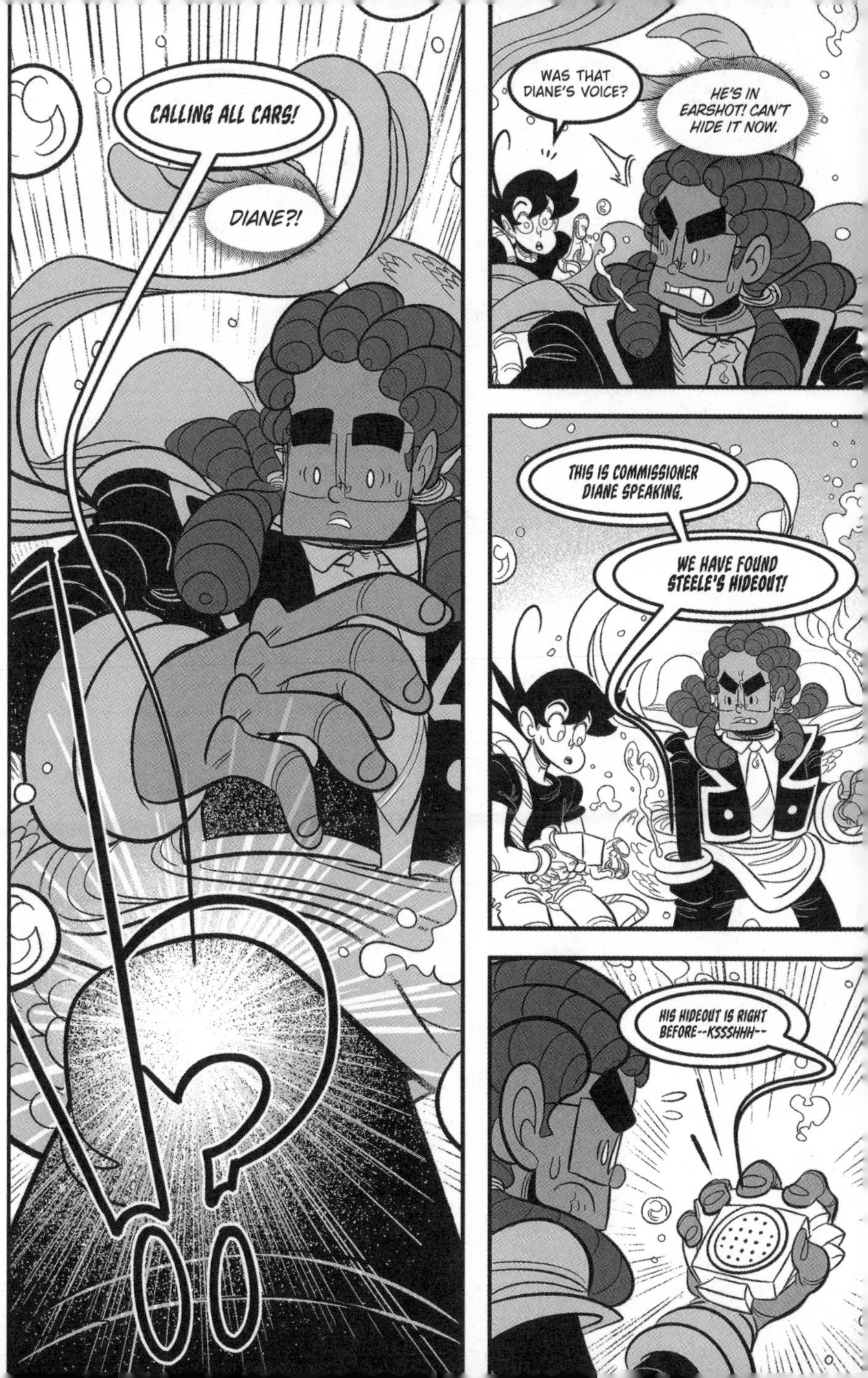
CALLING ALL CARS!
DIANE?!
WAS THAT DIANE'S VOICE?
HE'S IN EARSHOT! CAN'T HIDE IT NOW.
THIS IS COMMISSIONER DIANE SPEAKING.
WE HAVE FOUND STEELE'S HIDEOUT!
HIS HIDEOUT IS RIGHT BEFORE--KSSSHHH--

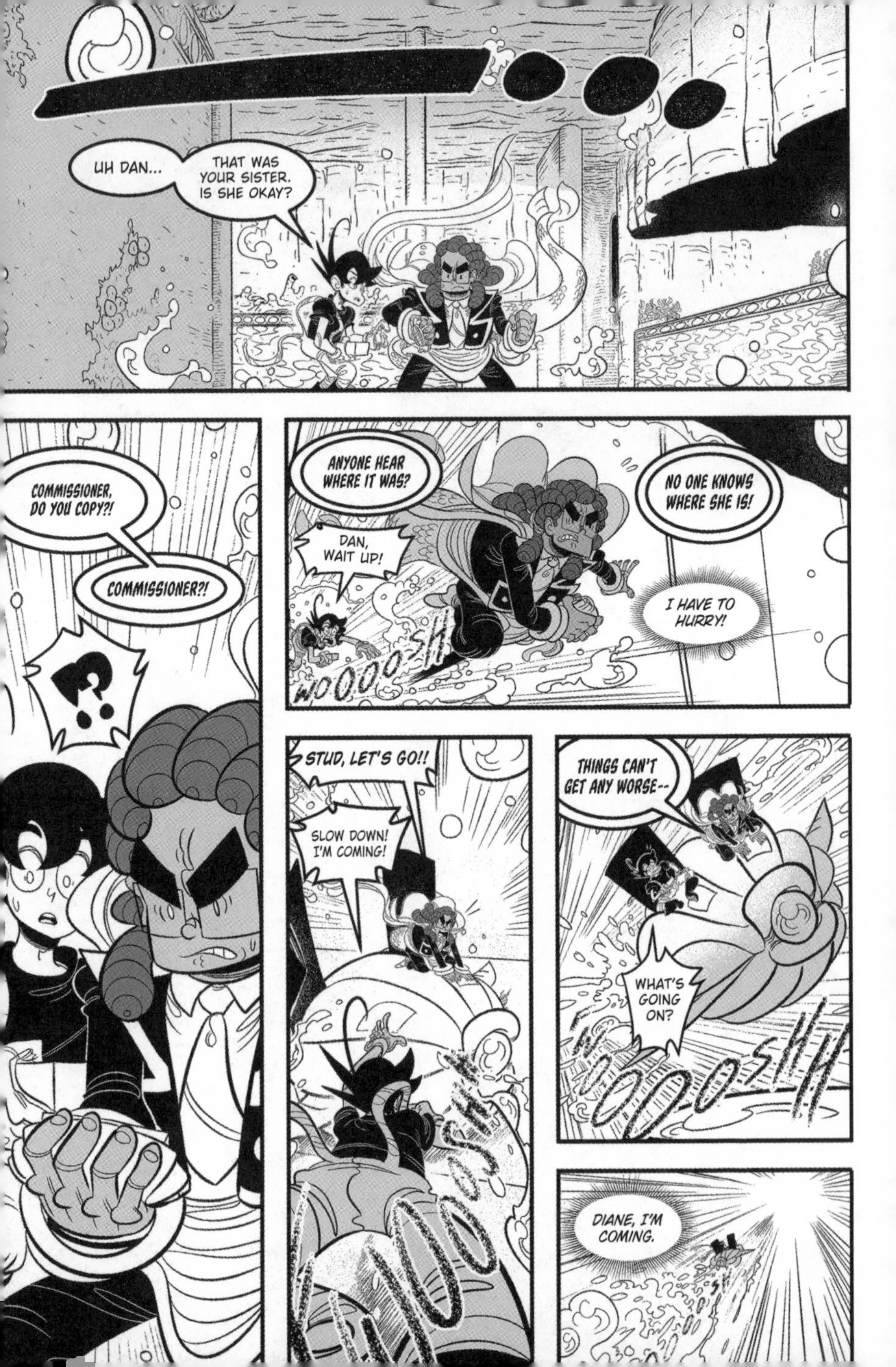
UH DAN...
THAT WAS YOUR SISTER. IS SHE OKAY?
COMMISSIONER, DO YOU COPY?!
COMMISSIONER?!
?
ANYONE HEAR WHERE IT WAS?
NO ONE KNOWS WHERE SHE IS!
DAN, WAIT UP!
I HAVE TO HURRY!
STUD, LET'S GO!!
SLOW DOWN! I'M COMING!
THINGS CAN'T GET ANY WORSE--
WHAT'S GOING ON?
DIANE, I'M COMING.

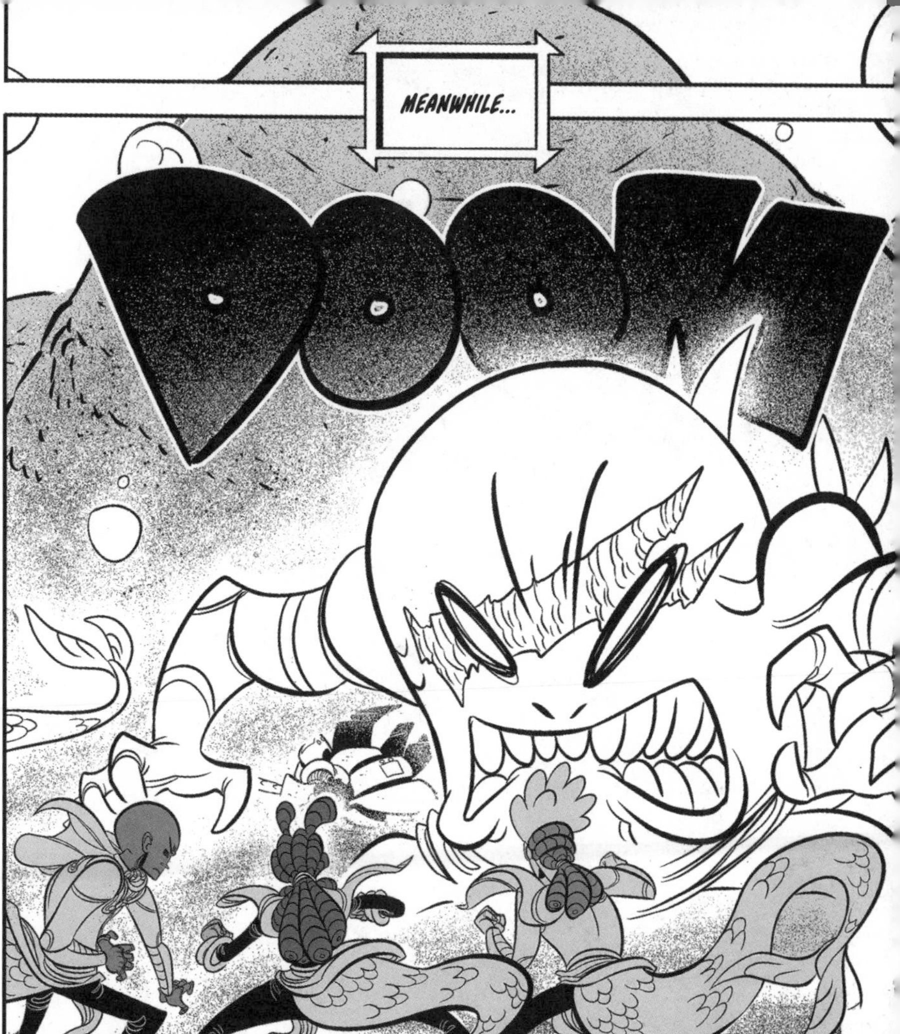
MEANWHILE...
DOOOM
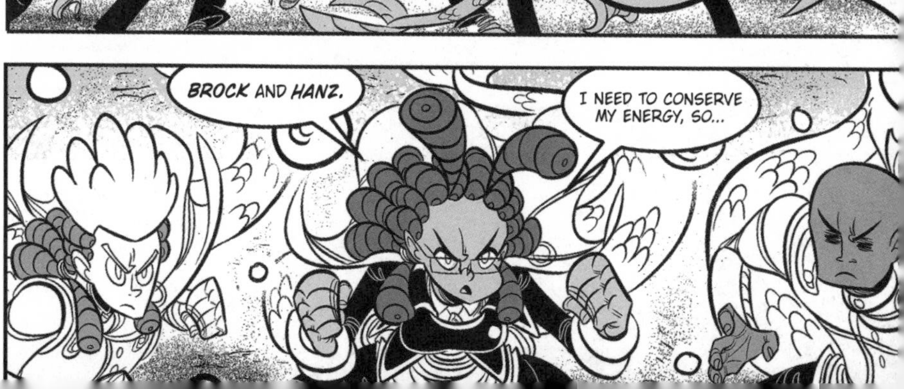
BROCK AND HANZ.
I NEED TO CONSERVE MY ENERGY, SO...

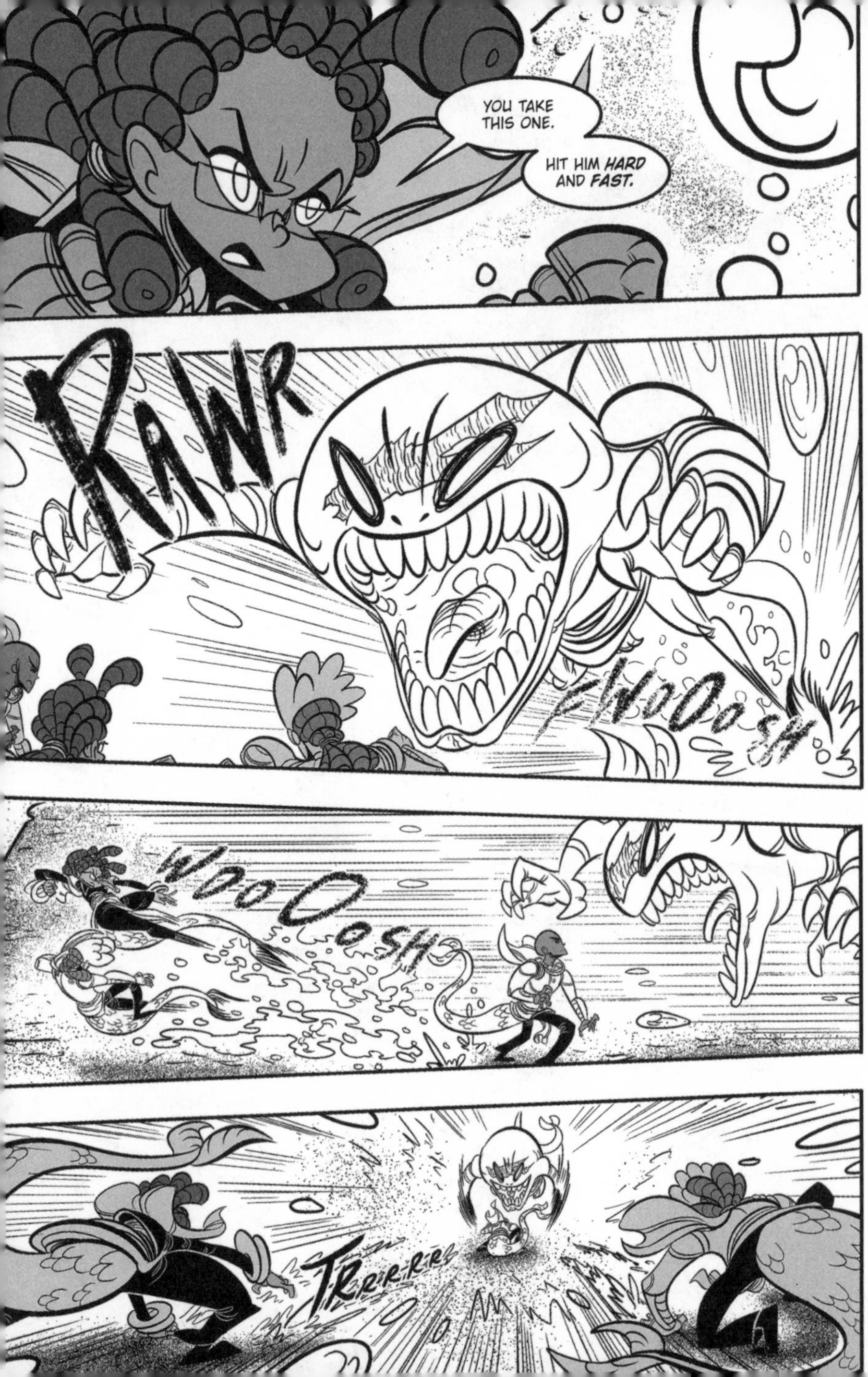
YOU TAKE THIS ONE.
HIT HIM HARD AND FAST.
RAWR
FWOOOOSH
WOOOOSH
TRRRRR

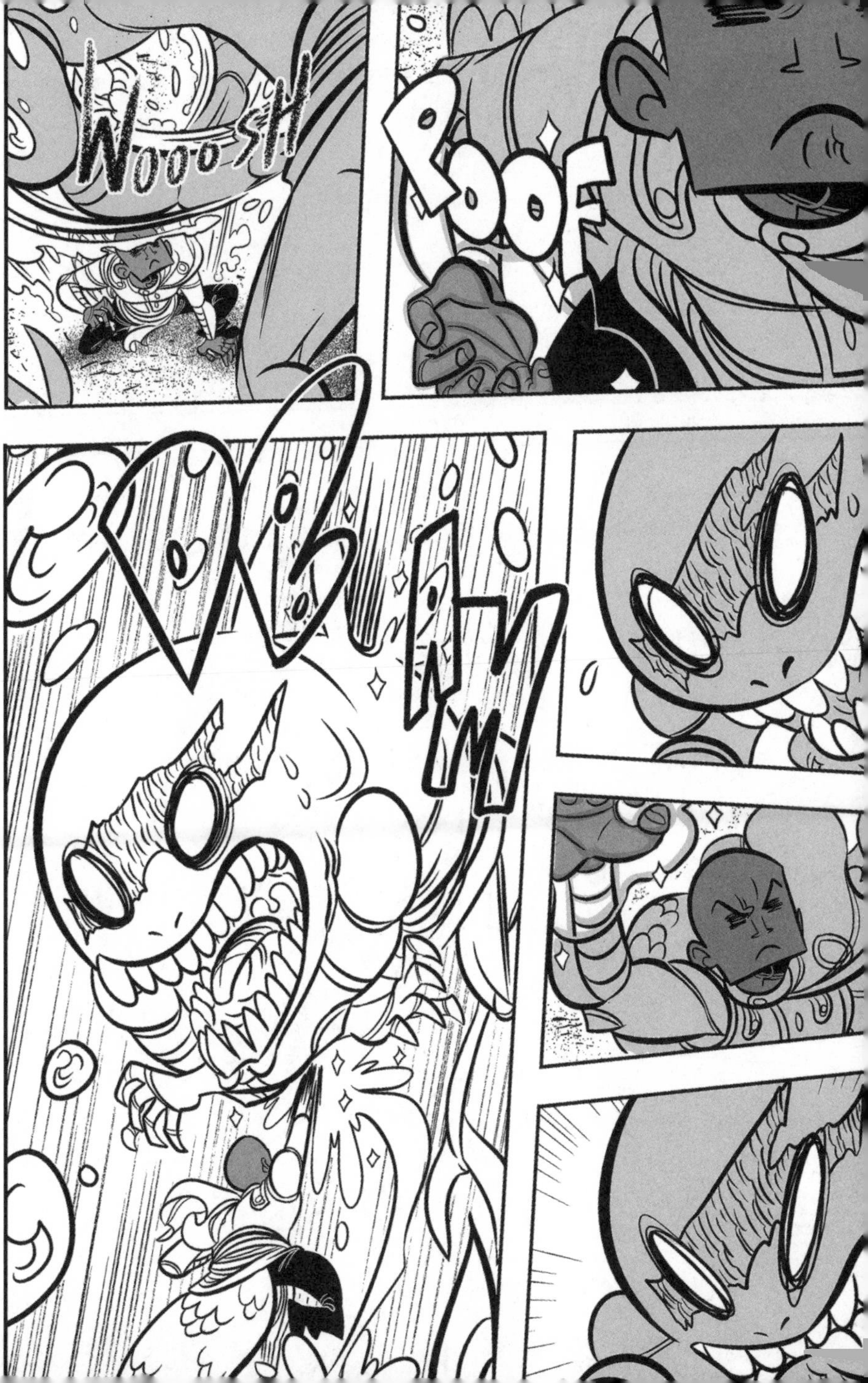
WOOOOSH
POOF

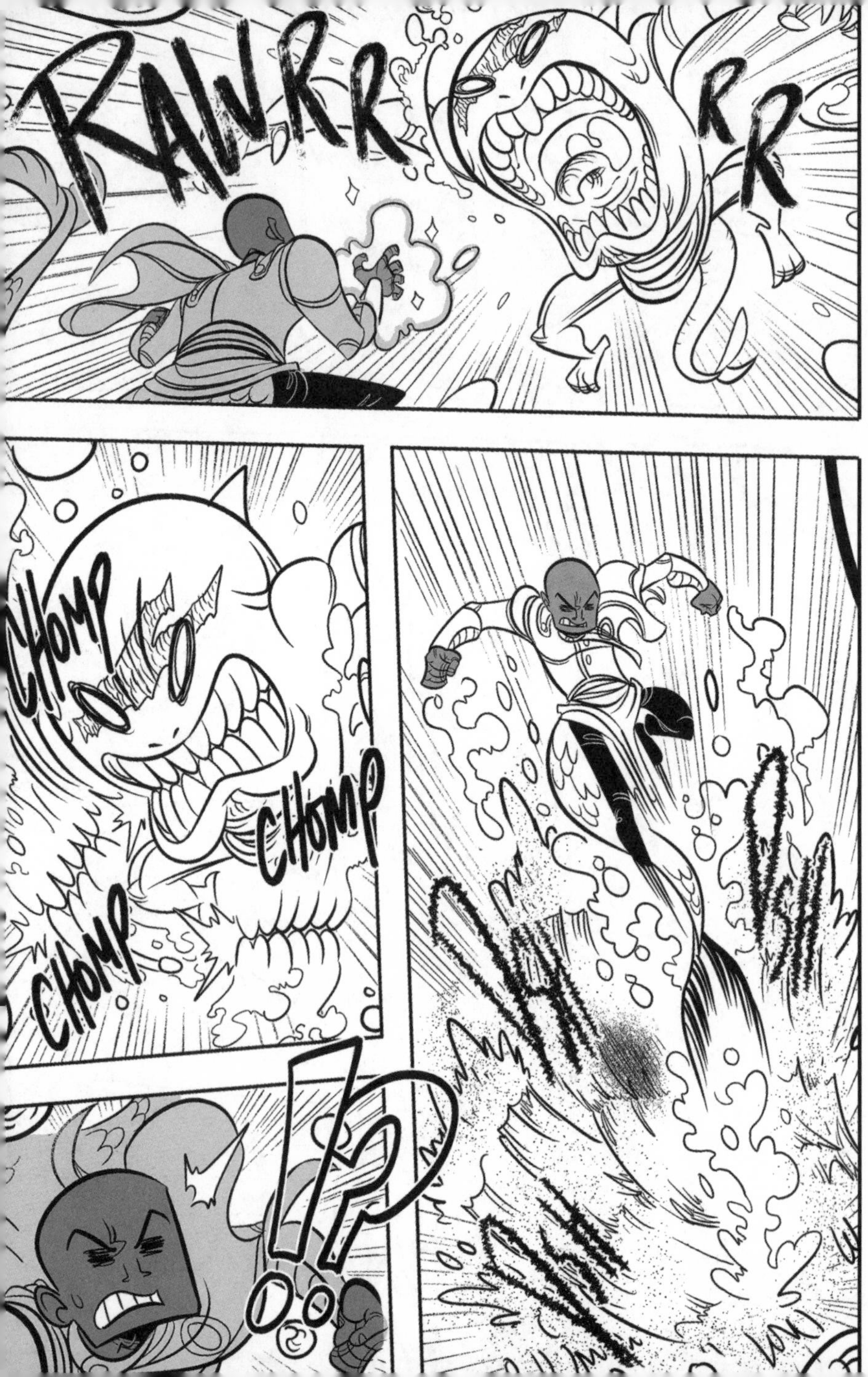
RAWRR
RR
CHOMP
CHOMP
CHOMP
VSH
!?

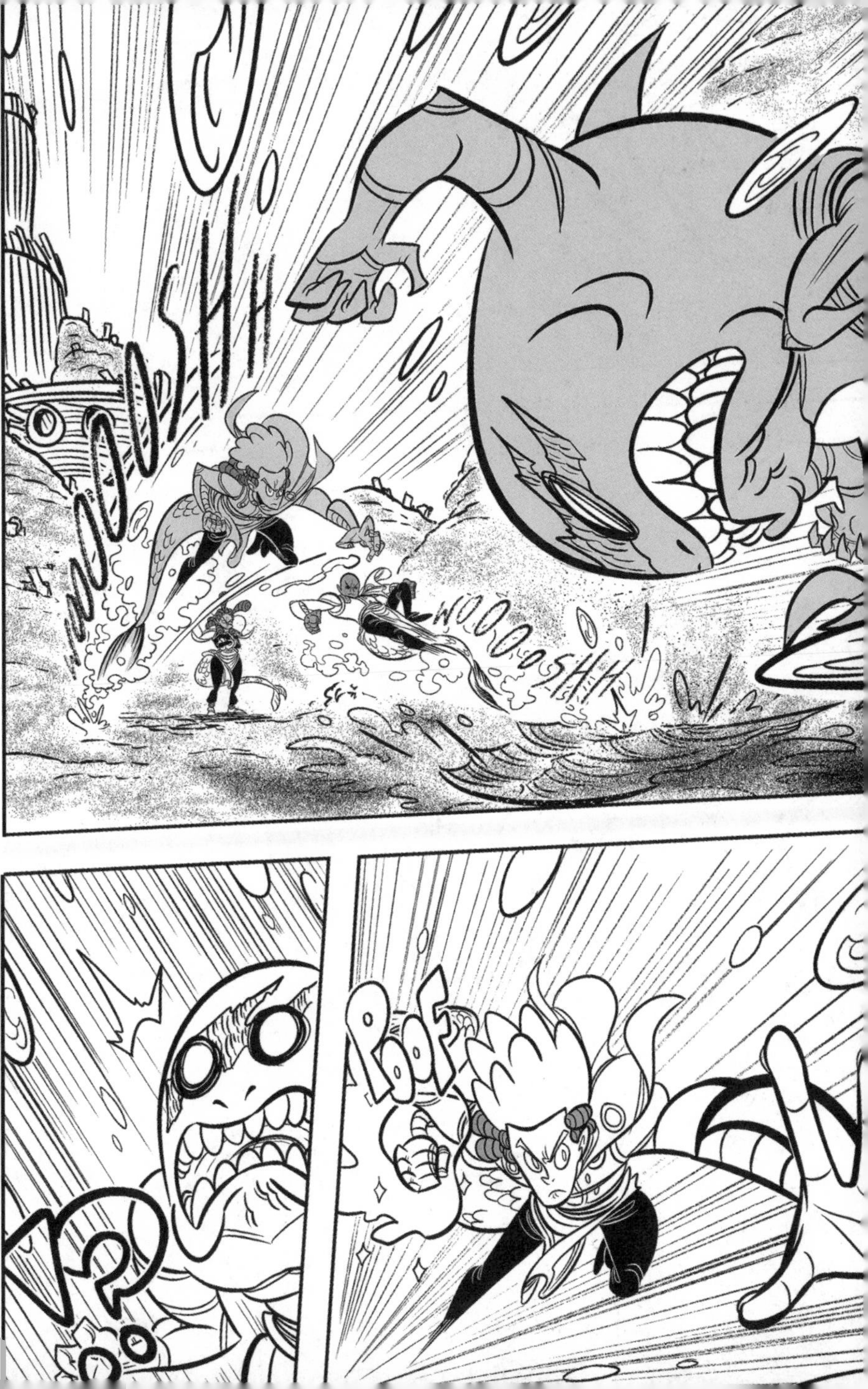
WOOOOSHH
WOOOOOSHH
?
POOF

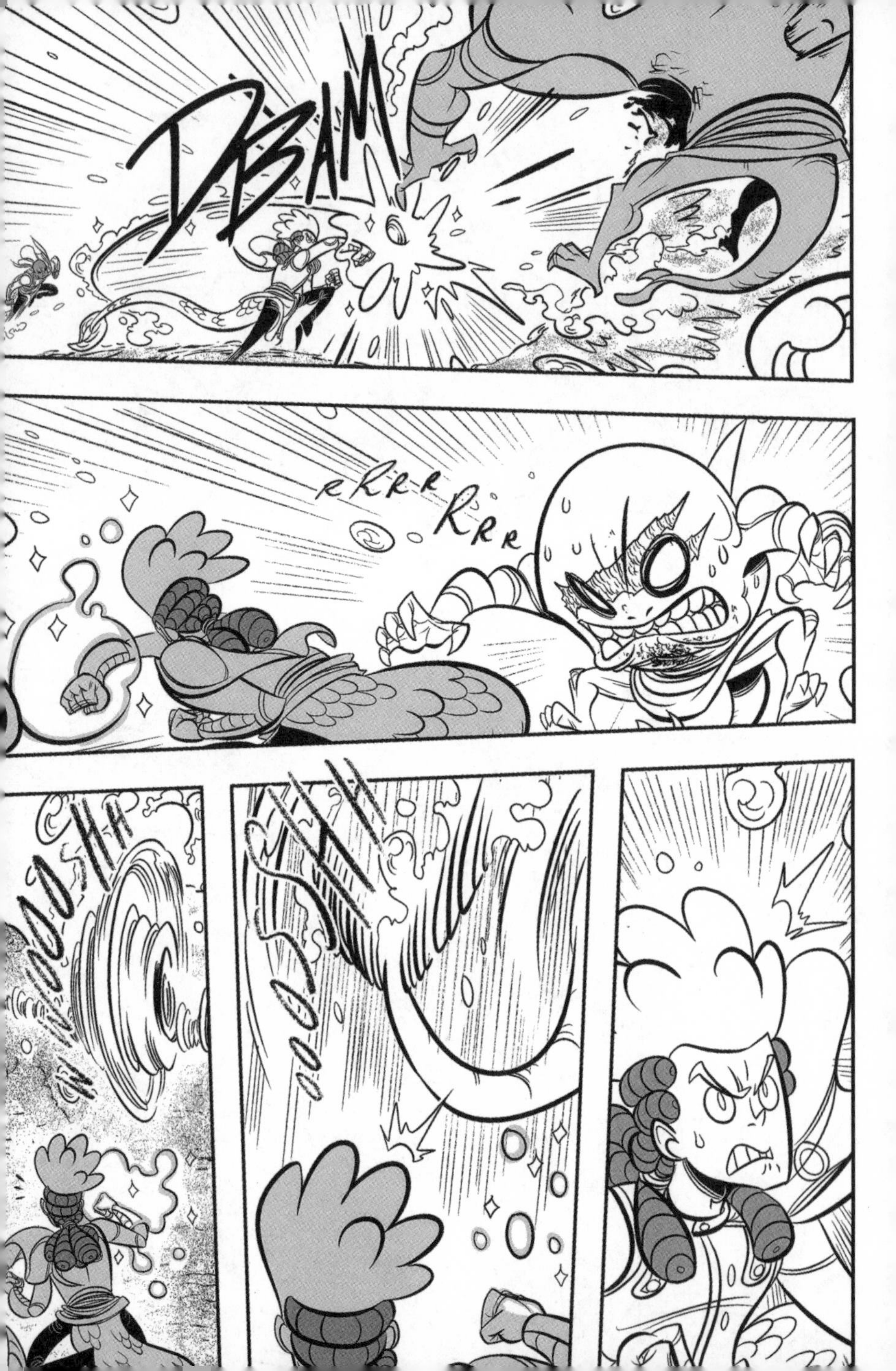
DBAM
RRRR
RRR
WHOOOSHH
WHOOOSHH

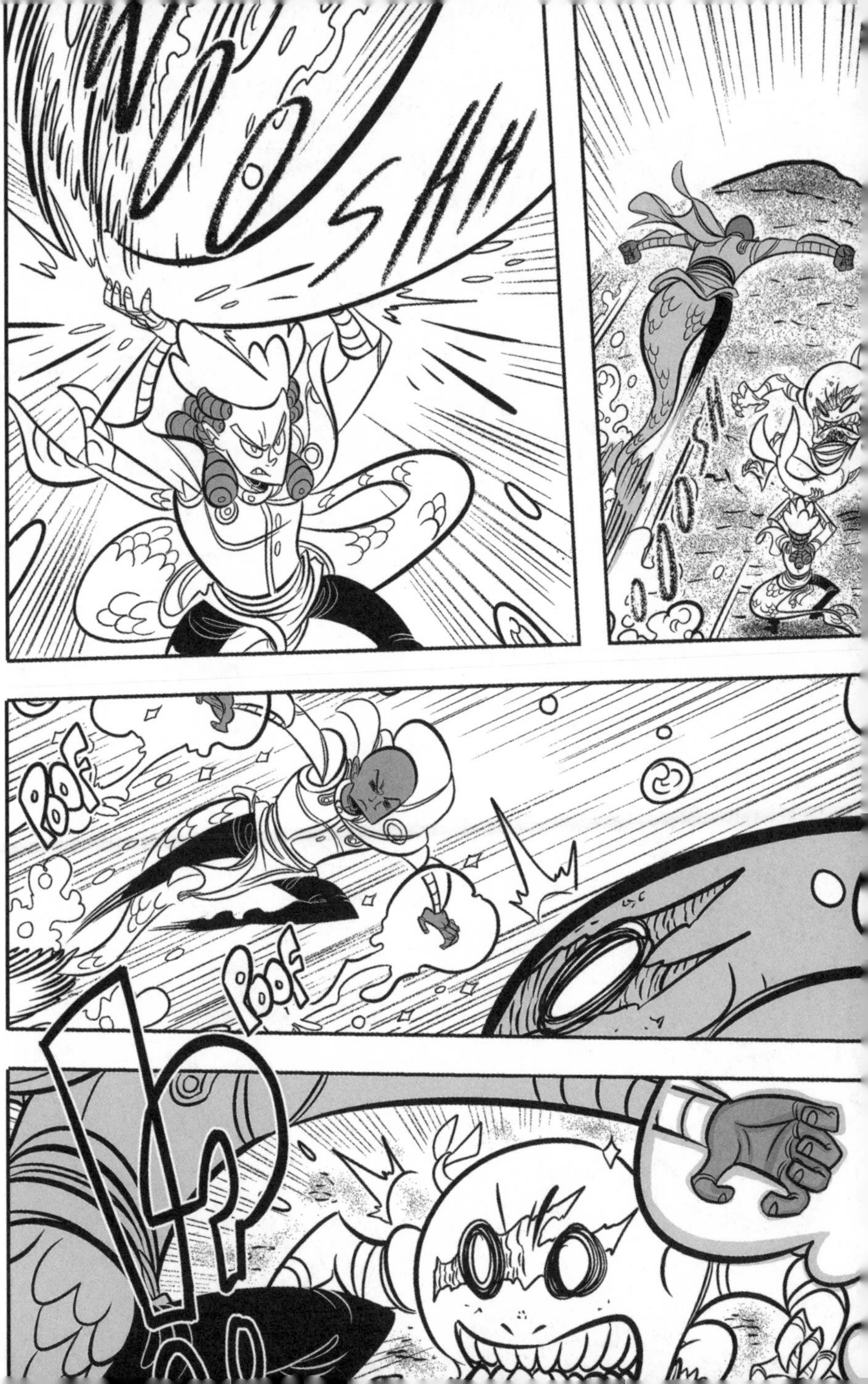
WOOSHH
OOOSH
POOF
POOF

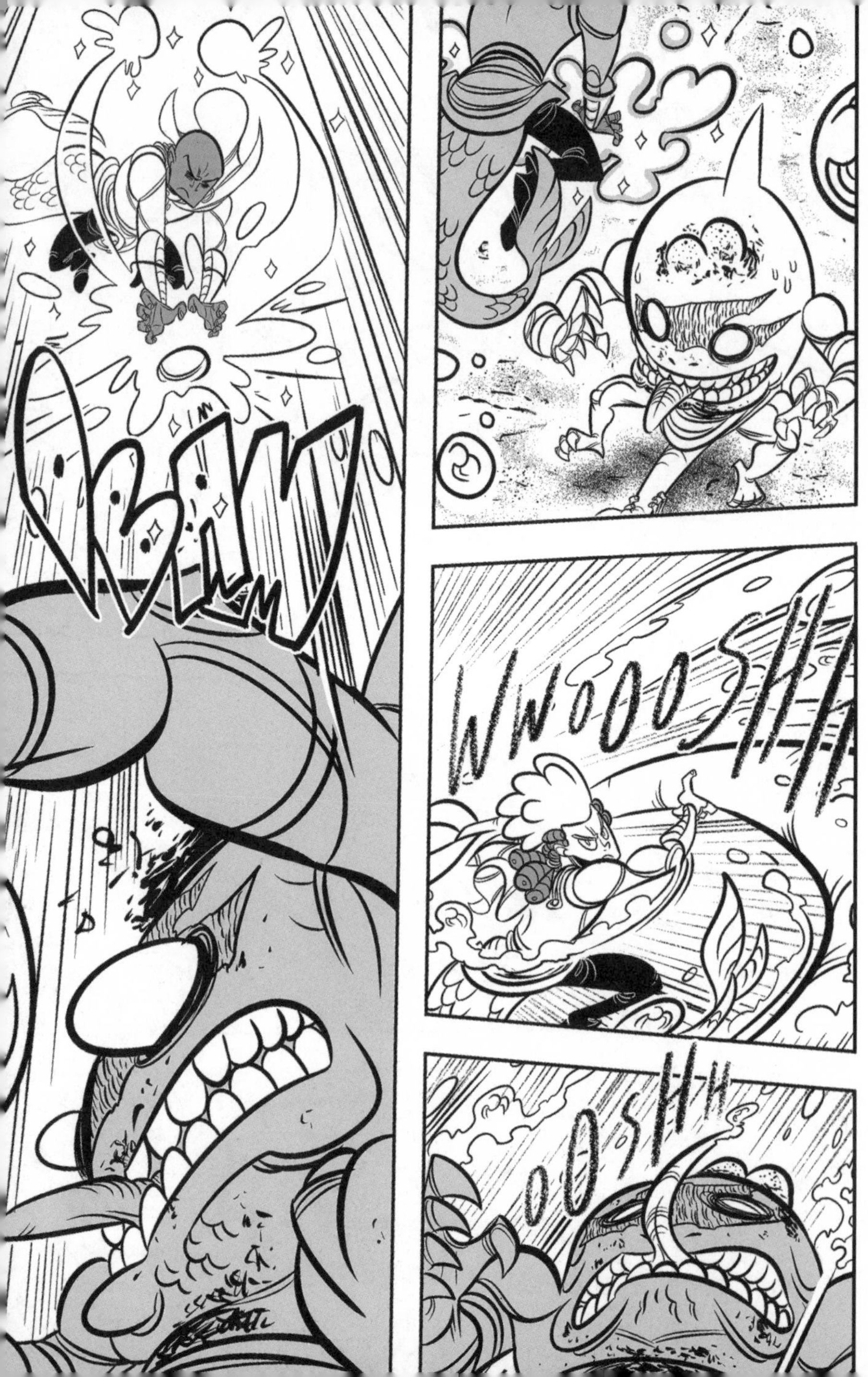
BAM
WWOOOSHH
OOSHH

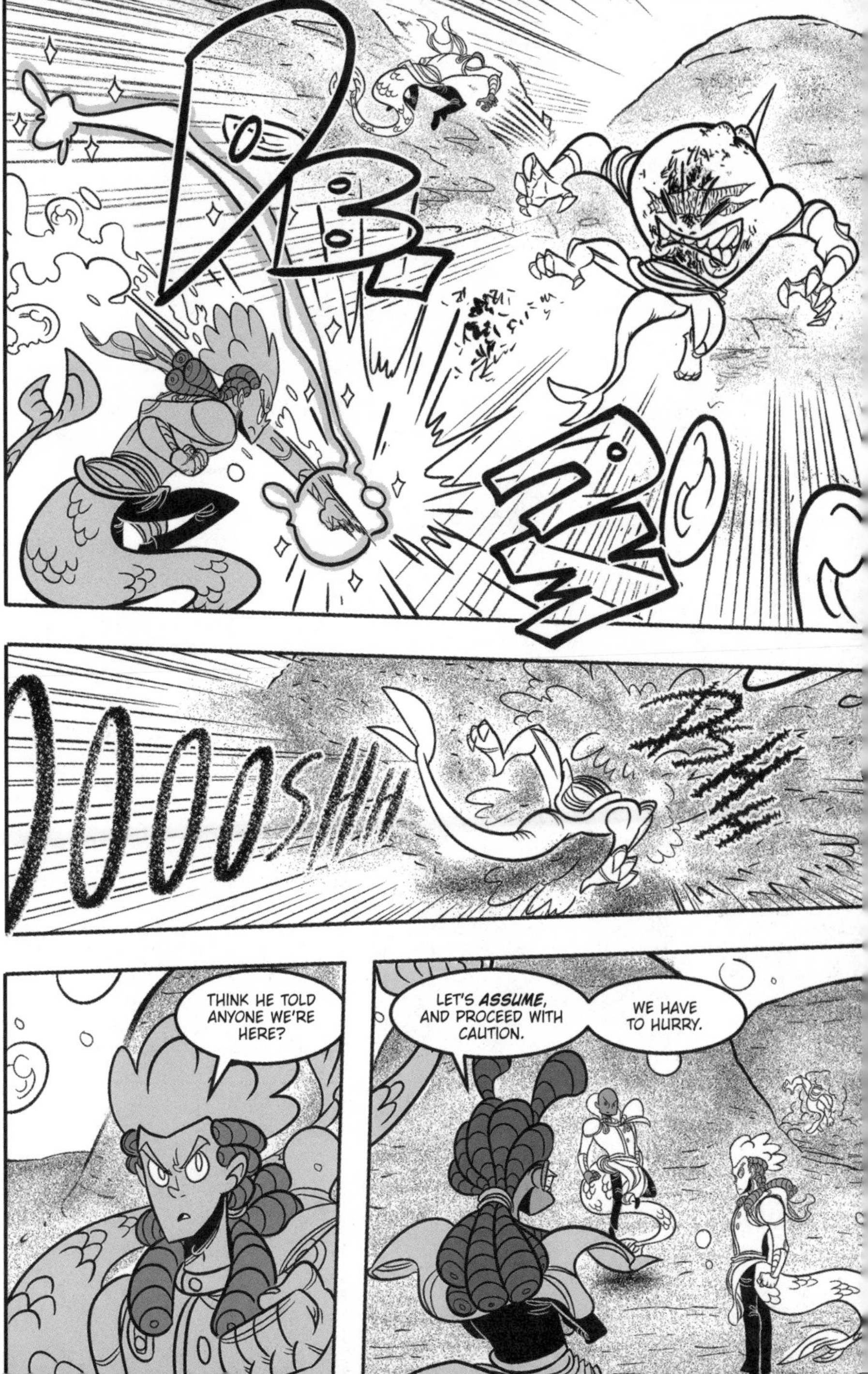
THINK HE TOLD ANYONE WE'RE HERE?
LET'S **ASSUME**, AND PROCEED WITH CAUTION.
WE HAVE TO HURRY.

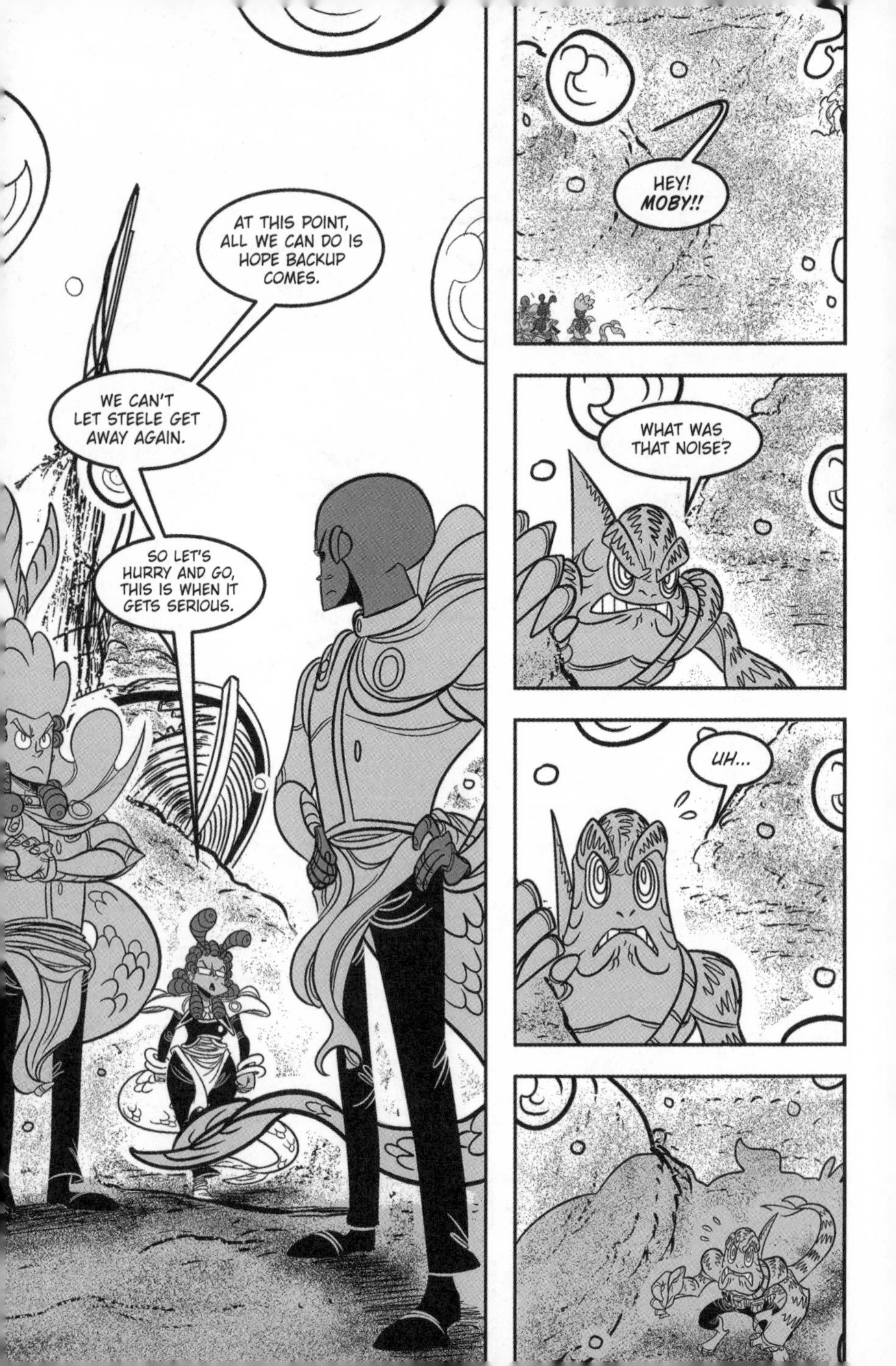
AT THIS POINT, ALL WE CAN DO IS HOPE BACKUP COMES.
WE CAN'T LET STEELE GET AWAY AGAIN.
SO LET'S HURRY AND GO, THIS IS WHEN IT GETS SERIOUS.
HEY! MOBY!!
WHAT WAS THAT NOISE?
UH...

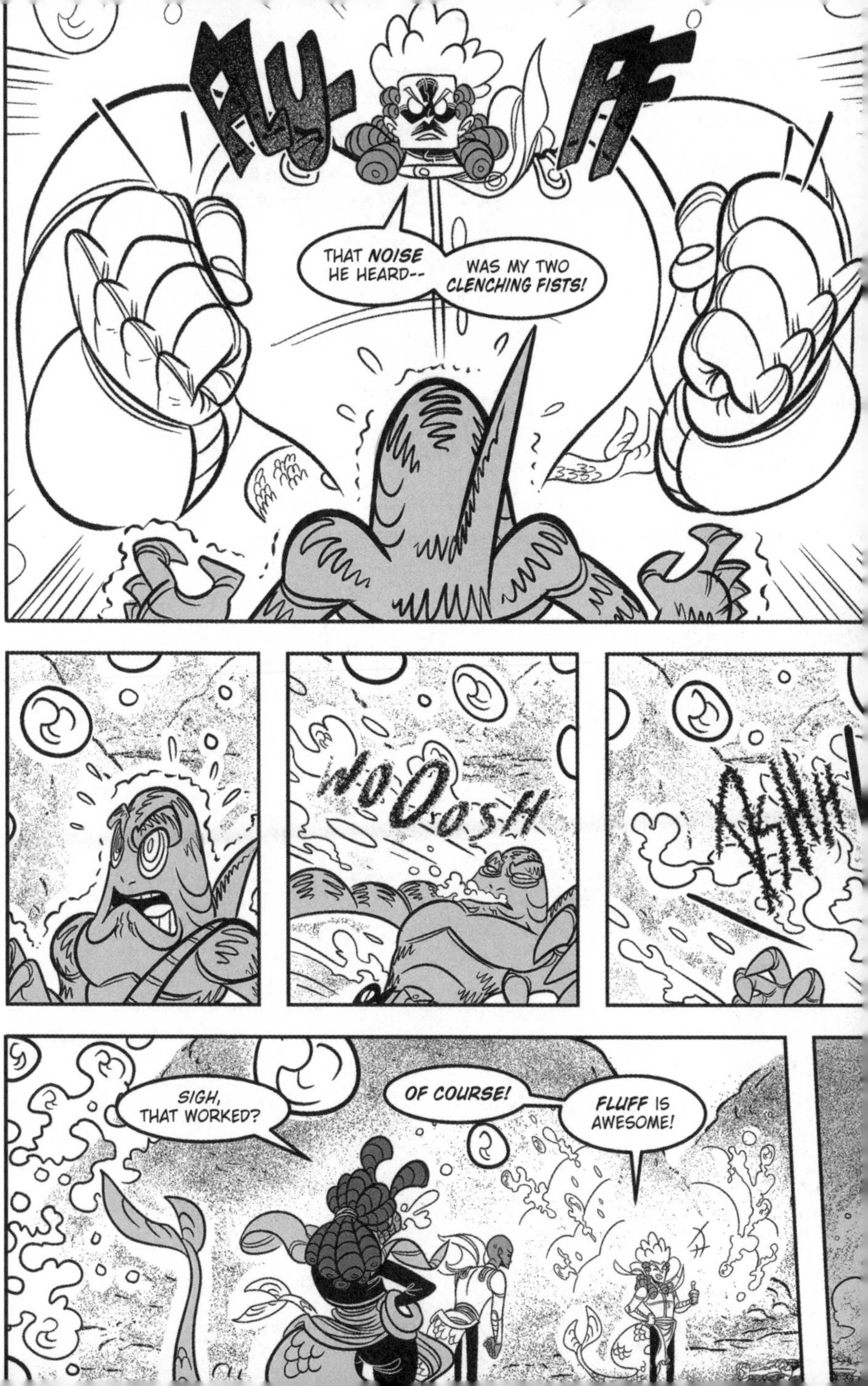
THAT NOISE HE HEARD--
WAS MY TWO CLENCHING FISTS!
WOOOSH
SIGH, THAT WORKED?
OF COURSE!
FLUFF IS AWESOME!

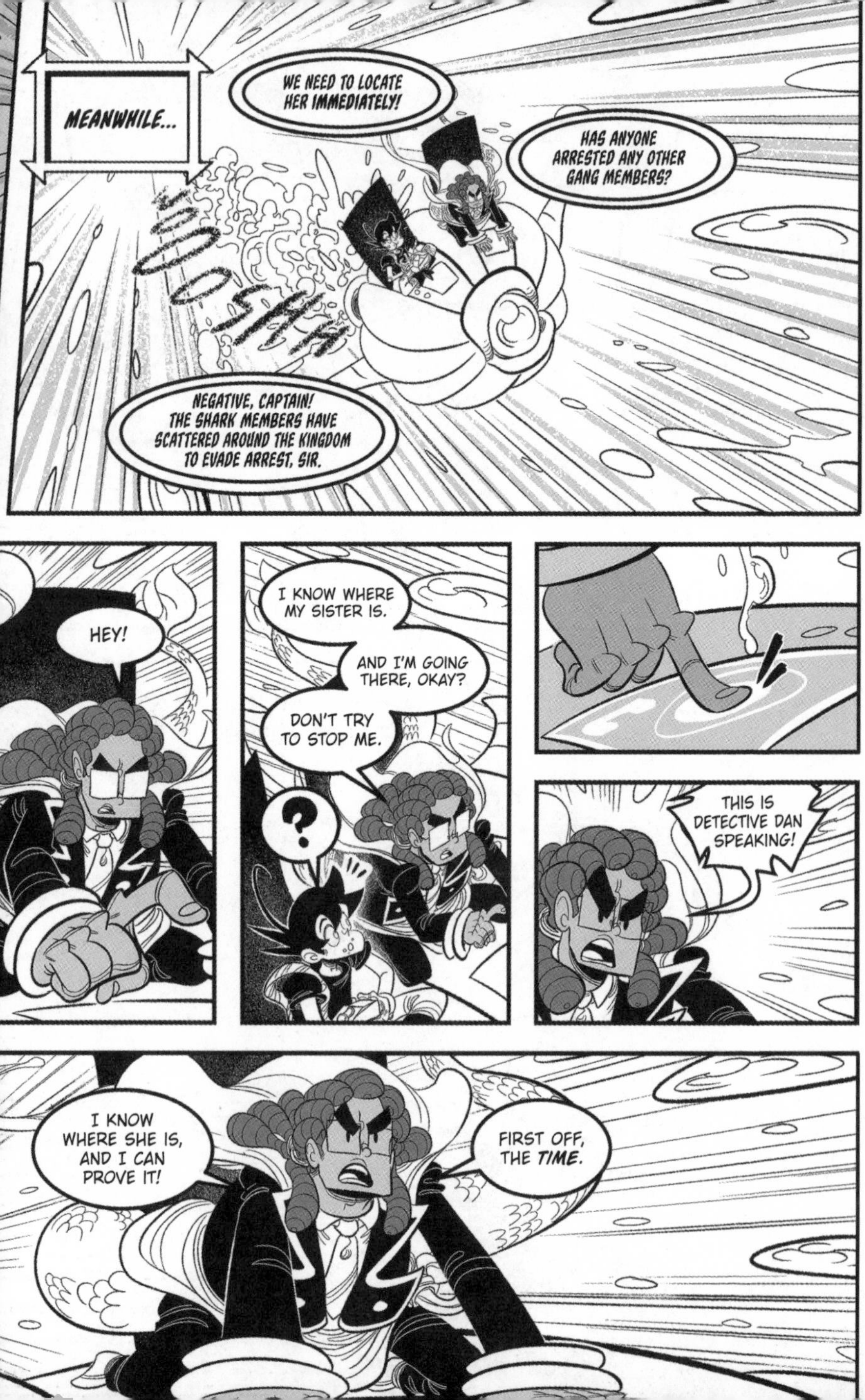

MEANWHILE...
WE NEED TO LOCATE HER IMMEDIATELY!
HAS ANYONE ARRESTED ANY OTHER GANG MEMBERS?
NEGATIVE, CAPTAIN! THE SHARK MEMBERS HAVE SCATTERED AROUND THE KINGDOM TO EVADE ARREST, SIR.
HEY!
I KNOW WHERE MY SISTER IS.
AND I'M GOING THERE, OKAY?
DON'T TRY TO STOP ME.
?
THIS IS DETECTIVE DAN SPEAKING!
I KNOW WHERE SHE IS, AND I CAN PROVE IT!
FIRST OFF, THE *TIME*.

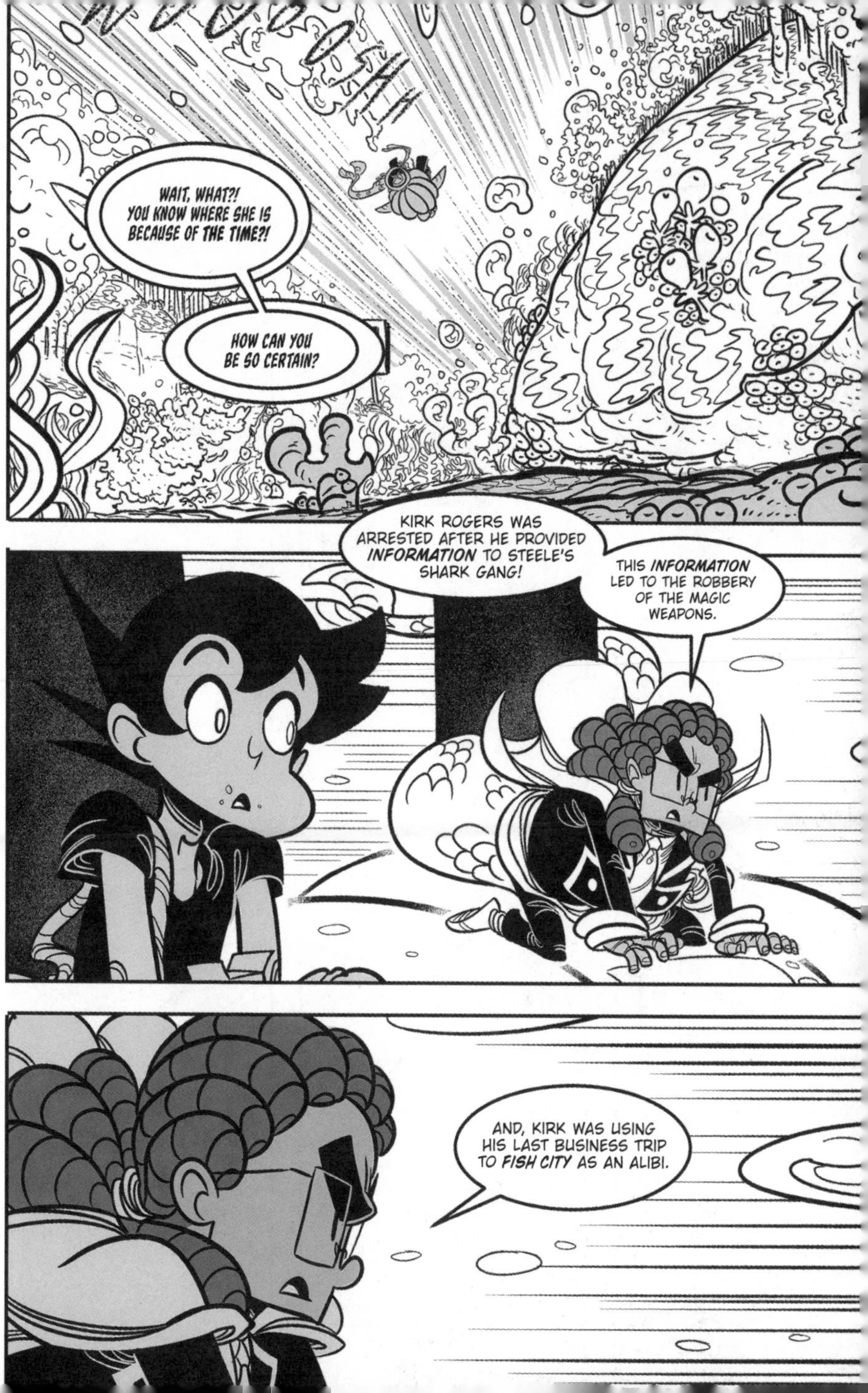
WAIT, WHAT?! YOU KNOW WHERE SHE IS BECAUSE OF THE TIME?!
HOW CAN YOU BE SO CERTAIN?
KIRK ROGERS WAS ARRESTED AFTER HE PROVIDED INFORMATION TO STEELE'S SHARK GANG!
THIS INFORMATION LED TO THE ROBBERY OF THE MAGIC WEAPONS.
AND, KIRK WAS USING HIS LAST BUSINESS TRIP TO FISH CITY AS AN ALIBI.

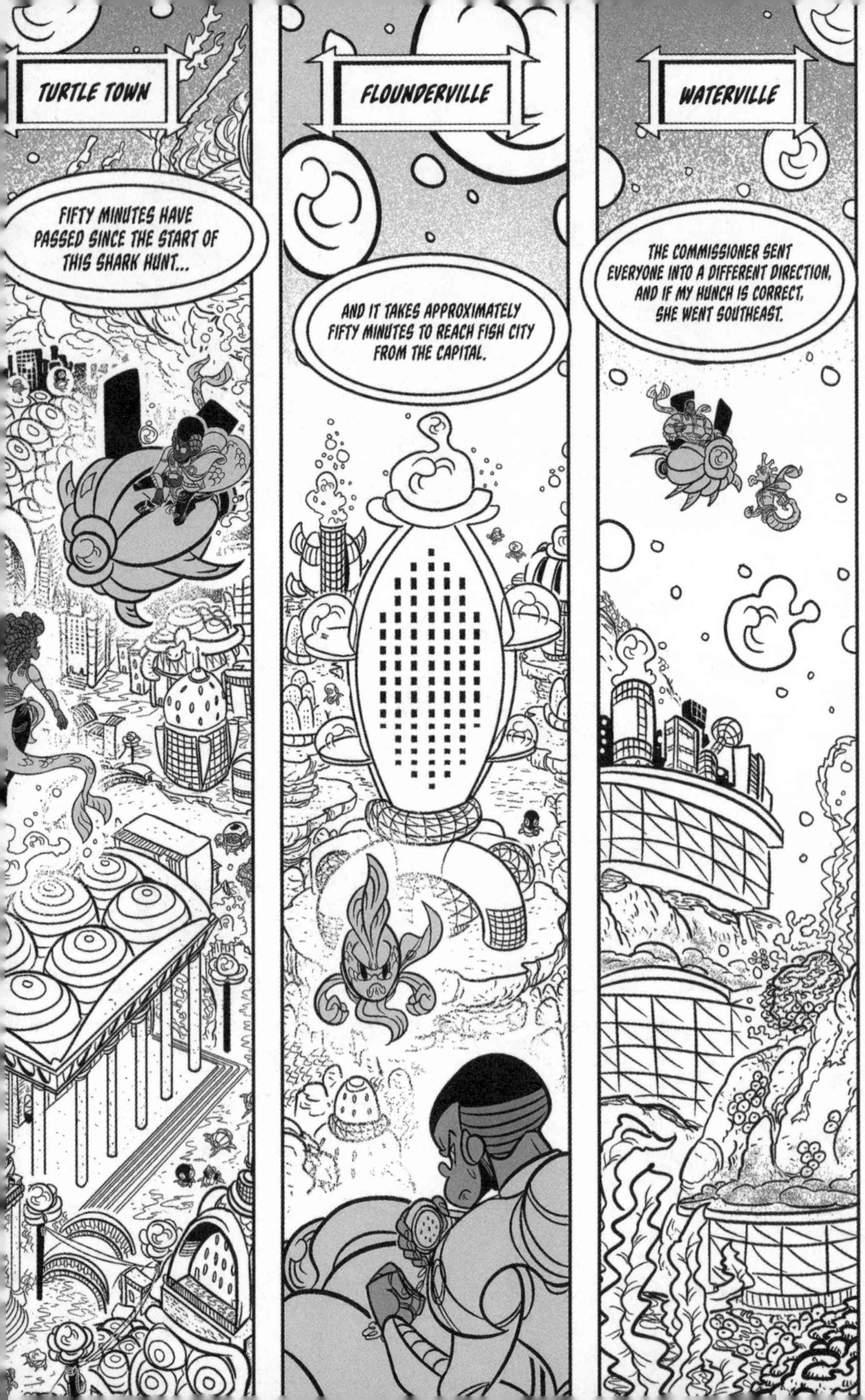
TURTLE TOWN
FIFTY MINUTES HAVE PASSED SINCE THE START OF THIS SHARK HUNT...
FLOUNDERVILLE
AND IT TAKES APPROXIMATELY FIFTY MINUTES TO REACH FISH CITY FROM THE CAPITAL.
WATERVILLE
THE COMMISSIONER SENT EVERYONE INTO A DIFFERENT DIRECTION, AND IF MY HUNCH IS CORRECT, SHE WENT SOUTHEAST.

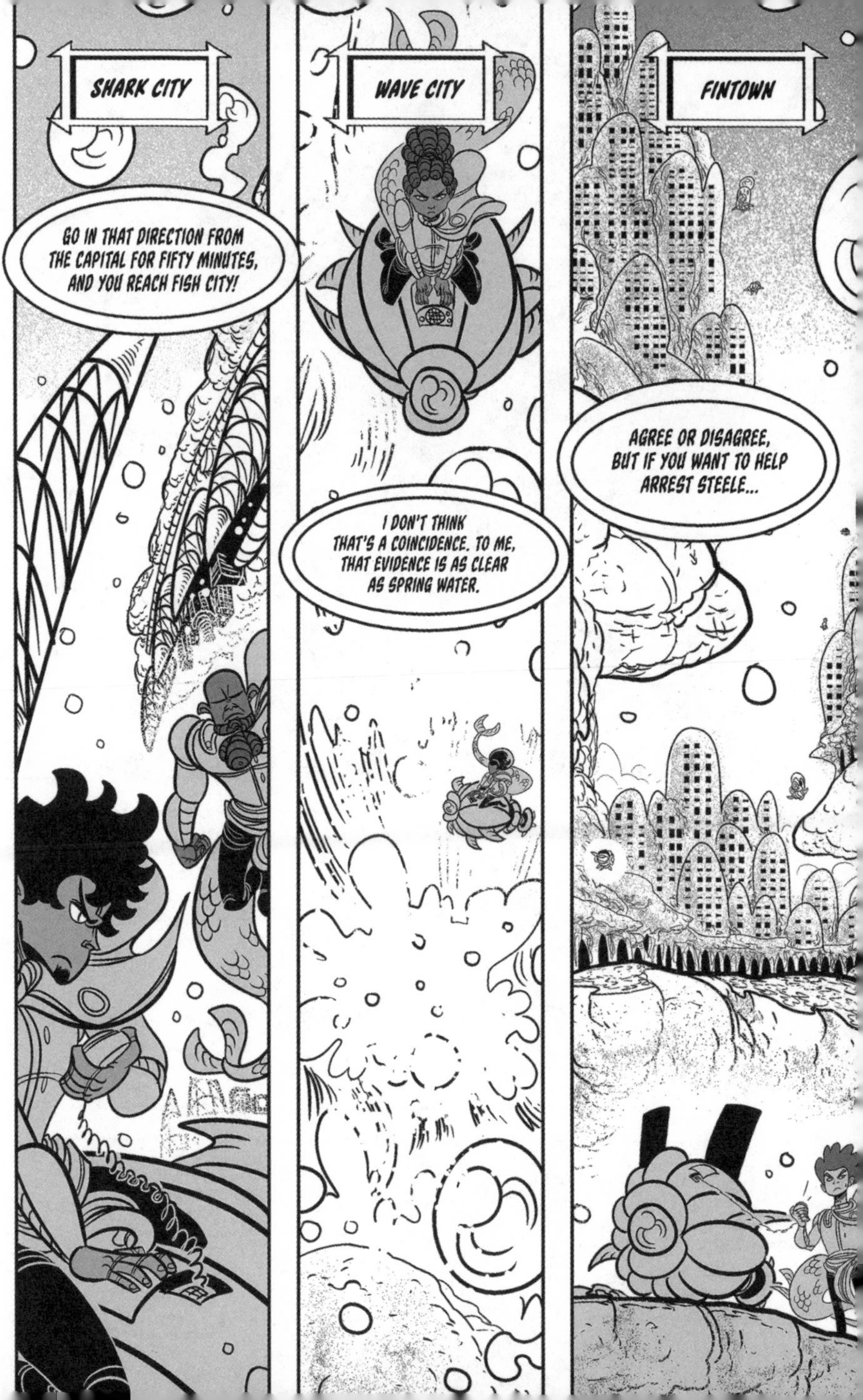
SHARK CITY
GO IN THAT DIRECTION FROM THE CAPITAL FOR FIFTY MINUTES, AND YOU REACH FISH CITY!
WAVE CITY
I DON'T THINK THAT'S A COINCIDENCE. TO ME, THAT EVIDENCE IS AS CLEAR AS SPRING WATER.
FINTOWN
AGREE OR DISAGREE, BUT IF YOU WANT TO HELP ARREST STEELE...

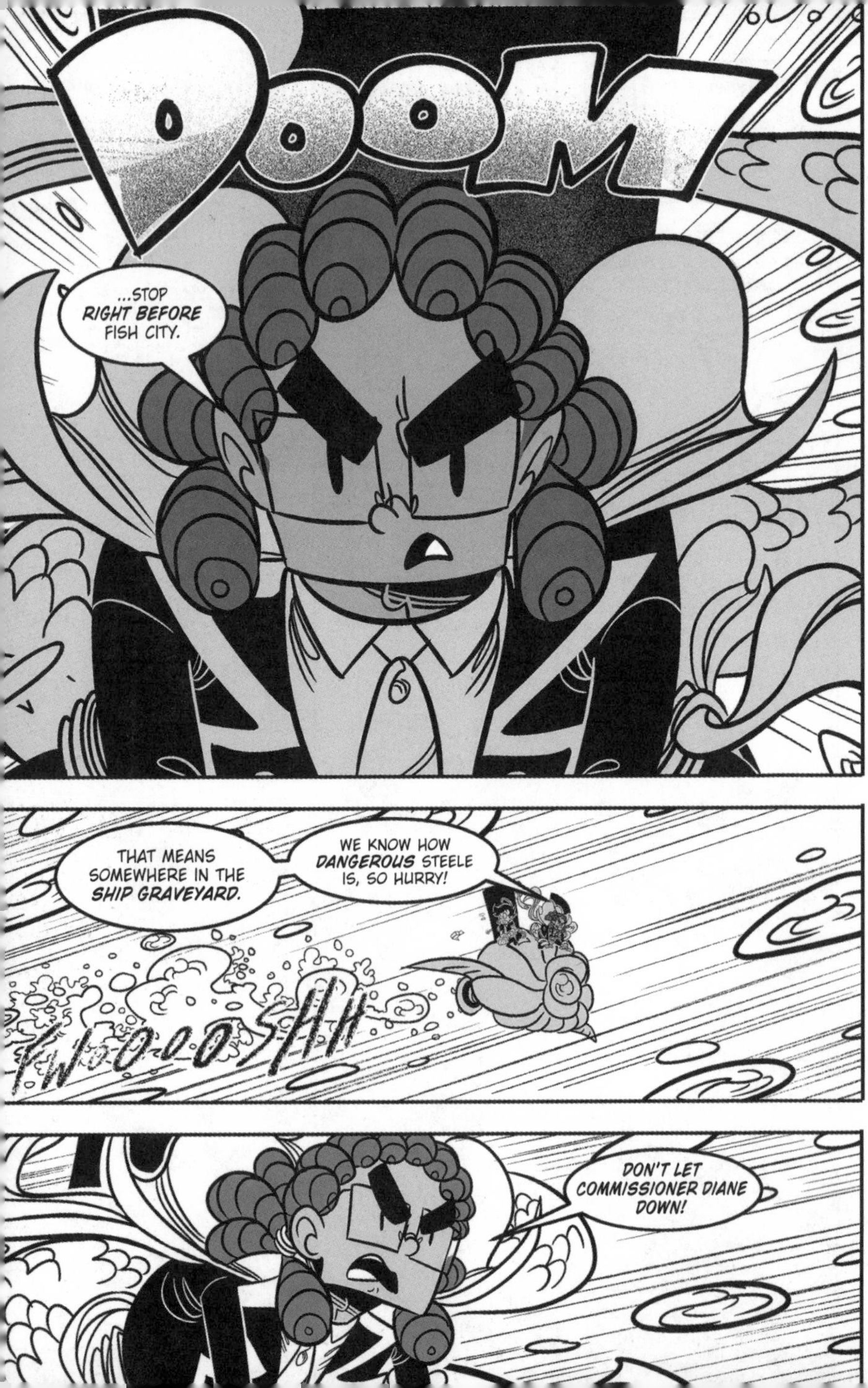
DOOM!
...STOP RIGHT BEFORE FISH CITY.
THAT MEANS SOMEWHERE IN THE SHIP GRAVEYARD.
WE KNOW HOW DANGEROUS STEELE IS, SO HURRY!
FWOOOOOSHH
DON'T LET COMMISSIONER DIANE DOWN!

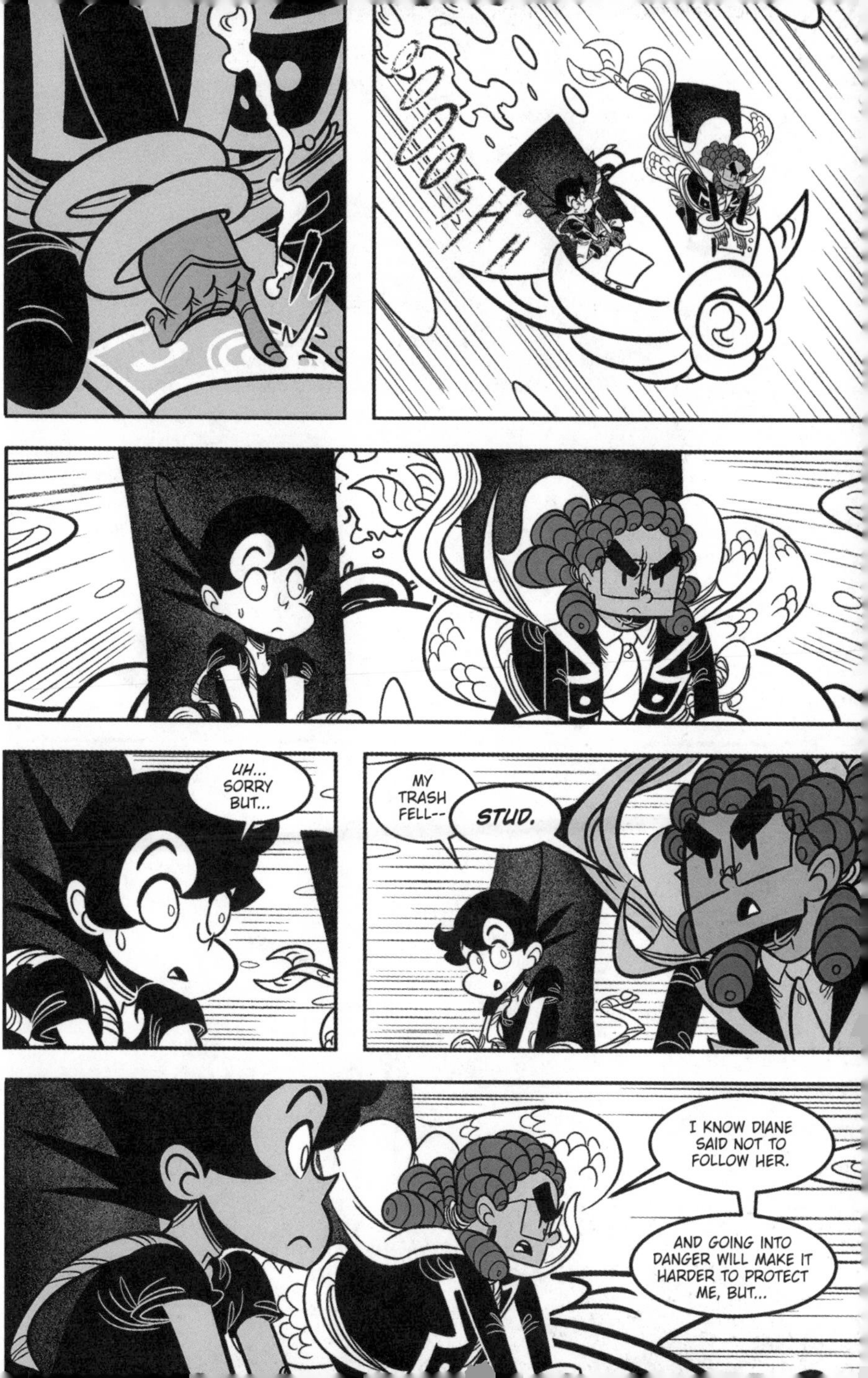
SHWOOOO
UH... SORRY BUT...
MY TRASH FELL--
STUD.
I KNOW DIANE SAID NOT TO FOLLOW HER.
AND GOING INTO DANGER WILL MAKE IT HARDER TO PROTECT ME, BUT...

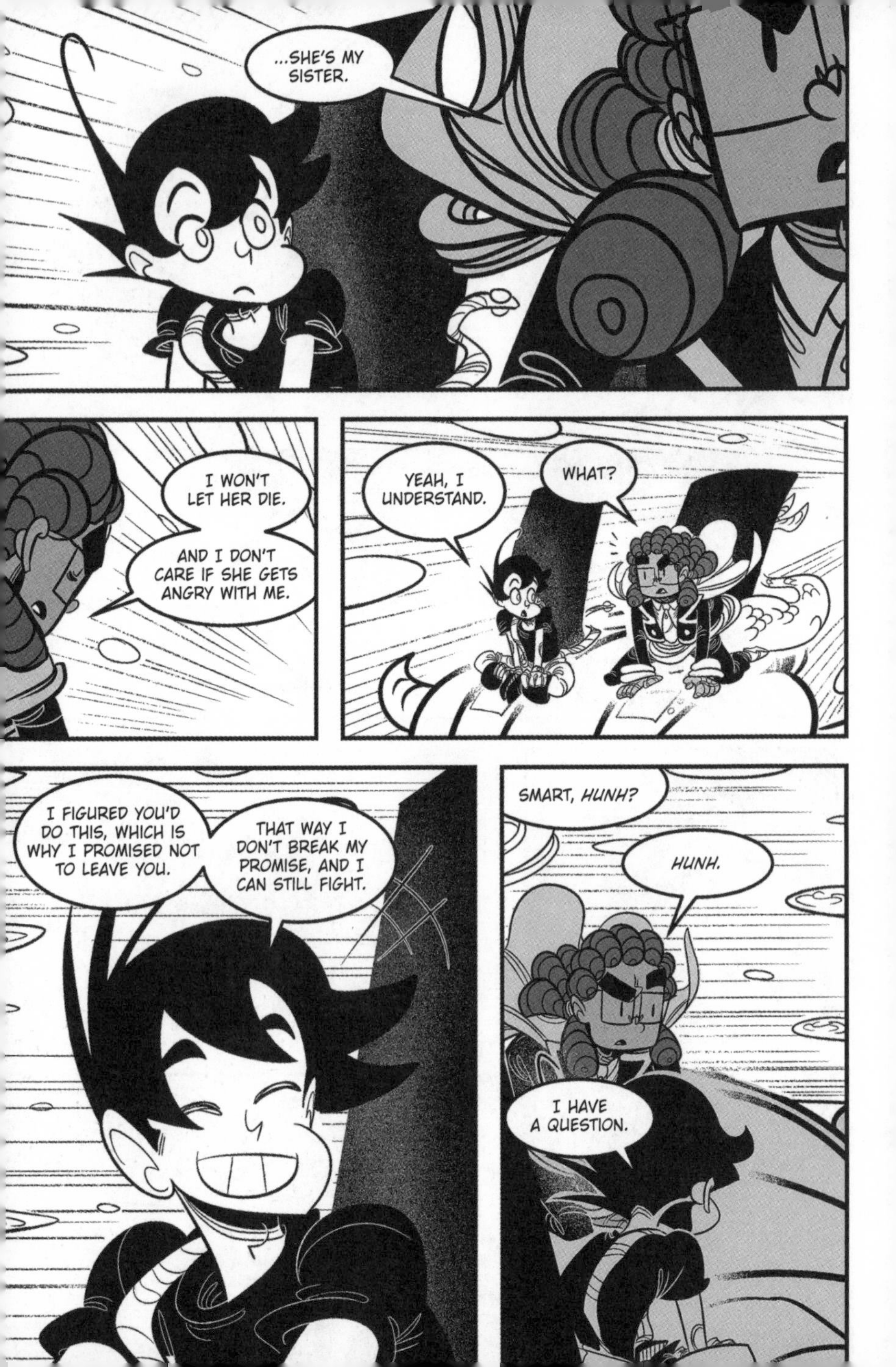
...SHE'S MY SISTER.
I WON'T LET HER DIE.
AND I DON'T CARE IF SHE GETS ANGRY WITH ME.
YEAH, I UNDERSTAND.
WHAT?
I FIGURED YOU'D DO THIS, WHICH IS WHY I PROMISED NOT TO LEAVE YOU.
THAT WAY I DON'T BREAK MY PROMISE, AND I CAN STILL FIGHT.
SMART, *HUNH?*
HUNH.
I HAVE A QUESTION.

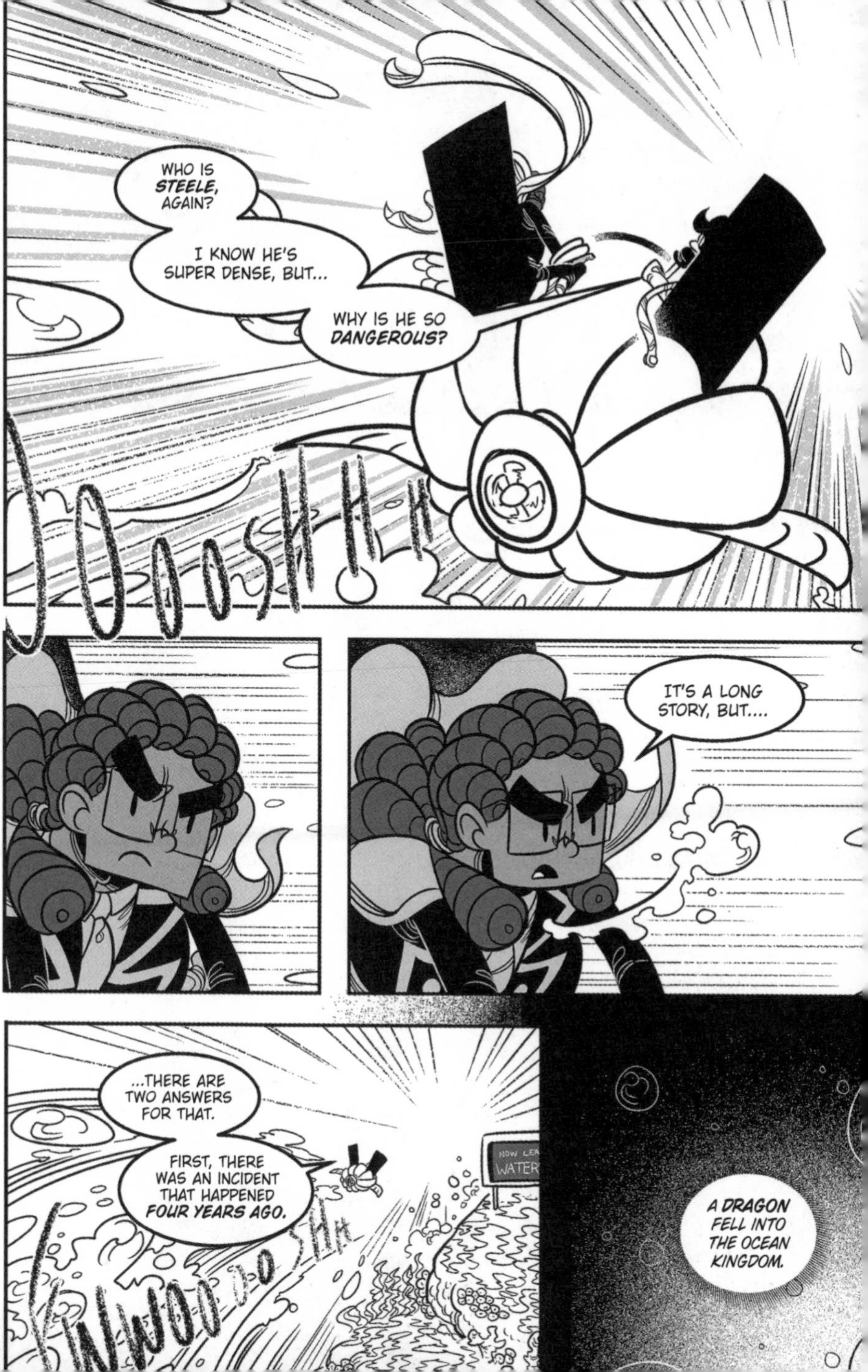

WHO IS **STEELE,** AGAIN?
I KNOW HE'S SUPER DENSE, BUT...
WHY IS HE SO **DANGEROUS?**
IT'S A LONG STORY, BUT....
...THERE ARE TWO ANSWERS FOR THAT.
FIRST, THERE WAS AN INCIDENT THAT HAPPENED **FOUR YEARS AGO.**
*A **DRAGON** FELL INTO THE OCEAN KINGDOM.*

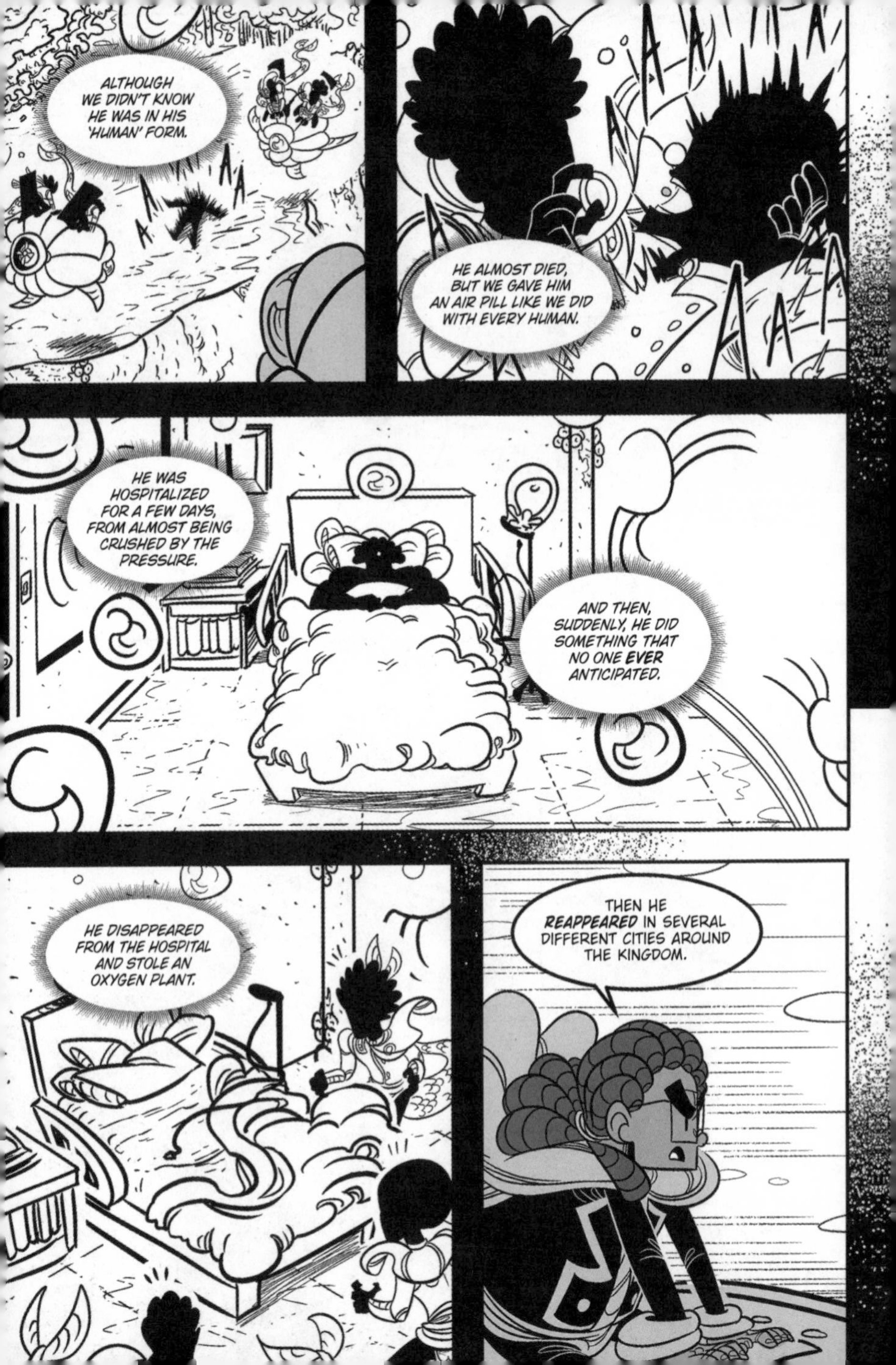
ALTHOUGH WE DIDN'T KNOW HE WAS IN HIS 'HUMAN' FORM.
HE ALMOST DIED, BUT WE GAVE HIM AN AIR PILL LIKE WE DID WITH EVERY HUMAN.
HE WAS HOSPITALIZED FOR A FEW DAYS, FROM ALMOST BEING CRUSHED BY THE PRESSURE.
AND THEN, SUDDENLY, HE DID SOMETHING THAT NO ONE **EVER** ANTICIPATED.
HE DISAPPEARED FROM THE HOSPITAL AND STOLE AN OXYGEN PLANT.
THEN HE **REAPPEARED** IN SEVERAL DIFFERENT CITIES AROUND THE KINGDOM.

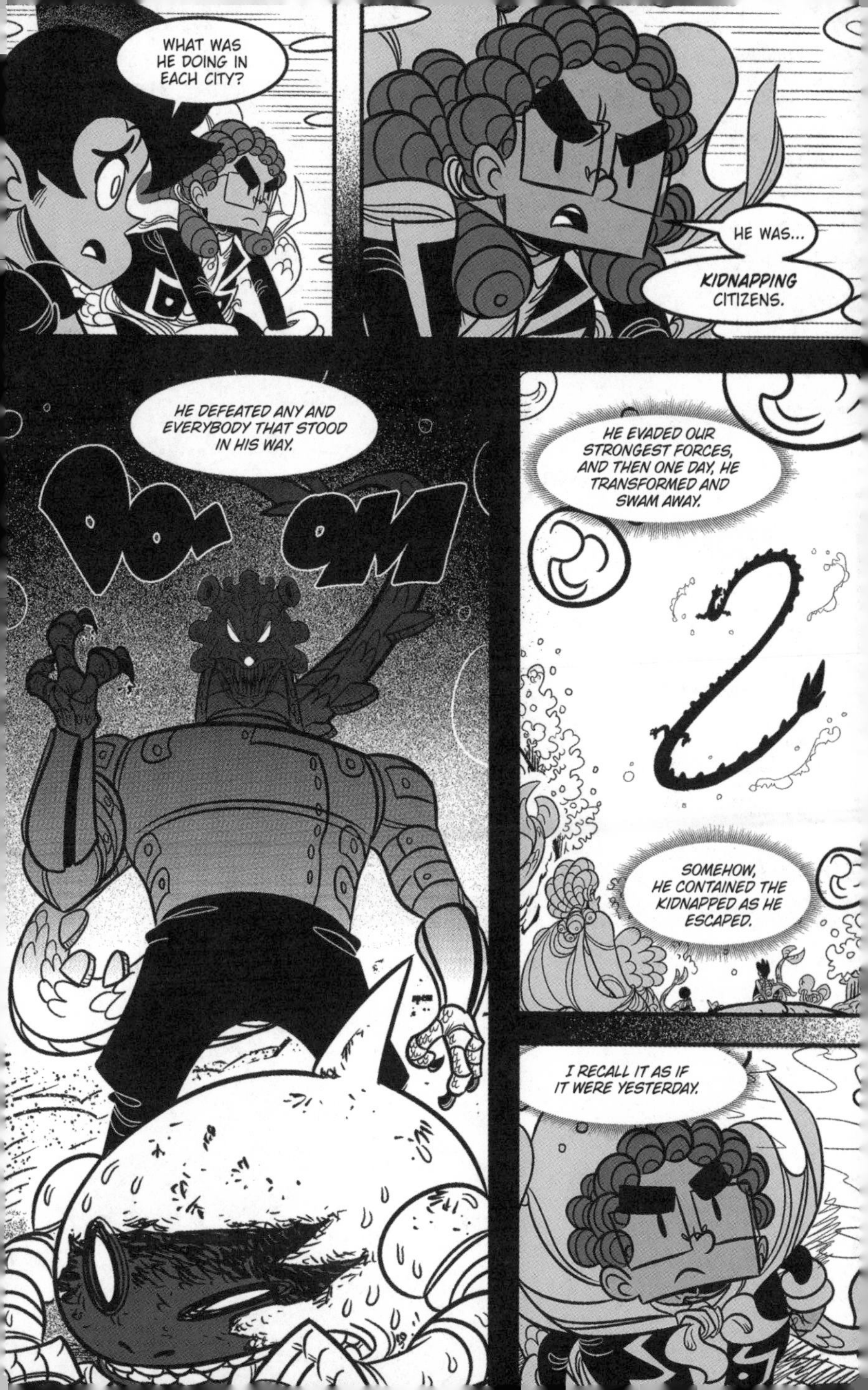

WHAT WAS HE DOING IN EACH CITY?
HE WAS...
KIDNAPPING CITIZENS.
HE DEFEATED ANY AND EVERYBODY THAT STOOD IN HIS WAY.
BOOM
HE EVADED OUR STRONGEST FORCES, AND THEN ONE DAY, HE TRANSFORMED AND SWAM AWAY.
SOMEHOW, HE CONTAINED THE KIDNAPPED AS HE ESCAPED.
I RECALL IT AS IF IT WERE YESTERDAY.

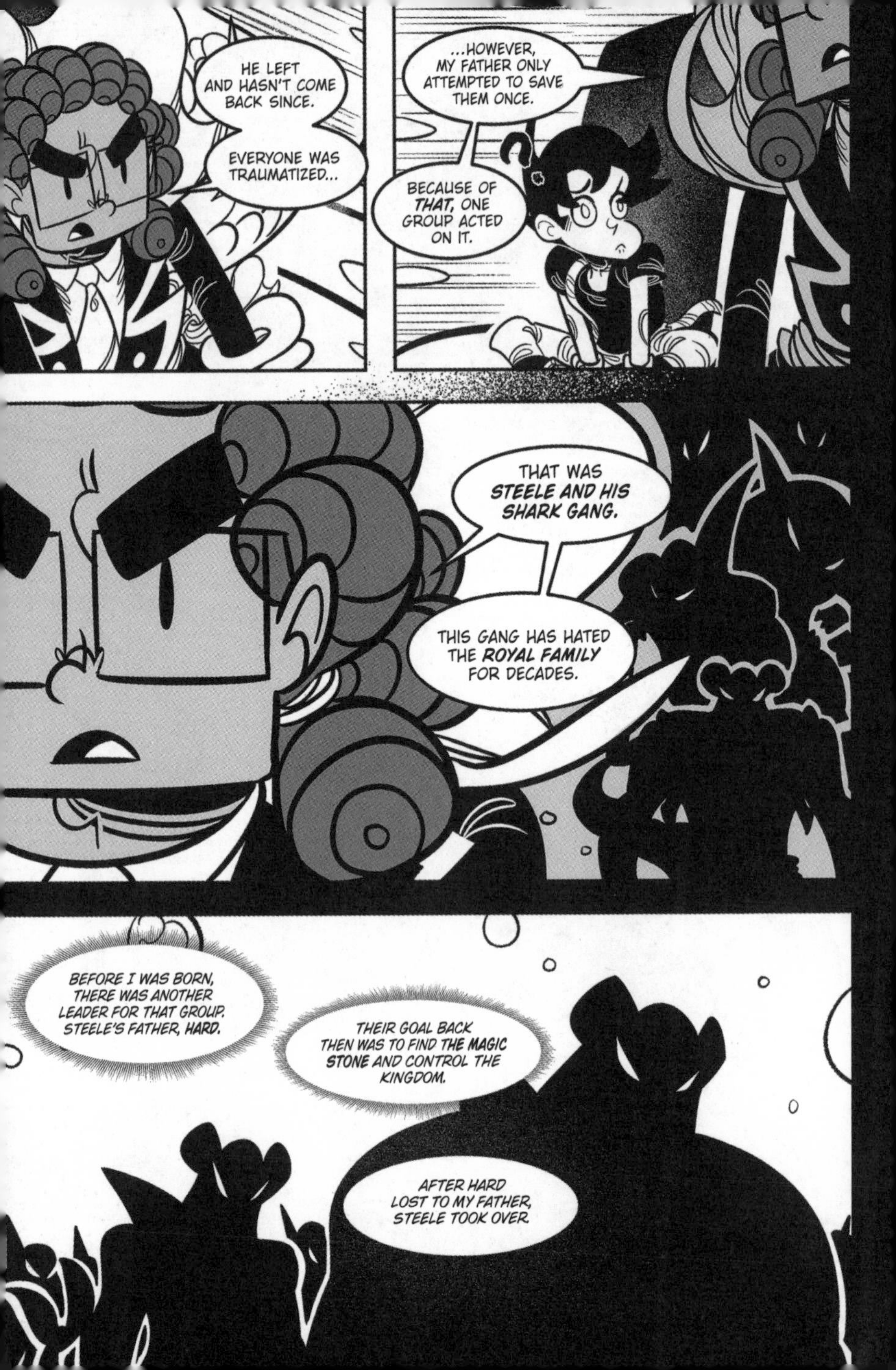
HE LEFT AND HASN'T COME BACK SINCE.
EVERYONE WAS TRAUMATIZED...
...HOWEVER, MY FATHER ONLY ATTEMPTED TO SAVE THEM ONCE.
BECAUSE OF THAT, ONE GROUP ACTED ON IT.
THAT WAS STEELE AND HIS SHARK GANG.
THIS GANG HAS HATED THE ROYAL FAMILY FOR DECADES.
BEFORE I WAS BORN, THERE WAS ANOTHER LEADER FOR THAT GROUP. STEELE'S FATHER, HARD.
THEIR GOAL BACK THEN WAS TO FIND THE MAGIC STONE AND CONTROL THE KINGDOM.
AFTER HARD LOST TO MY FATHER, STEELE TOOK OVER.

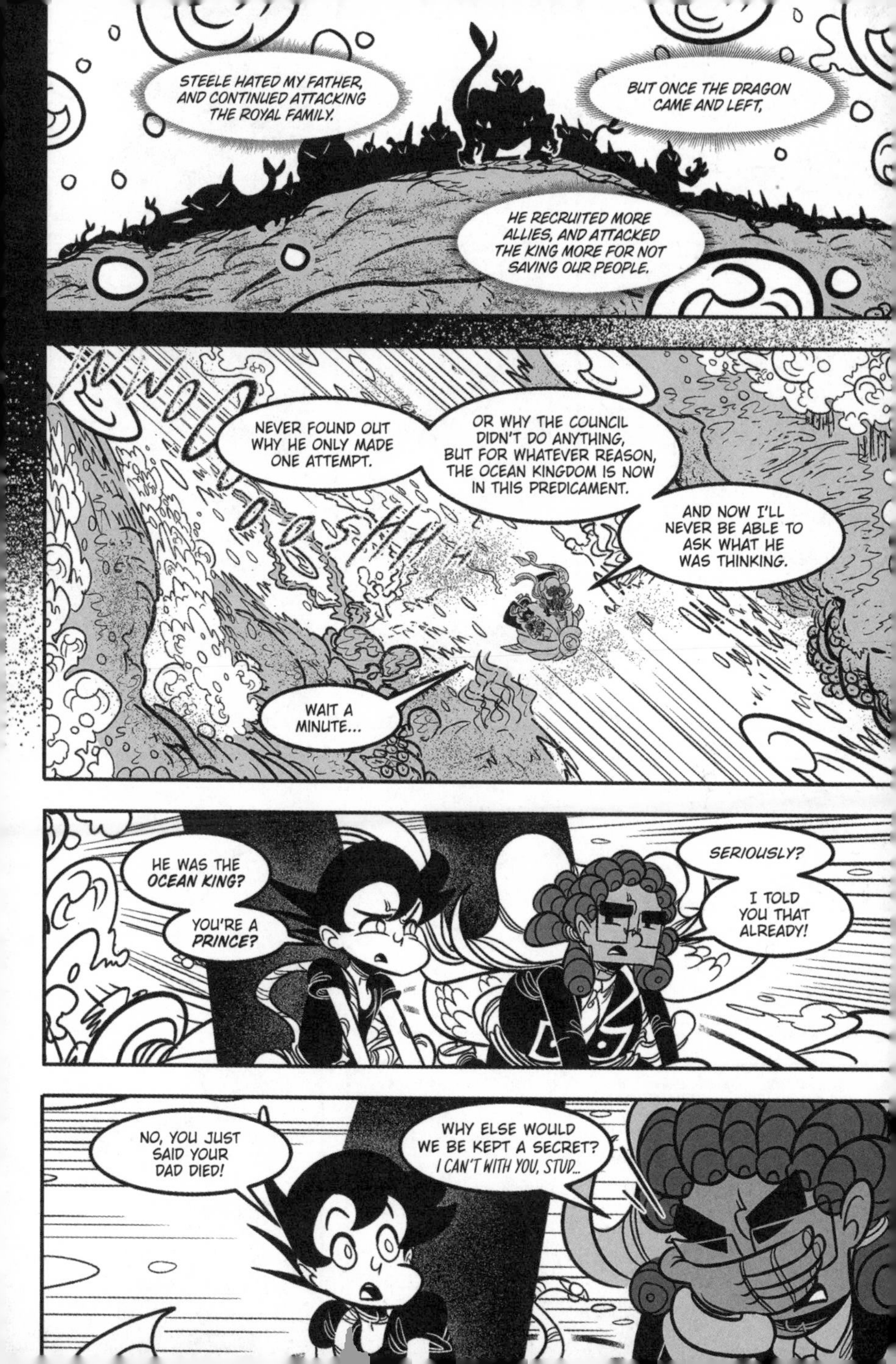
STEELE HATED MY FATHER, AND CONTINUED ATTACKING THE ROYAL FAMILY.
BUT ONCE THE DRAGON CAME AND LEFT,
HE RECRUITED MORE ALLIES, AND ATTACKED THE KING MORE FOR NOT SAVING OUR PEOPLE.
NEVER FOUND OUT WHY HE ONLY MADE ONE ATTEMPT.
OR WHY THE COUNCIL DIDN'T DO ANYTHING, BUT FOR WHATEVER REASON, THE OCEAN KINGDOM IS NOW IN THIS PREDICAMENT.
AND NOW I'LL NEVER BE ABLE TO ASK WHAT HE WAS THINKING.
WAIT A MINUTE...
HE WAS THE OCEAN KING?
YOU'RE A PRINCE?
SERIOUSLY?
I TOLD YOU THAT ALREADY!
NO, YOU JUST SAID YOUR DAD DIED!
WHY ELSE WOULD WE BE KEPT A SECRET? I CAN'T WITH YOU, STUD...

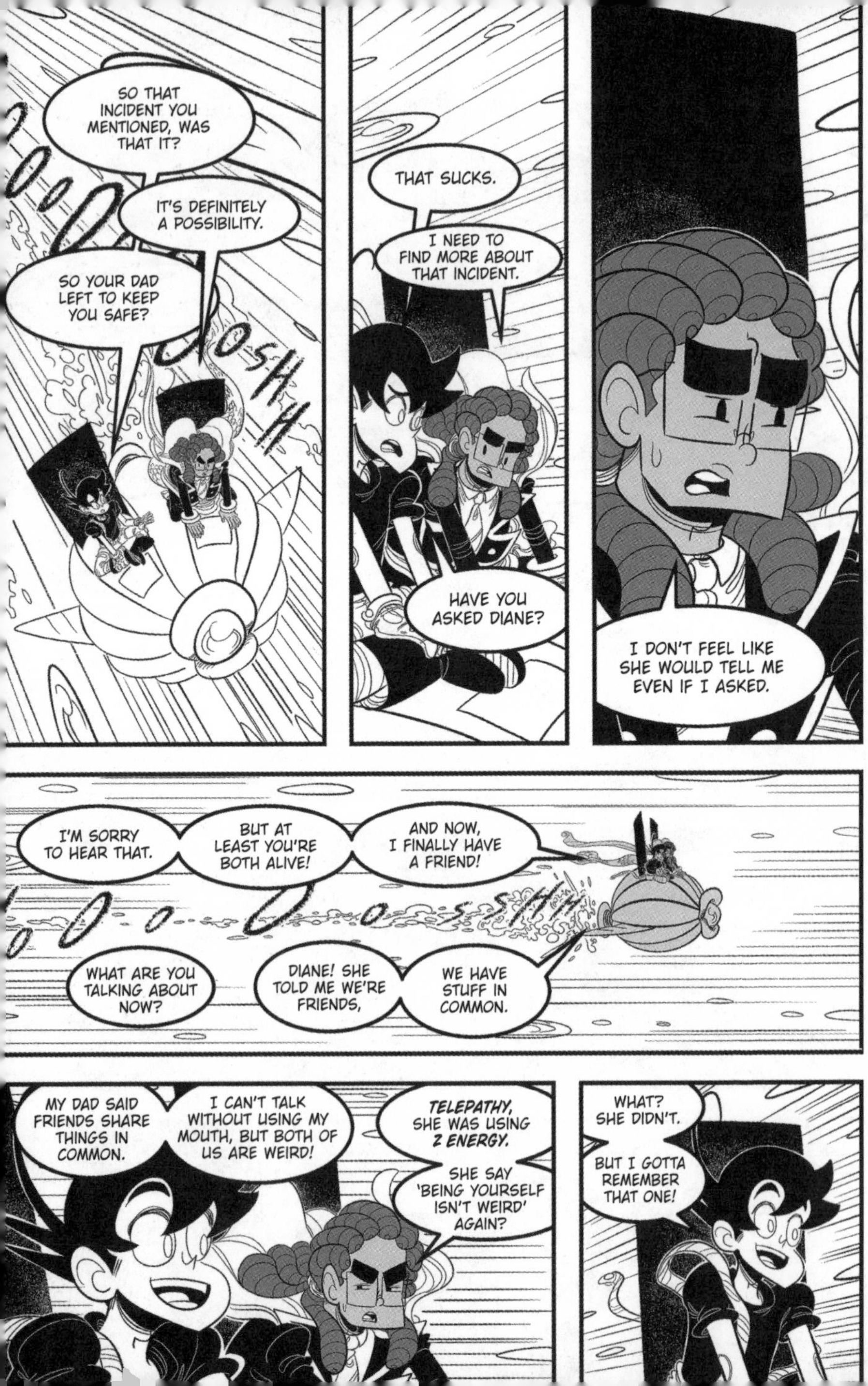
SO THAT INCIDENT YOU MENTIONED, WAS THAT IT?
IT'S DEFINITELY A POSSIBILITY.
SO YOUR DAD LEFT TO KEEP YOU SAFE?
THAT SUCKS.
I NEED TO FIND MORE ABOUT THAT INCIDENT.
HAVE YOU ASKED DIANE?
I DON'T FEEL LIKE SHE WOULD TELL ME EVEN IF I ASKED.
I'M SORRY TO HEAR THAT.
BUT AT LEAST YOU'RE BOTH ALIVE!
AND NOW, I FINALLY HAVE A FRIEND!
WHAT ARE YOU TALKING ABOUT NOW?
DIANE! SHE TOLD ME WE'RE FRIENDS,
WE HAVE STUFF IN COMMON.
MY DAD SAID FRIENDS SHARE THINGS IN COMMON.
I CAN'T TALK WITHOUT USING MY MOUTH, BUT BOTH OF US ARE WEIRD!
TELEPATHY, SHE WAS USING ***Z ENERGY.***
SHE SAY 'BEING YOURSELF ISN'T WEIRD' AGAIN?
WHAT? SHE DIDN'T.
BUT I GOTTA REMEMBER THAT ONE!

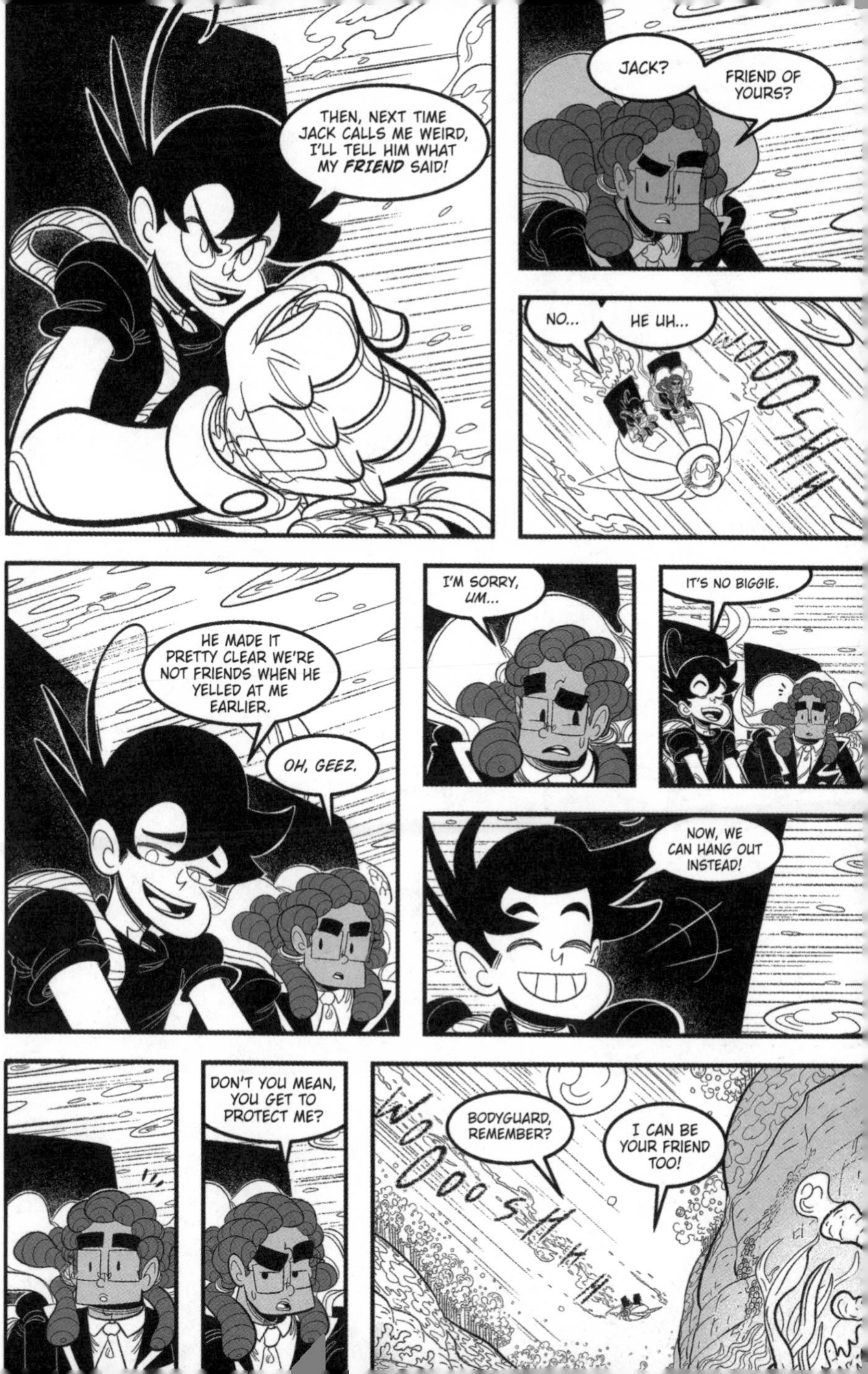
THEN, NEXT TIME JACK CALLS ME WEIRD, I'LL TELL HIM WHAT MY **FRIEND** SAID!
JACK?
FRIEND OF YOURS?
NO...
HE UH...
WHOOOSH
HE MADE IT PRETTY CLEAR WE'RE NOT FRIENDS WHEN HE YELLED AT ME EARLIER.
OH, GEEZ.
I'M SORRY, UM...
IT'S NO BIGGIE.
NOW, WE CAN HANG OUT INSTEAD!
DON'T YOU MEAN, YOU GET TO PROTECT ME?
BODYGUARD, REMEMBER?
I CAN BE YOUR FRIEND TOO!
WOOOOOOSHHH

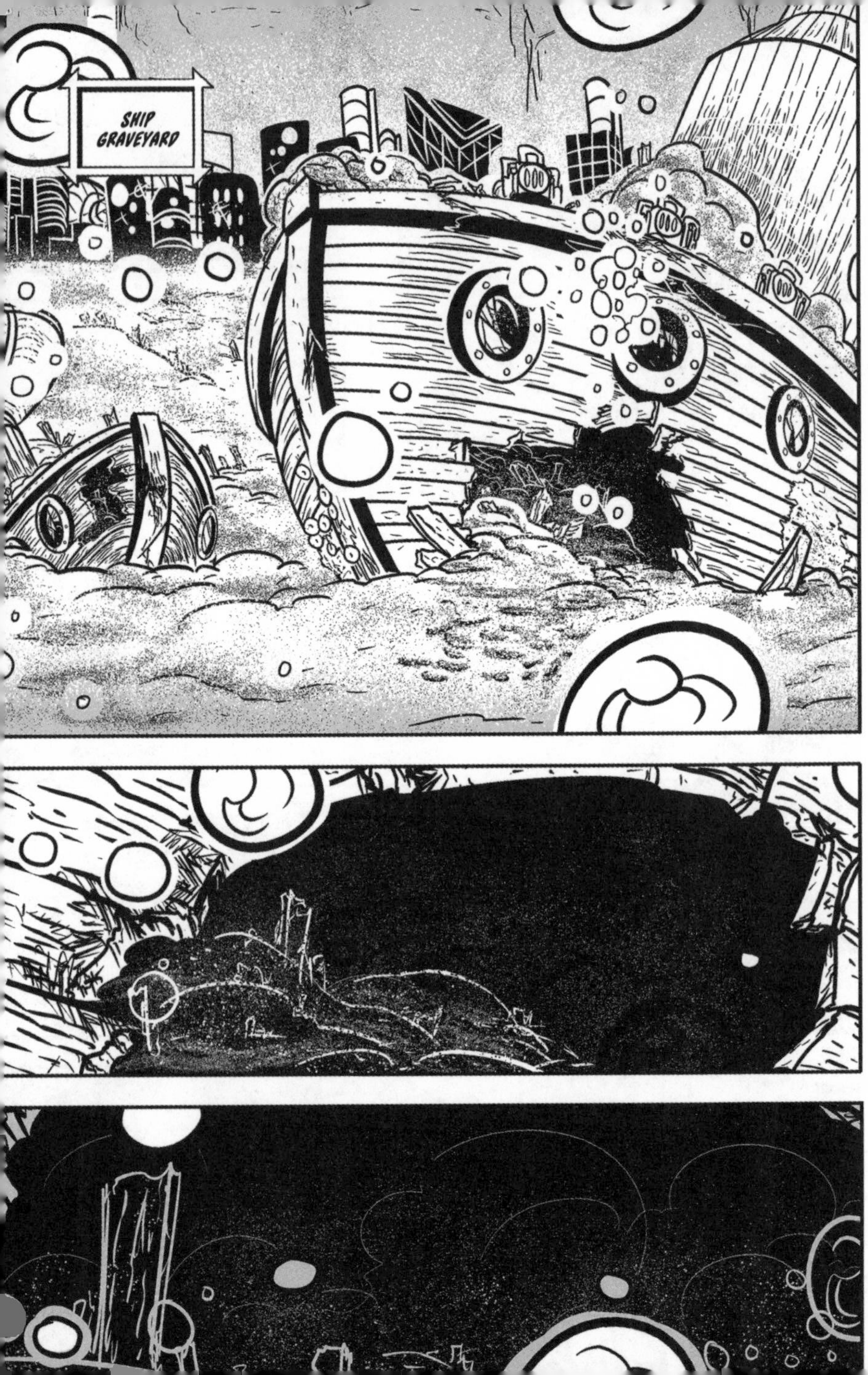
SHIP GRAVEYARD

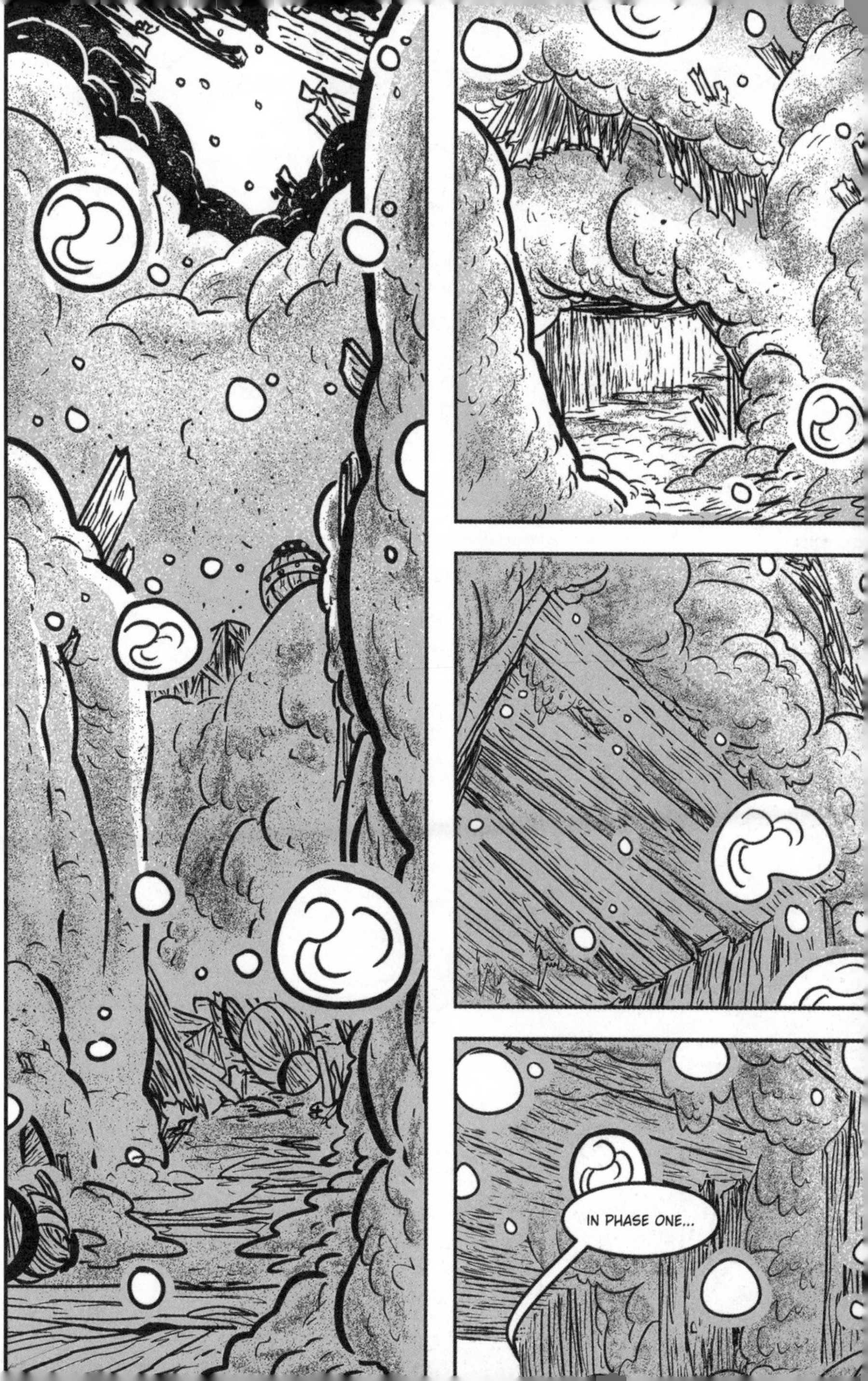
IN PHASE ONE...

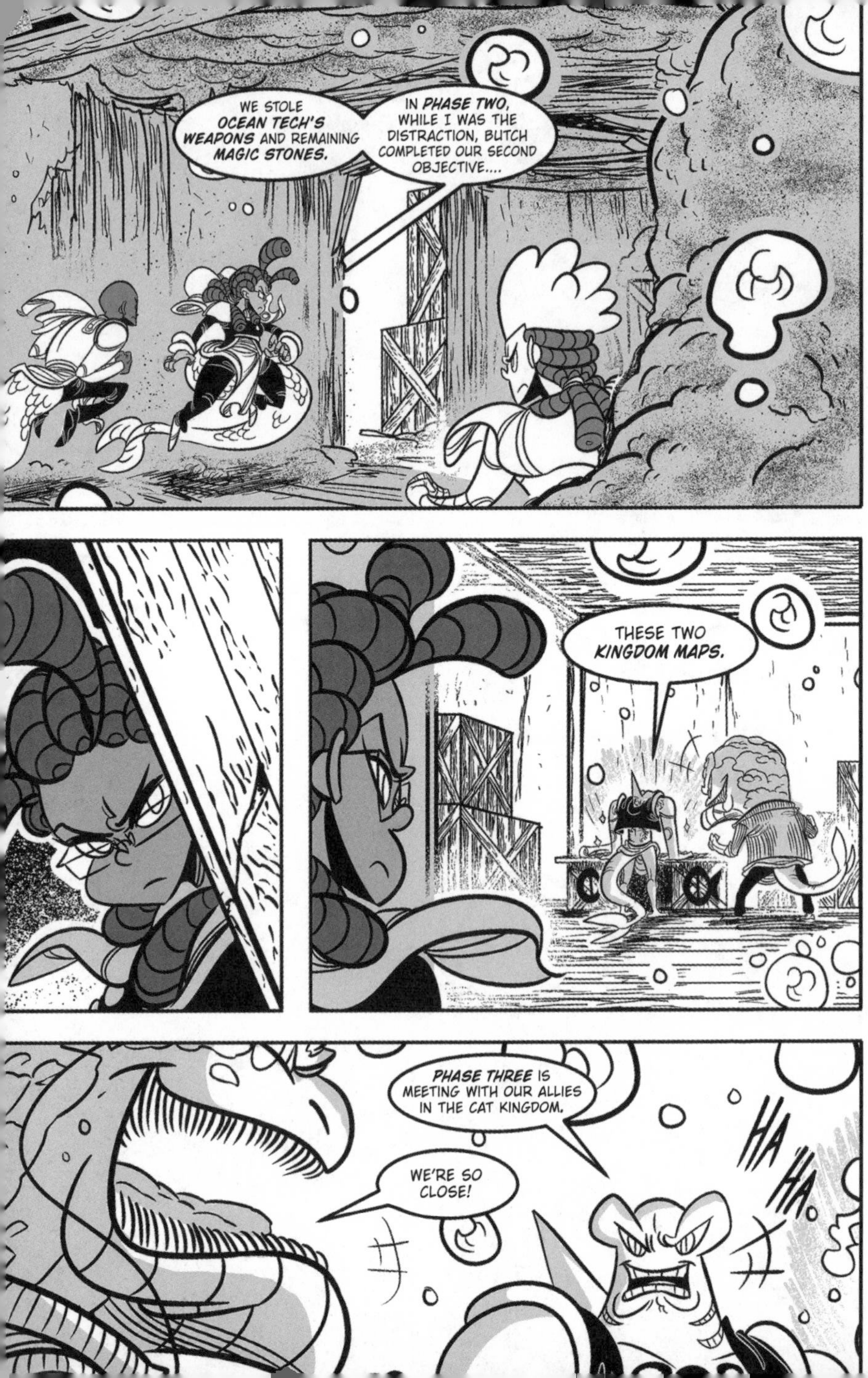
WE STOLE OCEAN TECH'S WEAPONS AND REMAINING MAGIC STONES.
IN PHASE TWO, WHILE I WAS THE DISTRACTION, BUTCH COMPLETED OUR SECOND OBJECTIVE....
THESE TWO KINGDOM MAPS.
PHASE THREE IS MEETING WITH OUR ALLIES IN THE CAT KINGDOM.
WE'RE SO CLOSE!
HA HA HA

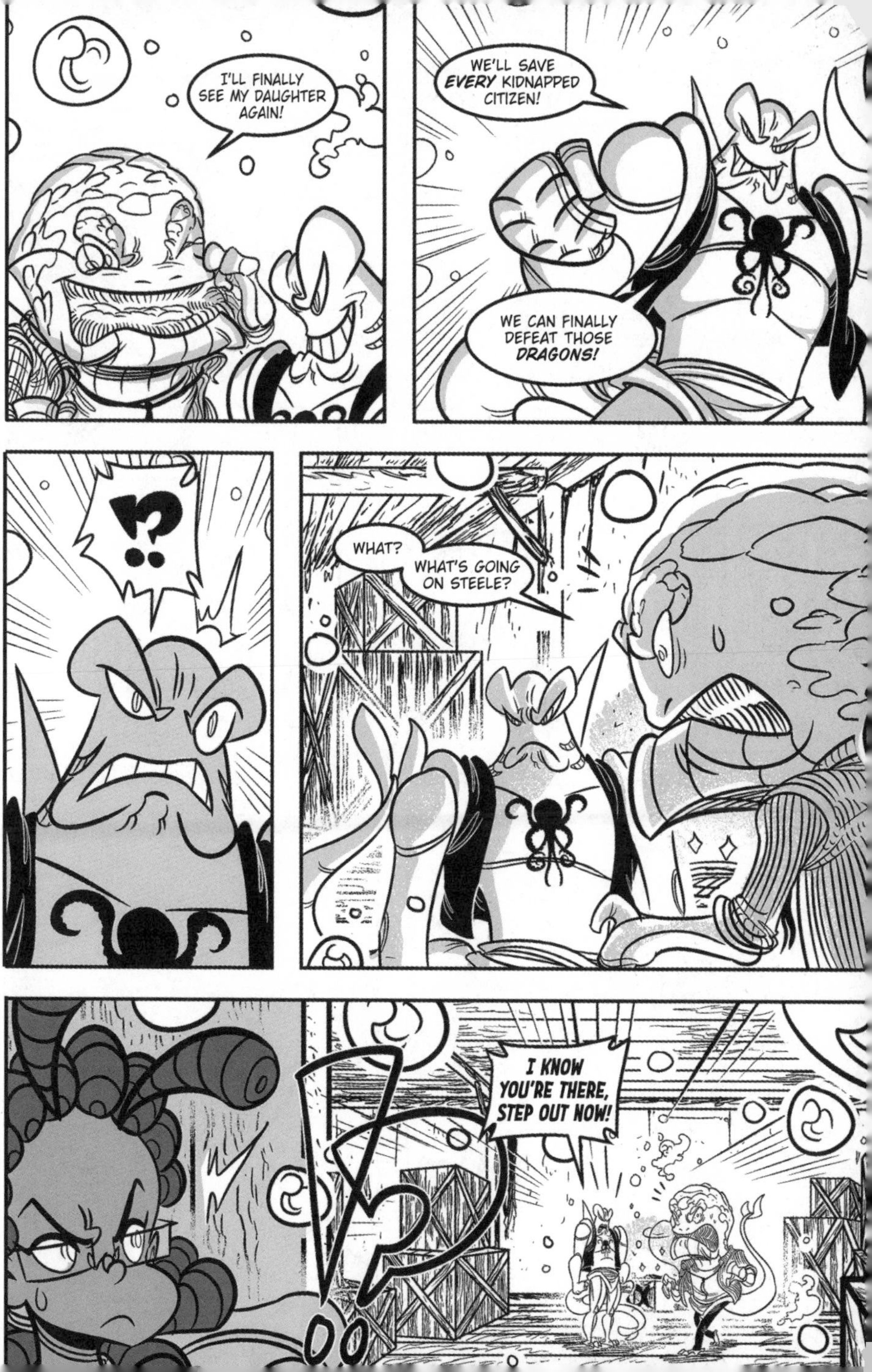
I'LL FINALLY SEE MY DAUGHTER AGAIN!
WE'LL SAVE EVERY KIDNAPPED CITIZEN!
WE CAN FINALLY DEFEAT THOSE DRAGONS!
!?
WHAT?
WHAT'S GOING ON STEELE?
I KNOW YOU'RE THERE, STEP OUT NOW!

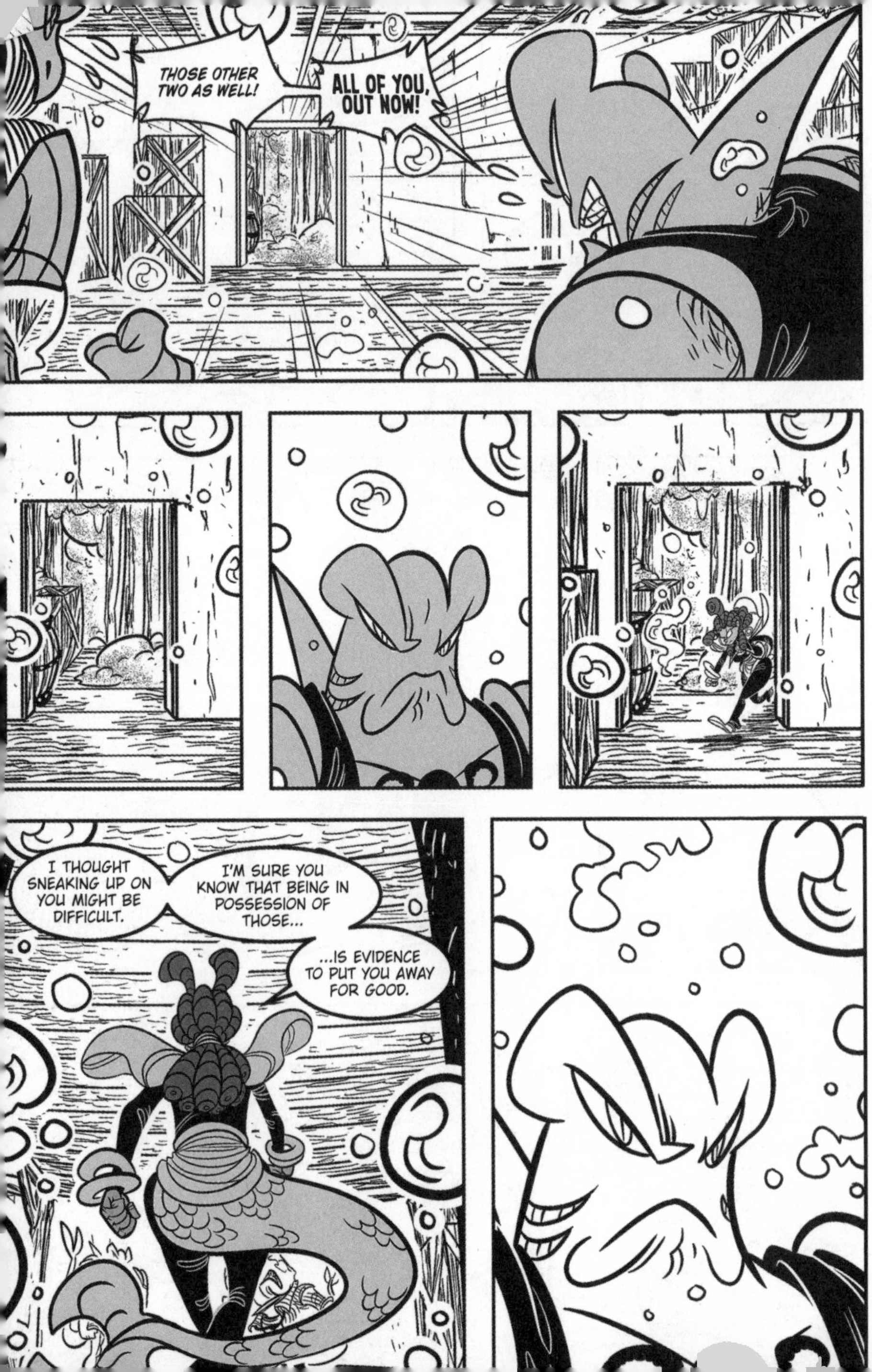
THOSE OTHER TWO AS WELL!
ALL OF YOU, OUT NOW!
I THOUGHT SNEAKING UP ON YOU MIGHT BE DIFFICULT.
I'M SURE YOU KNOW THAT BEING IN POSSESSION OF THOSE...
...IS EVIDENCE TO PUT YOU AWAY FOR GOOD.

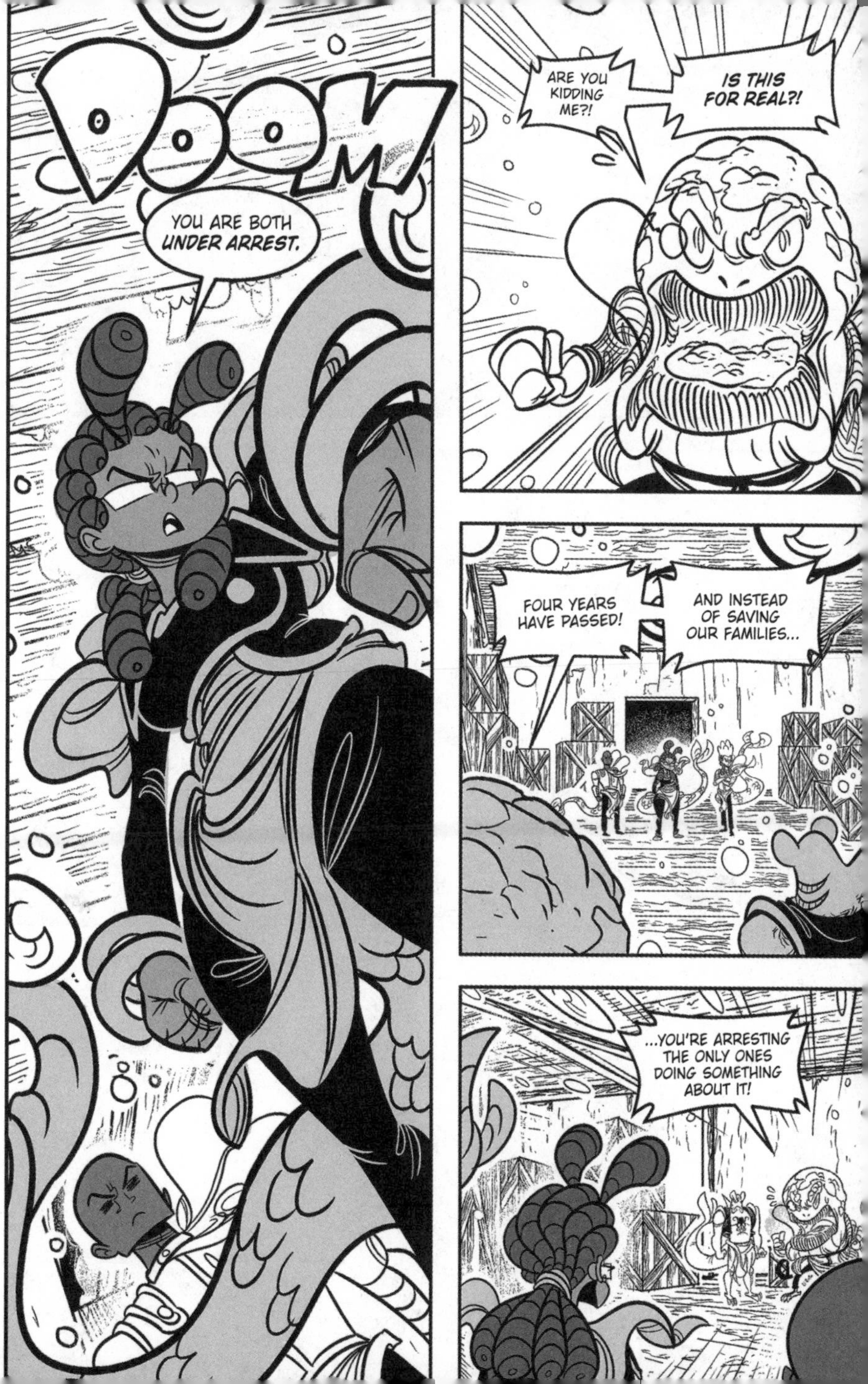
DOOM
YOU ARE BOTH UNDER ARREST.
ARE YOU KIDDING ME?!
IS THIS FOR REAL?!
FOUR YEARS HAVE PASSED!
AND INSTEAD OF SAVING OUR FAMILIES...
...YOU'RE ARRESTING THE ONLY ONES DOING SOMETHING ABOUT IT!

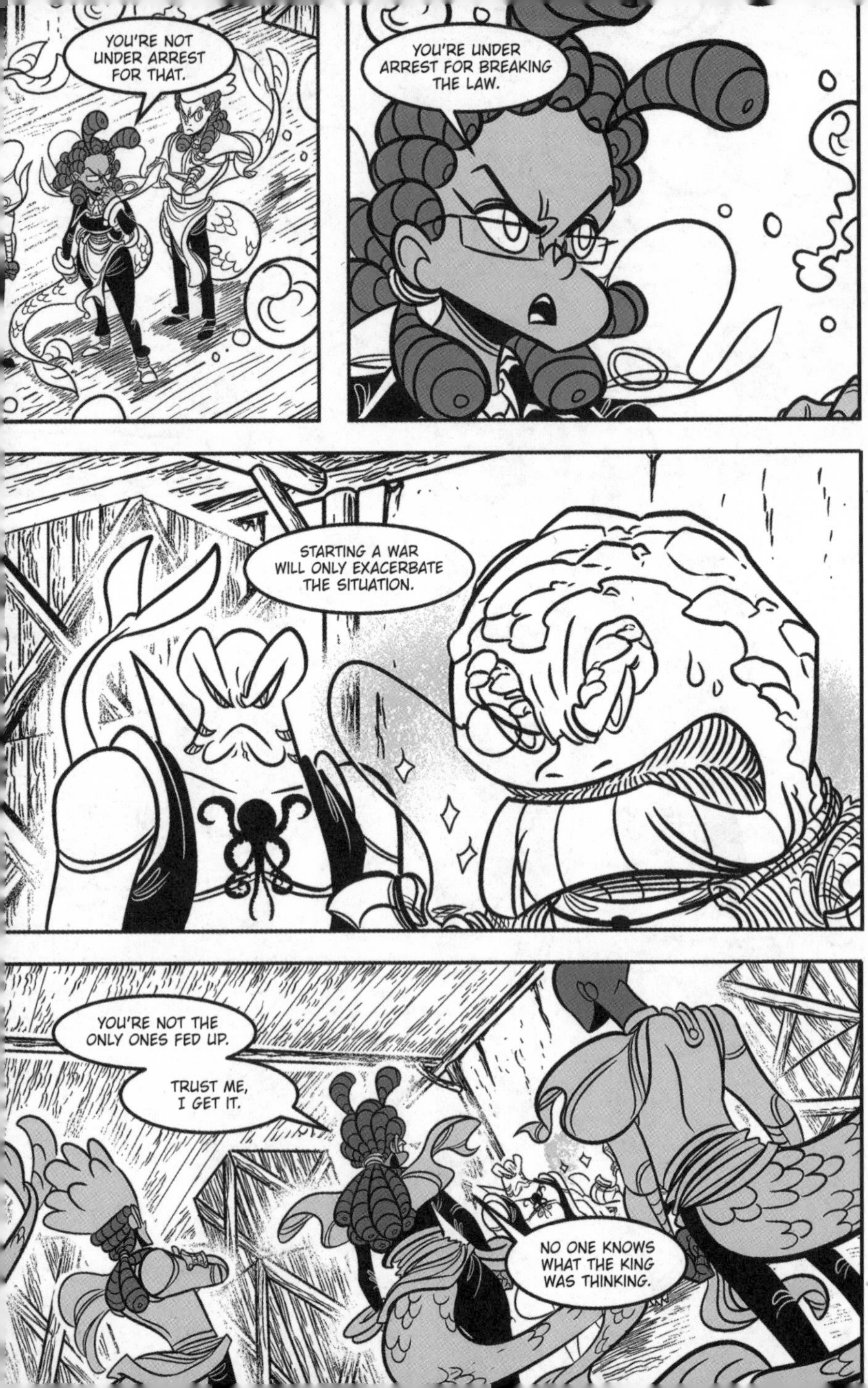
YOU'RE NOT UNDER ARREST FOR THAT.
YOU'RE UNDER ARREST FOR BREAKING THE LAW.
STARTING A WAR WILL ONLY EXACERBATE THE SITUATION.
YOU'RE NOT THE ONLY ONES FED UP.
TRUST ME, I GET IT.
NO ONE KNOWS WHAT THE KING WAS THINKING.

BUT I *DO* KNOW STEALING *GOVERNMENT WEAPONS*--

--AND TERRORIZING THE CITY IS A *CRIME!*

NOW, *SURRENDER.* YOU'RE UNDER ARREST.

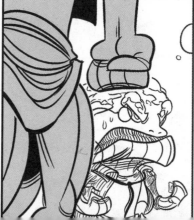

WOOOSHH

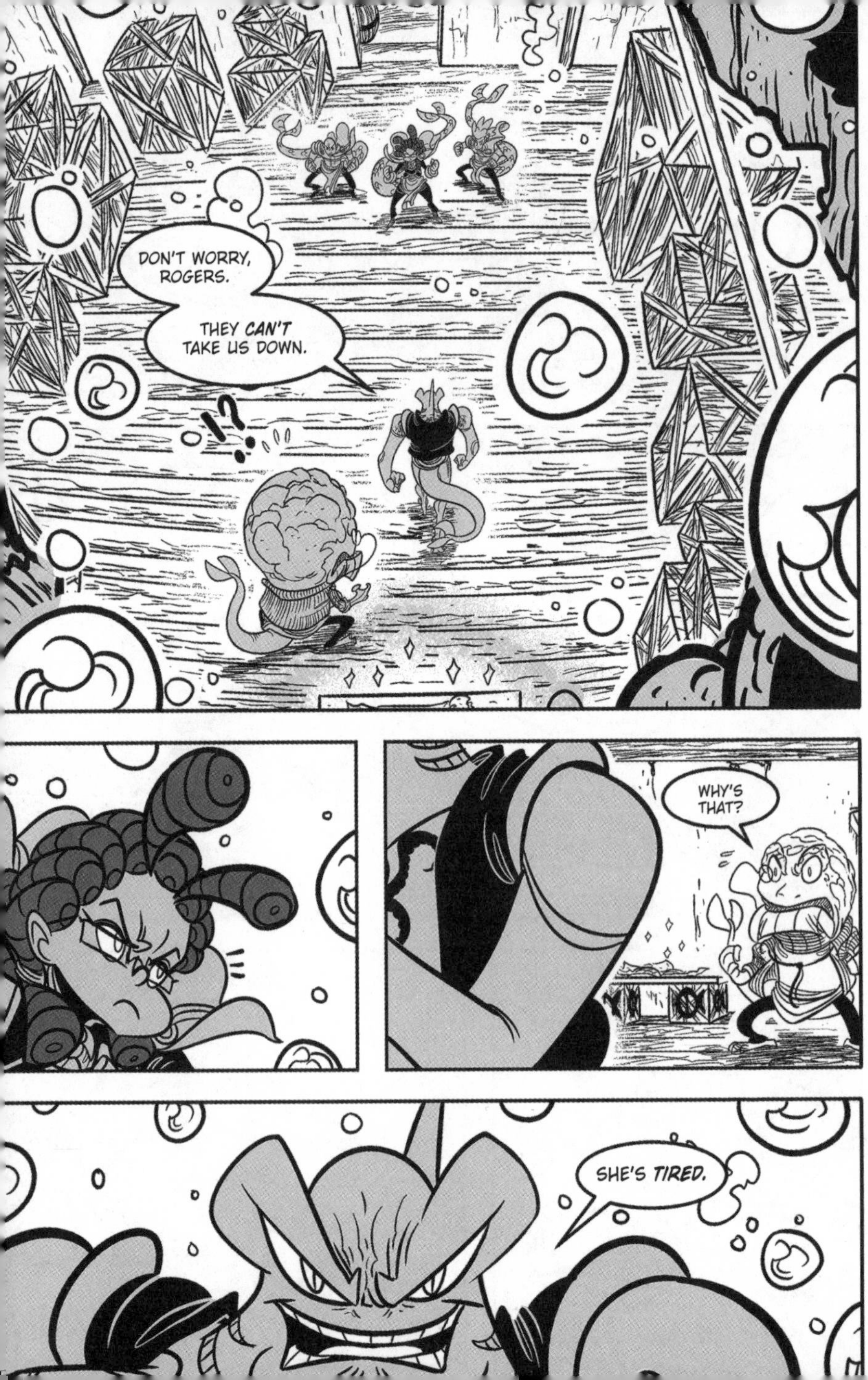
DON'T WORRY, ROGERS.
THEY CAN'T TAKE US DOWN.
!?
WHY'S THAT?
SHE'S TIRED.

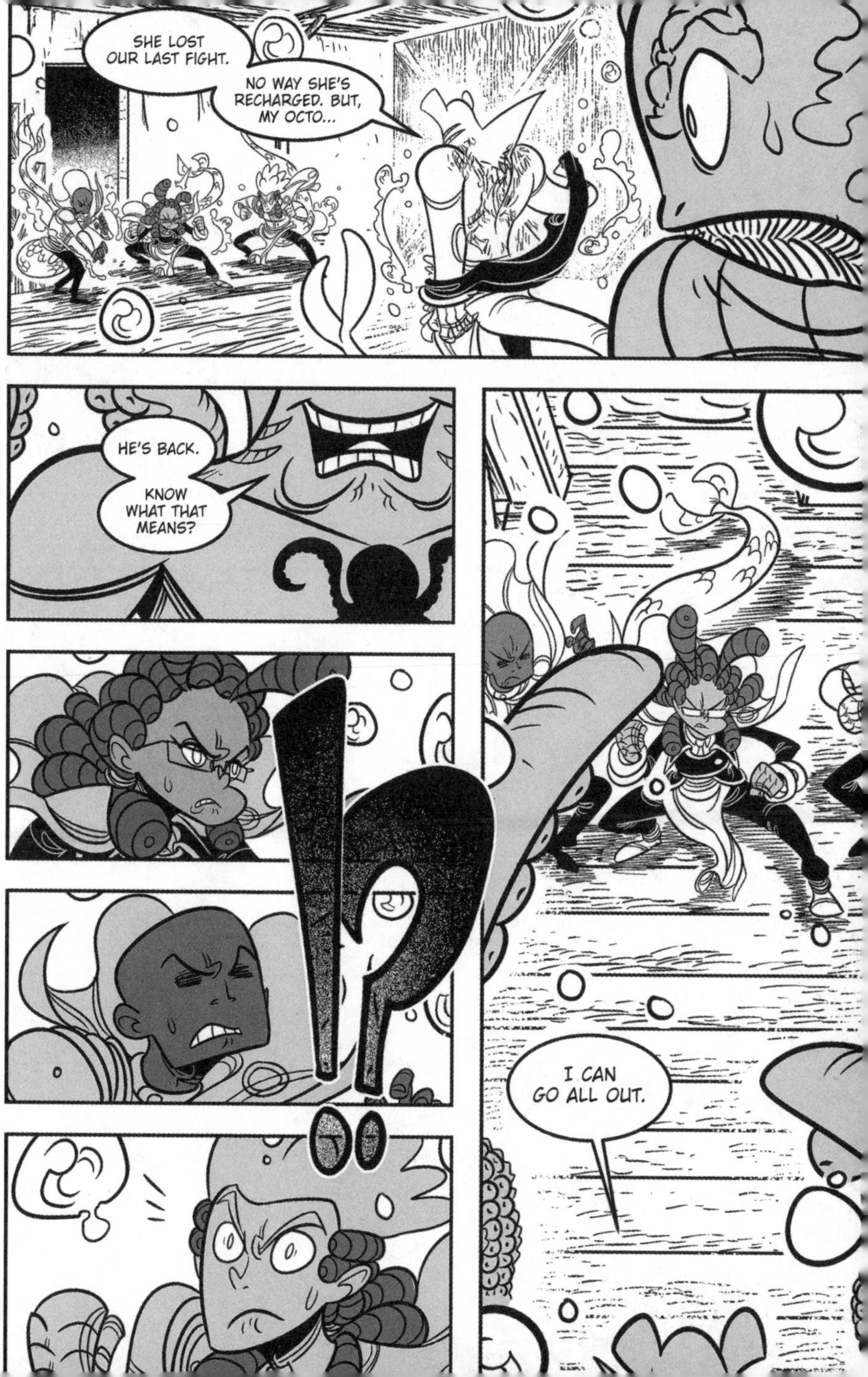
SHE LOST OUR LAST FIGHT.
NO WAY SHE'S RECHARGED. BUT, MY OCTO...
HE'S BACK.
KNOW WHAT THAT MEANS?
I CAN GO ALL OUT.

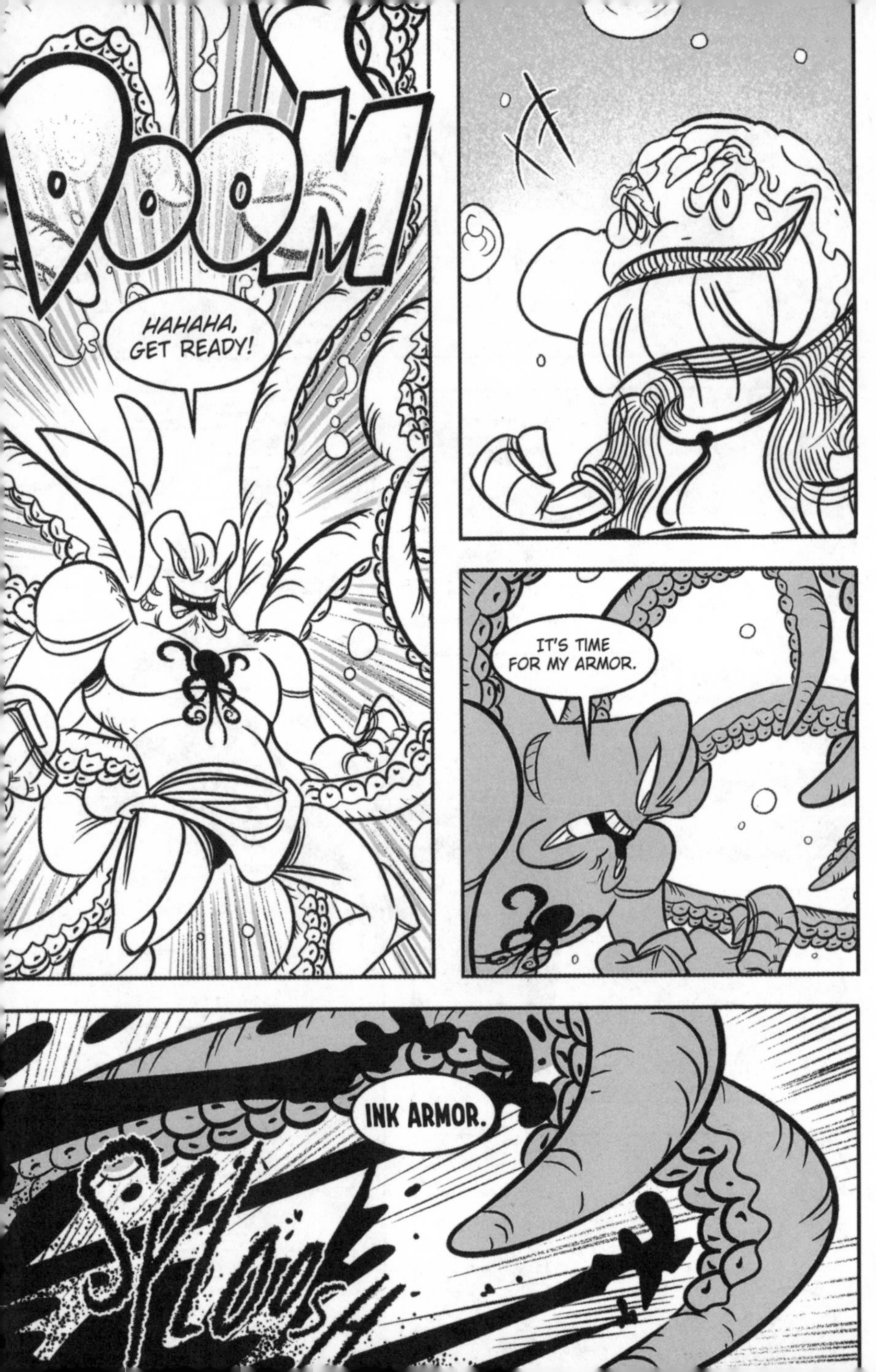
DOOM
HAHAHA, GET READY!
IT'S TIME FOR MY ARMOR.
INK ARMOR.
SPLOOSH

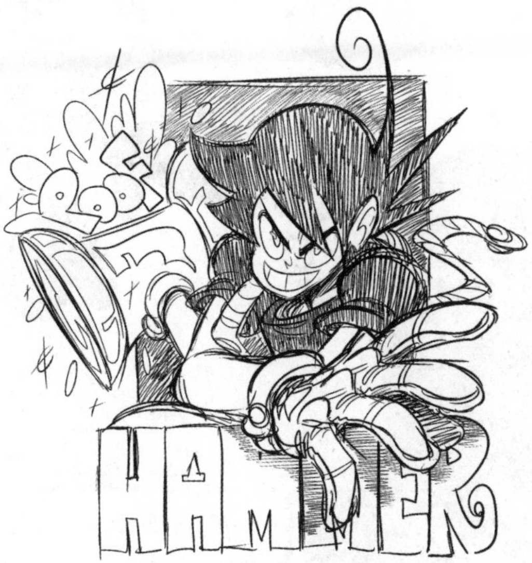
HAMMER

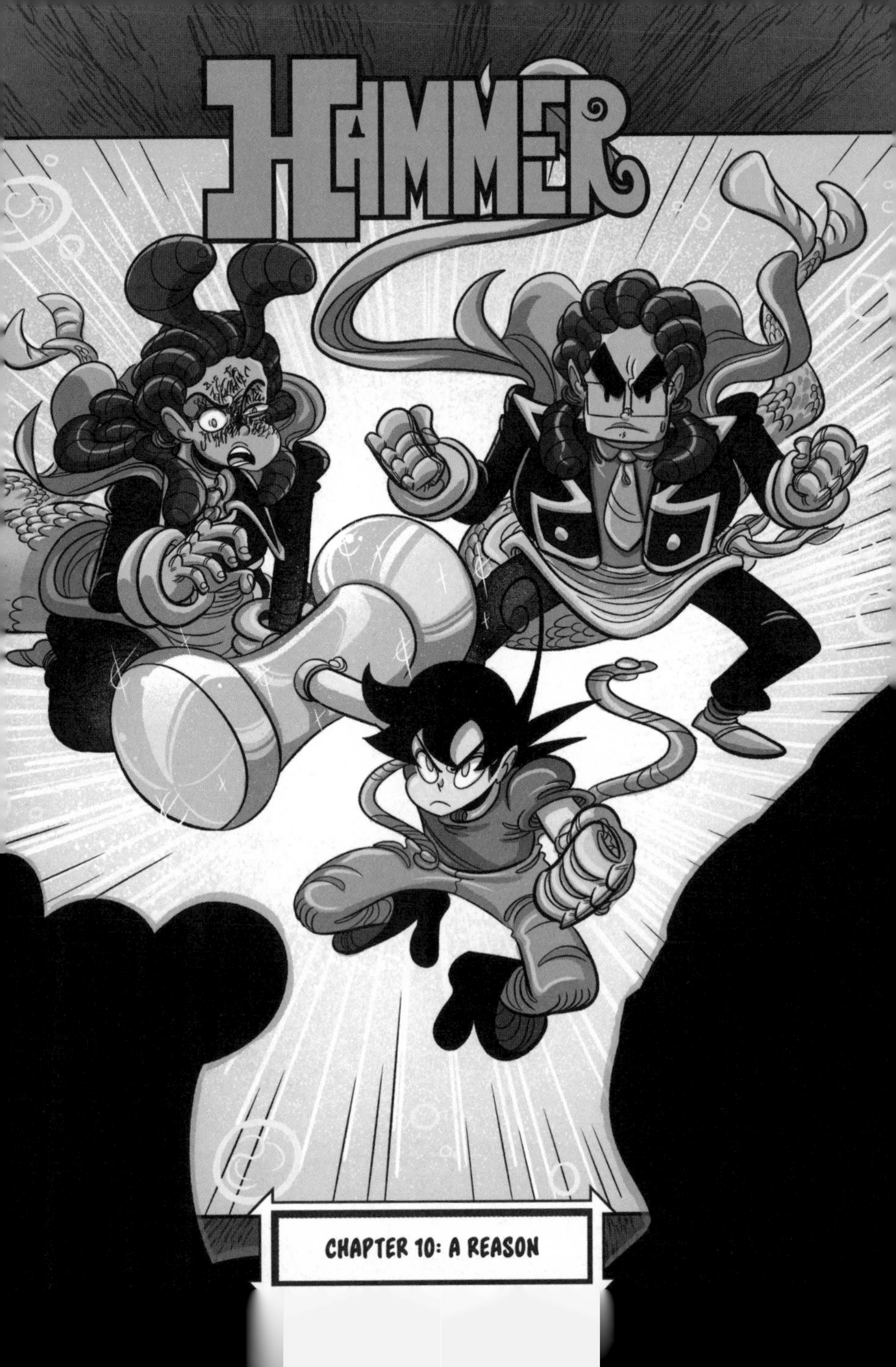
HAMMER
CHAPTER 10: A REASON

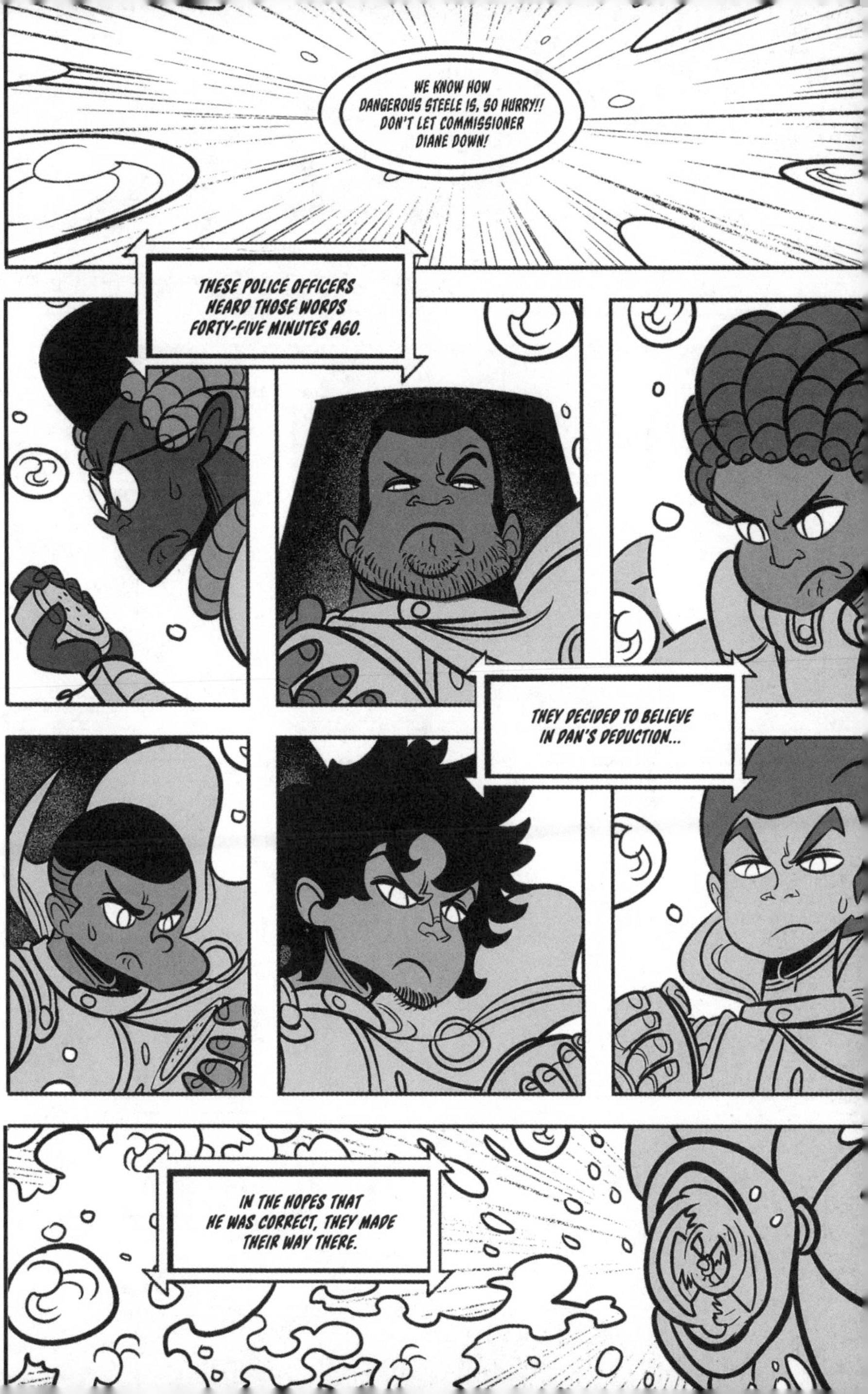
WE KNOW HOW DANGEROUS STEELE IS, SO HURRY!! DON'T LET COMMISSIONER DIANE DOWN!
THESE POLICE OFFICERS HEARD THOSE WORDS FORTY-FIVE MINUTES AGO.
THEY DECIDED TO BELIEVE IN DAN'S DEDUCTION...
IN THE HOPES THAT HE WAS CORRECT, THEY MADE THEIR WAY THERE.

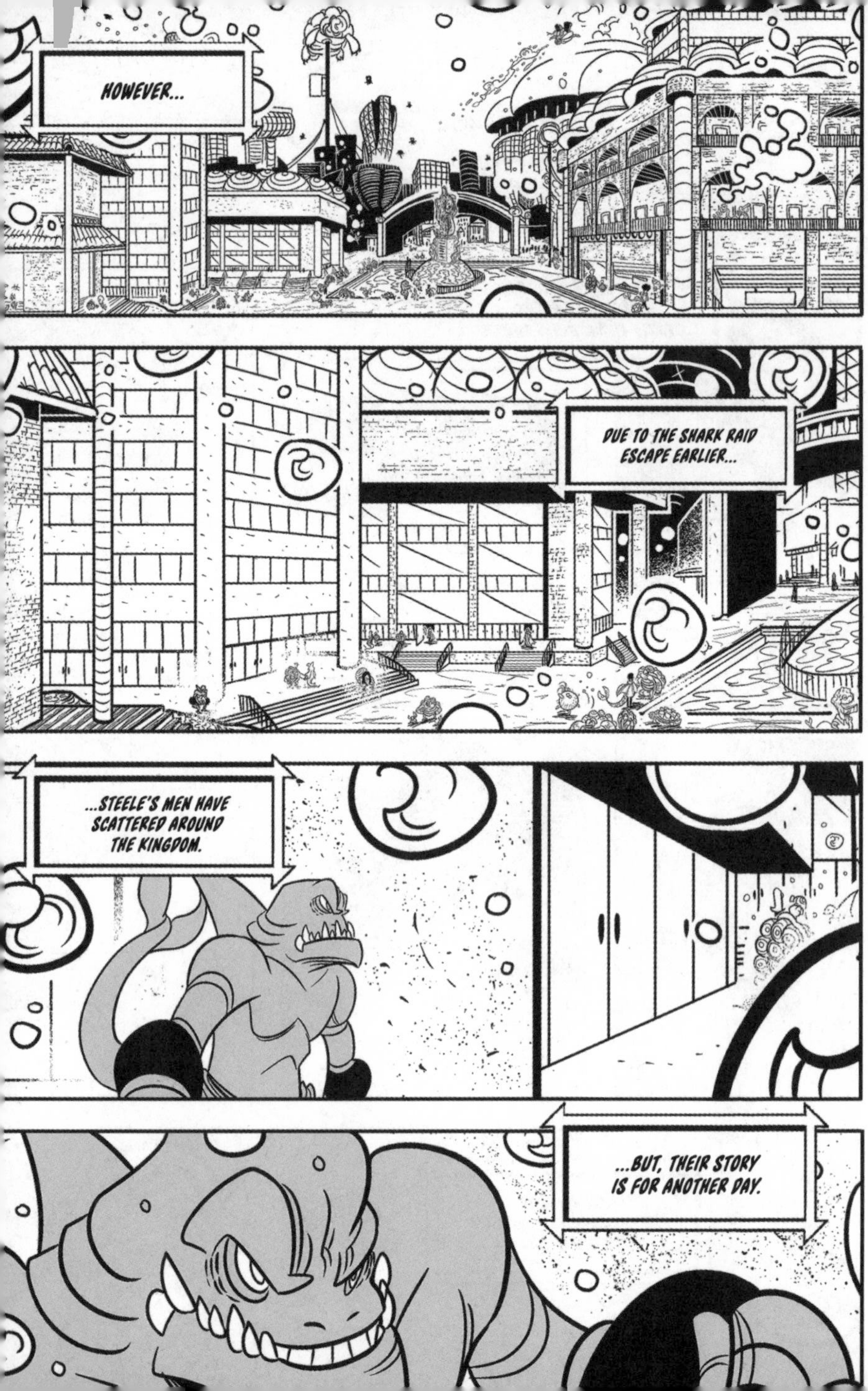
HOWEVER...
DUE TO THE SHARK RAID ESCAPE EARLIER...
...STEELE'S MEN HAVE SCATTERED AROUND THE KINGDOM.
...BUT, THEIR STORY IS FOR ANOTHER DAY.

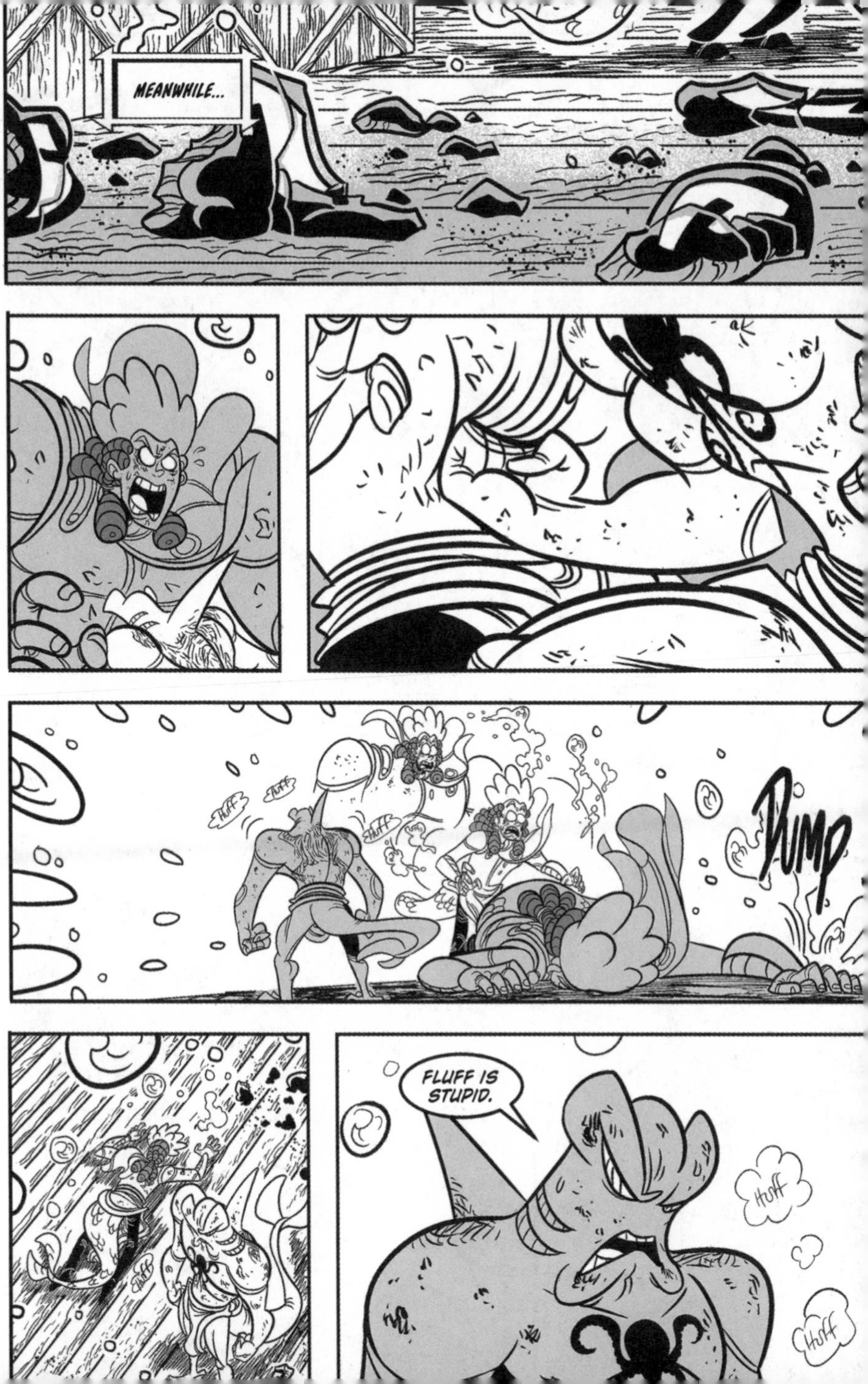
MEANWHILE...
HUFF
HUFF
HUFF
DUMP
FLUFF IS STUPID.
HUFF
HUFF

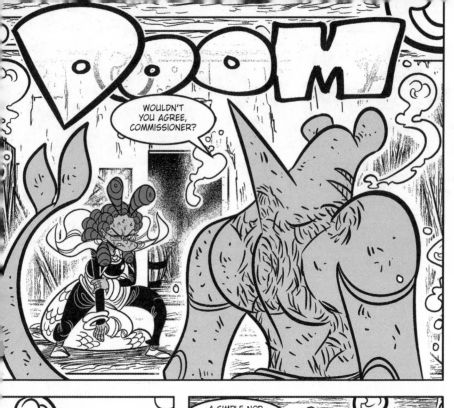

DOOM

WOULDN'T YOU AGREE, COMMISSIONER?

A SIMPLE NOD WILL DO. YOU MUST BE EXHAUSTED.

ESPECIALLY AFTER THAT BEAT DOWN.

YAWN   GOTTA GIVE YOU CREDIT THOUGH--

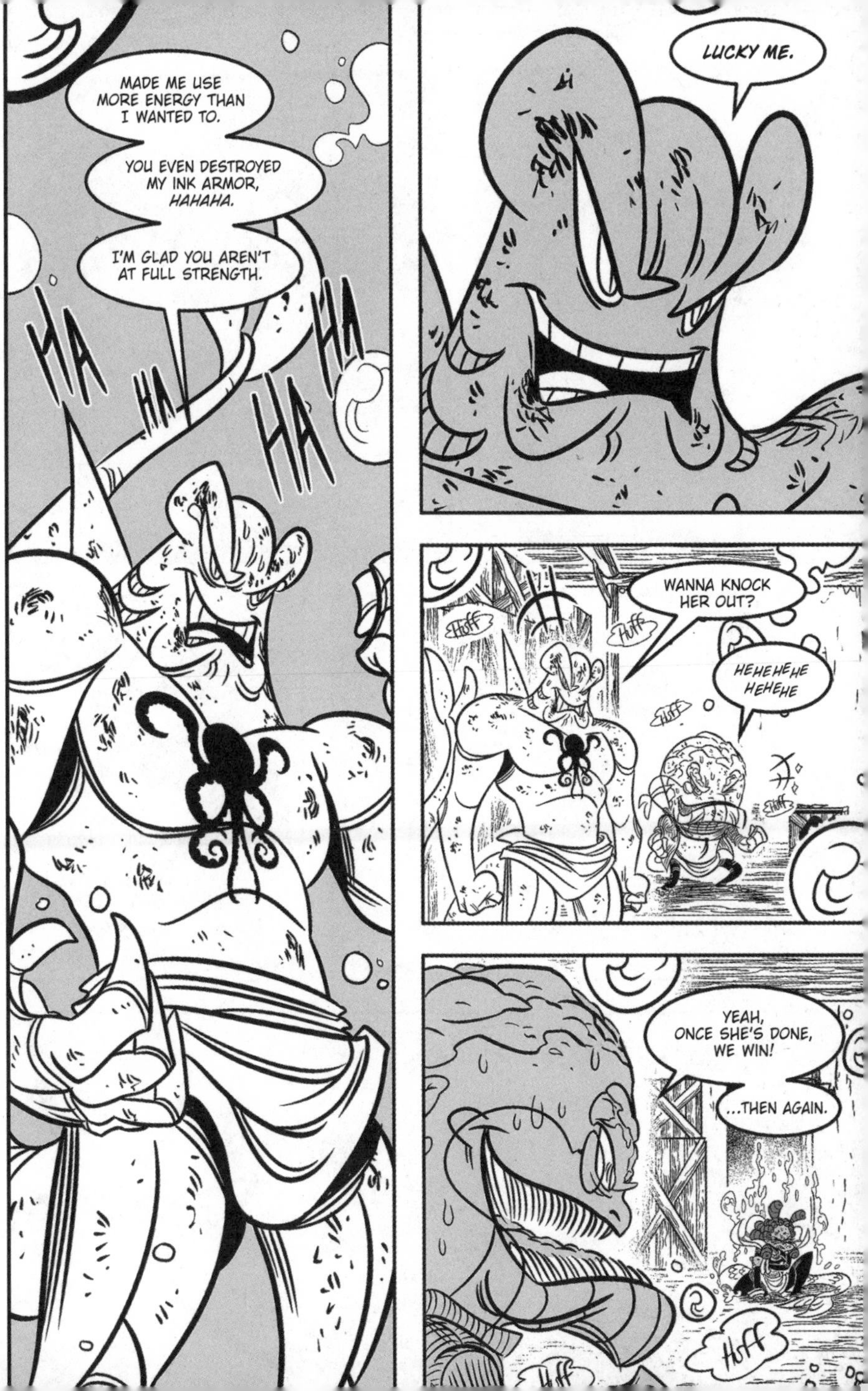
MADE ME USE MORE ENERGY THAN I WANTED TO.
YOU EVEN DESTROYED MY INK ARMOR, HAHAHA.
I'M GLAD YOU AREN'T AT FULL STRENGTH.
HA HA HA HA
LUCKY ME.
HUFF HUFF
WANNA KNOCK HER OUT?
HEHEHEHE HEHEHEHE
HUFF HUFF
YEAH, ONCE SHE'S DONE, WE WIN!
...THEN AGAIN.
HUFF HUFF

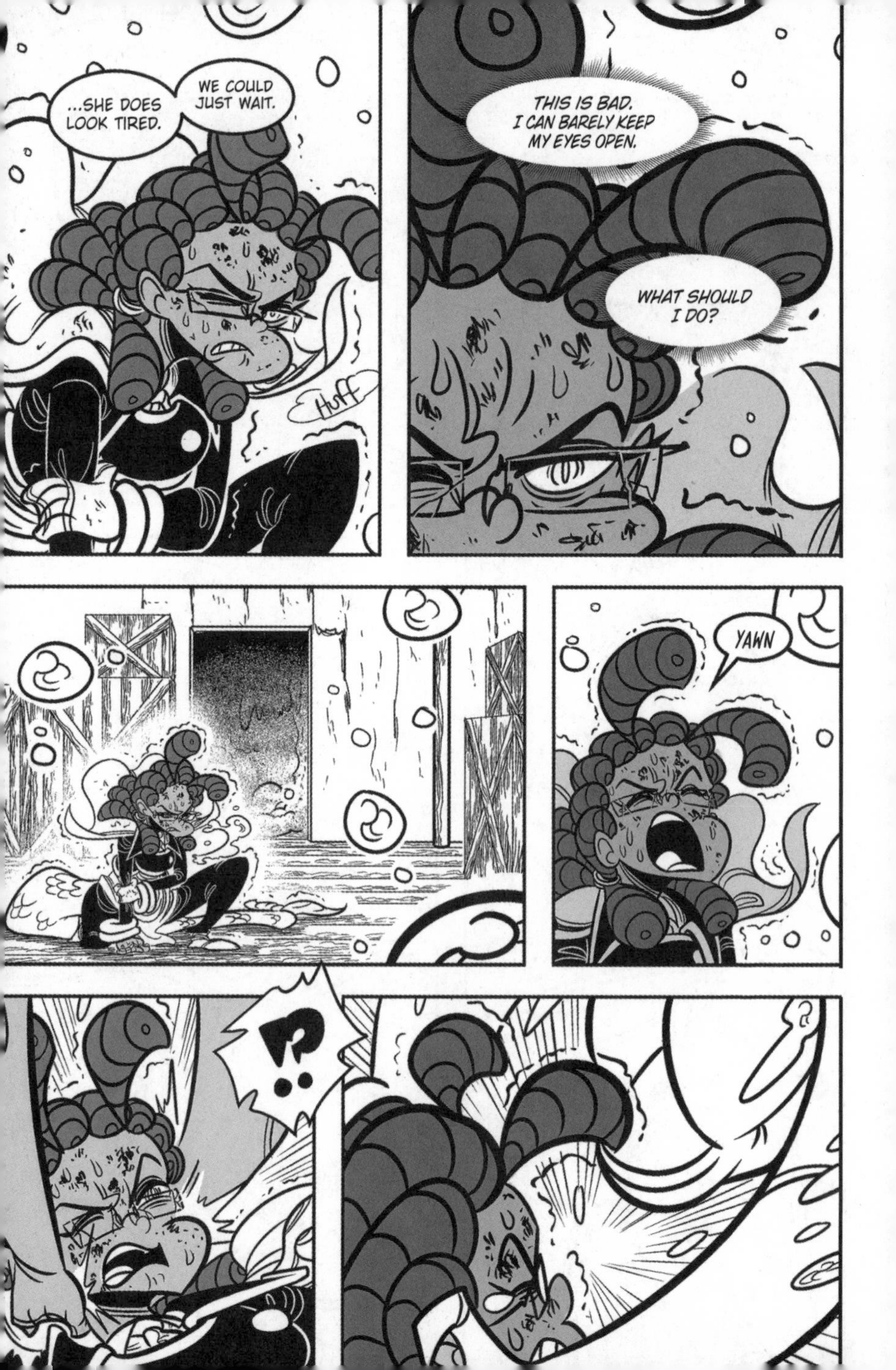
...SHE DOES LOOK TIRED.
WE COULD JUST WAIT.
HUFF
THIS IS BAD. I CAN BARELY KEEP MY EYES OPEN.
WHAT SHOULD I DO?
YAWN
!?

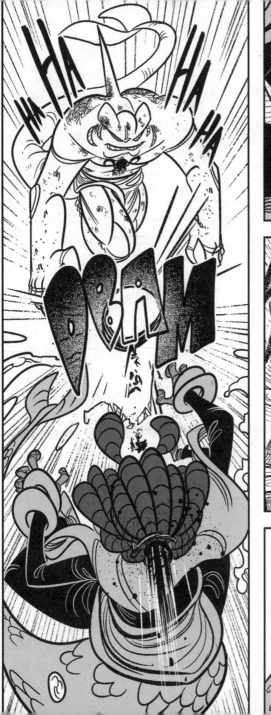

HA HA HA HA

VRRRM

WOOOOOOOO DOOSH

WE *COULD,* BUT... I'M IMPATIENT.

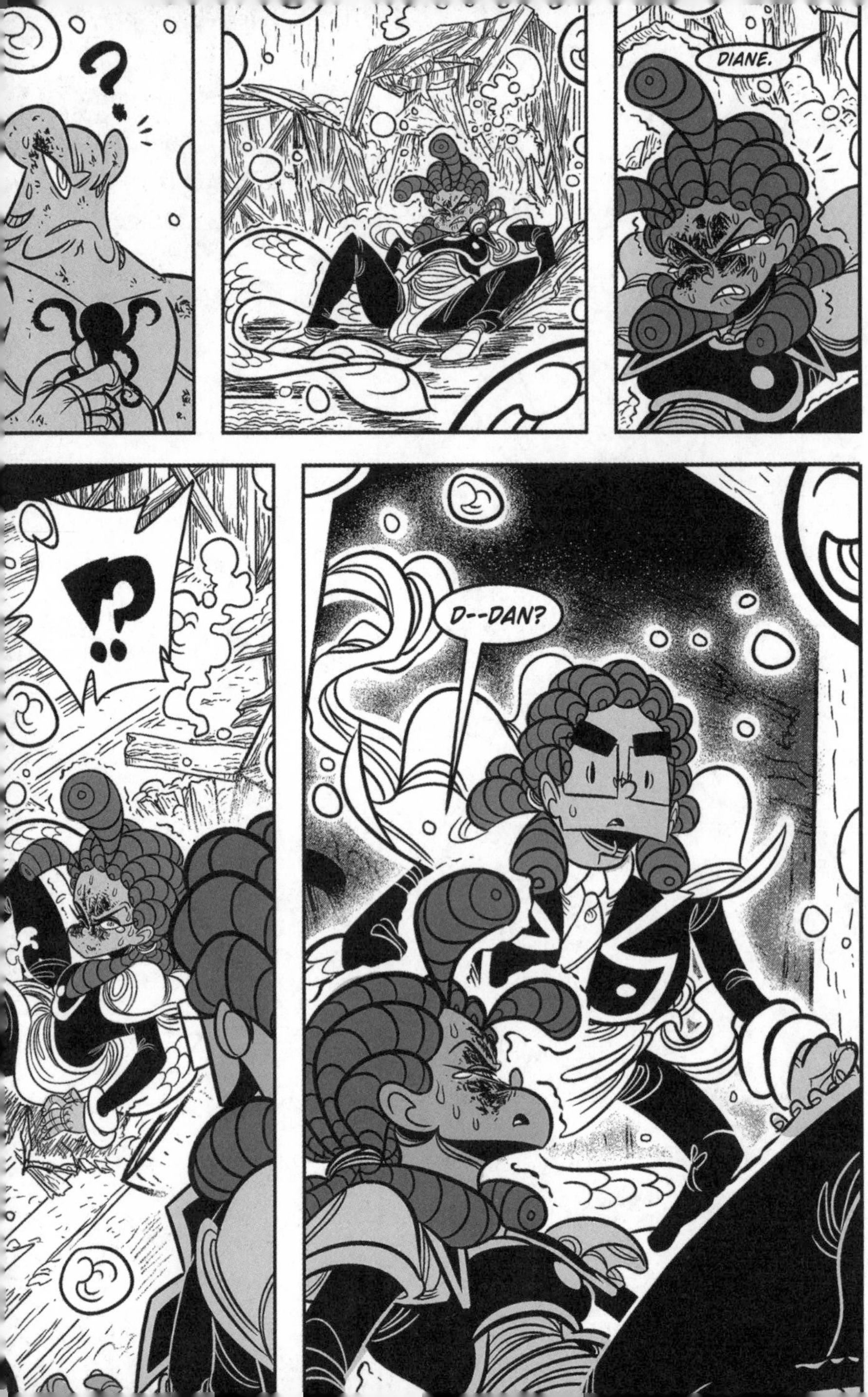

?
DIANE.
?!!
D--DAN?

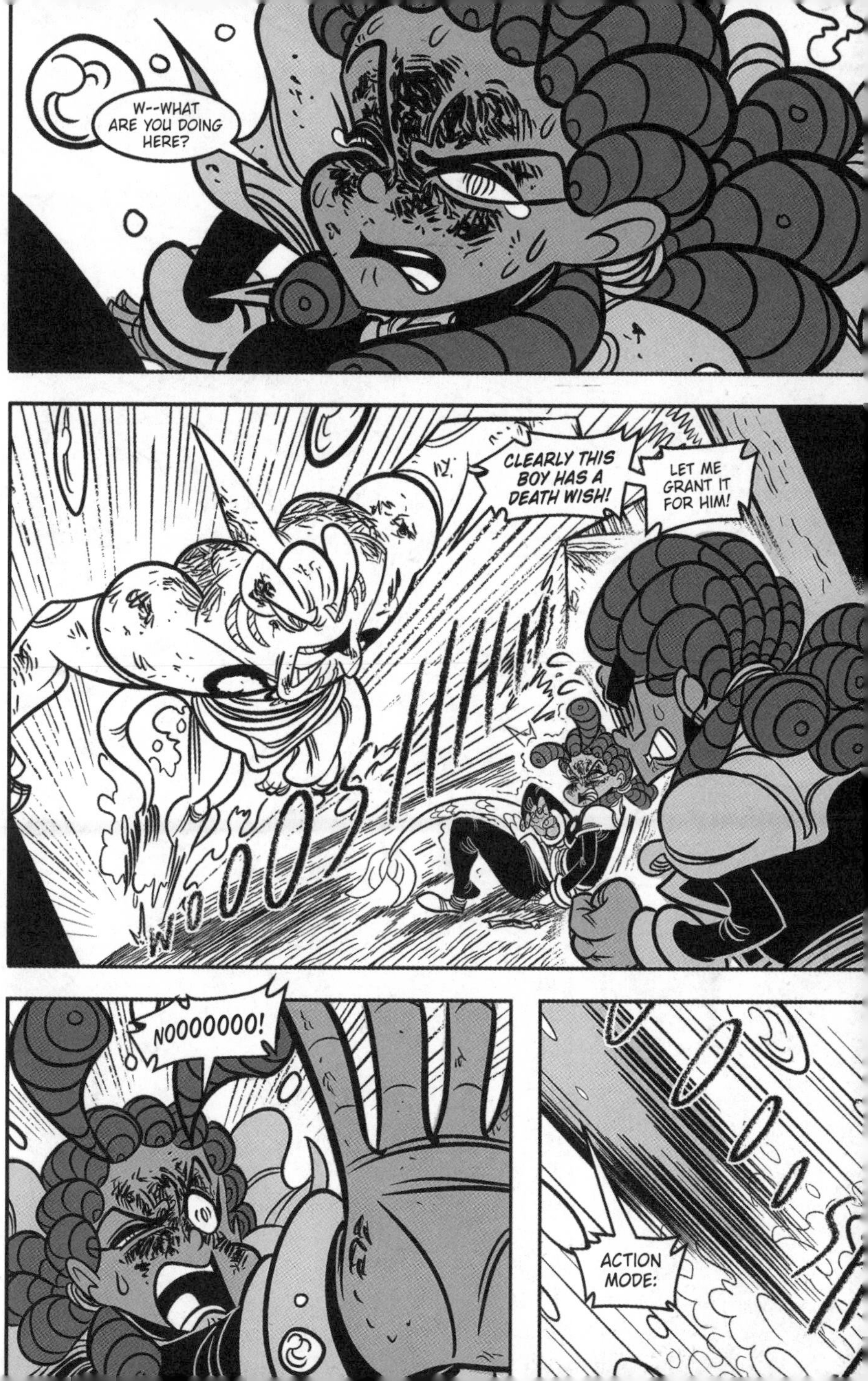
W--WHAT ARE YOU DOING HERE?
CLEARLY THIS BOY HAS A DEATH WISH!
LET ME GRANT IT FOR HIM!
NOOOOOOO!
ACTION MODE:

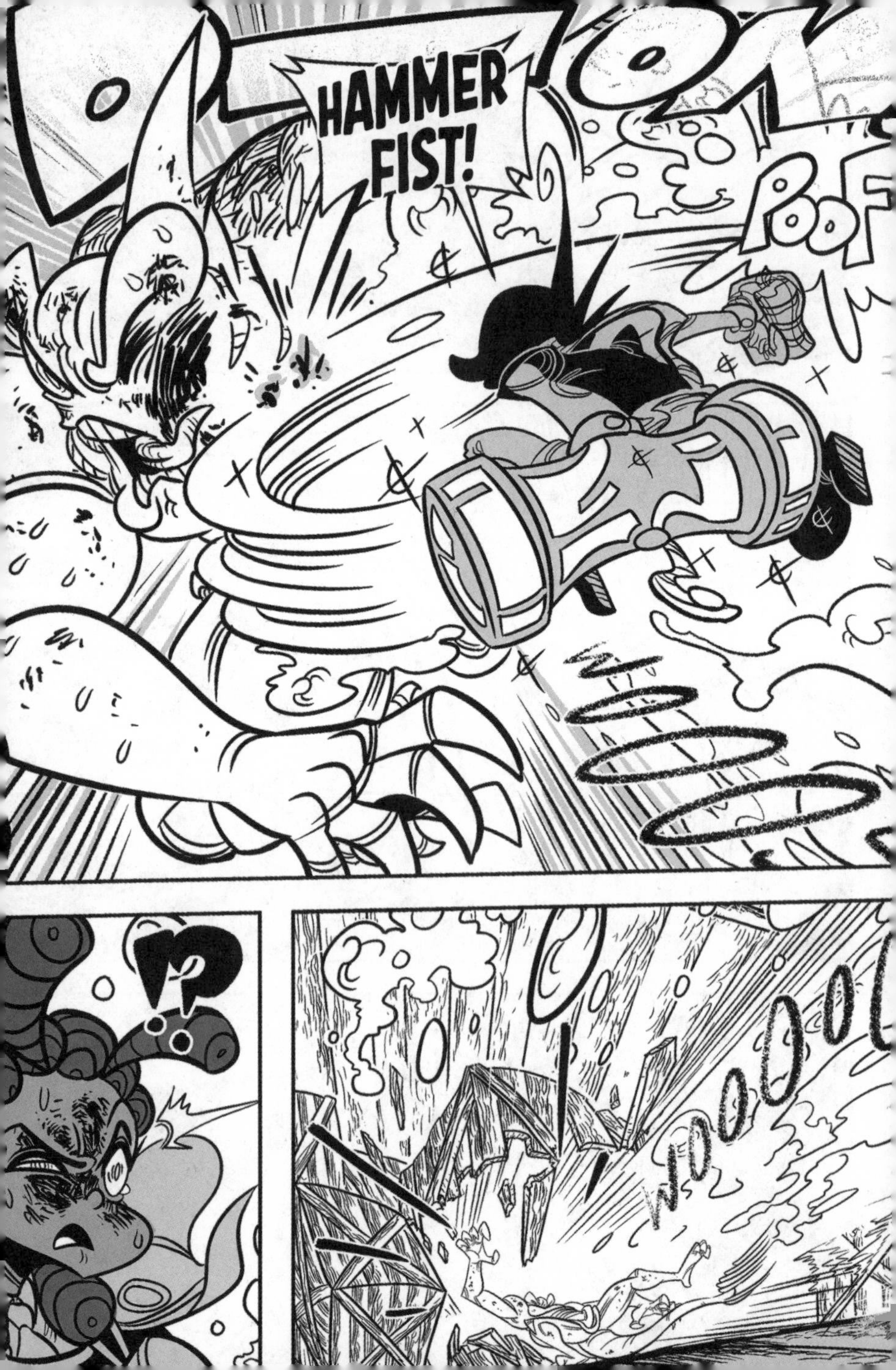
HAMMER FIST!
POOF
WOOOOOO
!?
WOOOOOO

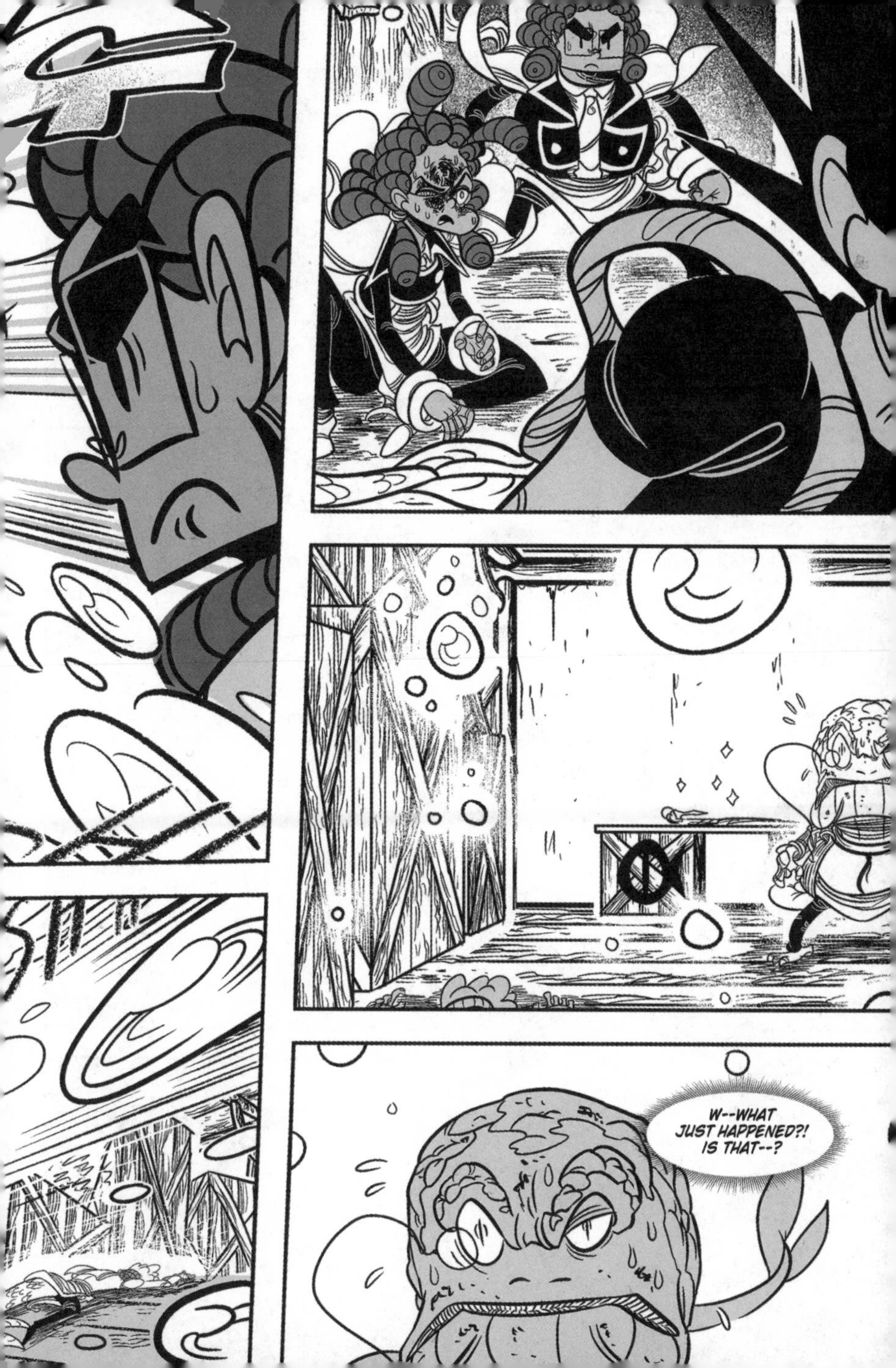
W--WHAT JUST HAPPENED?! IS THAT--?

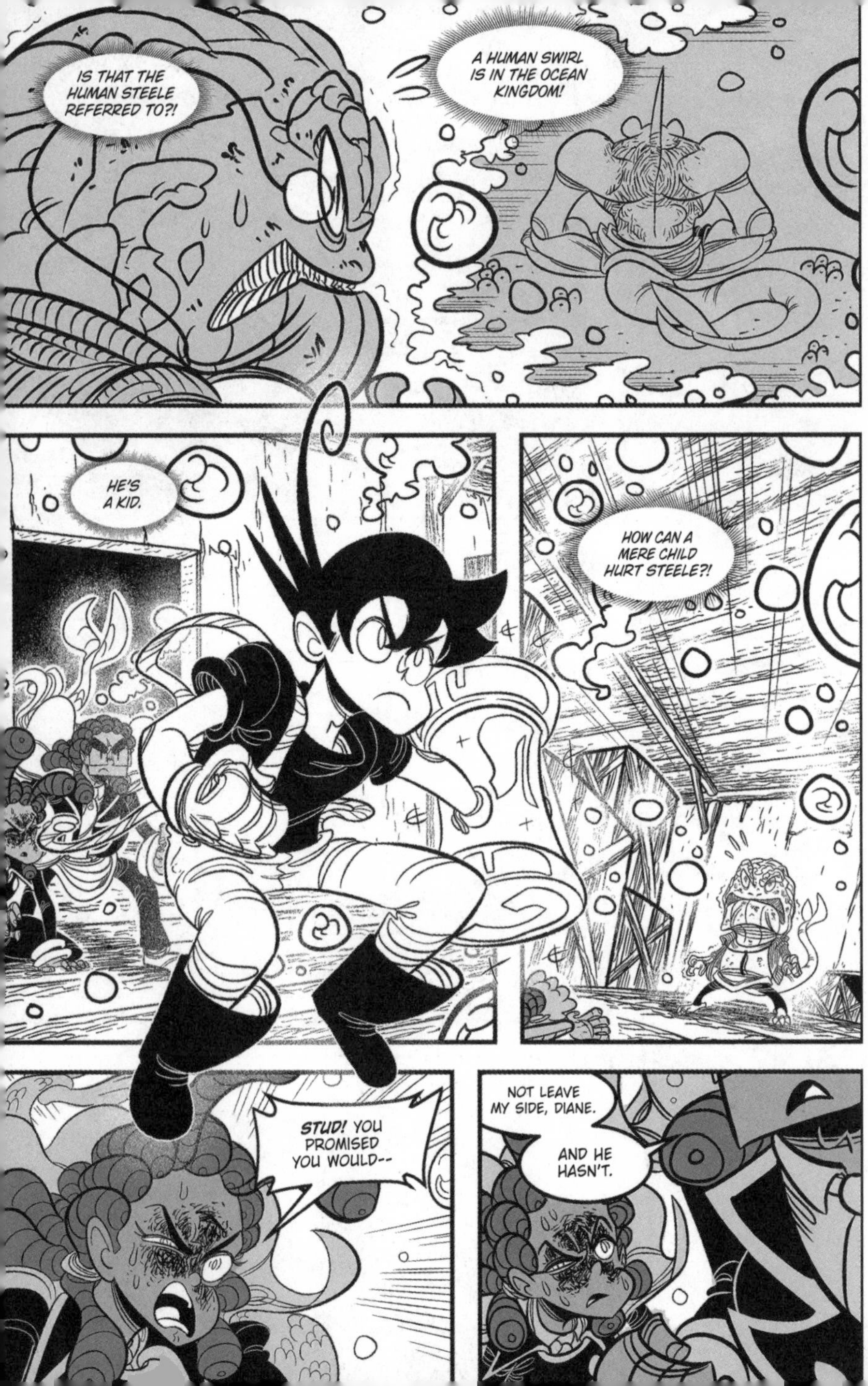
IS THAT THE HUMAN STEELE REFERRED TO?!
A HUMAN SWIRL IS IN THE OCEAN KINGDOM!
HE'S A KID.
HOW CAN A MERE CHILD HURT STEELE?!
STUD! YOU PROMISED YOU WOULD--
NOT LEAVE MY SIDE, DIANE.
AND HE HASN'T.

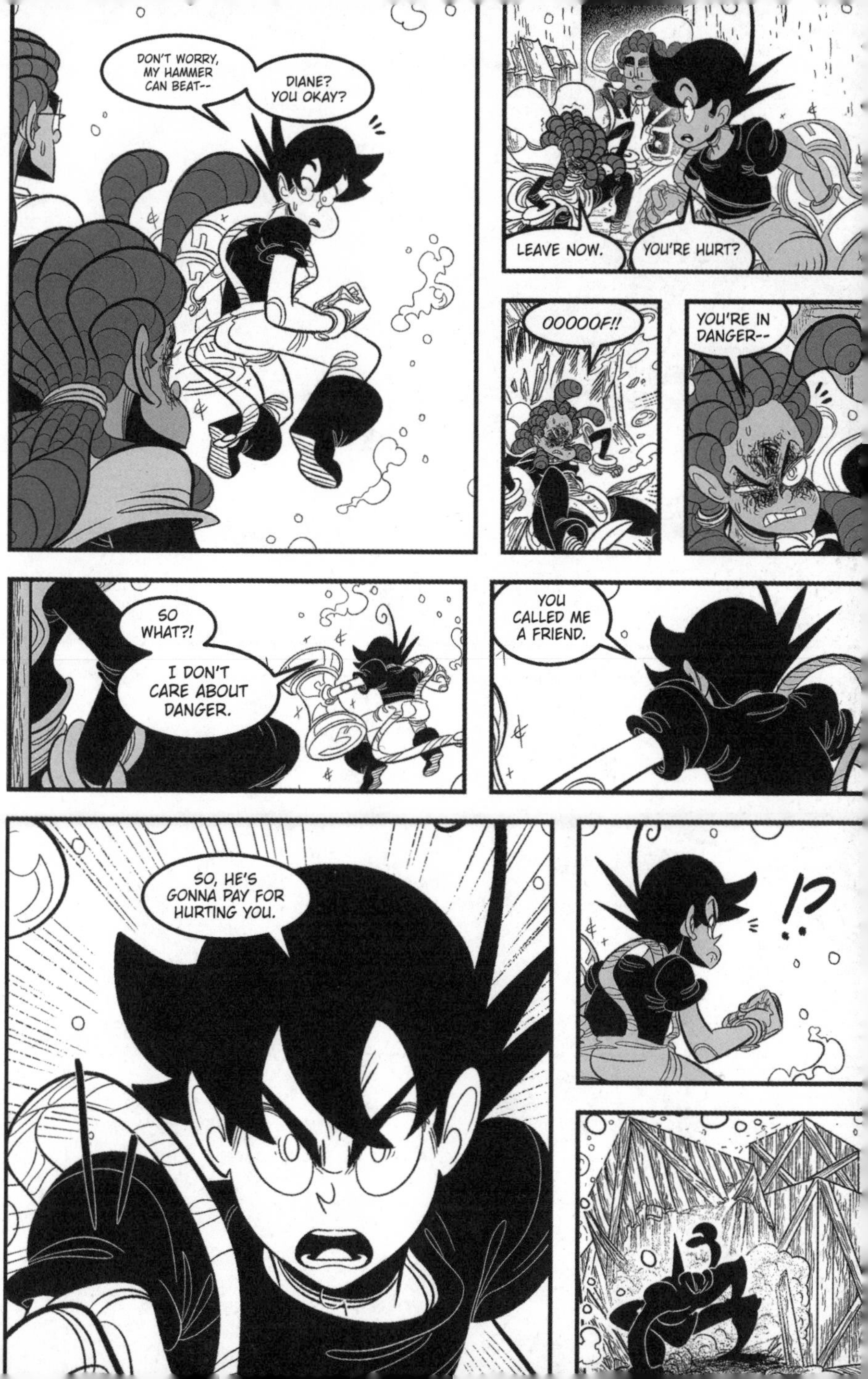
DON'T WORRY, MY HAMMER CAN BEAT--
DIANE? YOU OKAY?
LEAVE NOW.
YOU'RE HURT?
OOOOOF!!
YOU'RE IN DANGER--
SO WHAT?!
I DON'T CARE ABOUT DANGER.
YOU CALLED ME A FRIEND.
SO, HE'S GONNA PAY FOR HURTING YOU.
!?

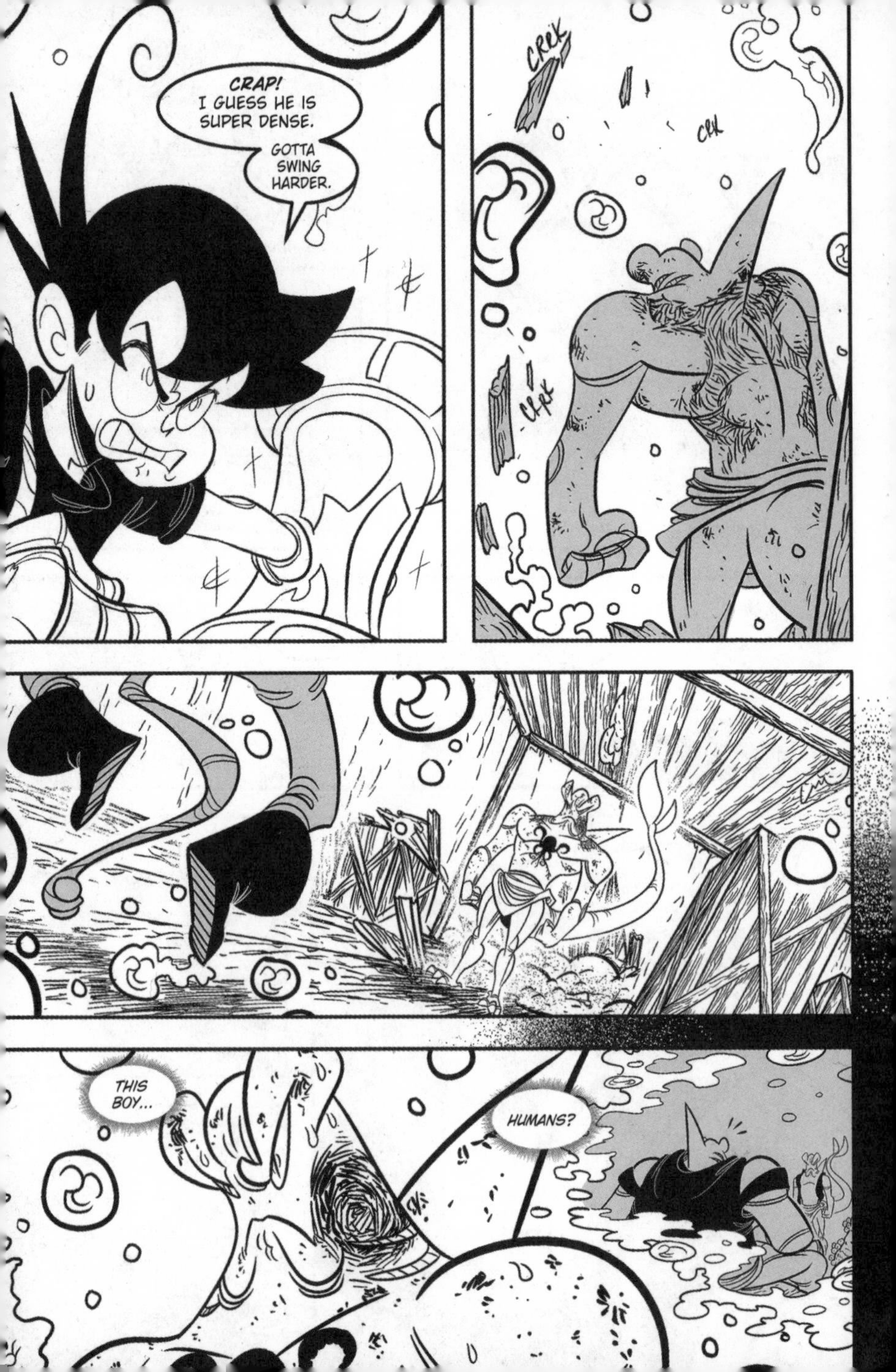
CRAP! I GUESS HE IS SUPER DENSE.
GOTTA SWING HARDER.
CRRK
CRK
CRRK
THIS BOY...
HUMANS?

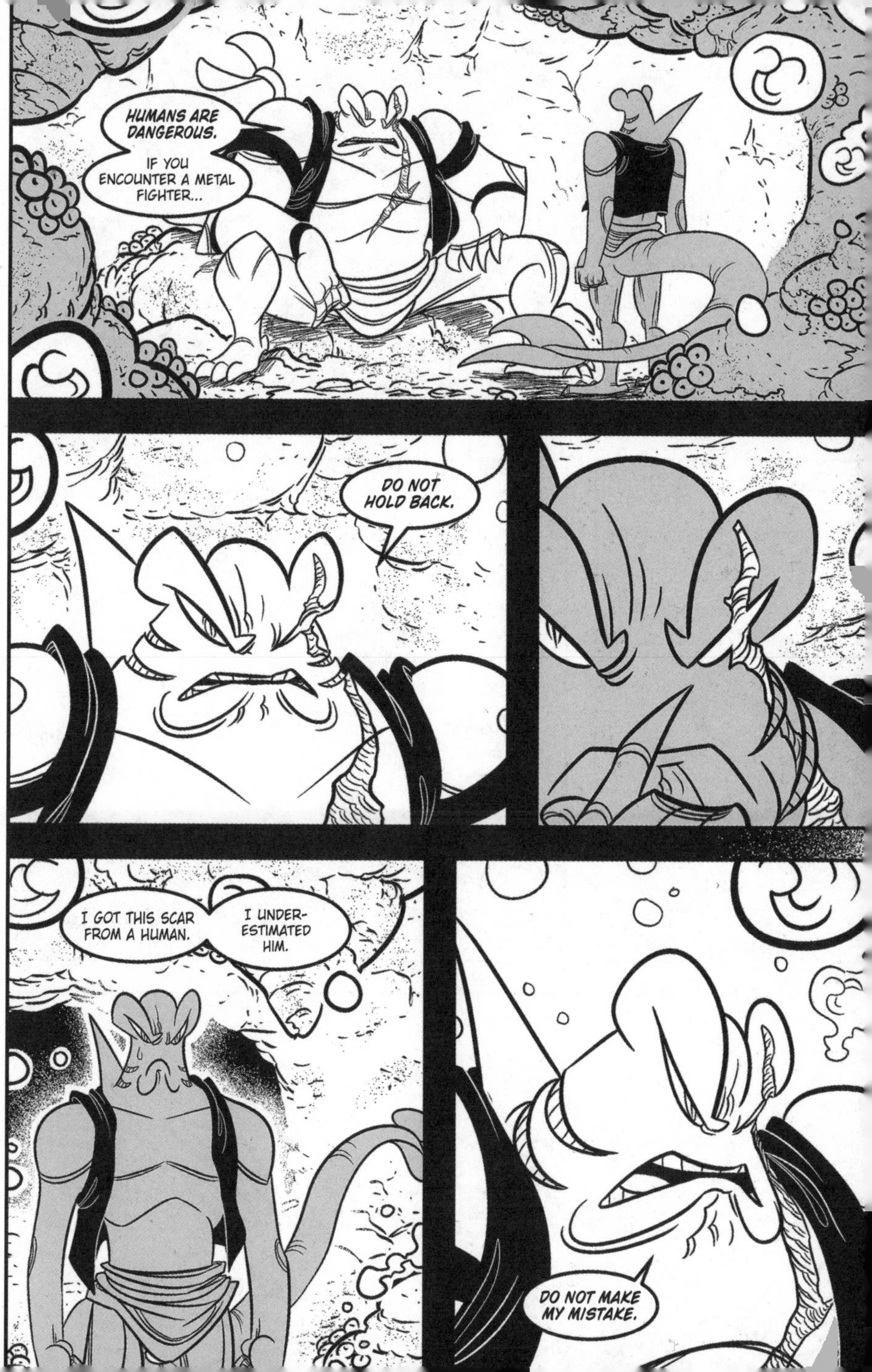
HUMANS ARE DANGEROUS.
IF YOU ENCOUNTER A METAL FIGHTER...
DO NOT HOLD BACK.
I GOT THIS SCAR FROM A HUMAN.
I UNDER-ESTIMATED HIM.
DO NOT MAKE MY MISTAKE.

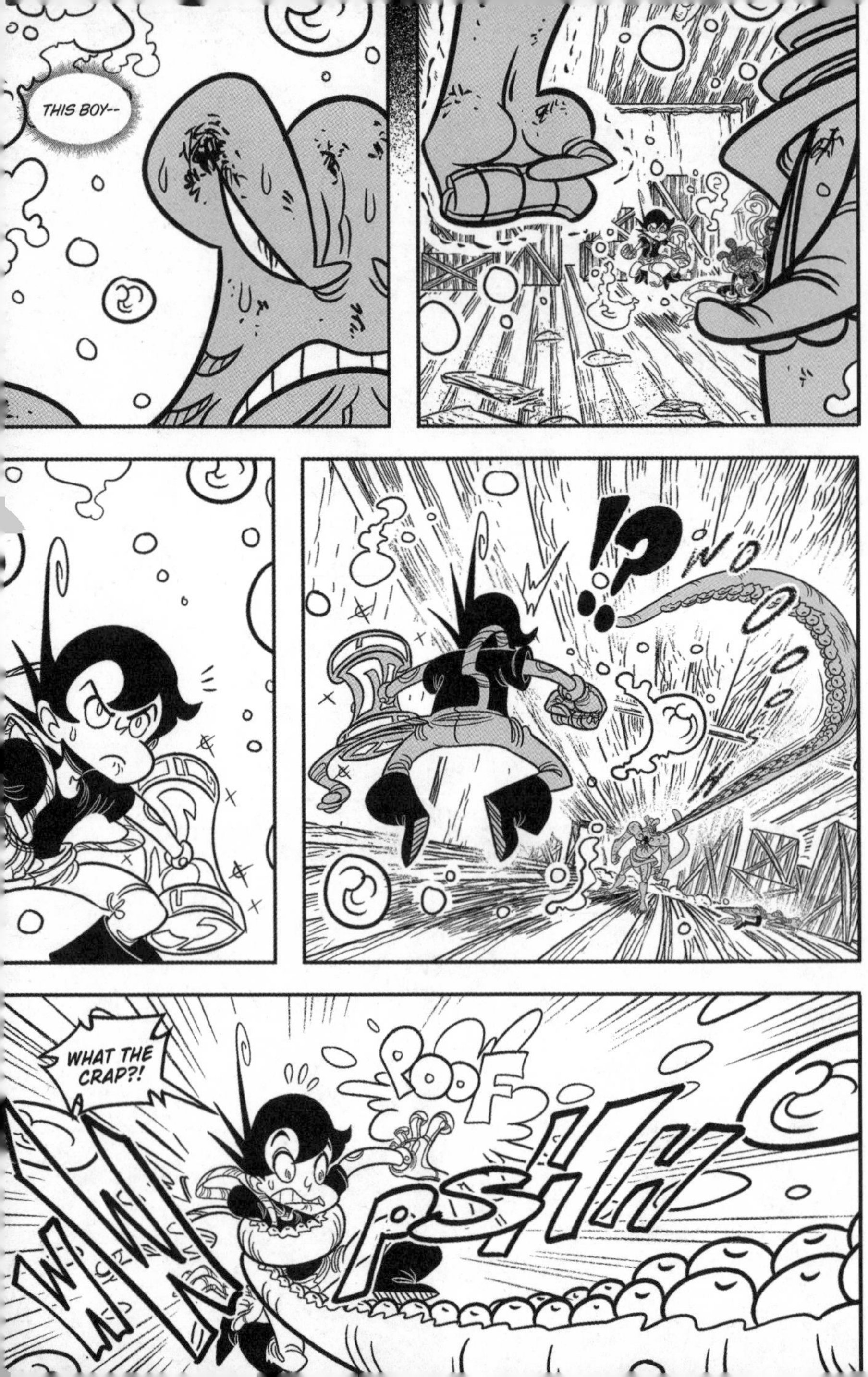
THIS BOY--
!?
WOOOOOSH
WHAT THE CRAP?!
POOF
PSHH

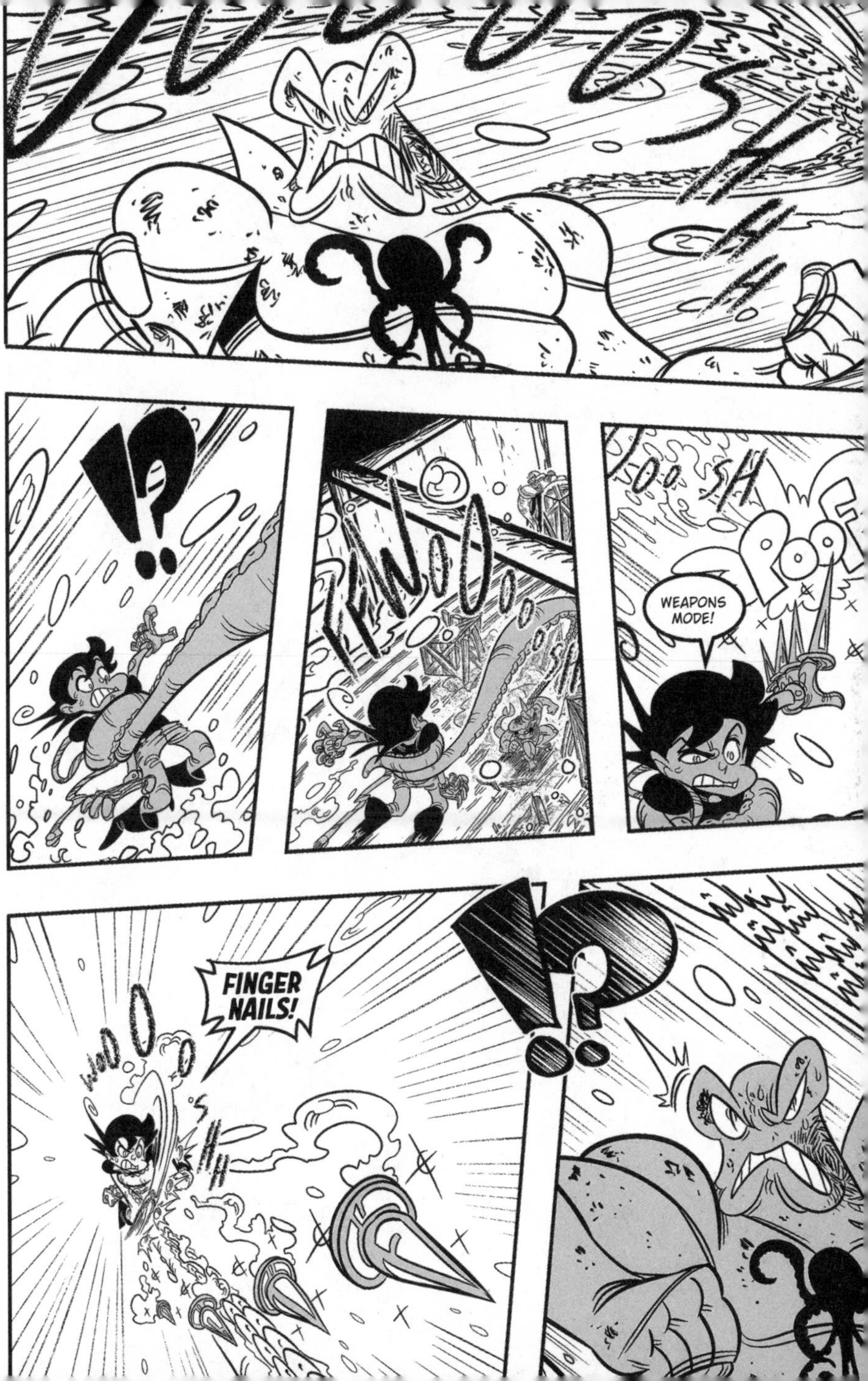
!?
POOF
WEAPONS MODE!
FINGER NAILS!
!?

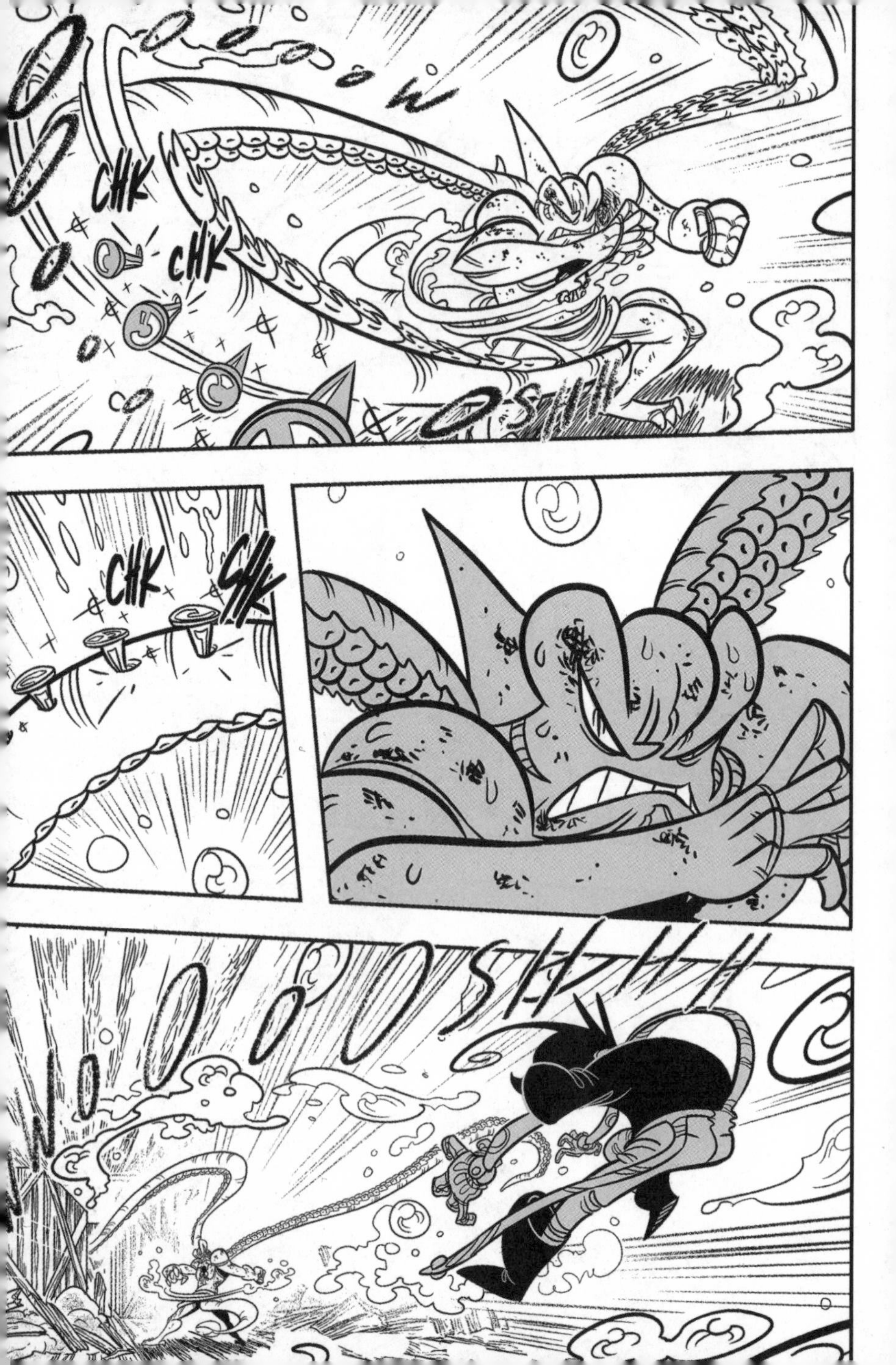
CHK
CHK
CHK
CHK
WOOOOSHHH

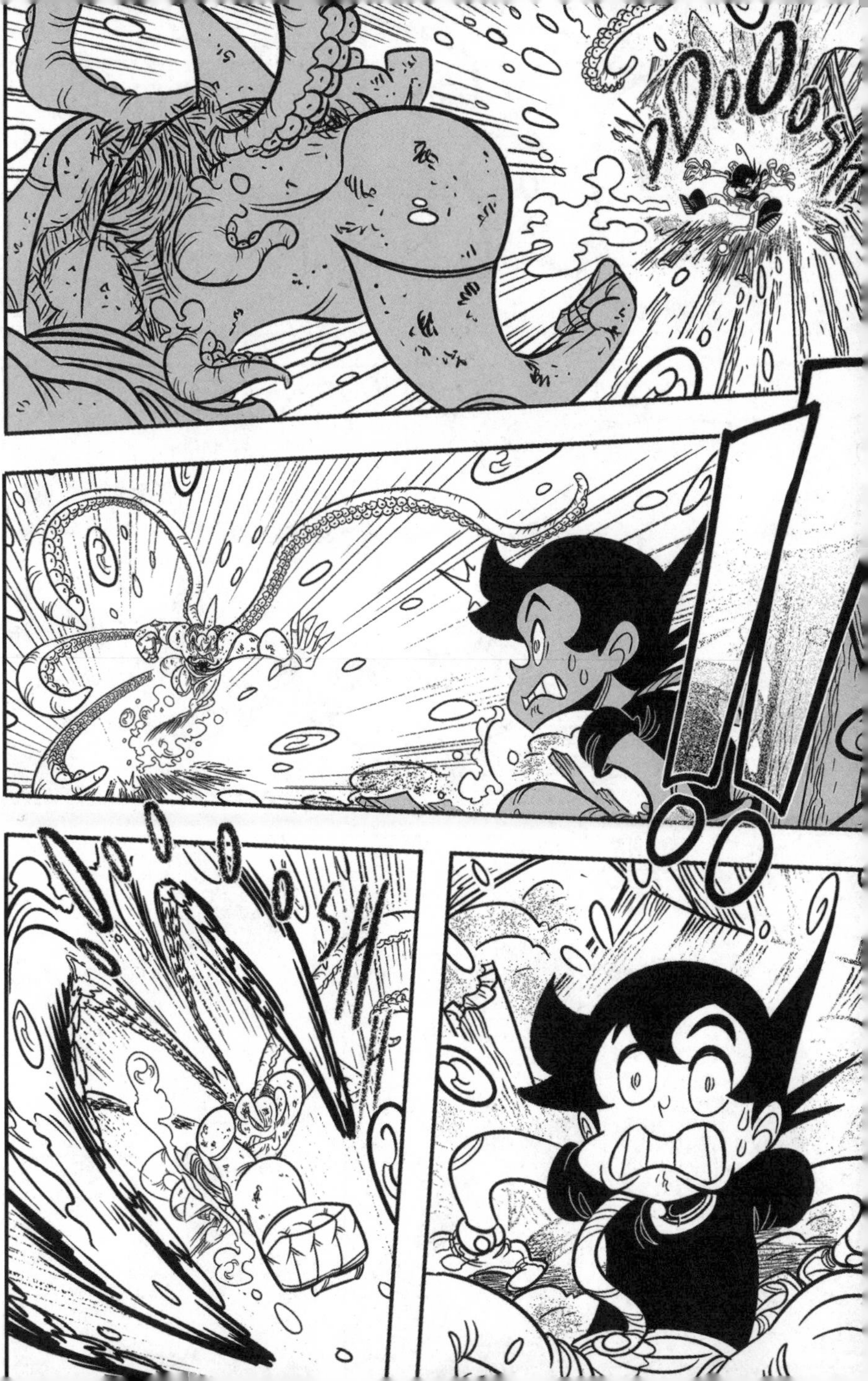

DDOOOSH
!!

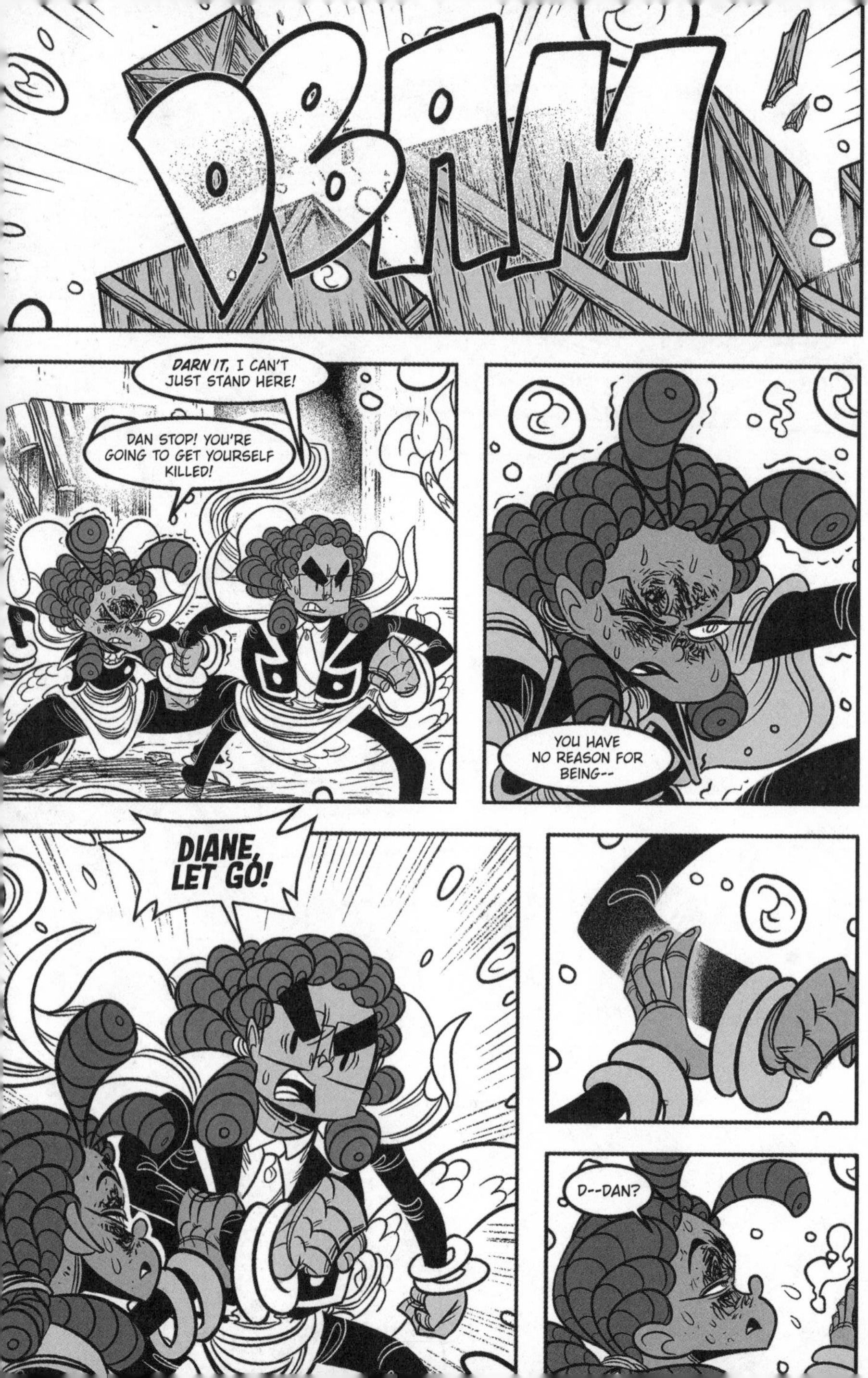
DBAM!
DARN IT, I CAN'T JUST STAND HERE!
DAN STOP! YOU'RE GOING TO GET YOURSELF KILLED!
YOU HAVE NO REASON FOR BEING--
DIANE, LET GO!
D--DAN?

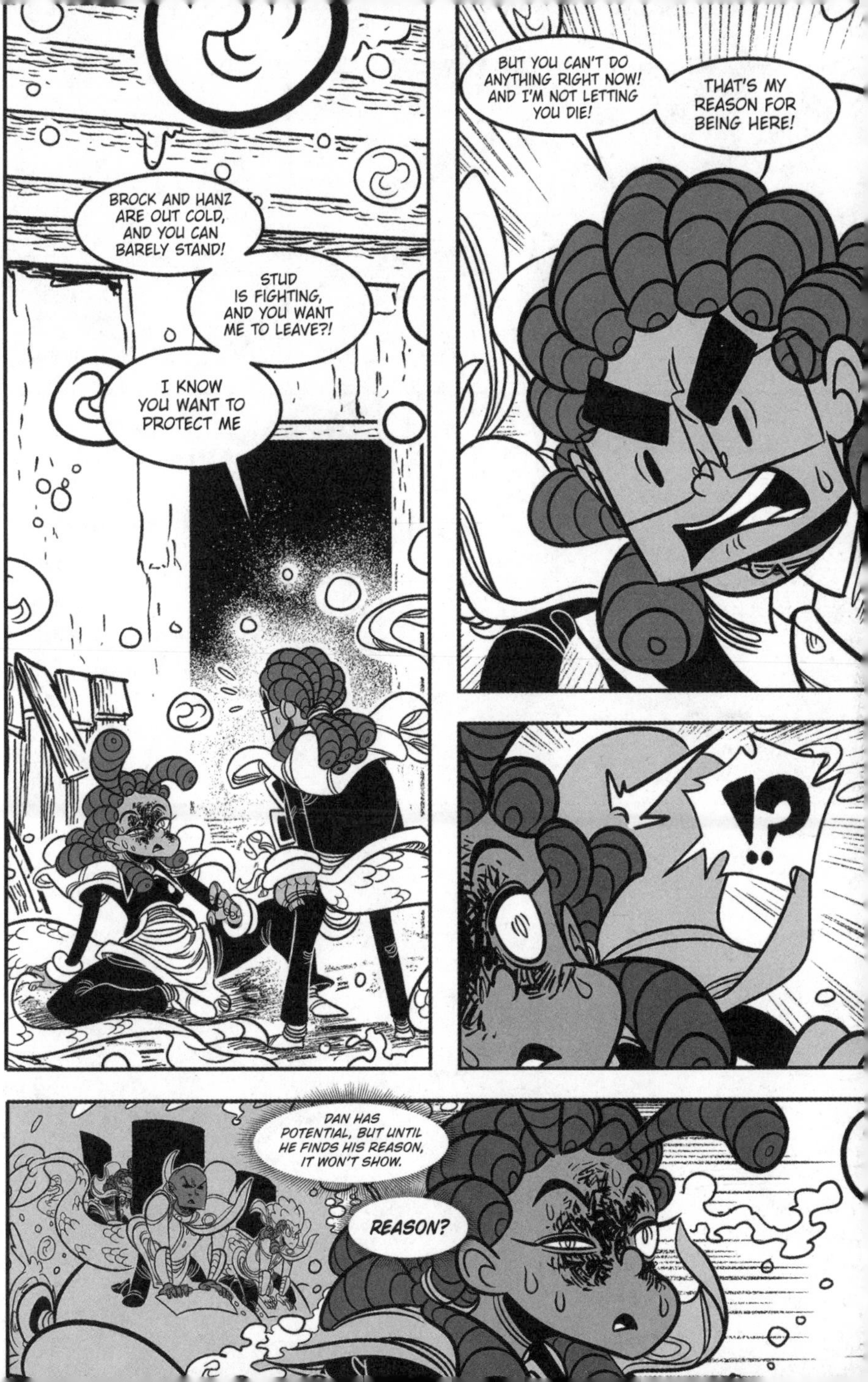
BROCK AND HANZ ARE OUT COLD, AND YOU CAN BARELY STAND!
STUD IS FIGHTING, AND YOU WANT ME TO LEAVE?!
I KNOW YOU WANT TO PROTECT ME
BUT YOU CAN'T DO ANYTHING RIGHT NOW! AND I'M NOT LETTING YOU DIE!
THAT'S MY REASON FOR BEING HERE!
!?
DAN HAS POTENTIAL, BUT UNTIL HE FINDS HIS REASON, IT WON'T SHOW.
REASON?

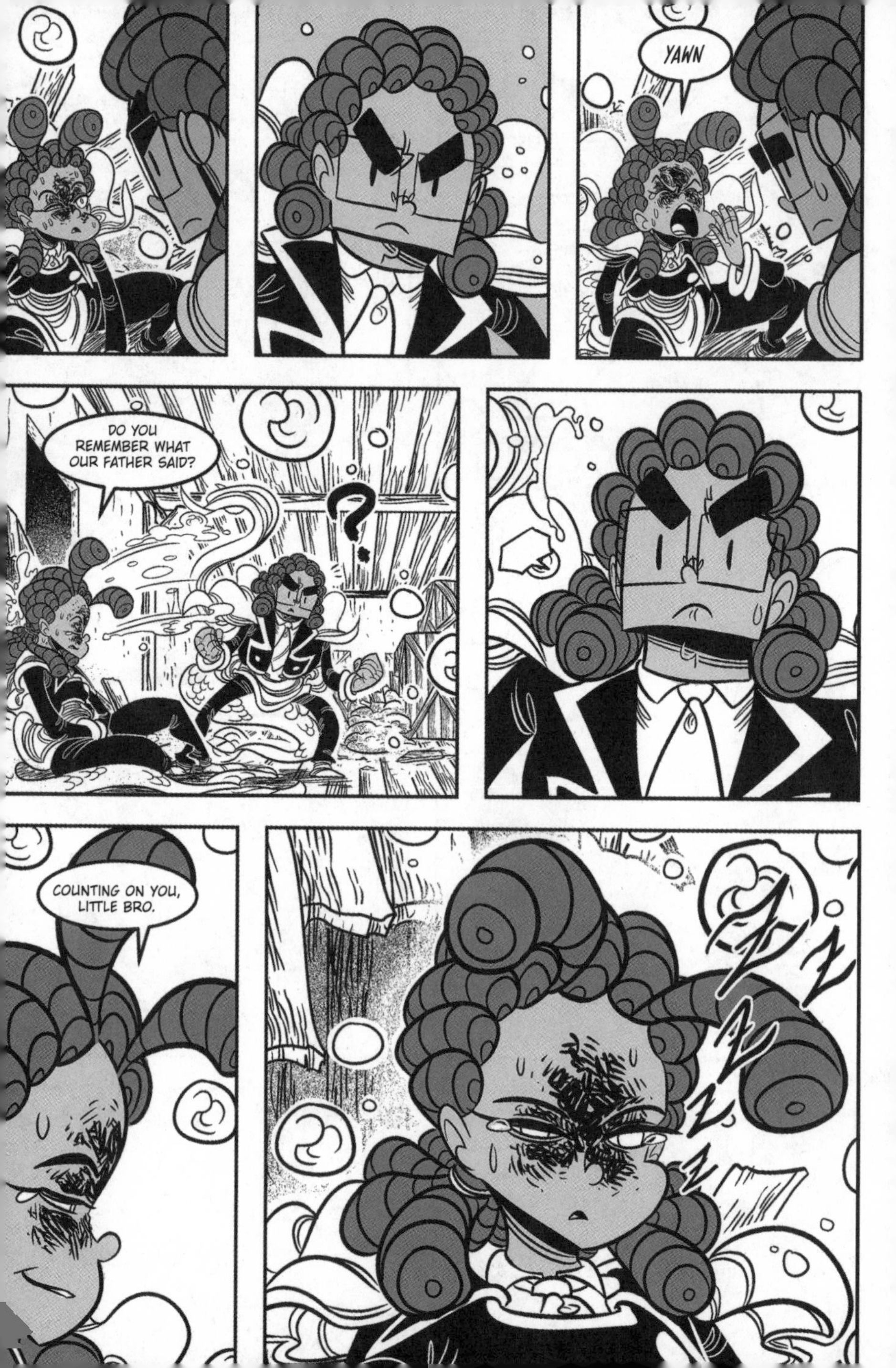
YAWN
DO YOU REMEMBER WHAT OUR FATHER SAID?
?
COUNTING ON YOU, LITTLE BRO.
ZZZZZ

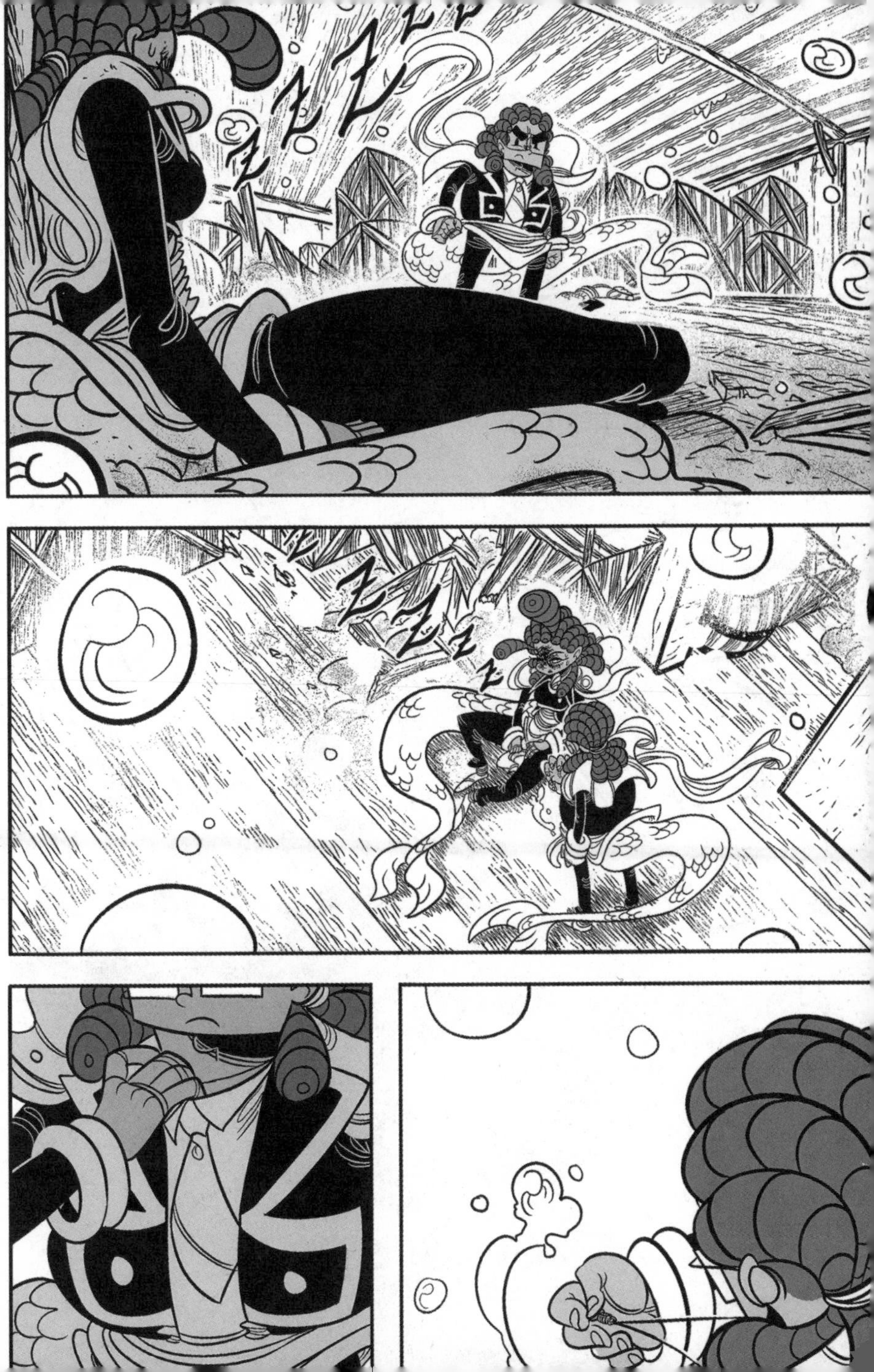

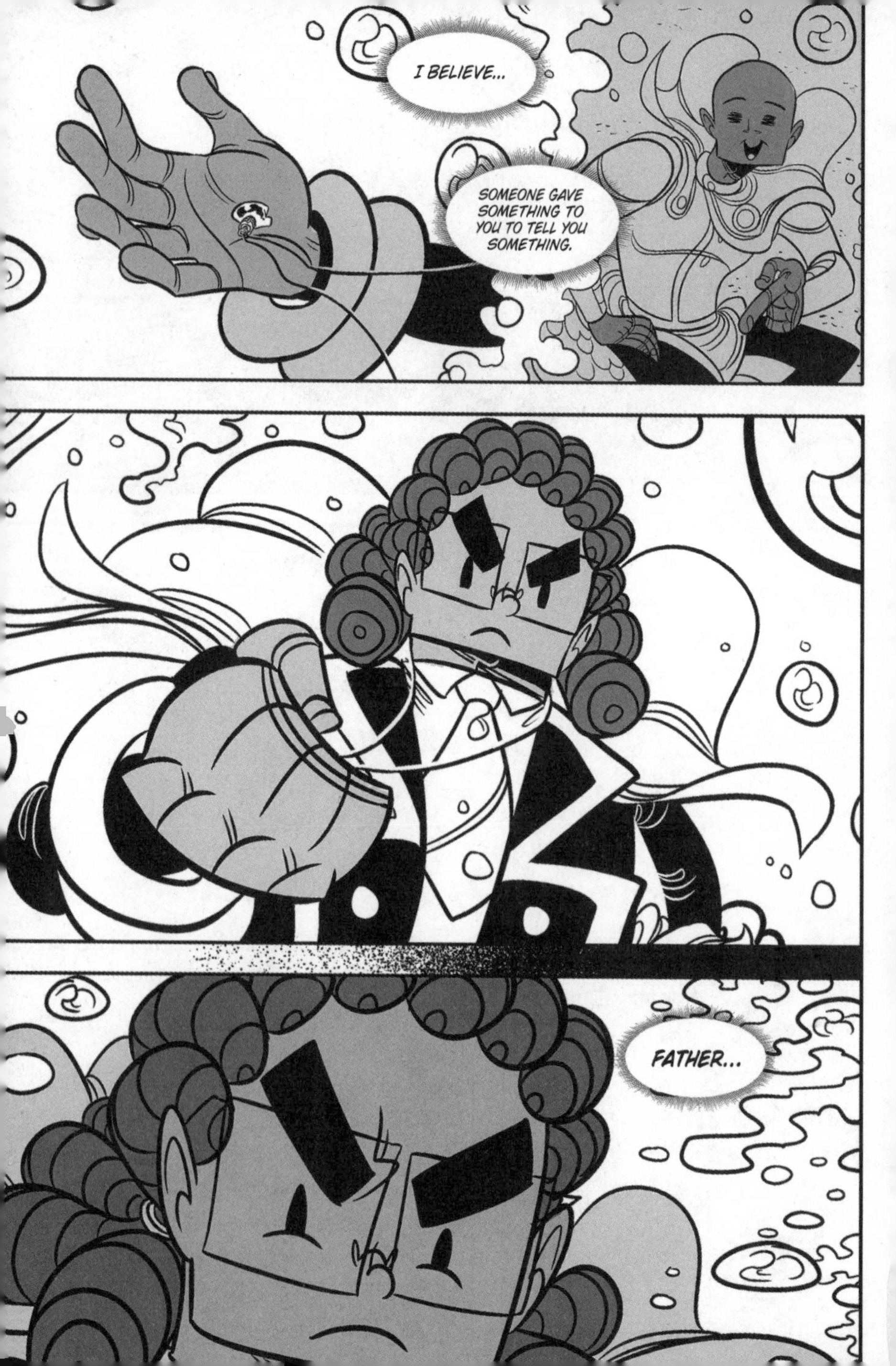
I BELIEVE...
SOMEONE GAVE SOMETHING TO YOU TO TELL YOU SOMETHING.
FATHER...

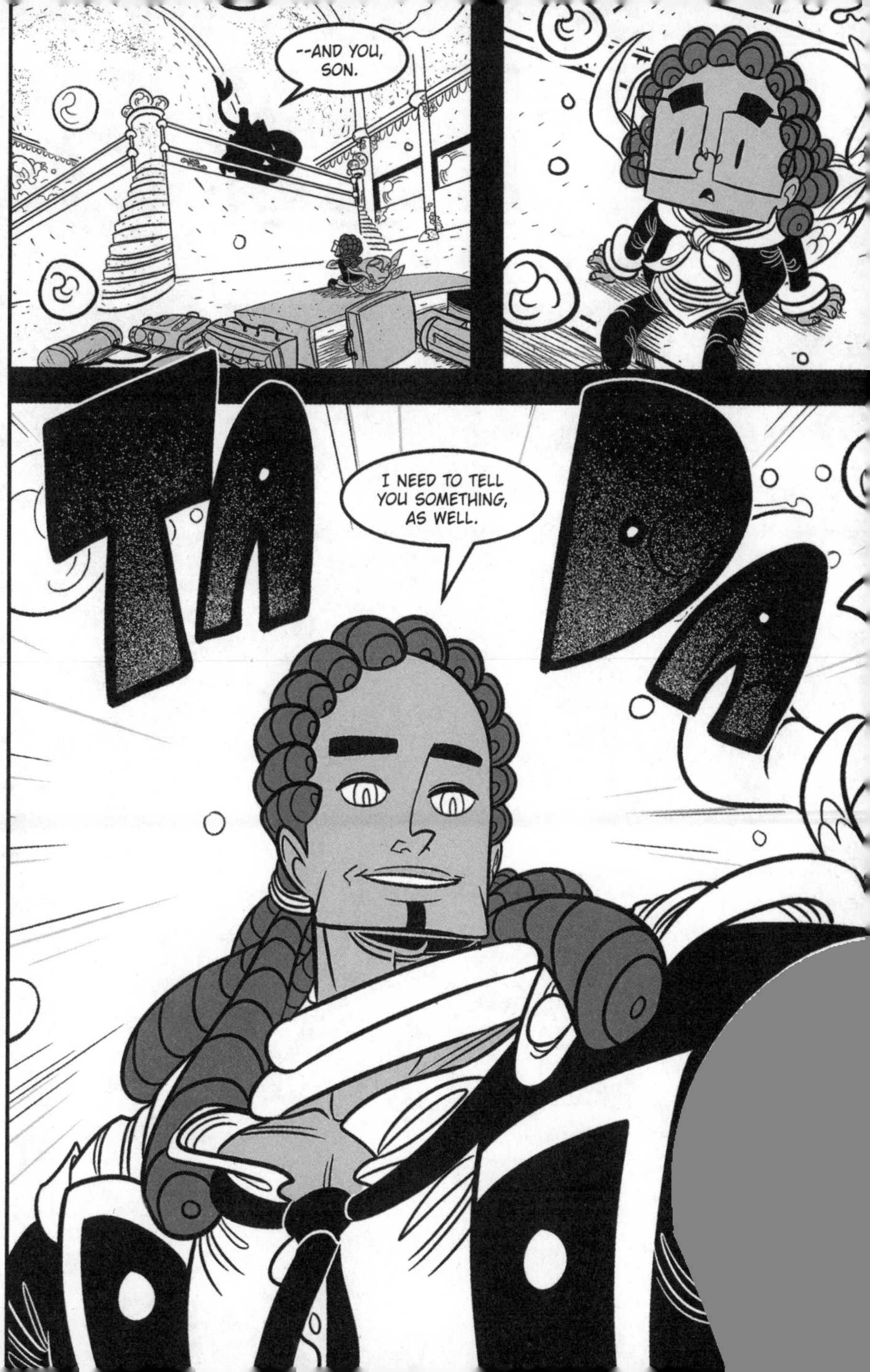
--AND YOU, SON.
TA DA
I NEED TO TELL YOU SOMETHING, AS WELL.

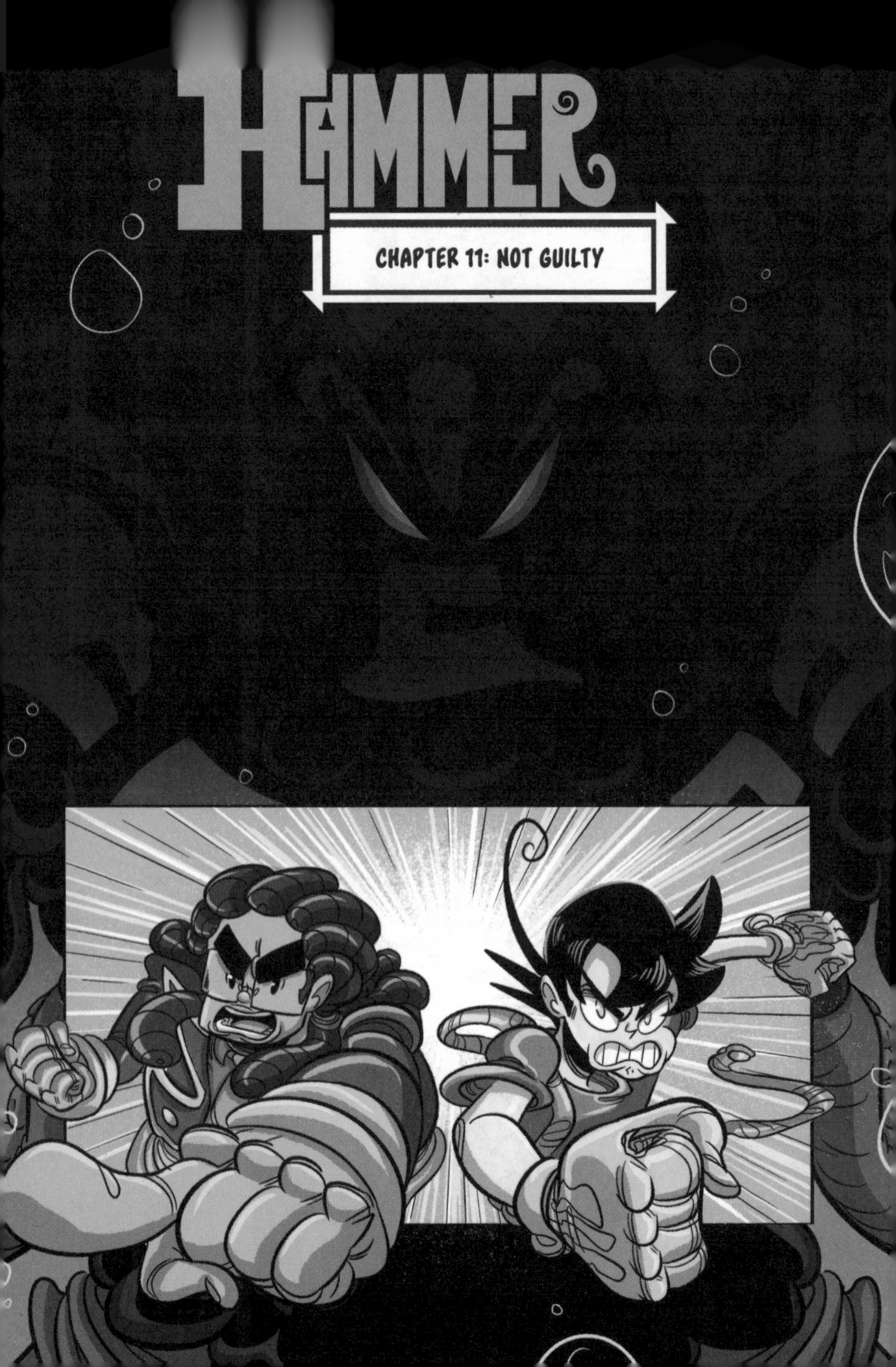
HAMMER
CHAPTER 11: NOT GUILTY

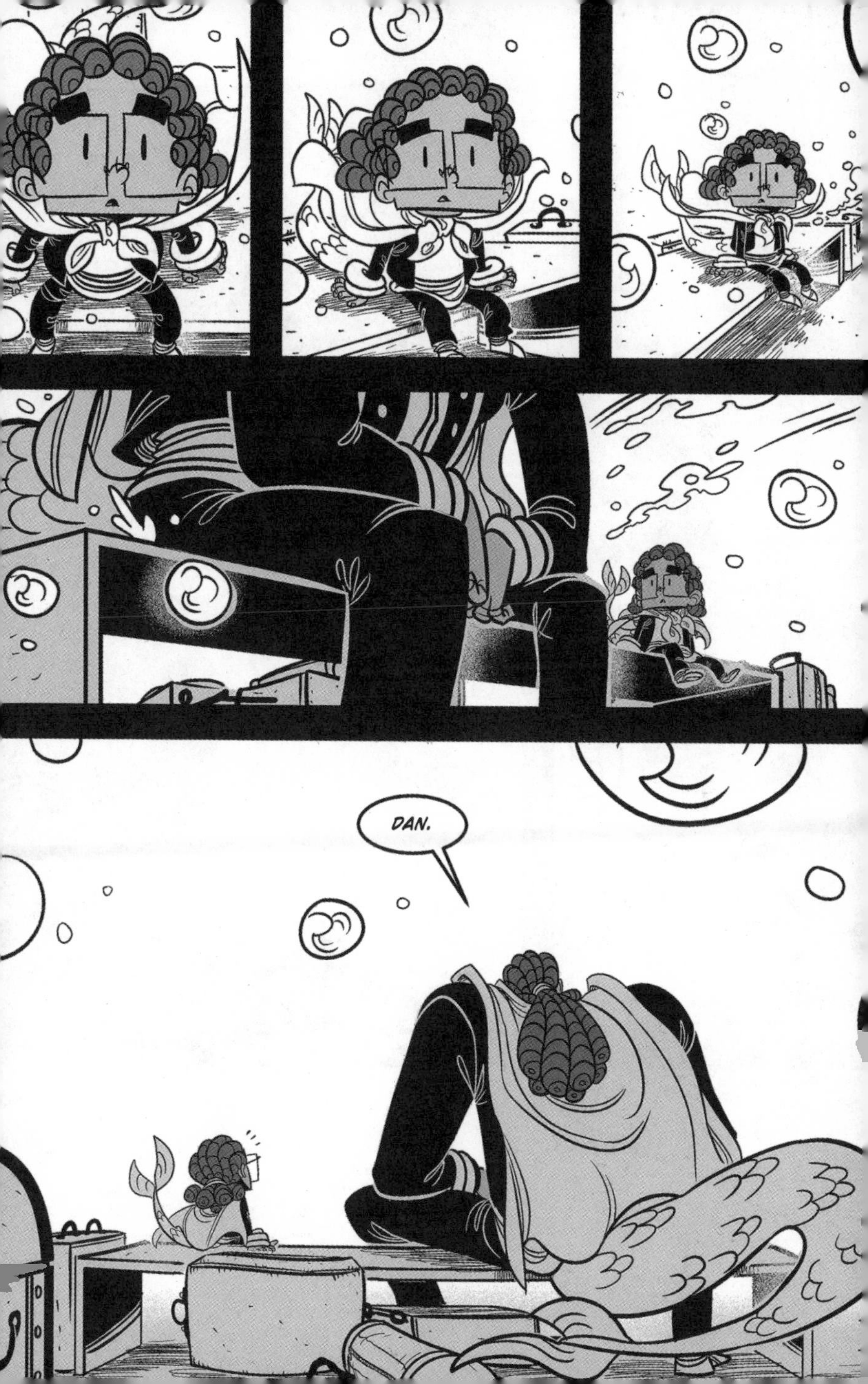
DAN.

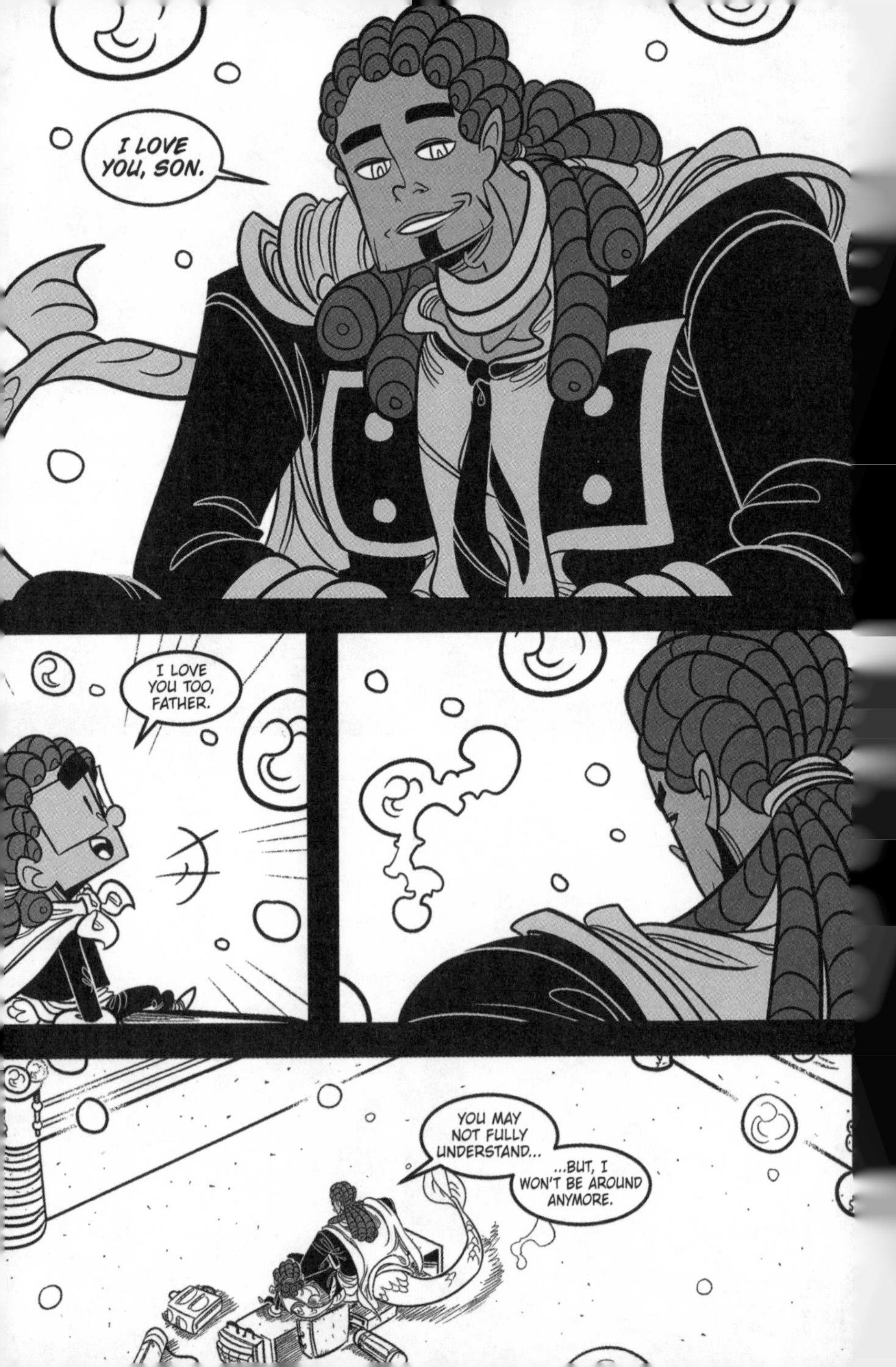
I LOVE YOU, SON.
I LOVE YOU TOO, FATHER.
YOU MAY NOT FULLY UNDERSTAND...
...BUT, I WON'T BE AROUND ANYMORE.

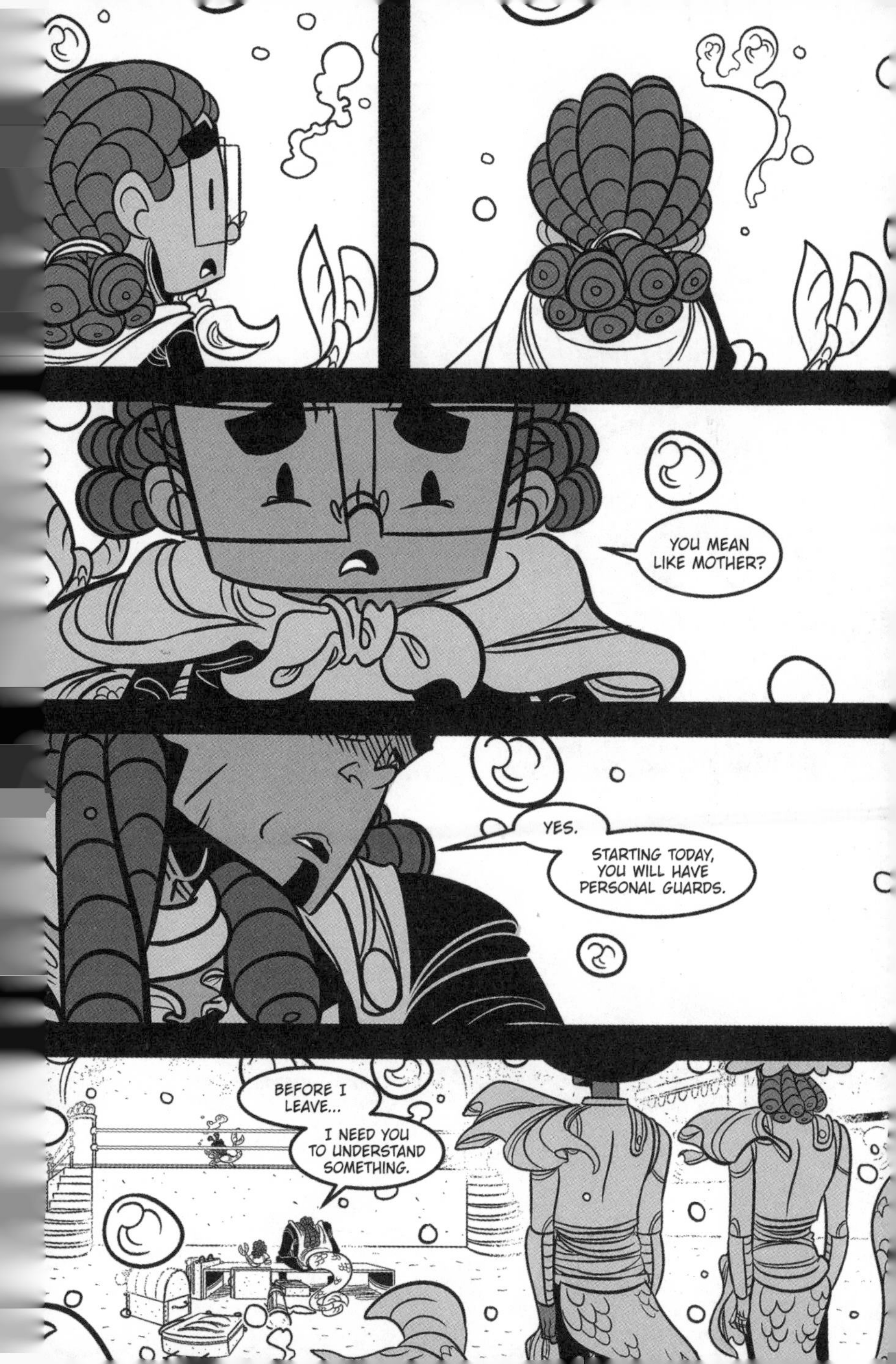
YOU MEAN LIKE MOTHER?
YES.
STARTING TODAY, YOU WILL HAVE PERSONAL GUARDS.
BEFORE I LEAVE...
I NEED YOU TO UNDERSTAND SOMETHING.

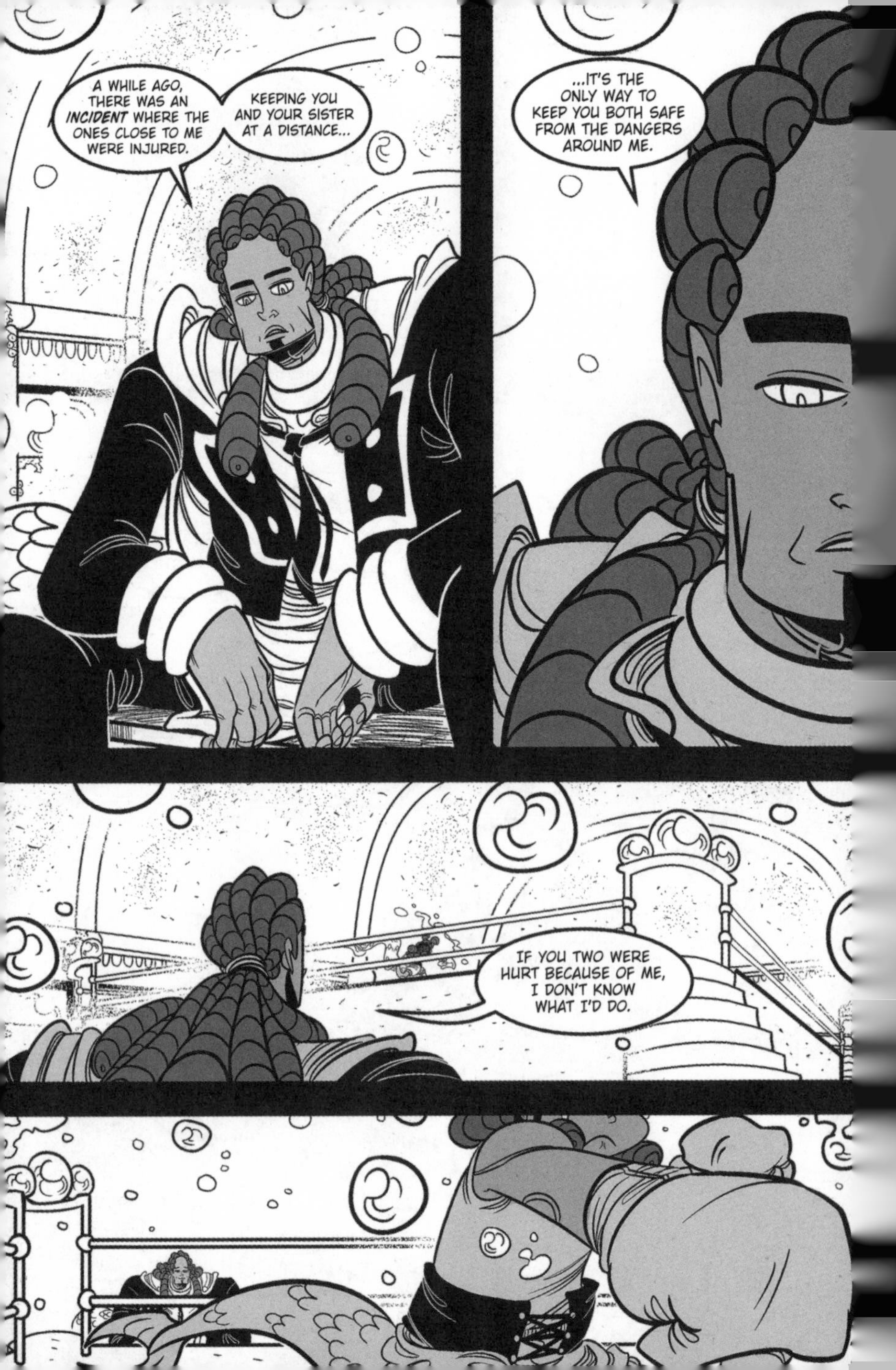
A WHILE AGO, THERE WAS AN *INCIDENT* WHERE THE ONES CLOSE TO ME WERE INJURED.
KEEPING YOU AND YOUR SISTER AT A DISTANCE...
...IT'S THE ONLY WAY TO KEEP YOU BOTH SAFE FROM THE DANGERS AROUND ME.
IF YOU TWO WERE HURT BECAUSE OF ME, I DON'T KNOW WHAT I'D DO.

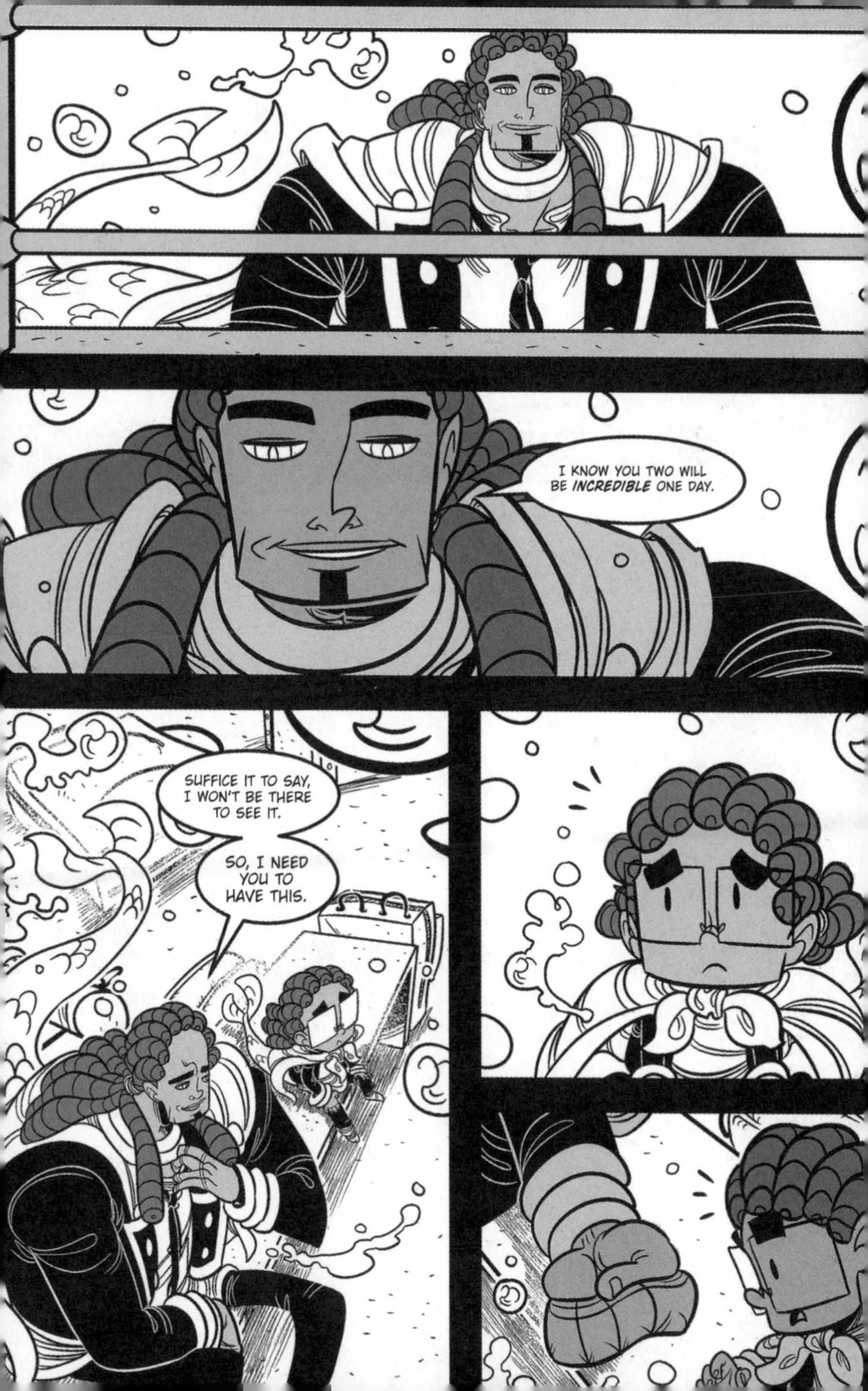
I KNOW YOU TWO WILL BE *INCREDIBLE* ONE DAY.
SUFFICE IT TO SAY, I WON'T BE THERE TO SEE IT.
SO, I NEED YOU TO HAVE THIS.

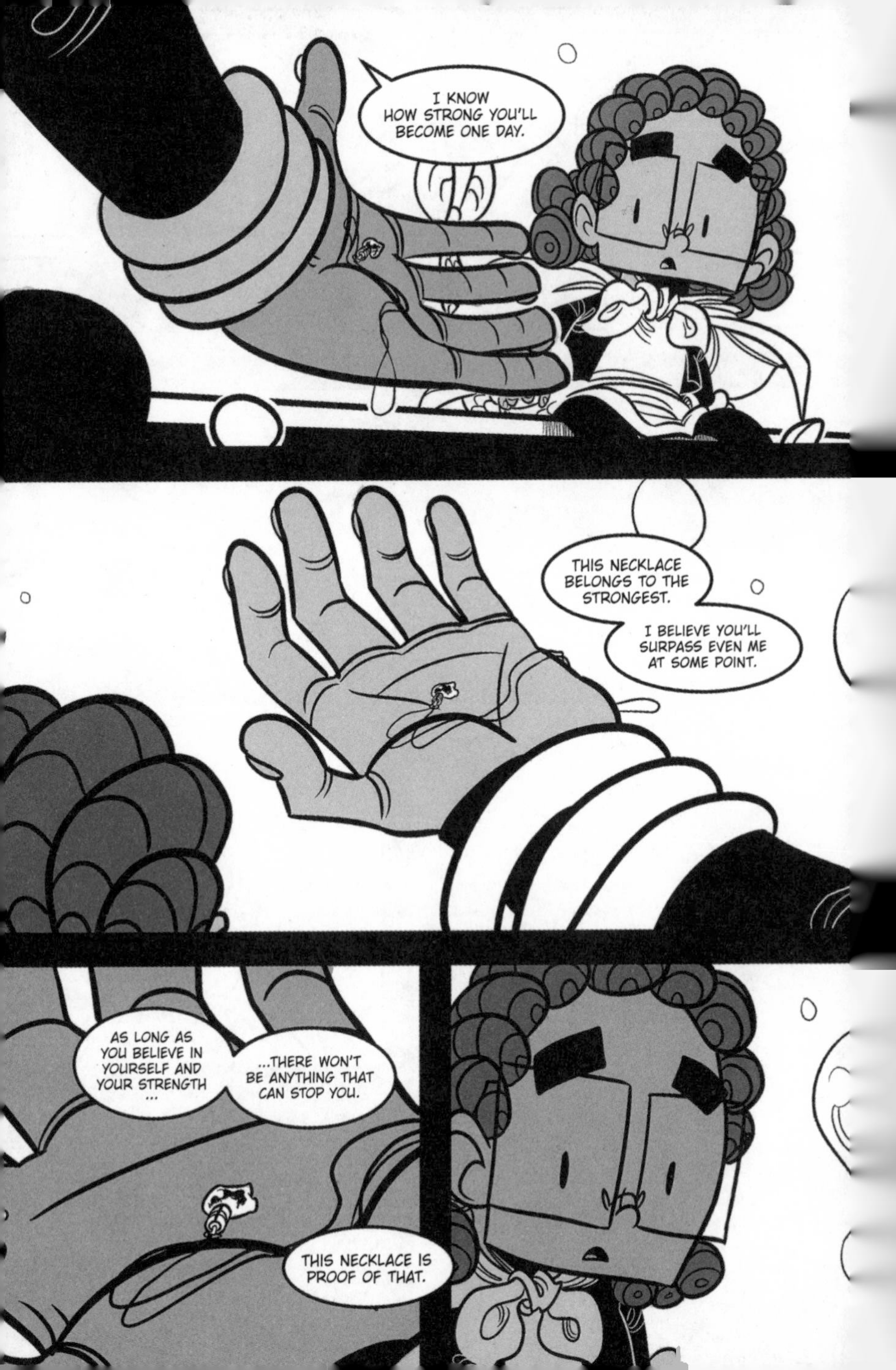
I KNOW HOW STRONG YOU'LL BECOME ONE DAY.
THIS NECKLACE BELONGS TO THE STRONGEST.
I BELIEVE YOU'LL SURPASS EVEN ME AT SOME POINT.
AS LONG AS YOU BELIEVE IN YOURSELF AND YOUR STRENGTH ...
...THERE WON'T BE ANYTHING THAT CAN STOP YOU.
THIS NECKLACE IS PROOF OF THAT.

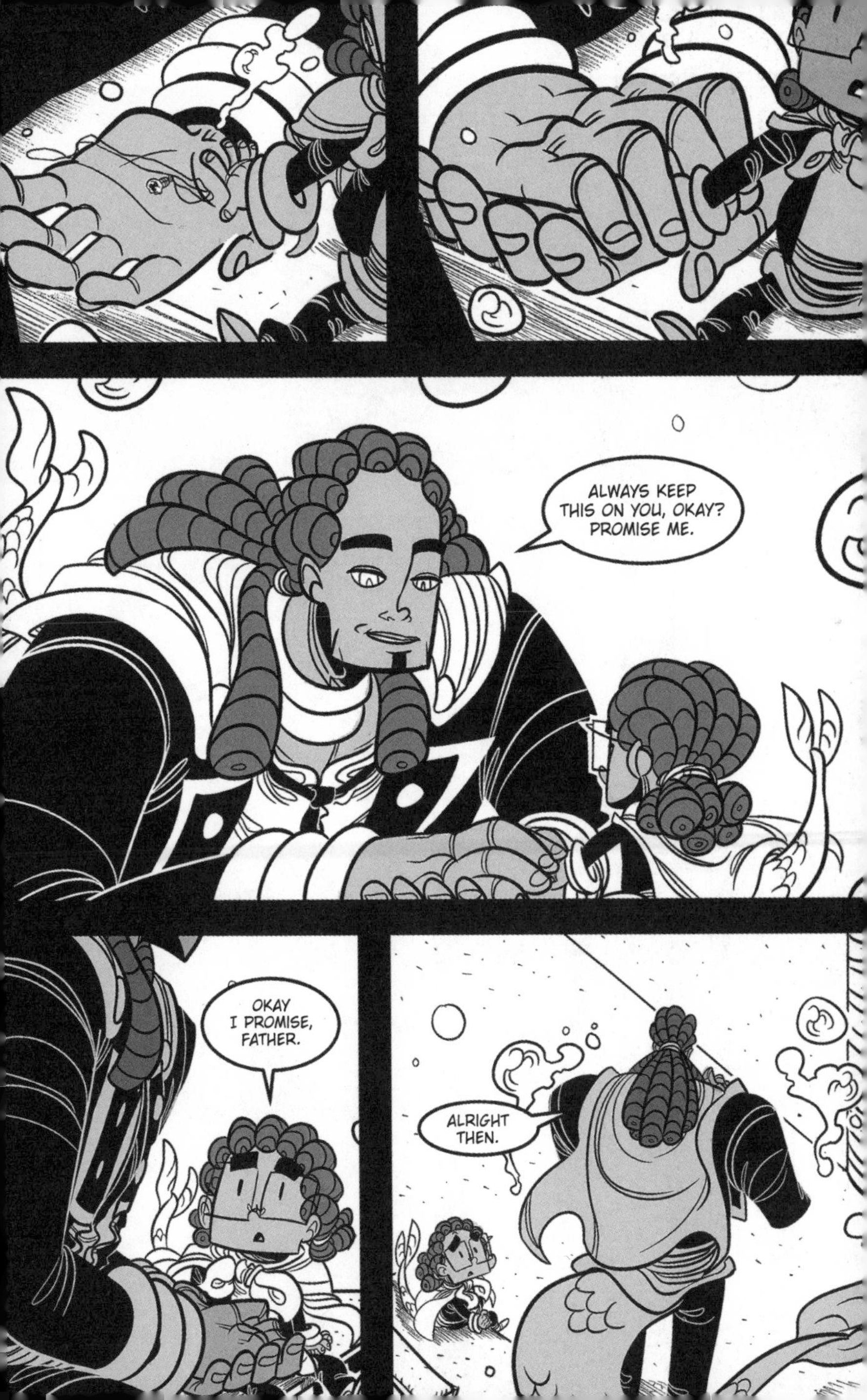
ALWAYS KEEP THIS ON YOU, OKAY? PROMISE ME.
OKAY I PROMISE, FATHER.
ALRIGHT THEN.

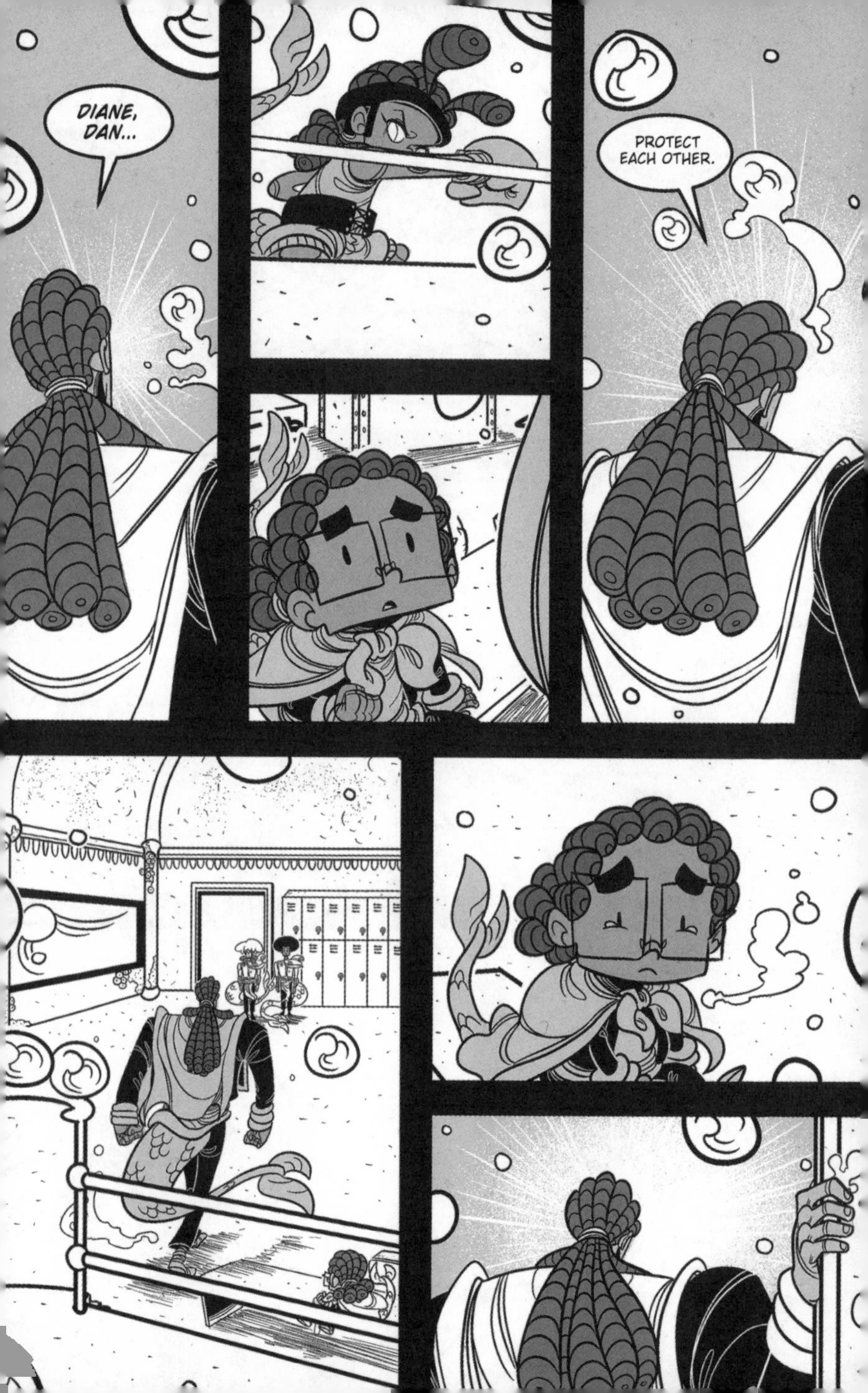
DIANE, DAN...
PROTECT EACH OTHER.

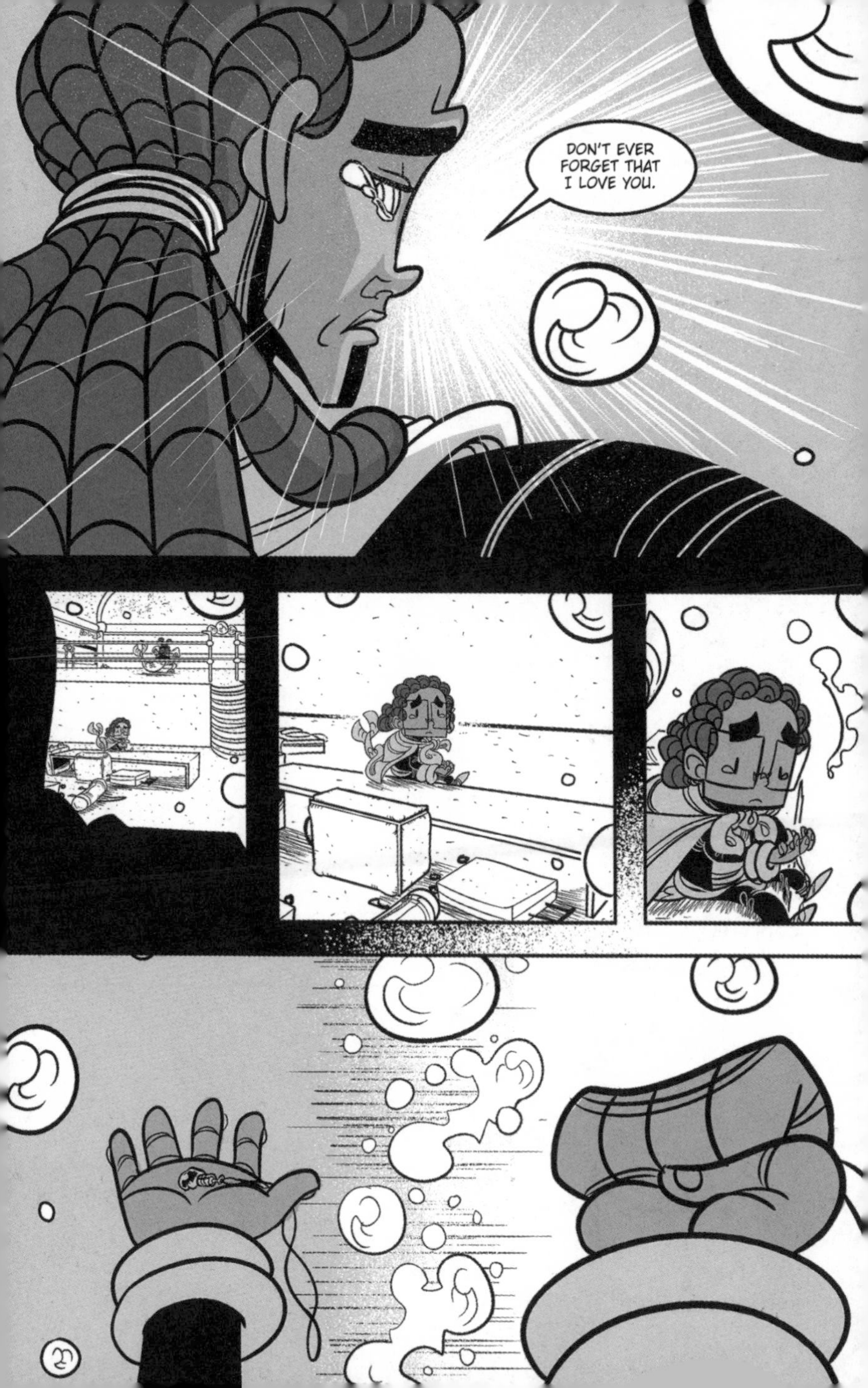
DON'T EVER FORGET THAT I LOVE YOU.

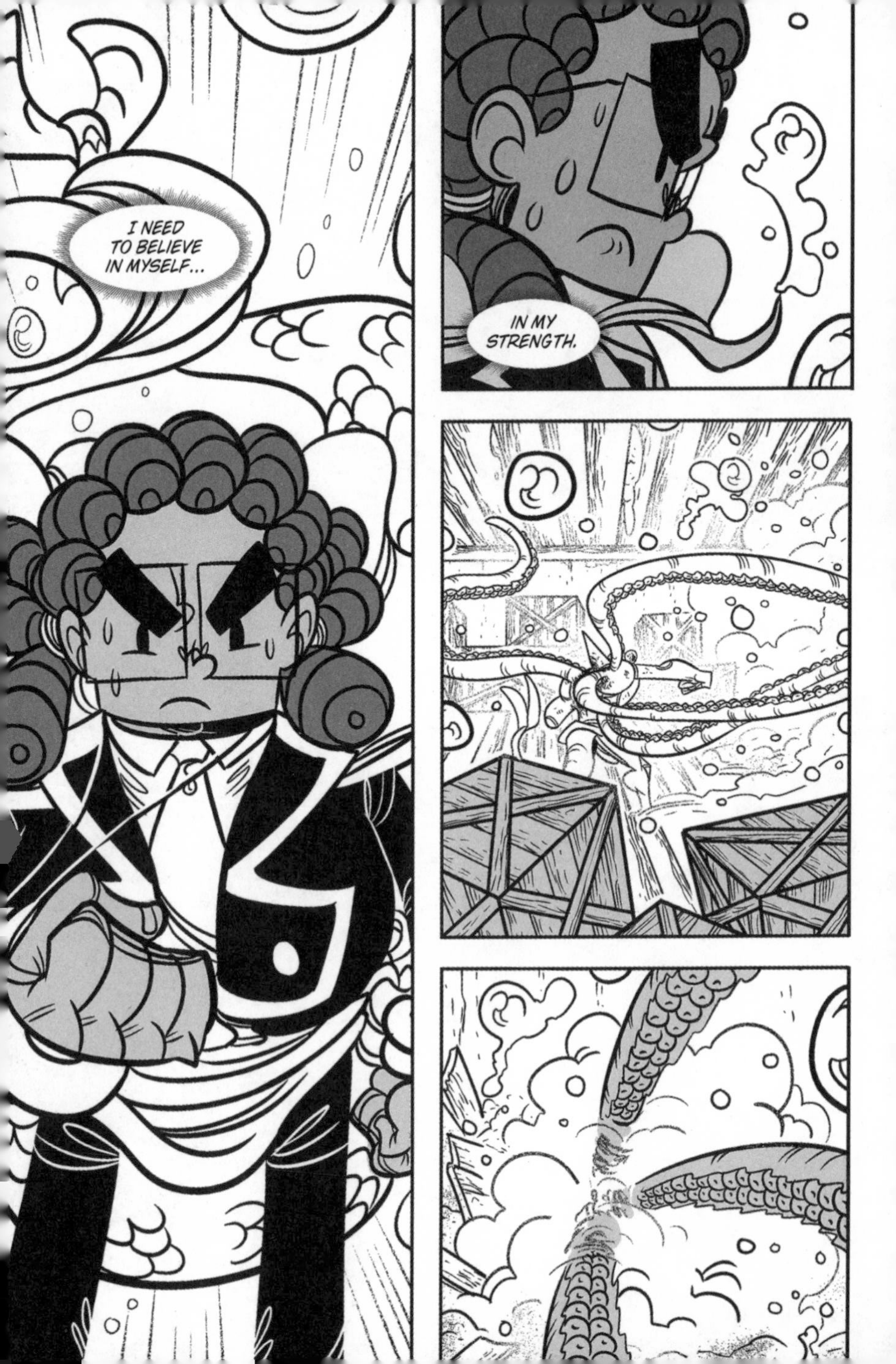
I NEED TO BELIEVE IN MYSELF...
IN MY STRENGTH.

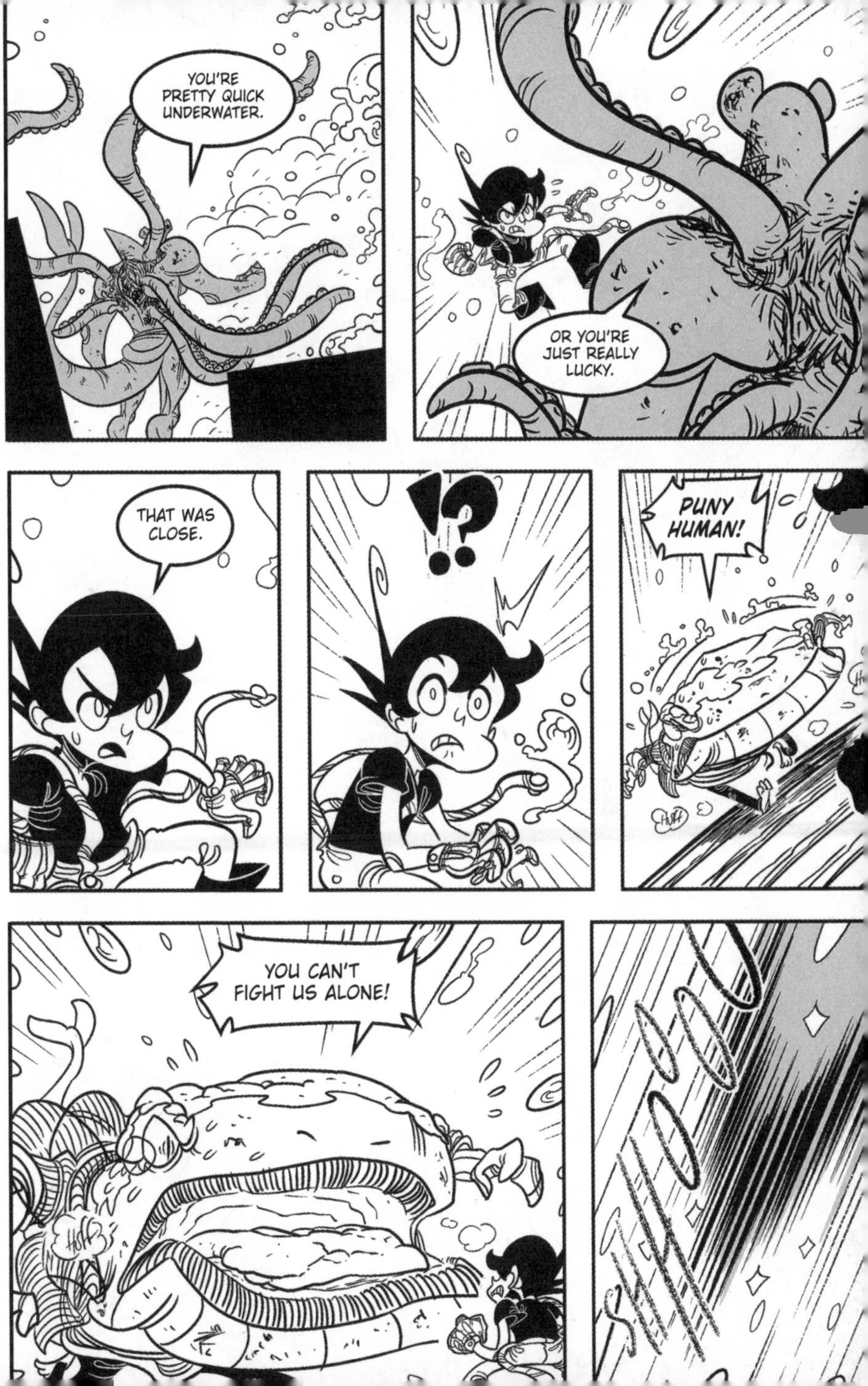
YOU'RE PRETTY QUICK UNDERWATER.
OR YOU'RE JUST REALLY LUCKY.
THAT WAS CLOSE.
!?
PUNY HUMAN!
HUFF
YOU CAN'T FIGHT US ALONE!
HUFF
SHOOOO

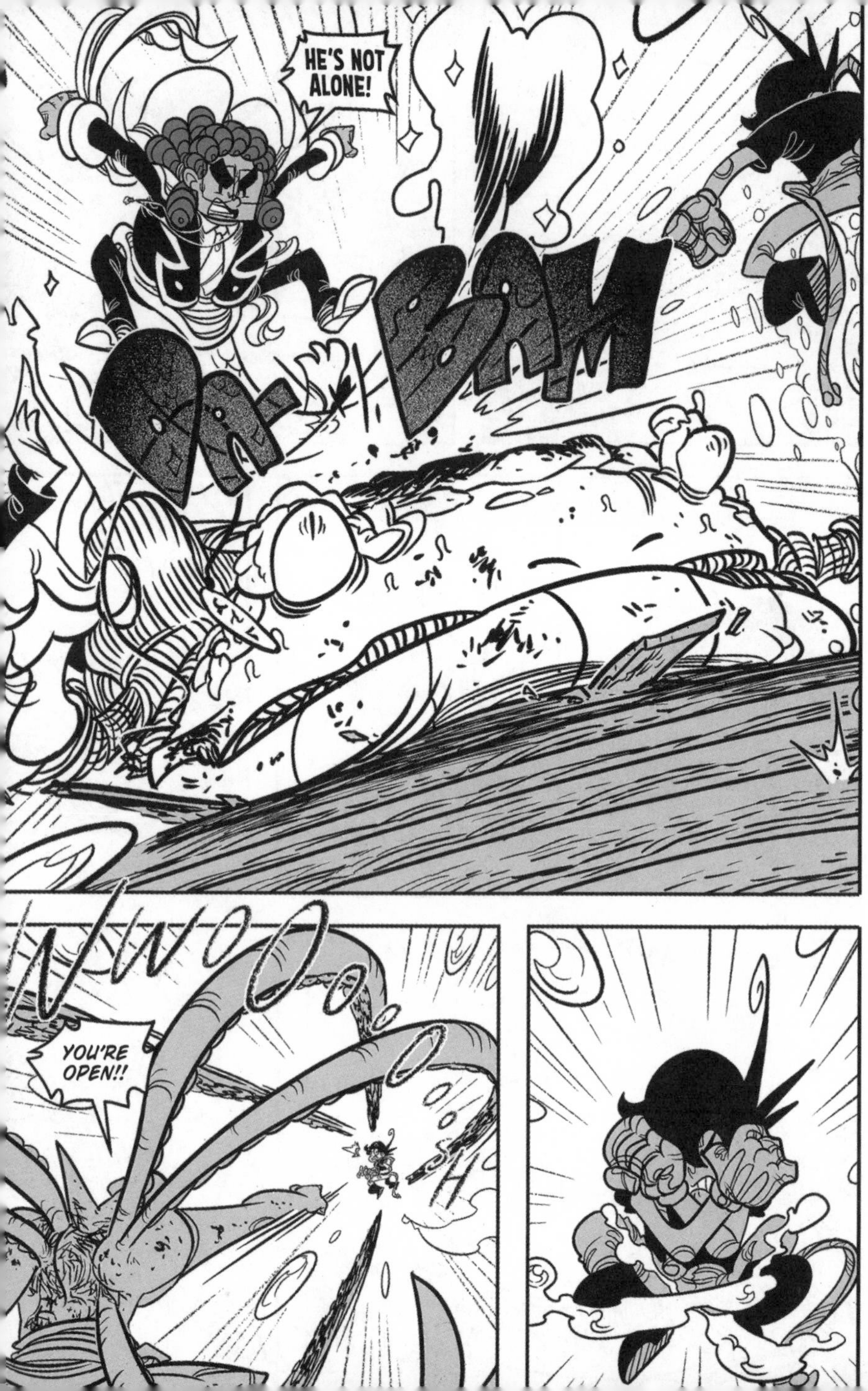
HE'S NOT ALONE!
BA-BAM
YOU'RE OPEN!!

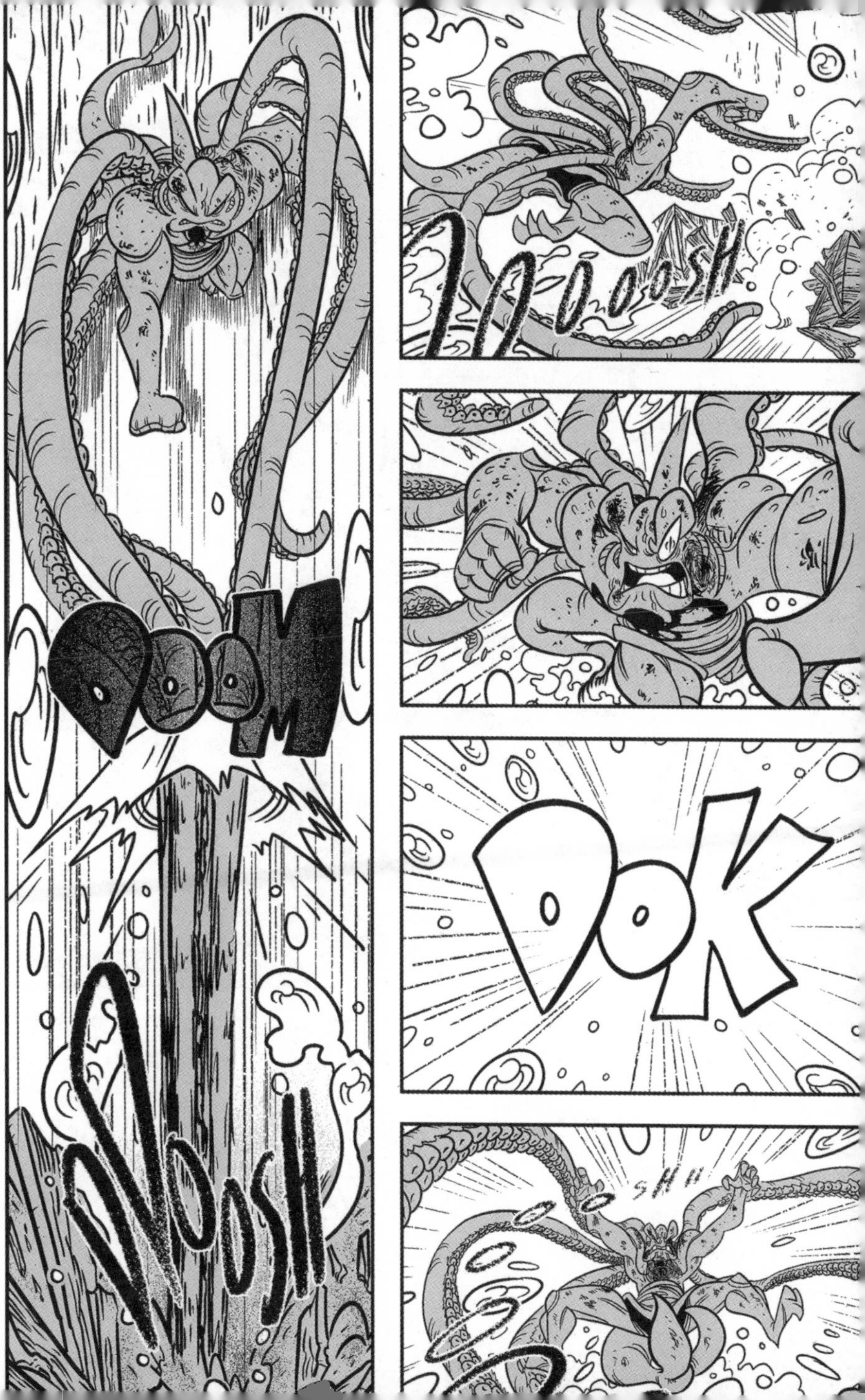

DOOM
WOOSH
WOOOOSH
DOK

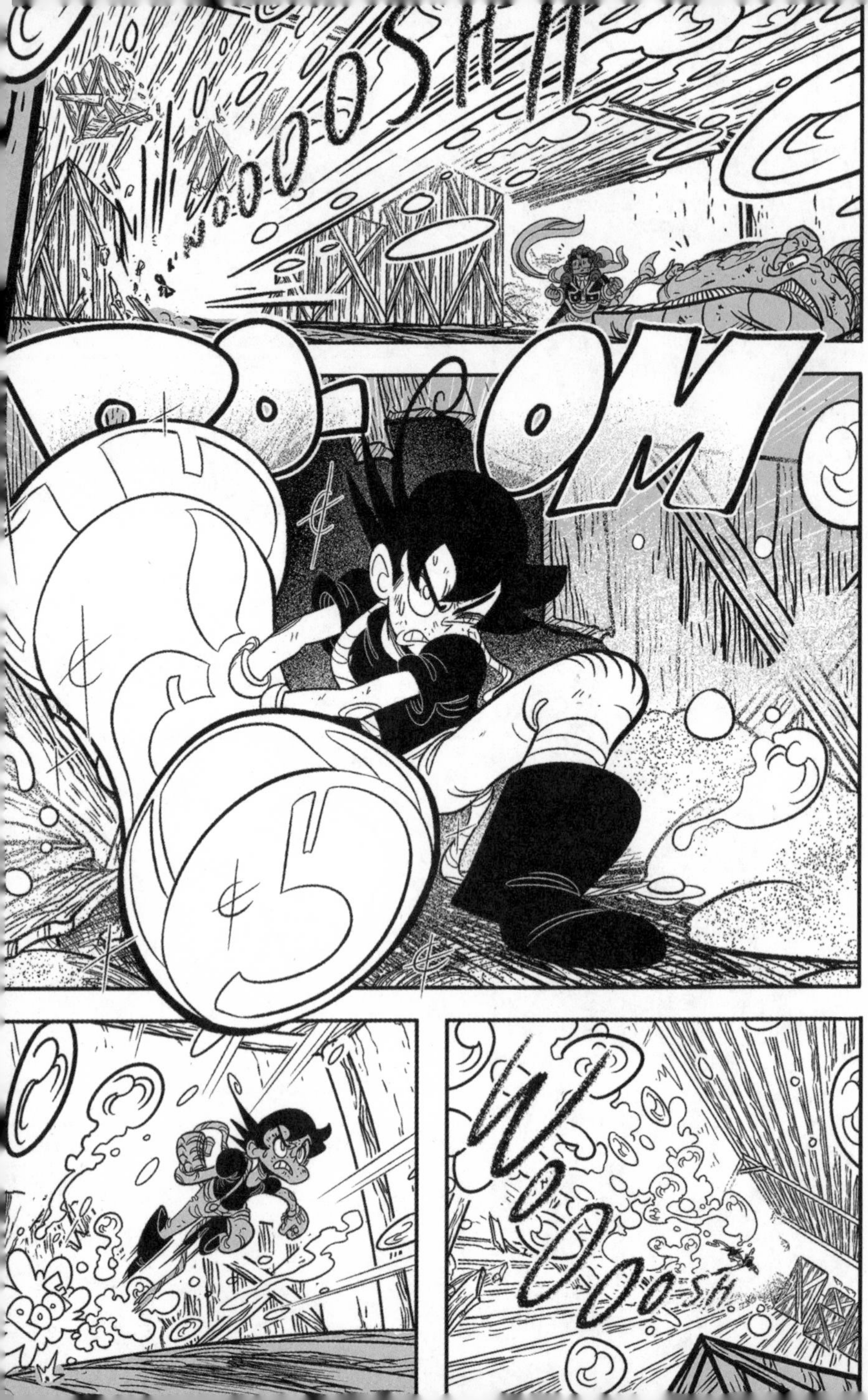

WOOOOOSHH
OOM
POOF
WOOOOOOSH

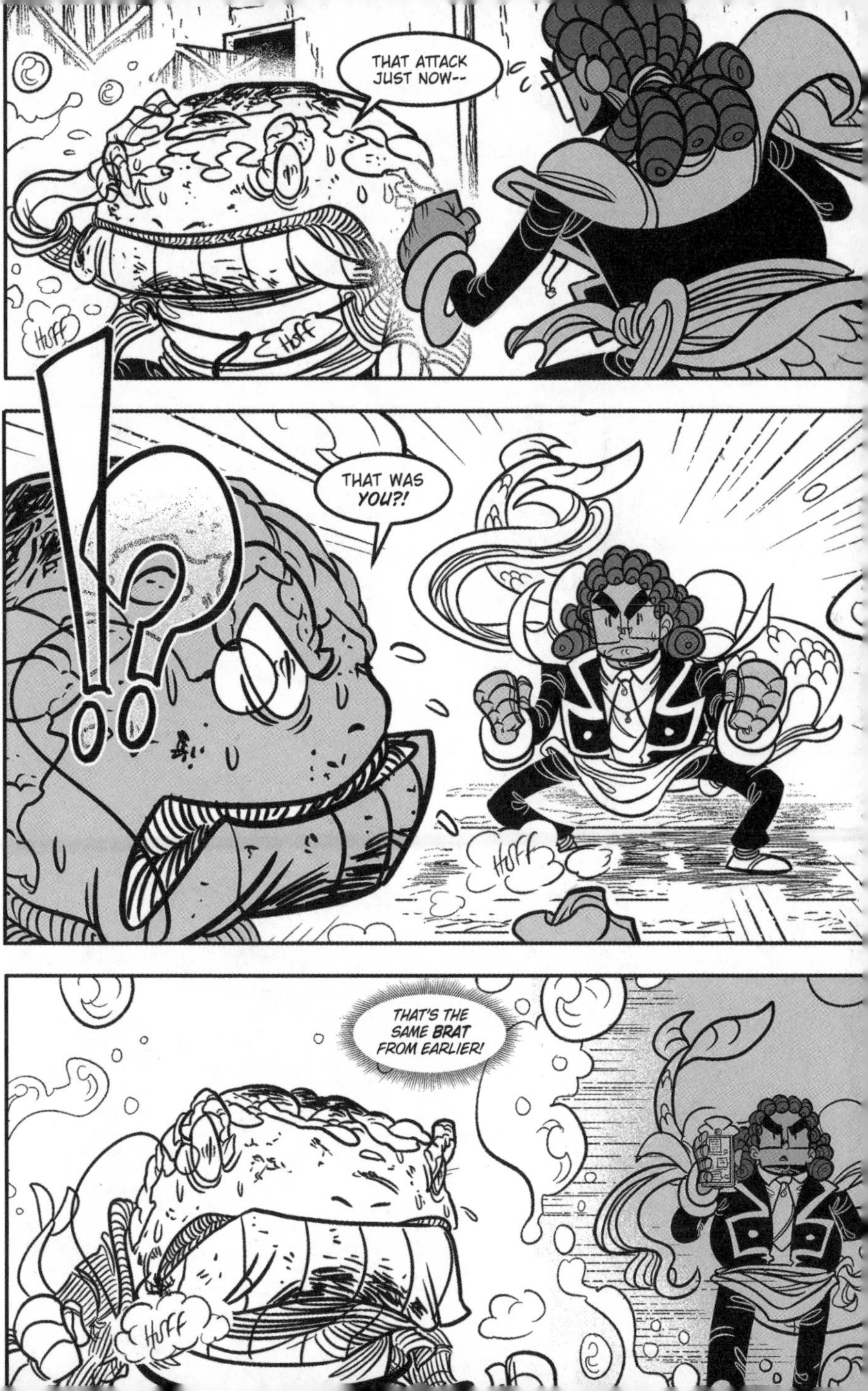
THAT ATTACK JUST NOW--
HUFF
HUFF
THAT WAS YOU?!
HUFF
THAT'S THE SAME BRAT FROM EARLIER!
HUFF

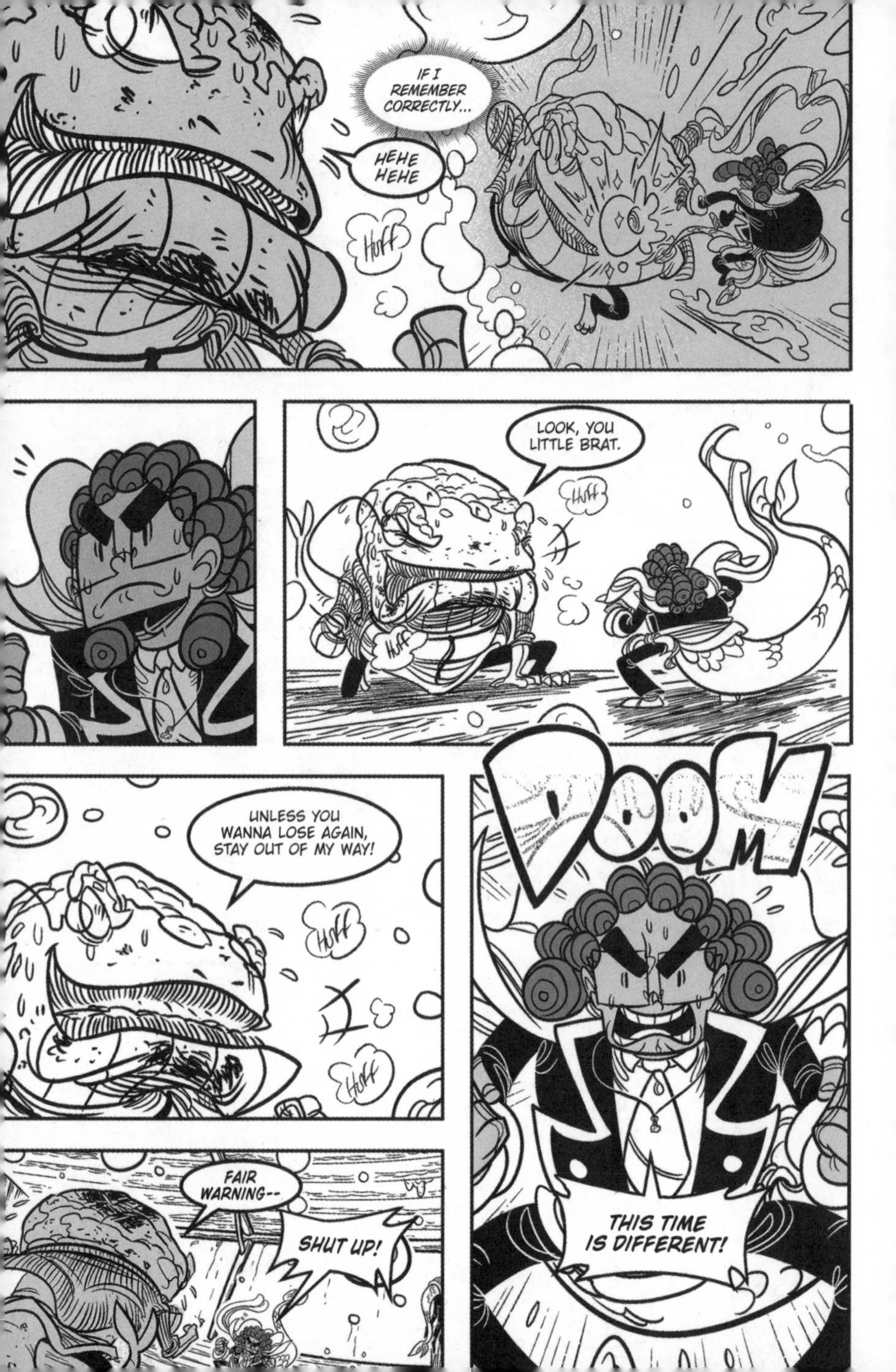
IF I REMEMBER CORRECTLY...
HEHE HEHE
HUFF
LOOK, YOU LITTLE BRAT.
HUFF
HUFF
UNLESS YOU WANNA LOSE AGAIN, STAY OUT OF MY WAY!
HUFF
HUFF
DOOM
FAIR WARNING--
SHUT UP!
THIS TIME IS DIFFERENT!

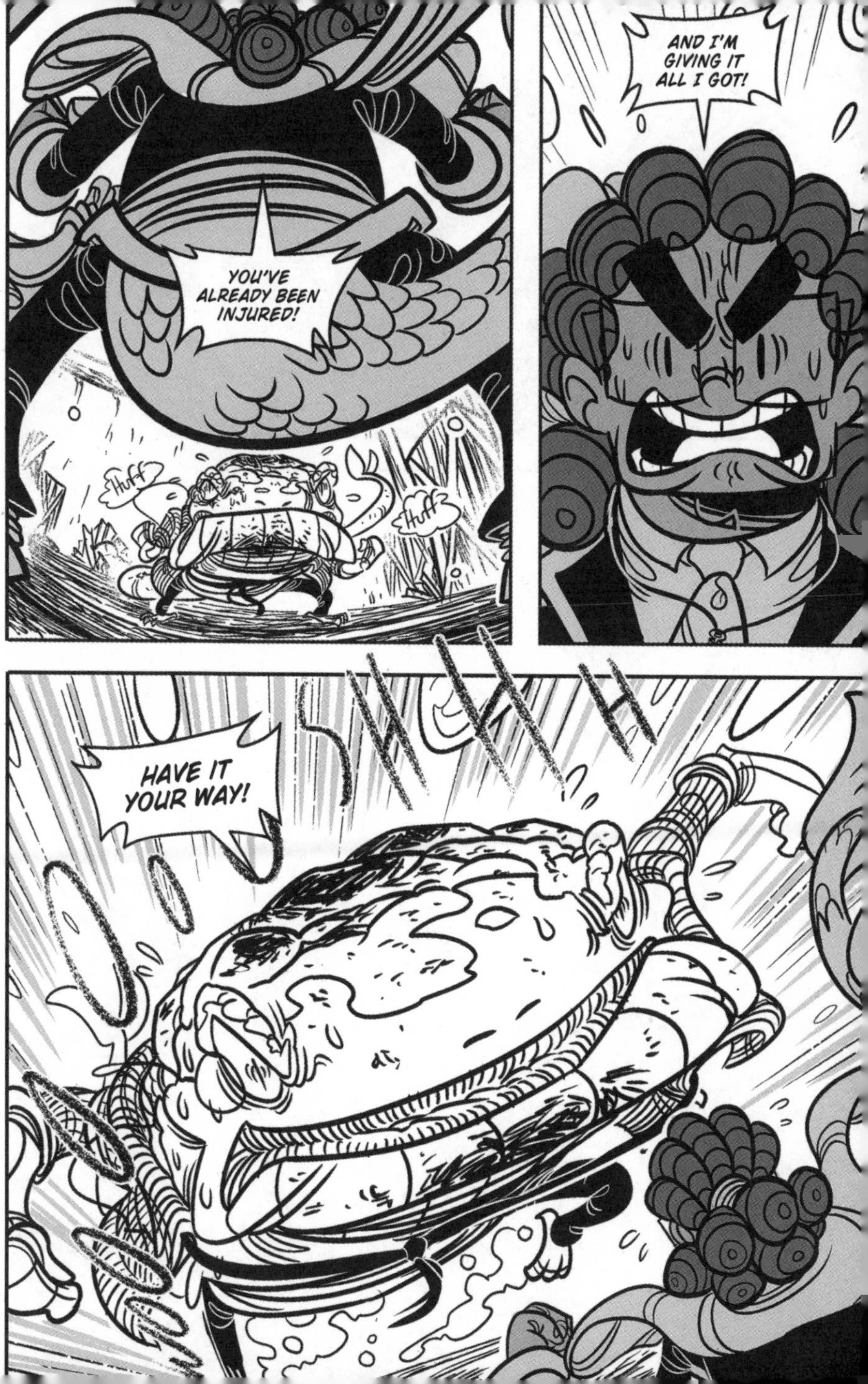
YOU'VE ALREADY BEEN INJURED!
HUFF
HUFF
AND I'M GIVING IT ALL I GOT!
SHHHH
HAVE IT YOUR WAY!

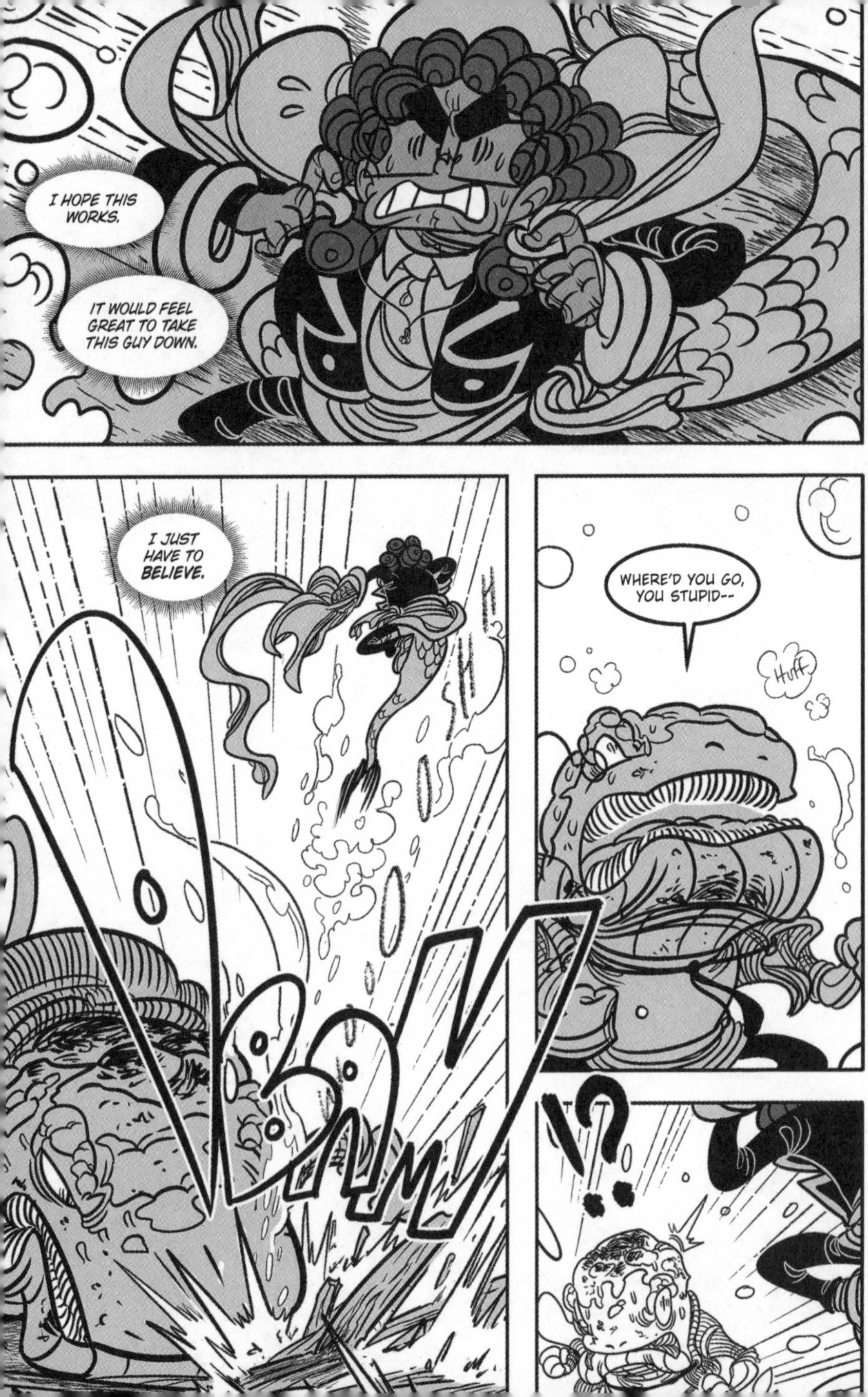
I HOPE THIS WORKS.
IT WOULD FEEL GREAT TO TAKE THIS GUY DOWN.
I JUST HAVE TO BELIEVE.
WHERE'D YOU GO, YOU STUPID--
Huff.
!?

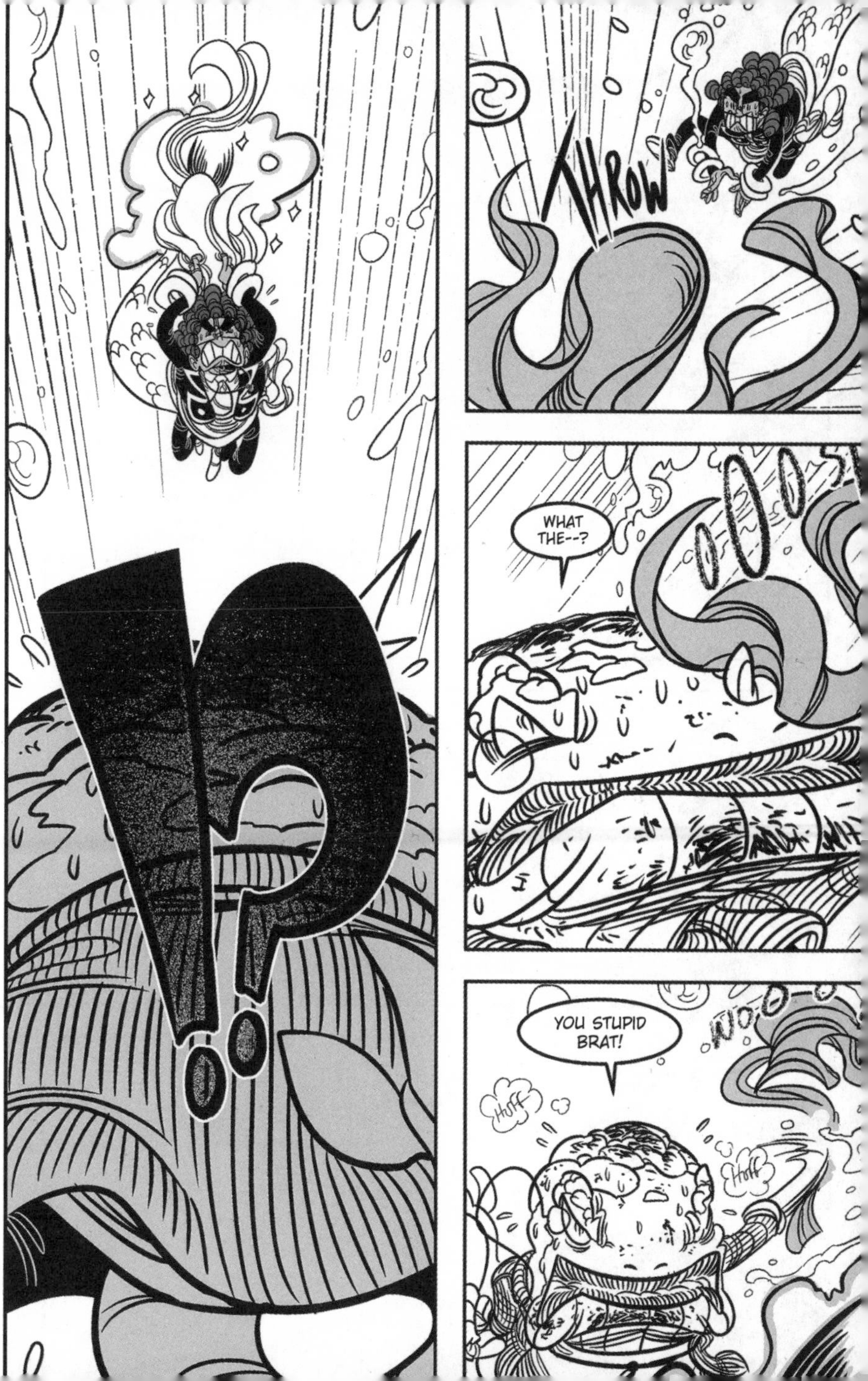
!?
THROW
WHAT THE--?
YOU STUPID BRAT!
HUFF
HUFF

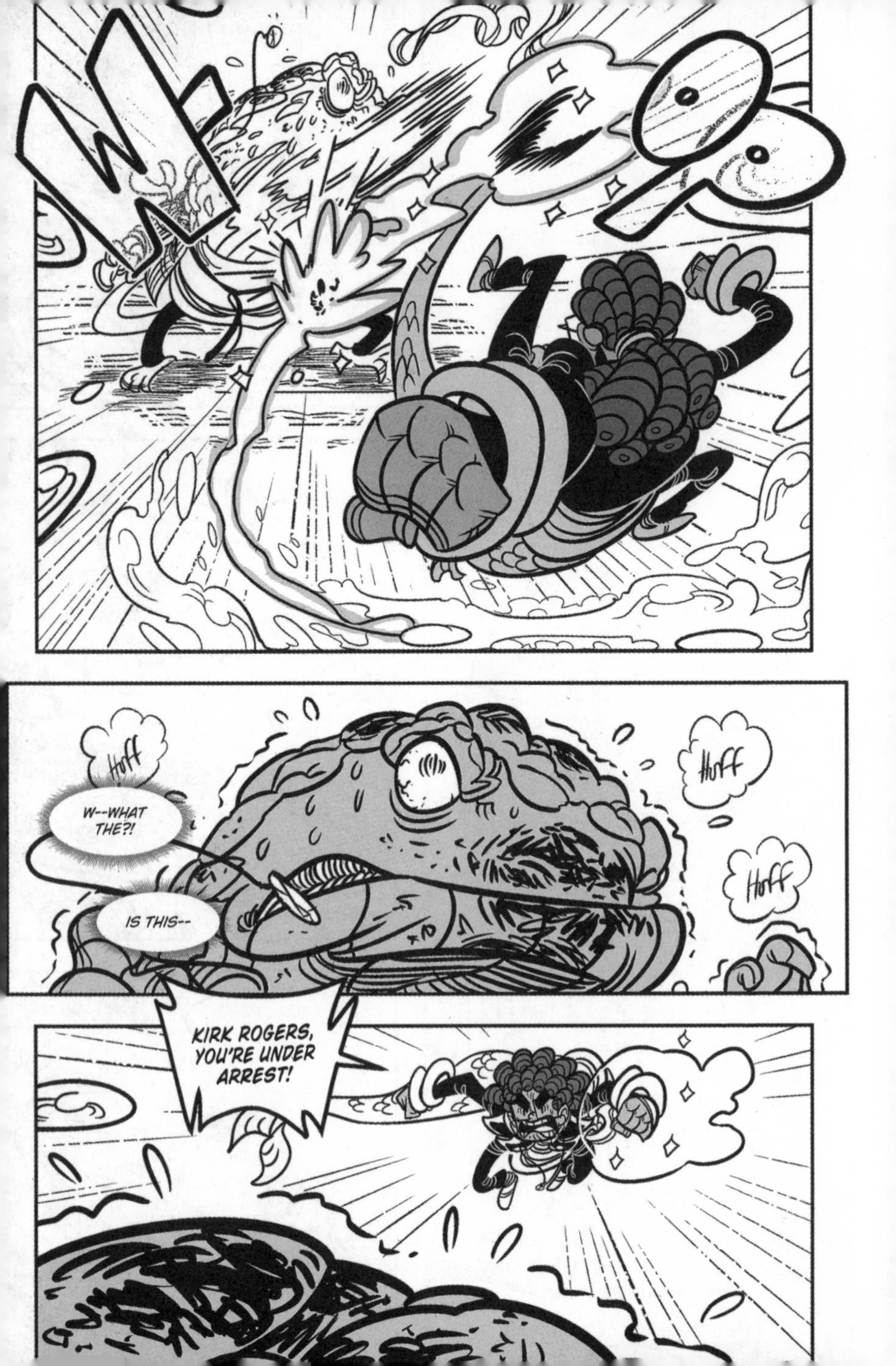
Huff
W--WHAT THE?!
IS THIS--
Huff
Huff
KIRK ROGERS, YOU'RE UNDER ARREST!

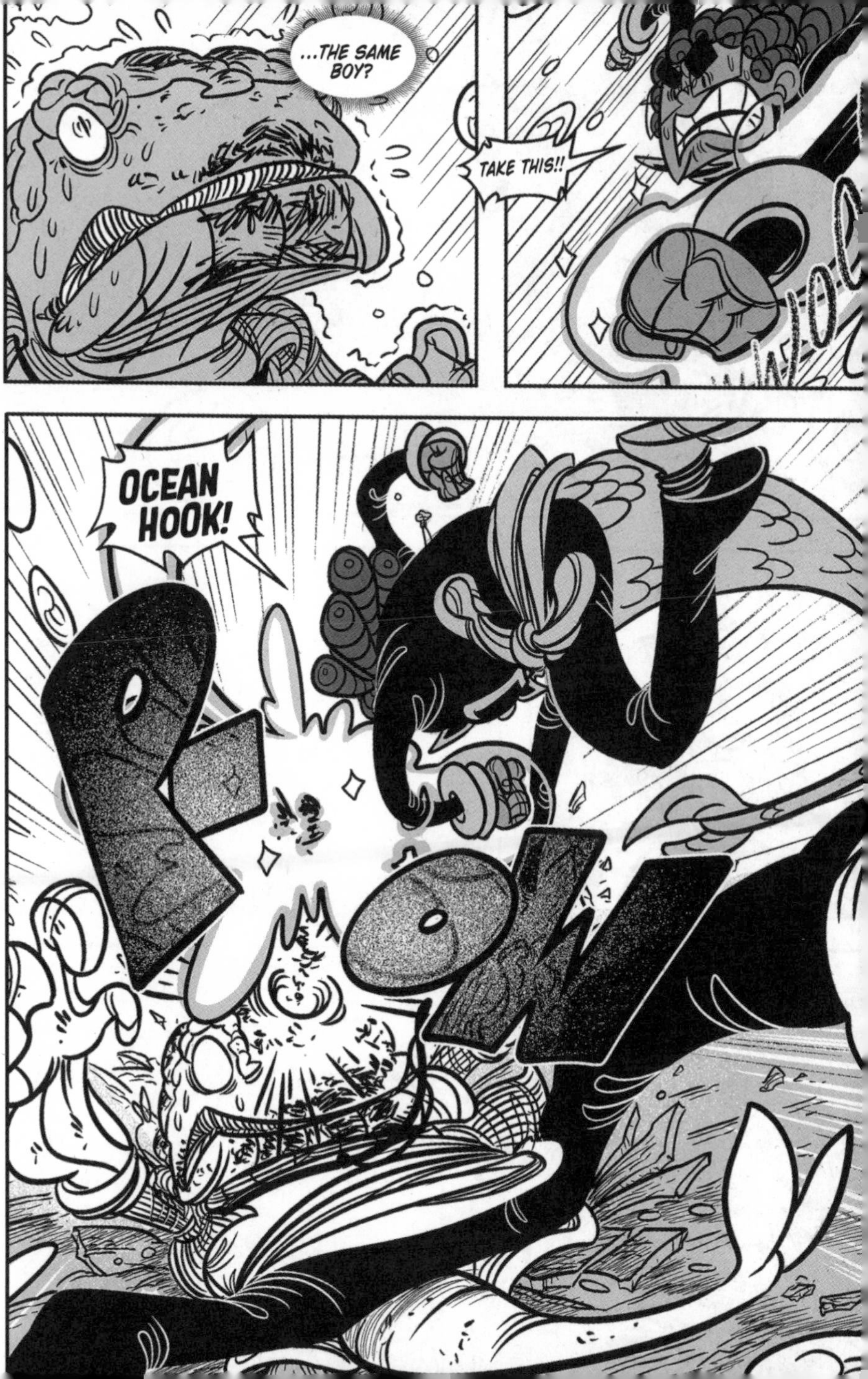
...THE SAME BOY?
TAKE THIS!!
OCEAN HOOK!
POW

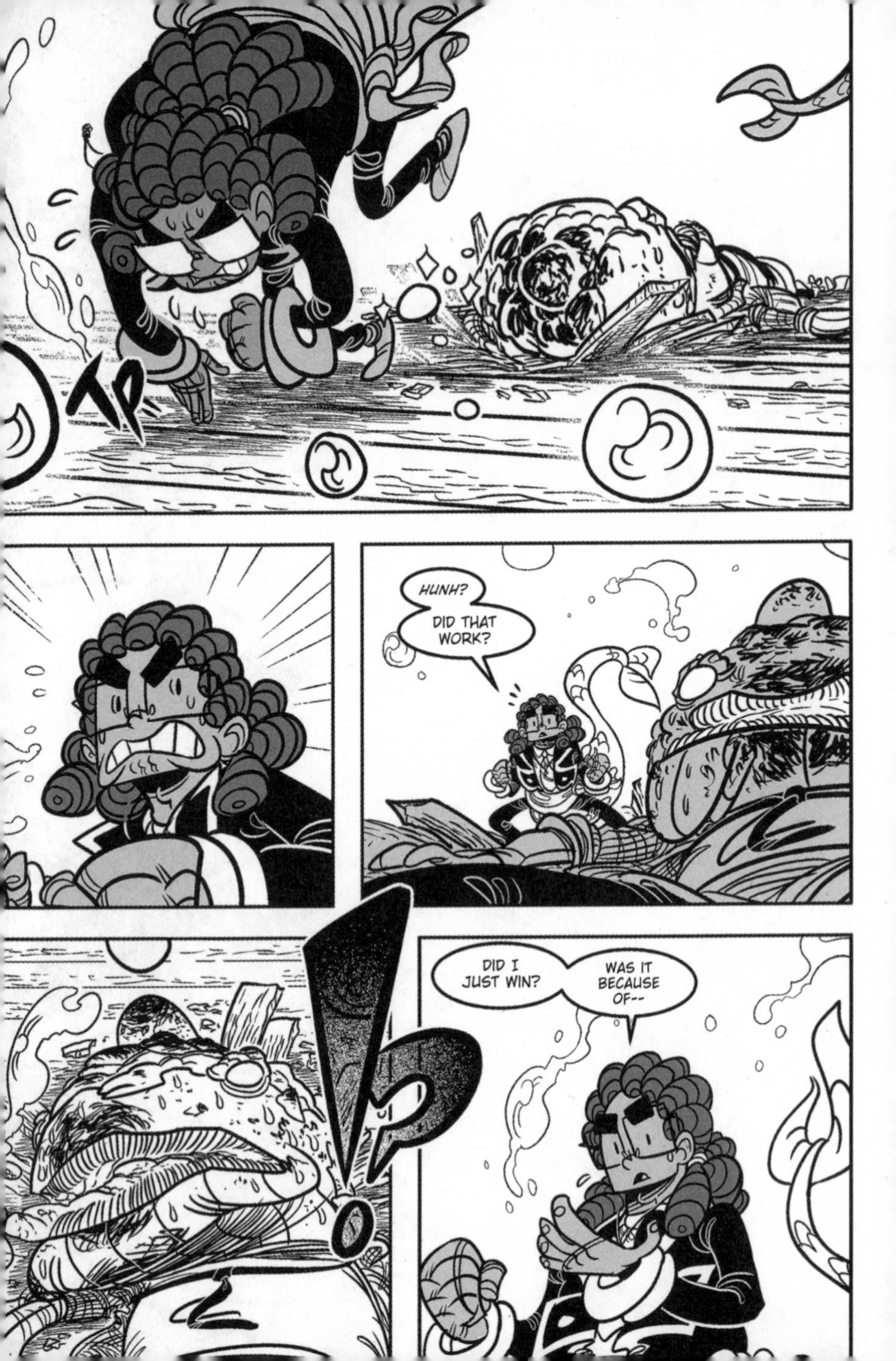
TP
HUNH?
DID THAT WORK?
DID I JUST WIN?
WAS IT BECAUSE OF--

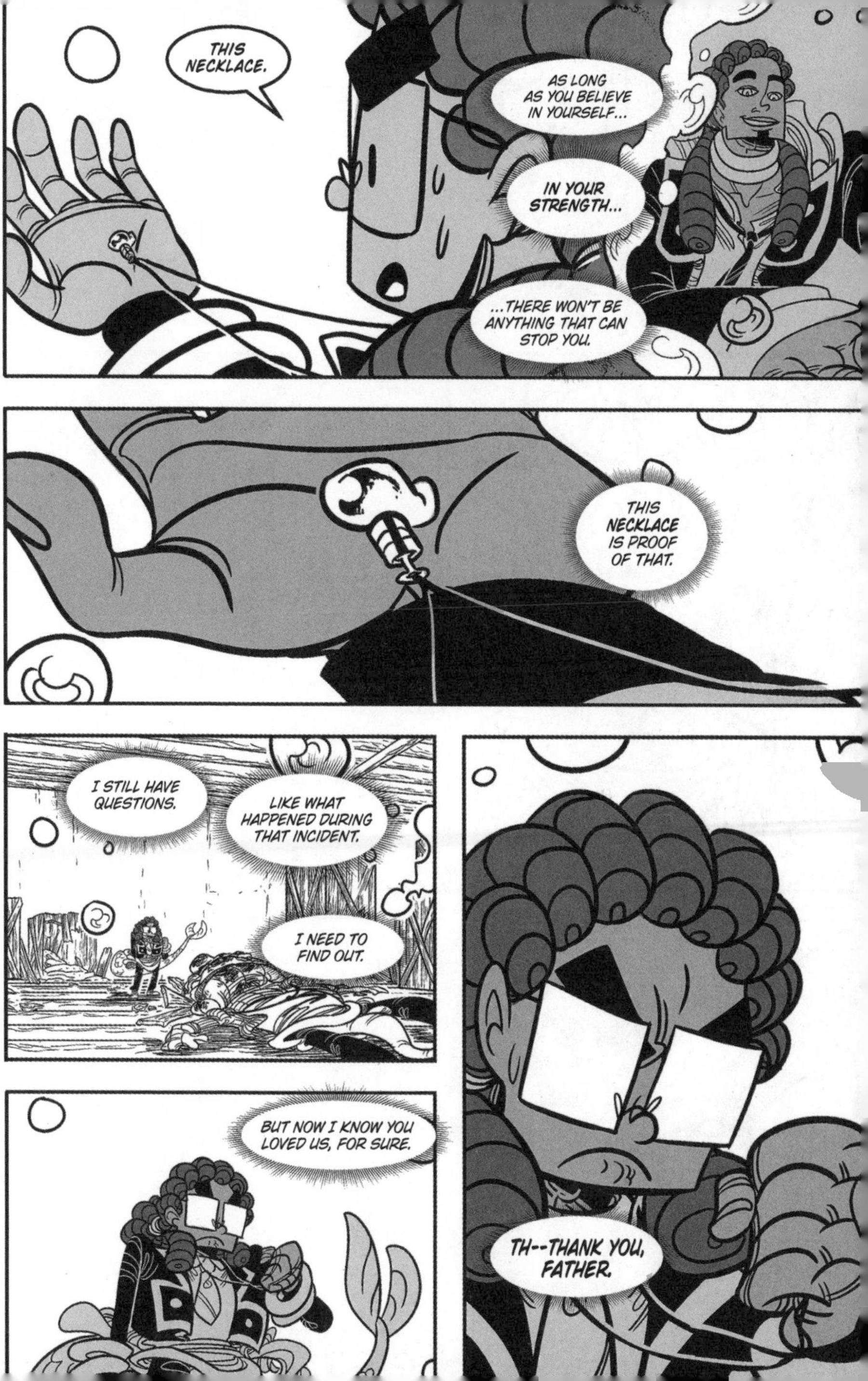
THIS NECKLACE.
AS LONG AS YOU BELIEVE IN YOURSELF...
IN YOUR STRENGTH...
...THERE WON'T BE ANYTHING THAT CAN STOP YOU.
THIS NECKLACE IS PROOF OF THAT.
I STILL HAVE QUESTIONS.
LIKE WHAT HAPPENED DURING THAT INCIDENT.
I NEED TO FIND OUT.
BUT NOW I KNOW YOU LOVED US, FOR SURE.
TH--THANK YOU, FATHER.

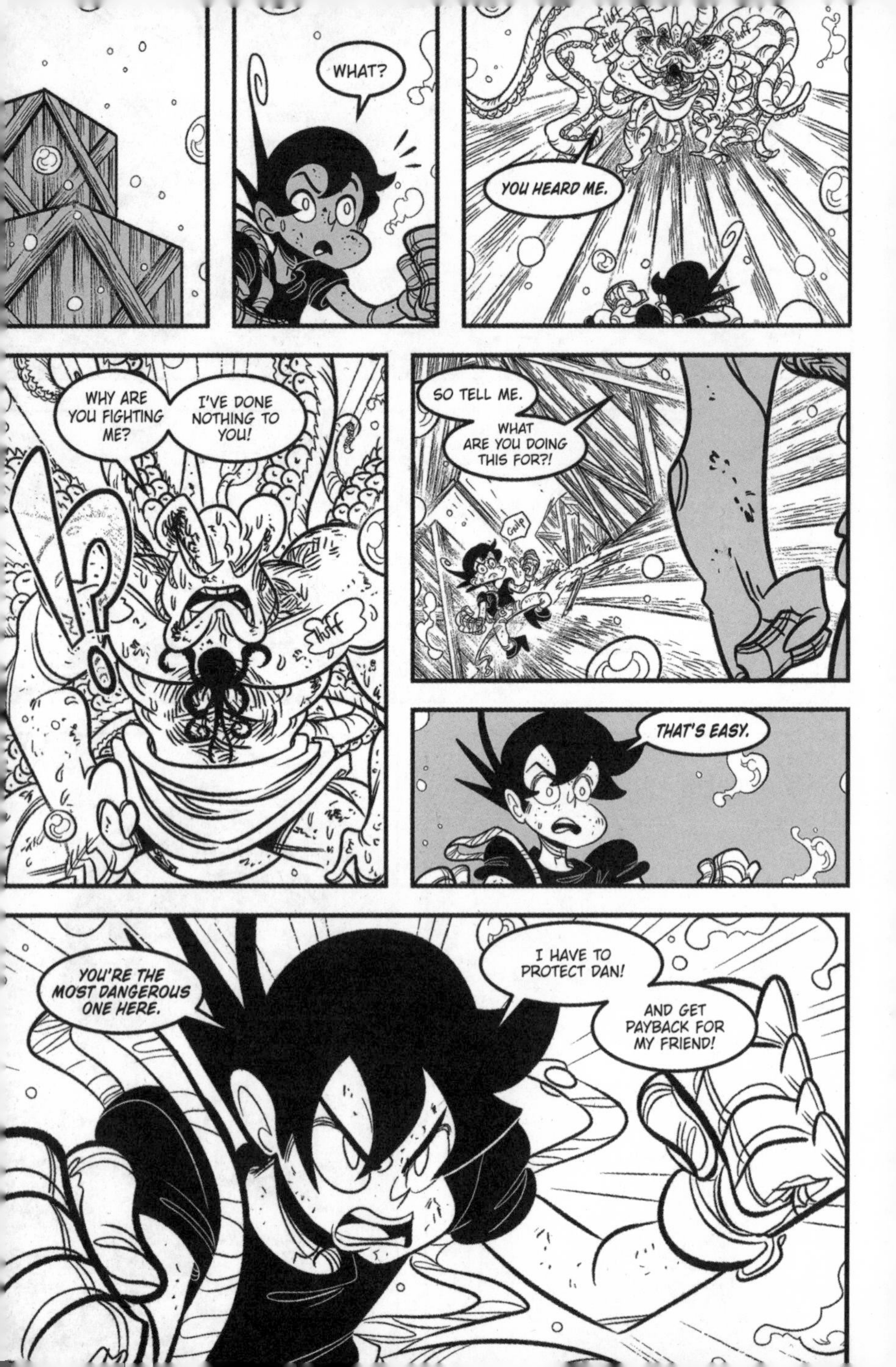
WHAT?
YOU HEARD ME.
WHY ARE YOU FIGHTING ME?
I'VE DONE NOTHING TO YOU!
Huff
SO TELL ME.
WHAT ARE YOU DOING THIS FOR?!
Gulp
THAT'S EASY.
YOU'RE THE MOST DANGEROUS ONE HERE.
I HAVE TO PROTECT DAN!
AND GET PAYBACK FOR MY FRIEND!

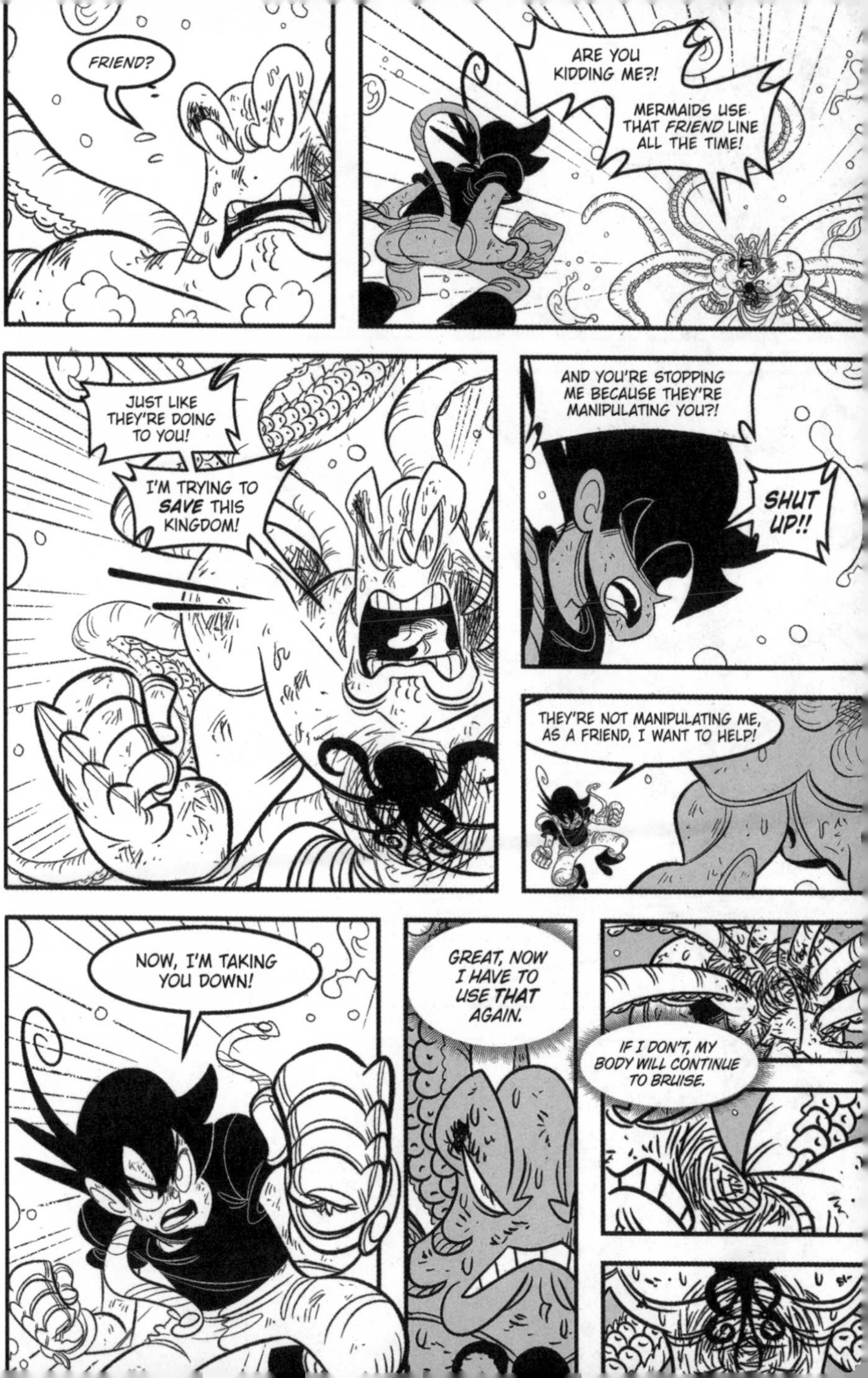
FRIEND?
ARE YOU KIDDING ME?!
MERMAIDS USE THAT FRIEND LINE ALL THE TIME!
JUST LIKE THEY'RE DOING TO YOU!
I'M TRYING TO SAVE THIS KINGDOM!
AND YOU'RE STOPPING ME BECAUSE THEY'RE MANIPULATING YOU?!
SHUT UP!!
THEY'RE NOT MANIPULATING ME, AS A FRIEND, I WANT TO HELP!
NOW, I'M TAKING YOU DOWN!
GREAT, NOW I HAVE TO USE THAT AGAIN.
IF I DON'T, MY BODY WILL CONTINUE TO BRUISE.

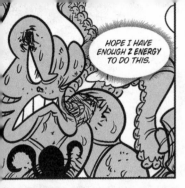

HOPE I HAVE ENOUGH Z ENERGY TO DO THIS.

THE MOST DANGEROUS?

TRUST ME BOY...

YOU'VE SEEN NOTHING YET.

SPLOOSH

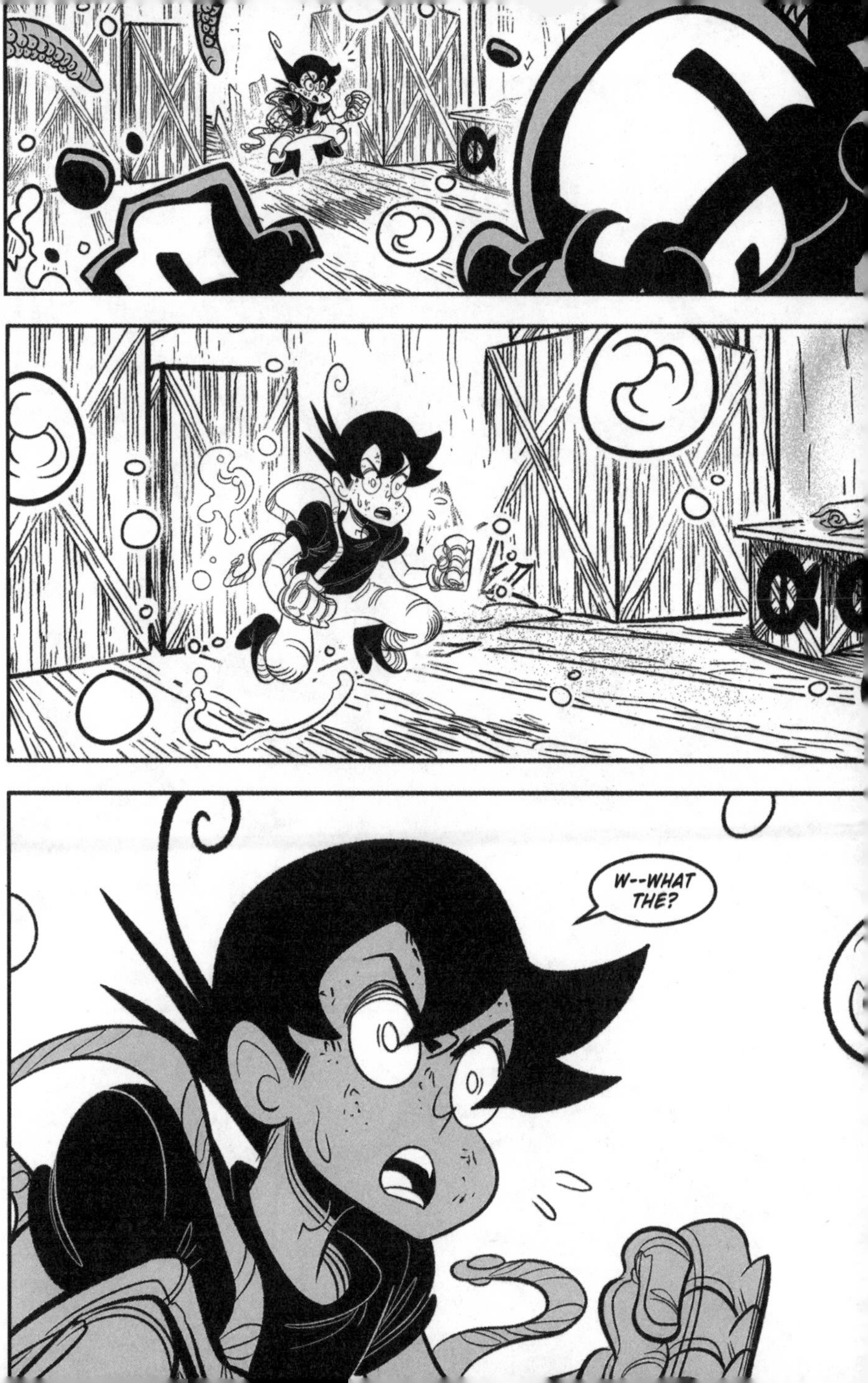
W--WHAT THE?

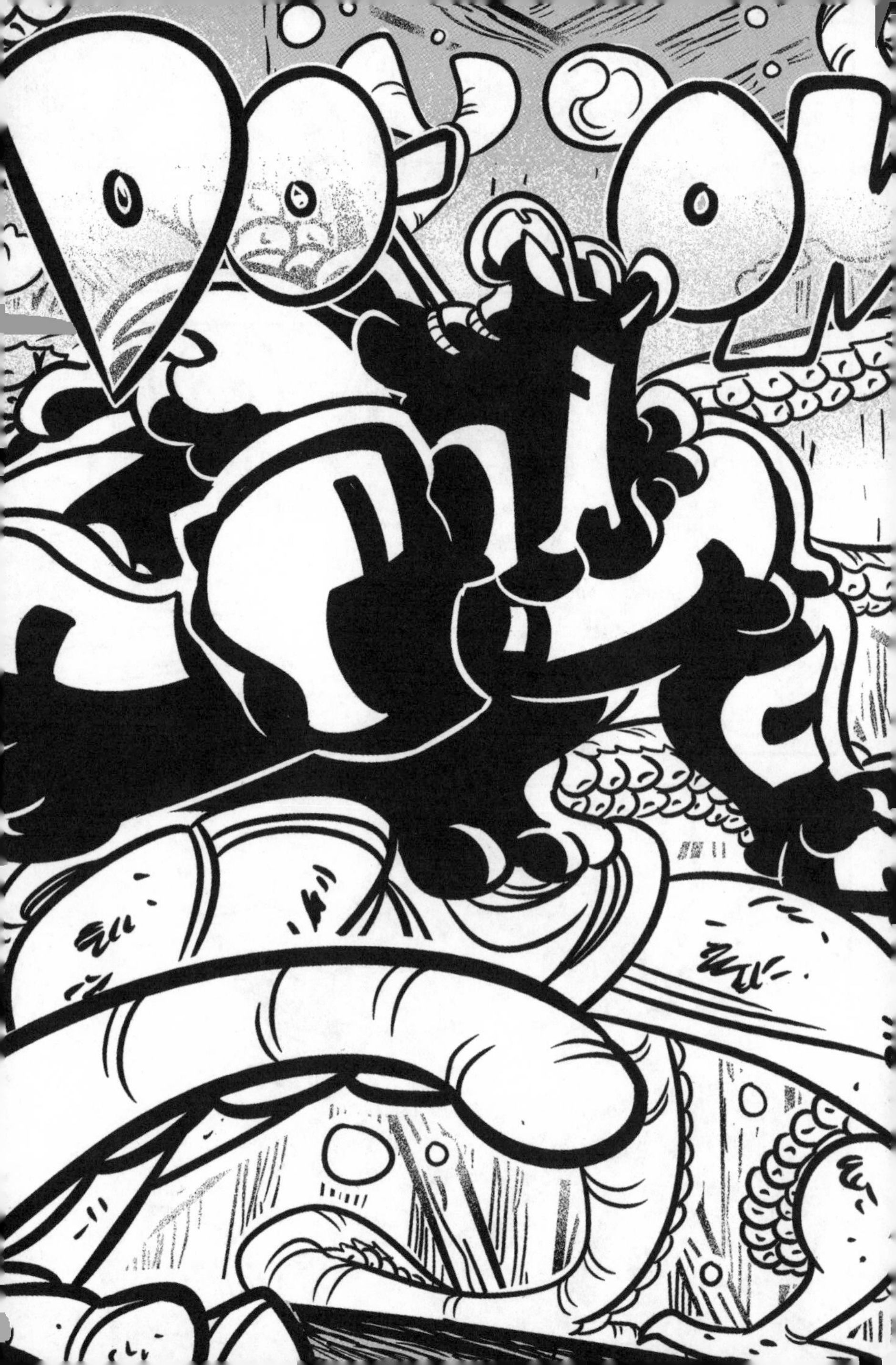

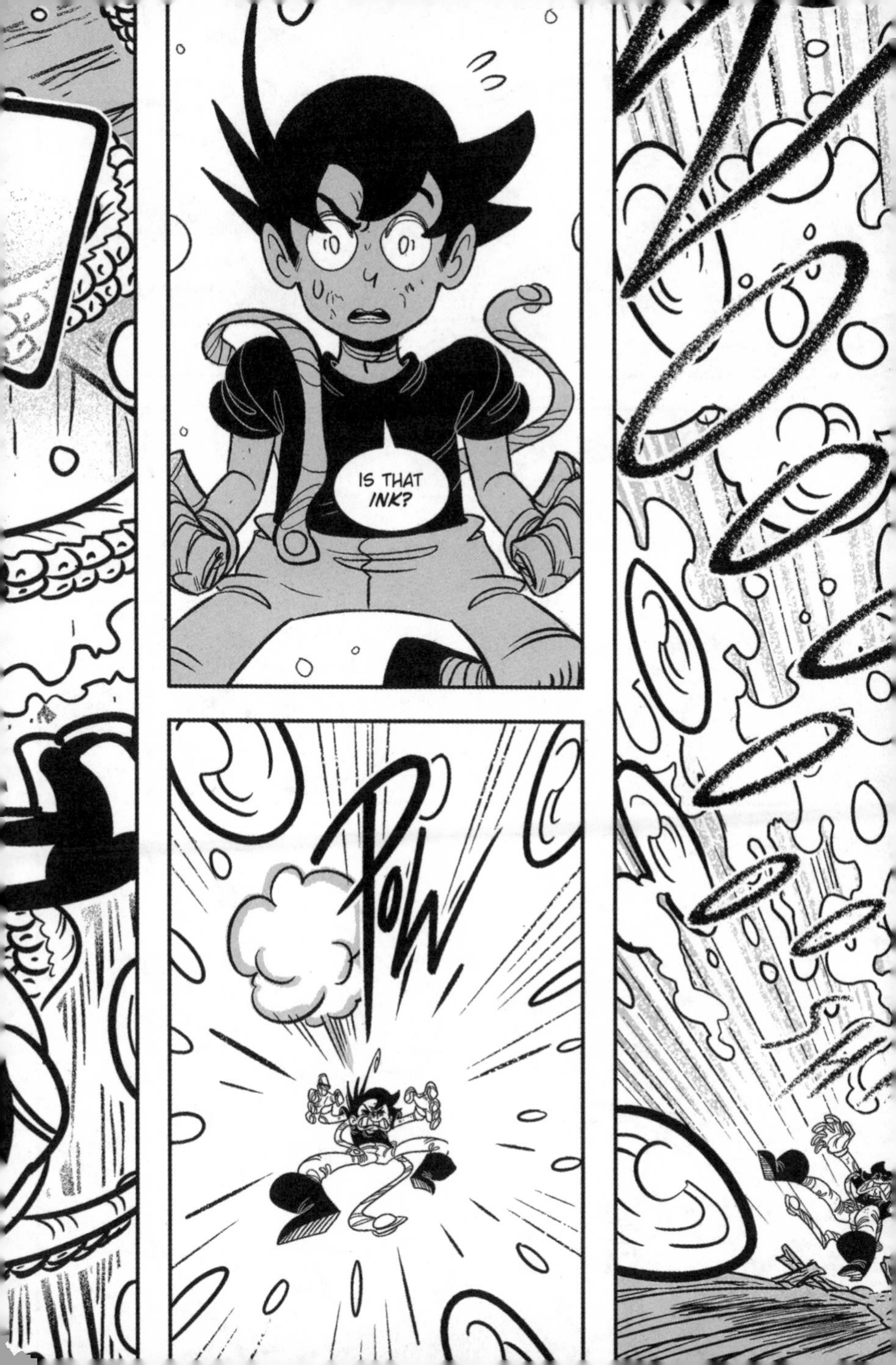
IS THAT INK?
POW

DID HE JUST *PUNCH ME?* HOW?

HE'S SO FAR AWAY.

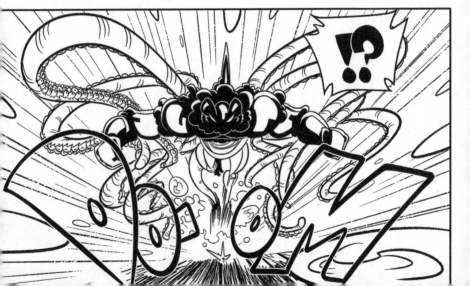

!?

DOOM

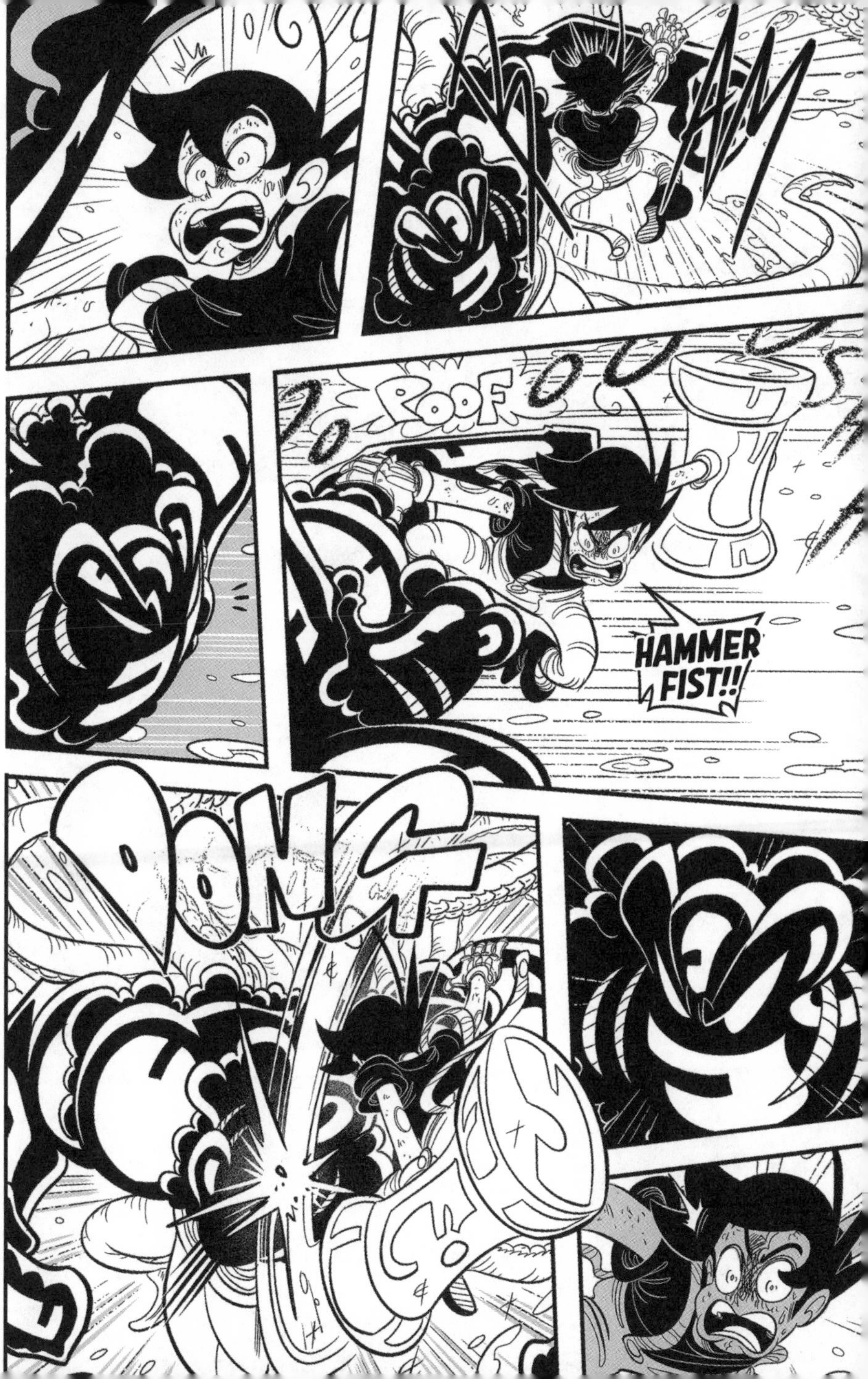
POOF
HAMMER FIST!!
DONG

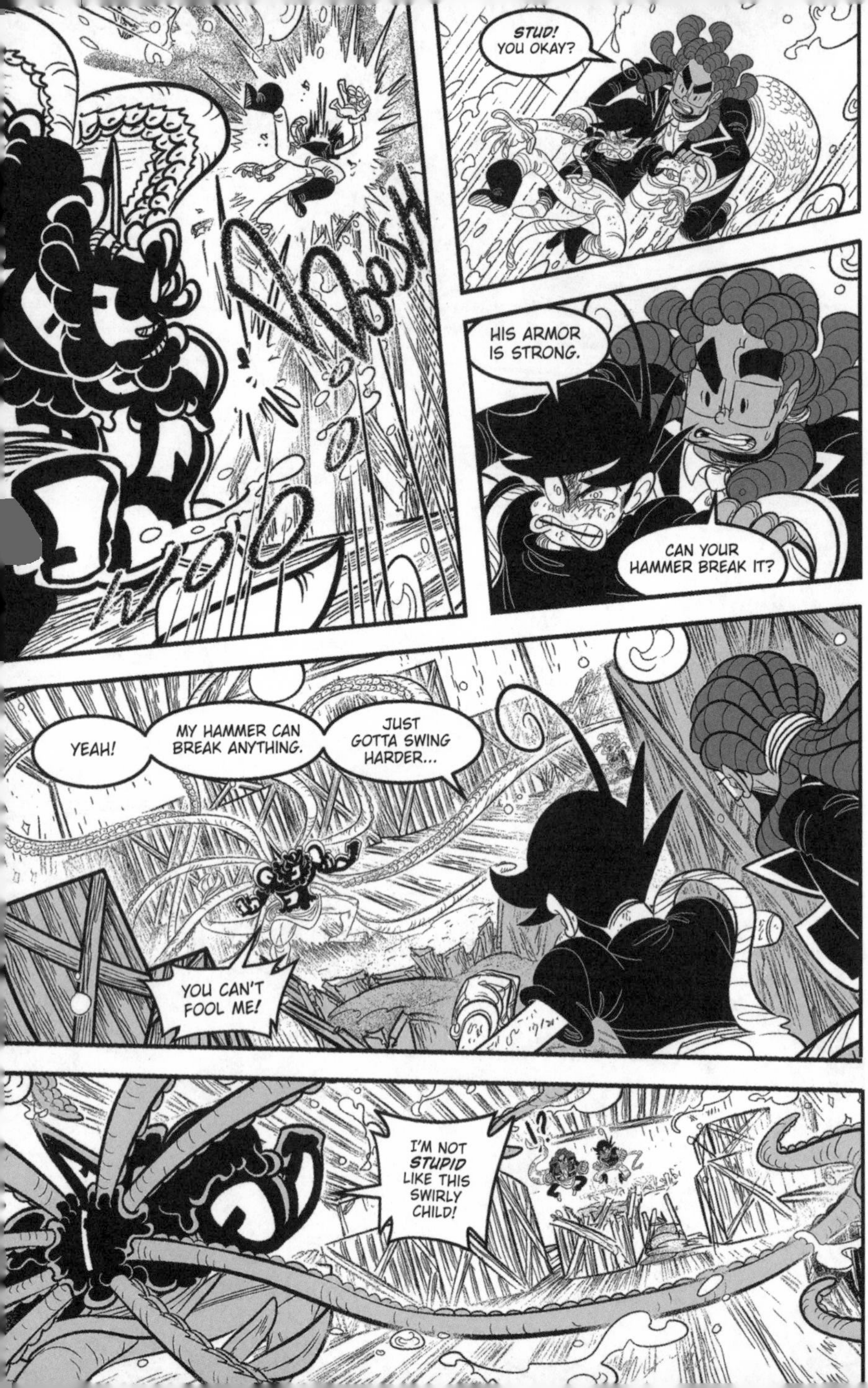
DOOSH
WOOO
STUD! YOU OKAY?
HIS ARMOR IS STRONG.
CAN YOUR HAMMER BREAK IT?
YEAH!
MY HAMMER CAN BREAK ANYTHING.
JUST GOTTA SWING HARDER...
YOU CAN'T FOOL ME!
I'M NOT **STUPID** LIKE THIS SWIRLY CHILD!
!?

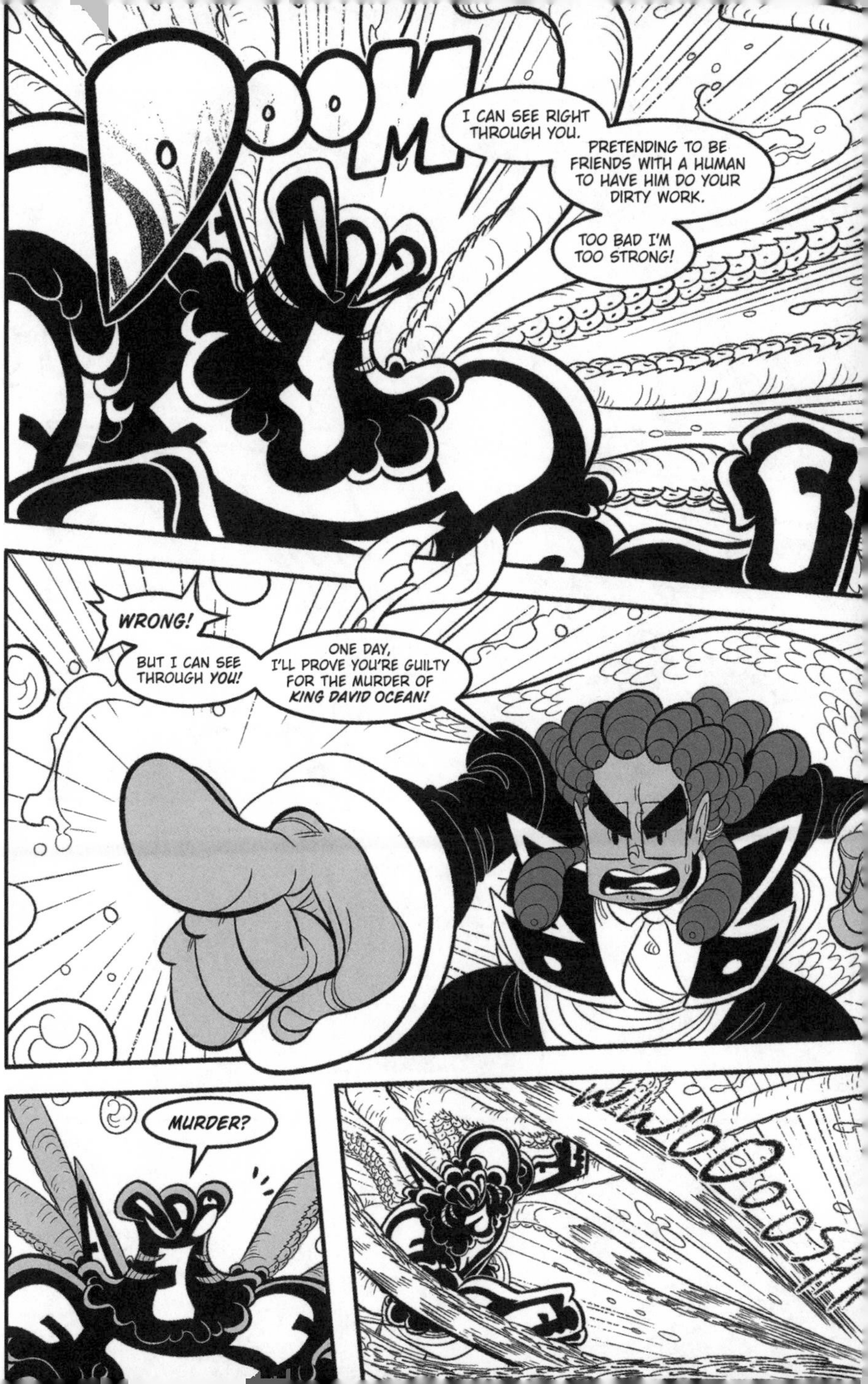
I CAN SEE RIGHT THROUGH YOU.
PRETENDING TO BE FRIENDS WITH A HUMAN TO HAVE HIM DO YOUR DIRTY WORK.
TOO BAD I'M TOO STRONG!
WRONG!
BUT I CAN SEE THROUGH YOU!
ONE DAY, I'LL PROVE YOU'RE GUILTY FOR THE MURDER OF KING DAVID OCEAN!
MURDER?

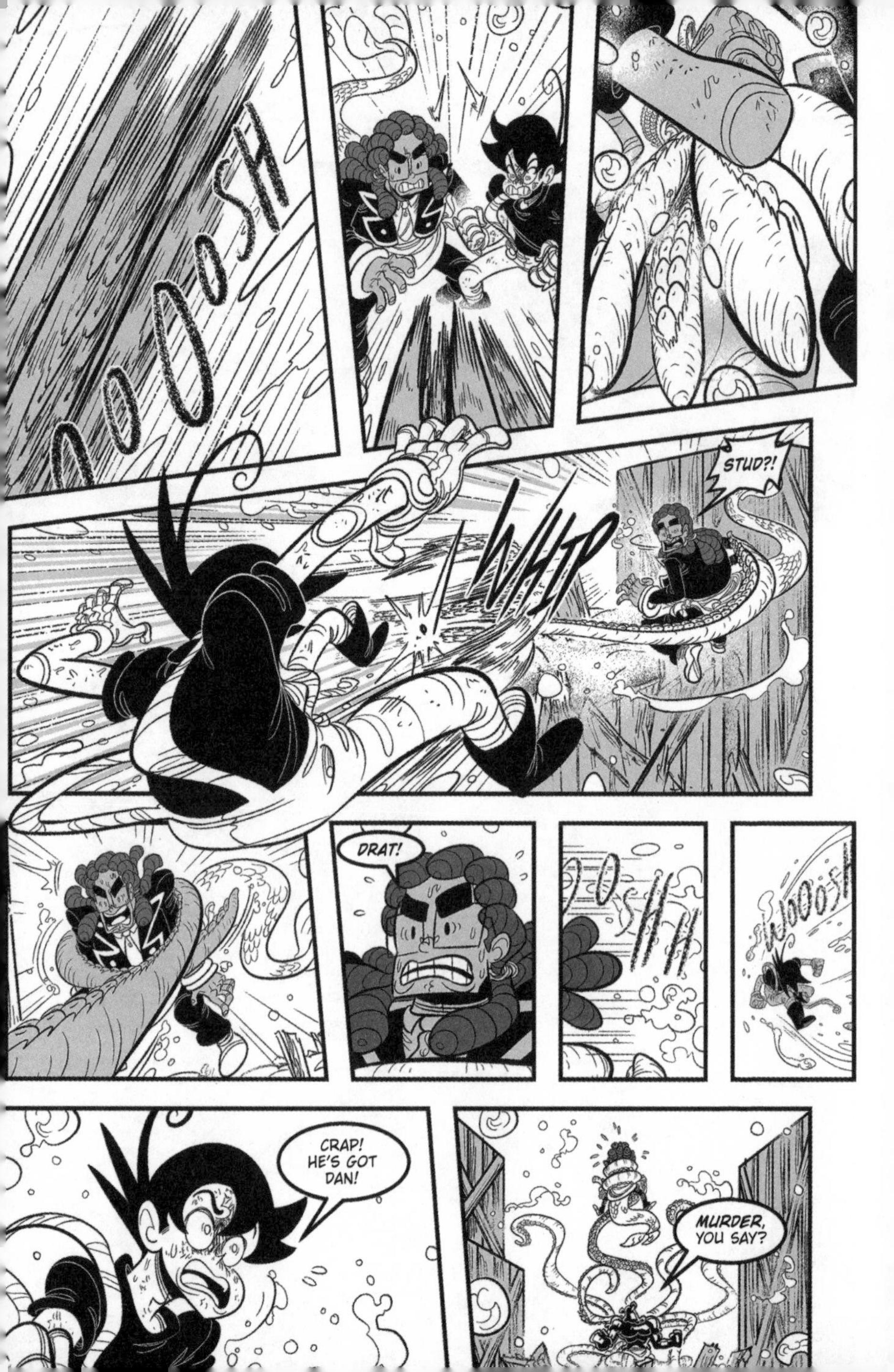
OoOoSH
STUD?!
WHIP
DRAT!
OOSHH
WOOOSH
CRAP! HE'S GOT DAN!
MURDER, YOU SAY?

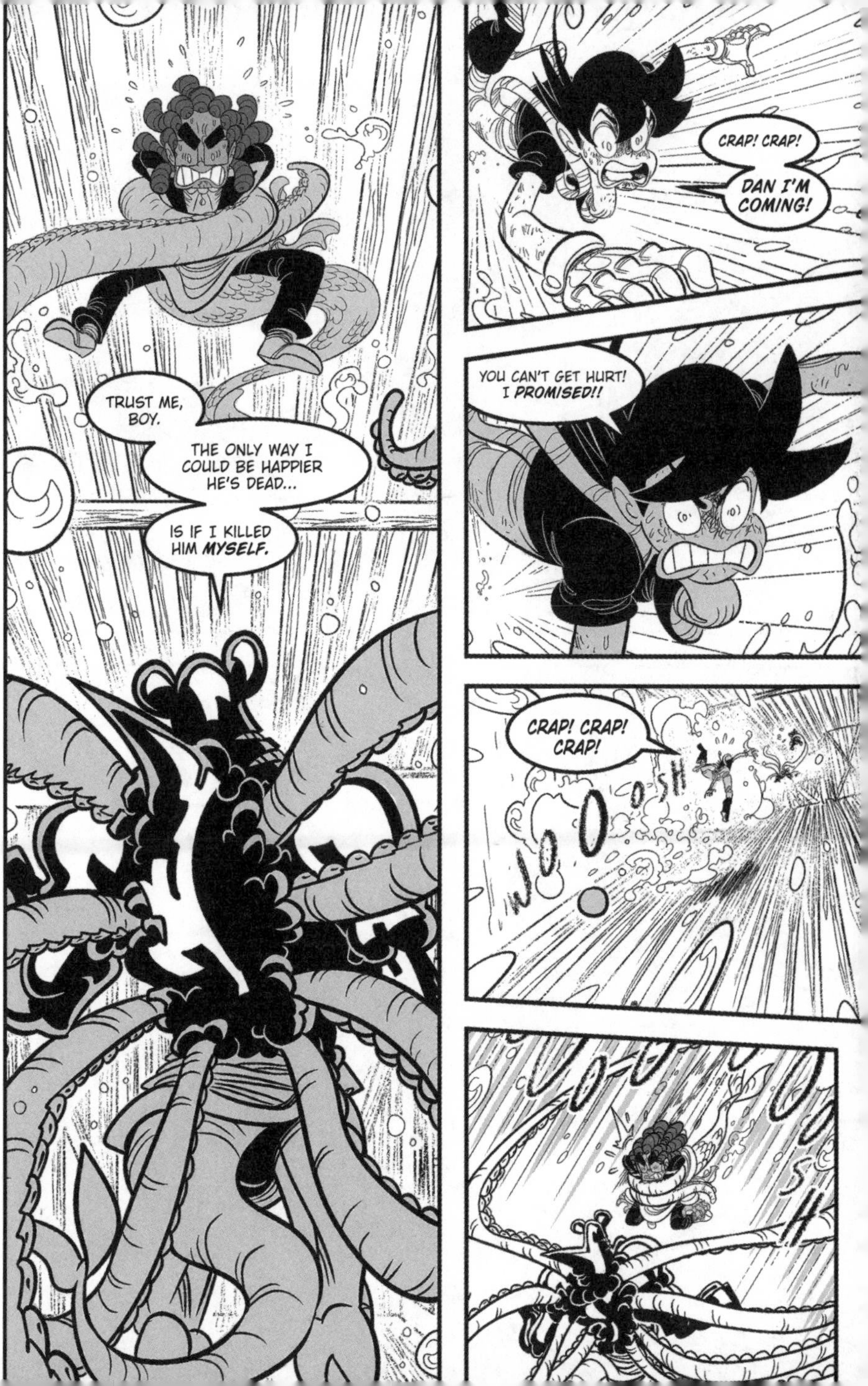
TRUST ME, BOY.
THE ONLY WAY I COULD BE HAPPIER HE'S DEAD...
IS IF I KILLED HIM *MYSELF*.
CRAP! CRAP!
DAN I'M COMING!
YOU CAN'T GET HURT! I *PROMISED!!*
CRAP! CRAP! CRAP!

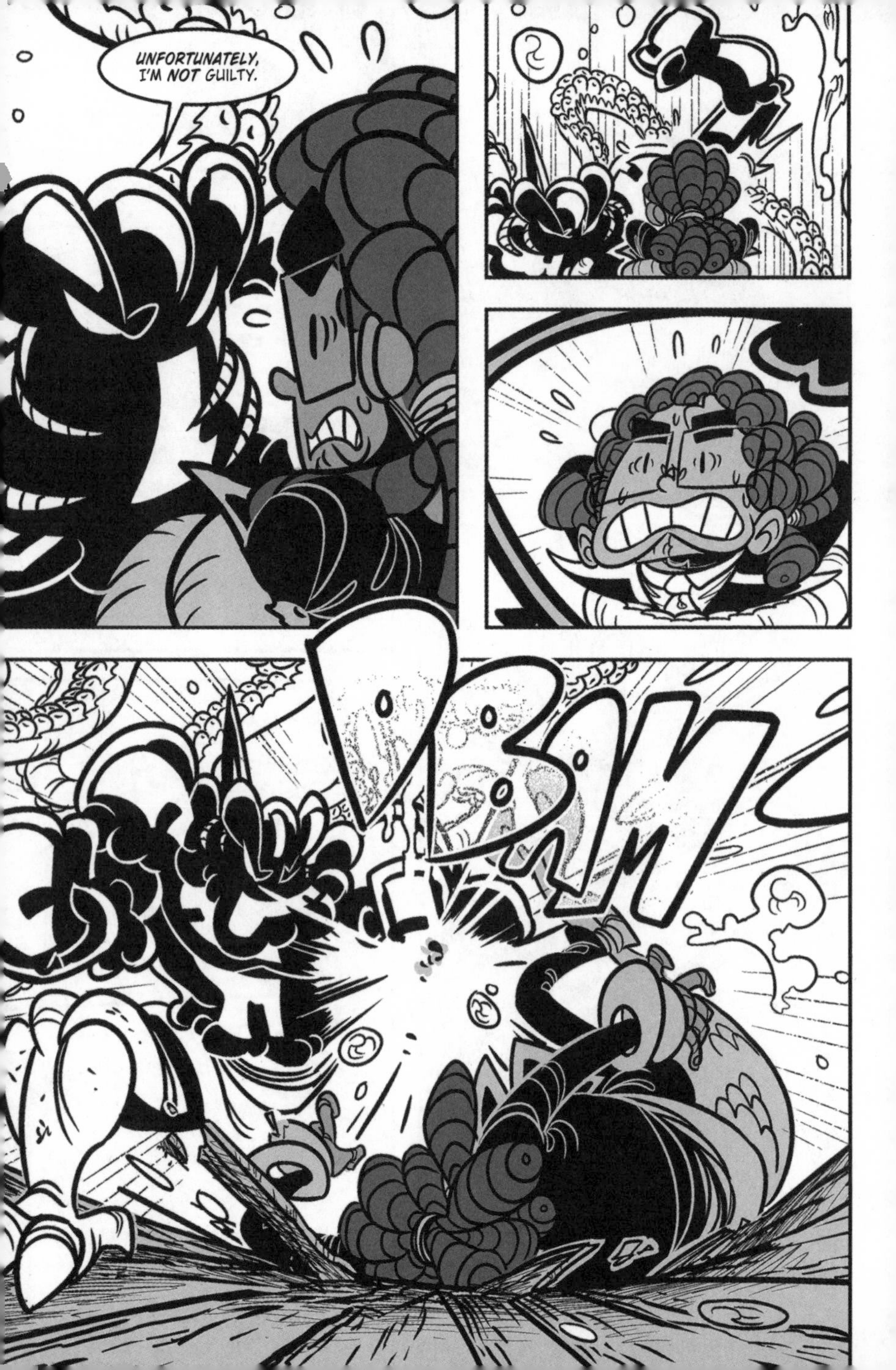
UNFORTUNATELY, I'M NOT GUILTY.
DOOM

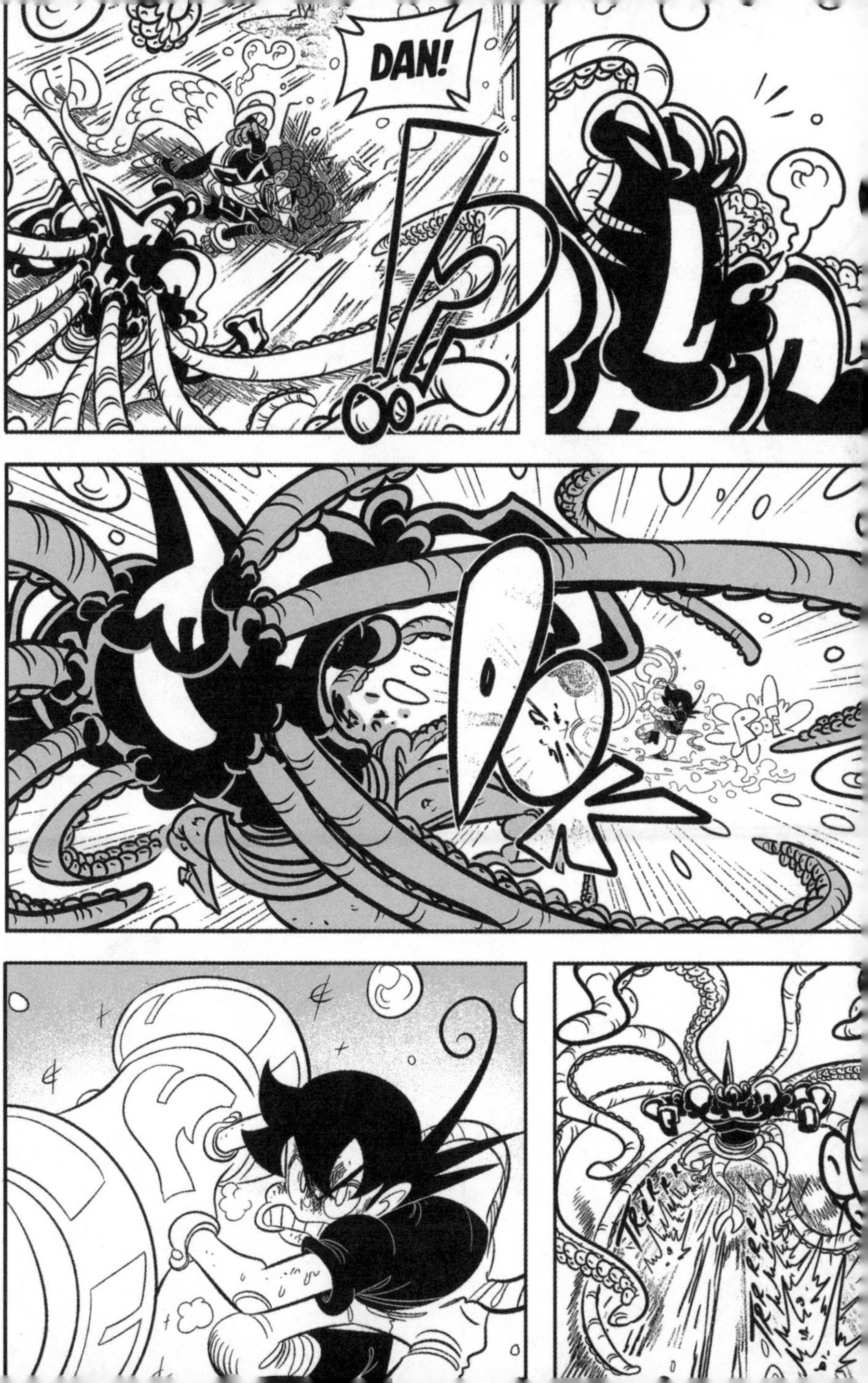
DAN!
POOF

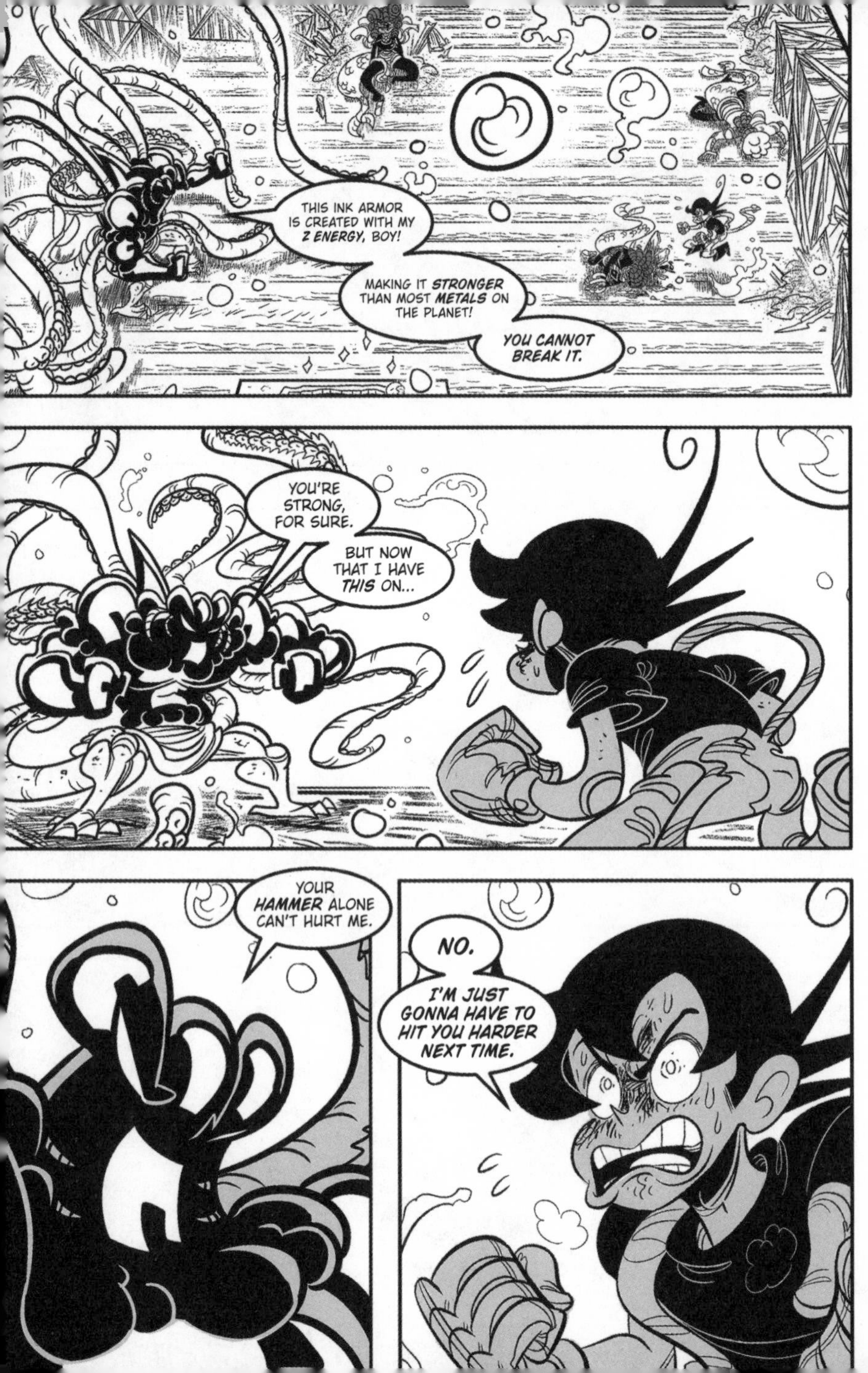
THIS INK ARMOR IS CREATED WITH MY Z ENERGY, BOY!
MAKING IT STRONGER THAN MOST METALS ON THE PLANET!
YOU CANNOT BREAK IT.
YOU'RE STRONG, FOR SURE.
BUT NOW THAT I HAVE THIS ON...
YOUR HAMMER ALONE CAN'T HURT ME.
NO.
I'M JUST GONNA HAVE TO HIT YOU HARDER NEXT TIME.

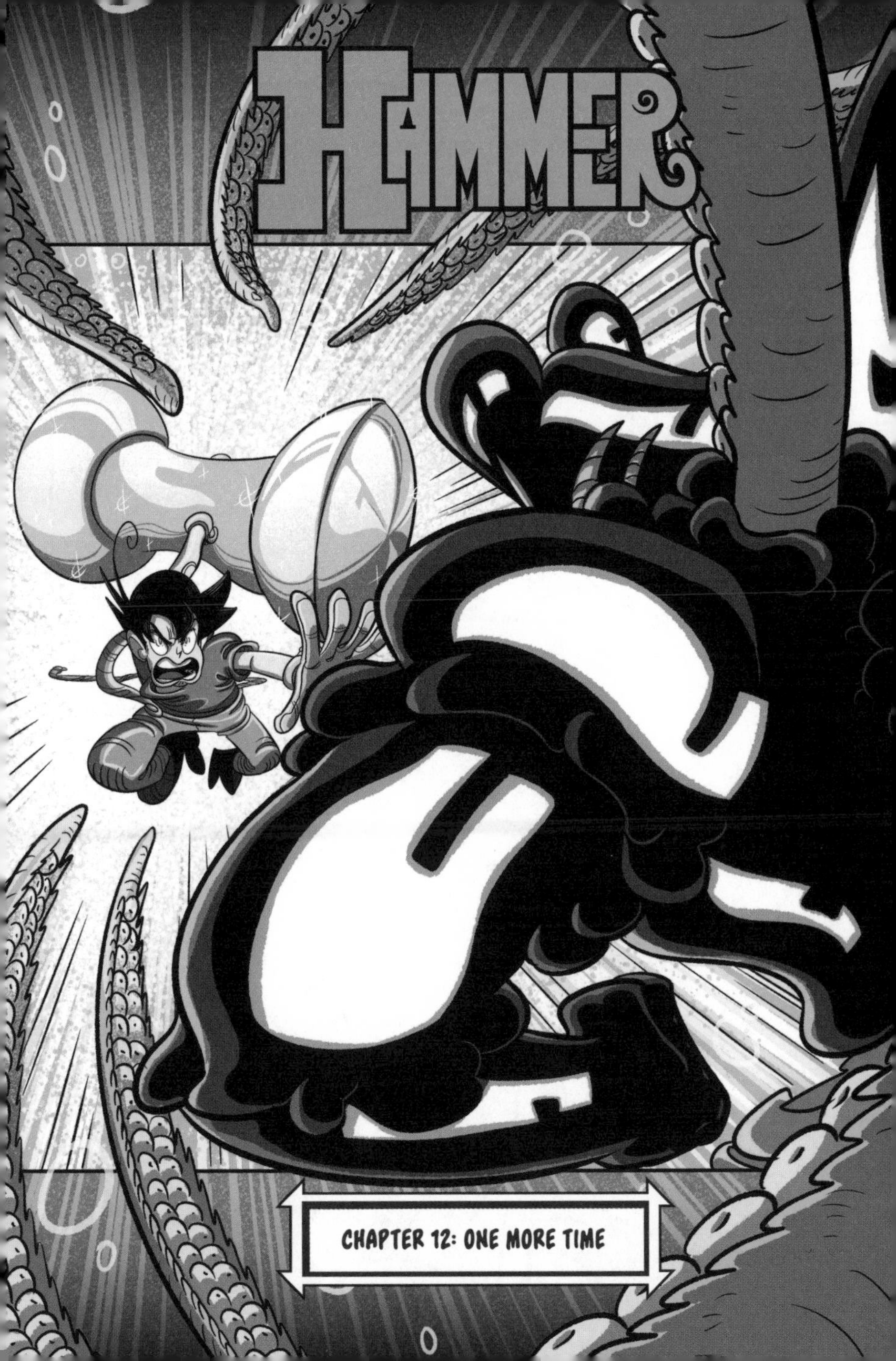
HAMMER
CHAPTER 12: ONE MORE TIME

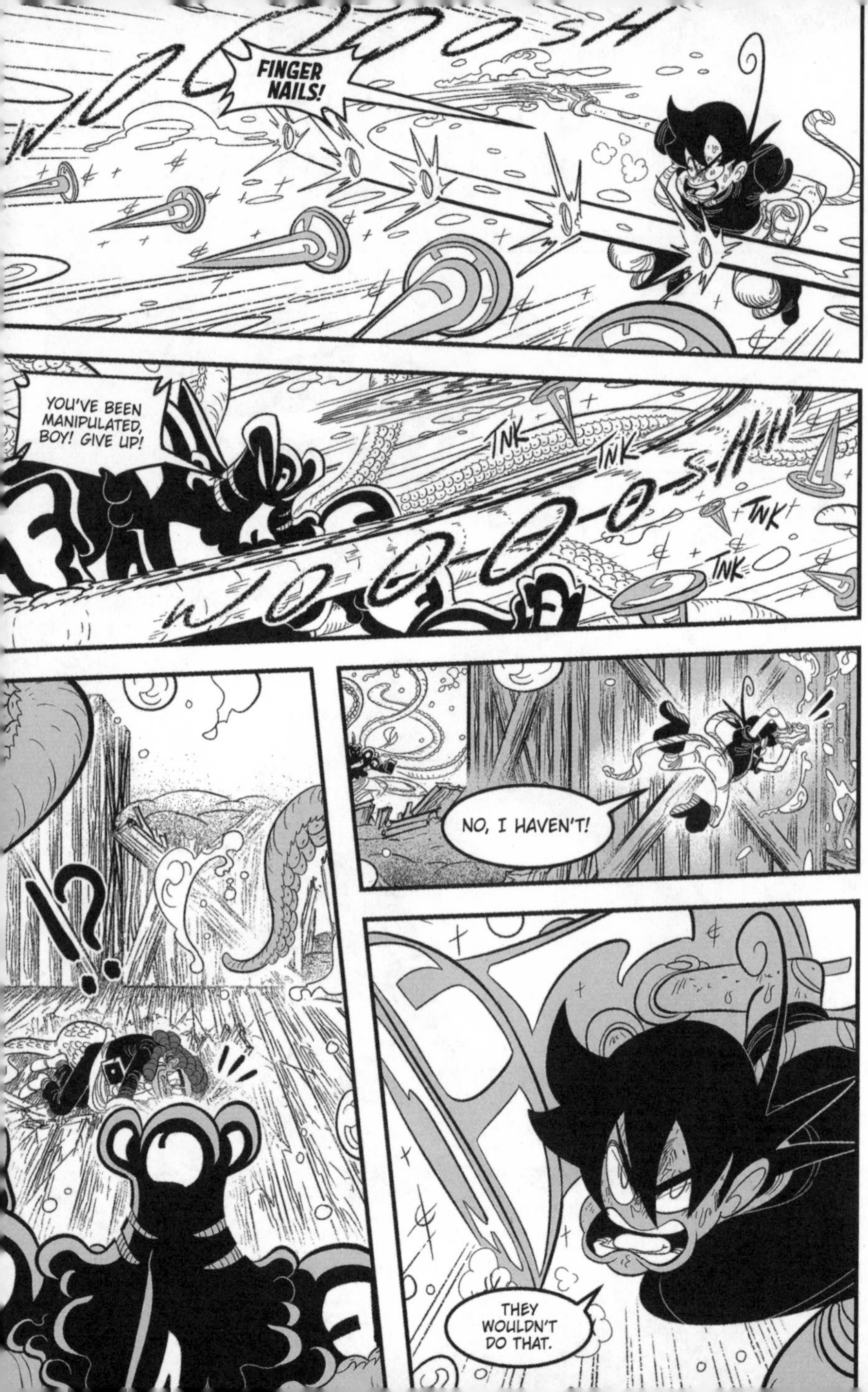
WOOOOSH
FINGER NAILS!
YOU'VE BEEN MANIPULATED, BOY! GIVE UP!
TNK
TNK
WOOOOOOSHHH
TNK
TNK
!?
NO, I HAVEN'T!
THEY WOULDN'T DO THAT.

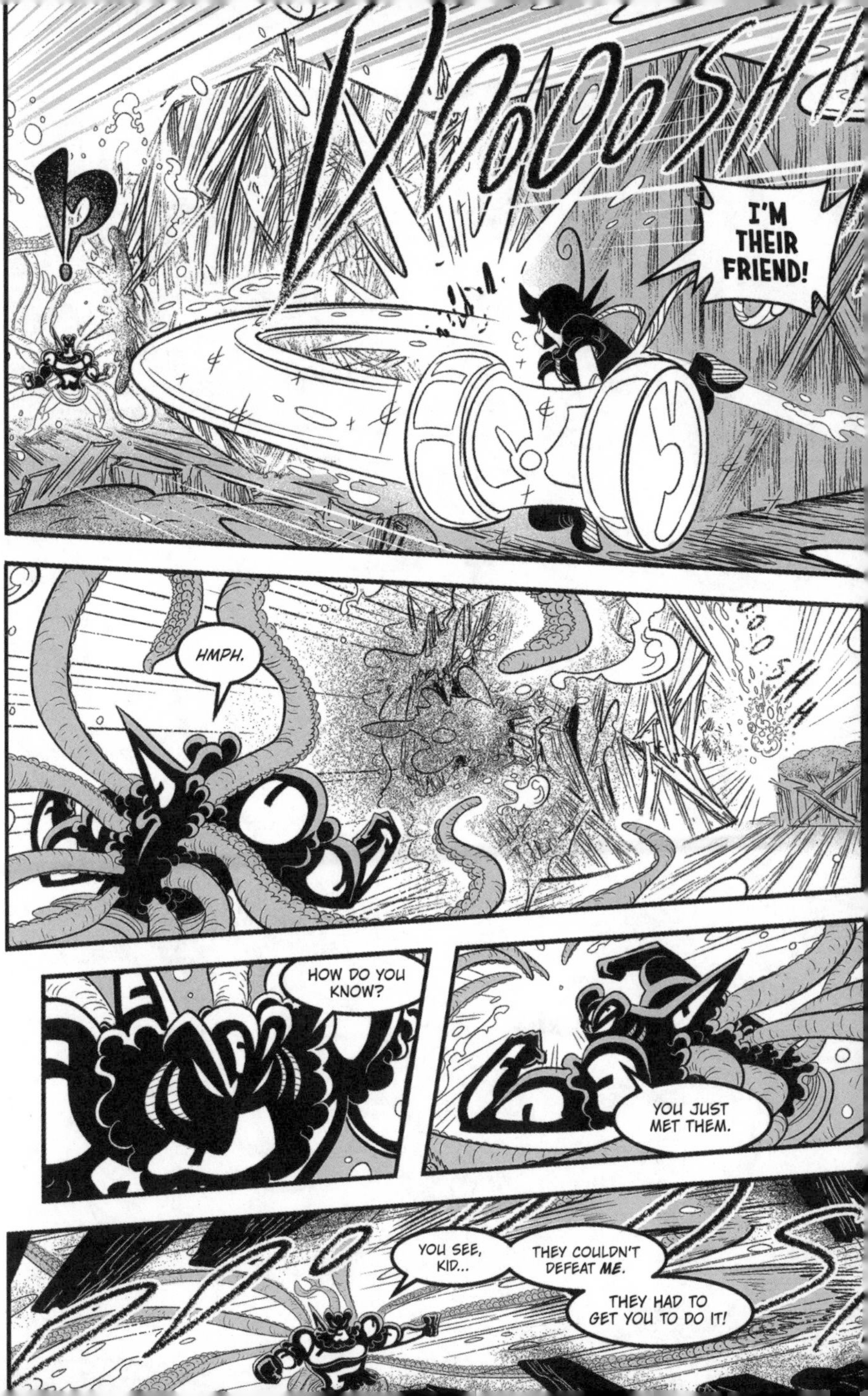

KWOOOSH
!
I'M THEIR FRIEND!
HMPH.
HOW DO YOU KNOW?
YOU JUST MET THEM.
YOU SEE, KID...
THEY COULDN'T DEFEAT ME.
THEY HAD TO GET YOU TO DO IT!

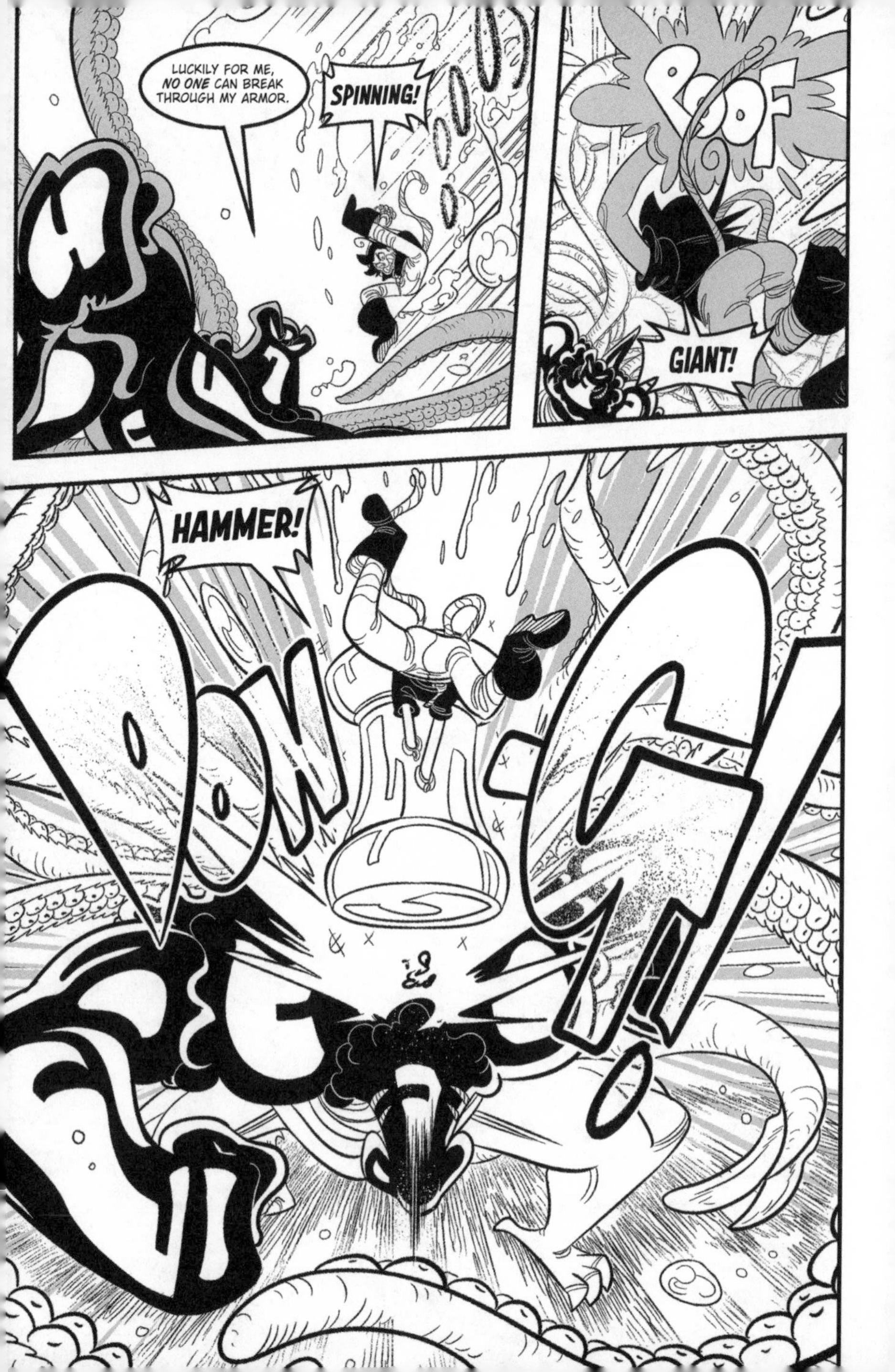
LUCKILY FOR ME, *NO ONE* CAN BREAK THROUGH MY ARMOR.
SPINNING!
POOF
GIANT!
HAMMER!

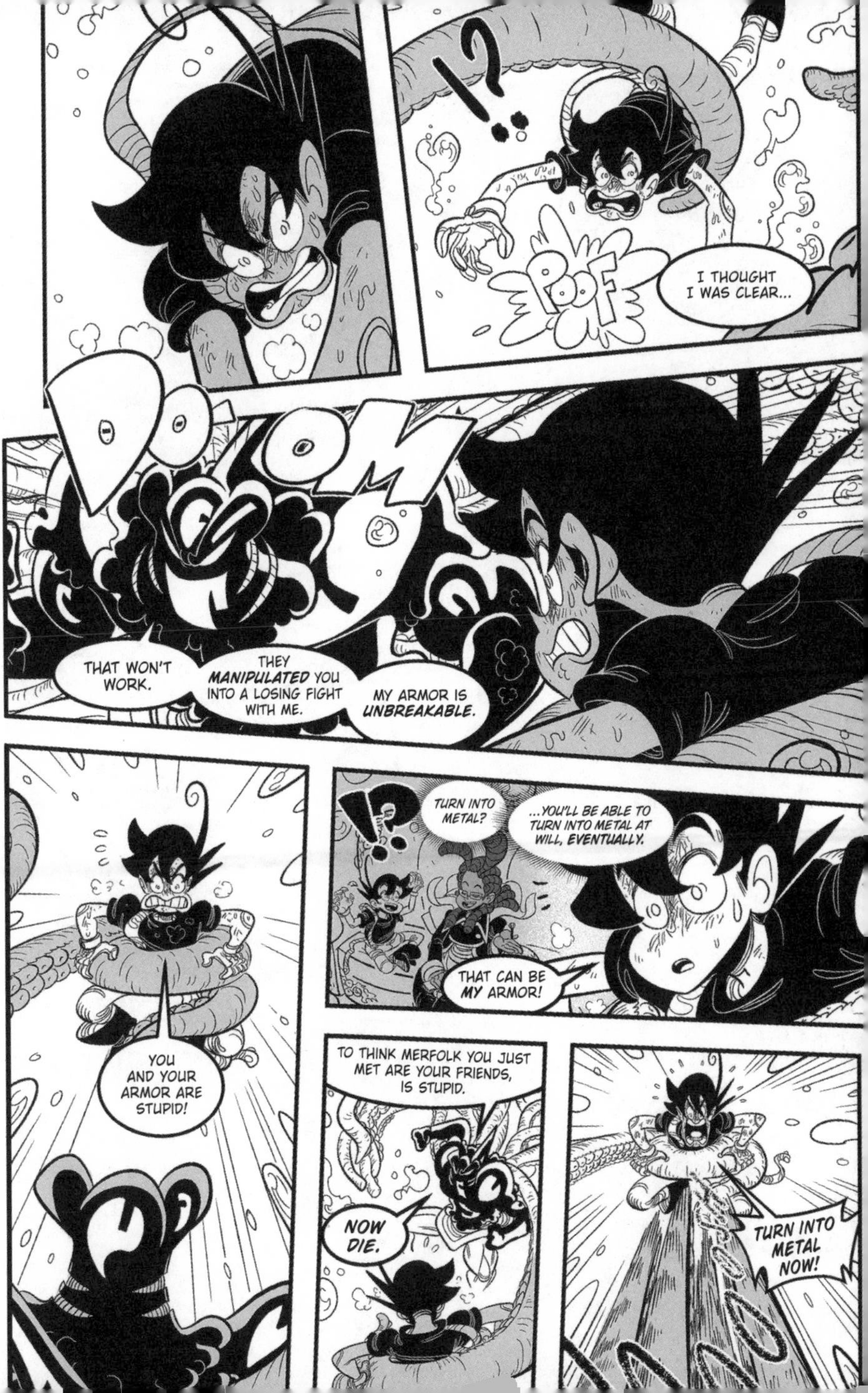
!?
POOF
I THOUGHT I WAS CLEAR...
DOOM
THAT WON'T WORK.
THEY **MANIPULATED** YOU INTO A LOSING FIGHT WITH ME.
MY ARMOR IS **UNBREAKABLE.**
YOU AND YOUR ARMOR ARE STUPID!
!?
TURN INTO METAL?
...YOU'LL BE ABLE TO TURN INTO METAL AT WILL, **EVENTUALLY.**
THAT CAN BE **MY** ARMOR!
TO THINK MERFOLK YOU JUST MET ARE YOUR FRIENDS, IS STUPID.
NOW DIE.
TURN INTO METAL NOW!

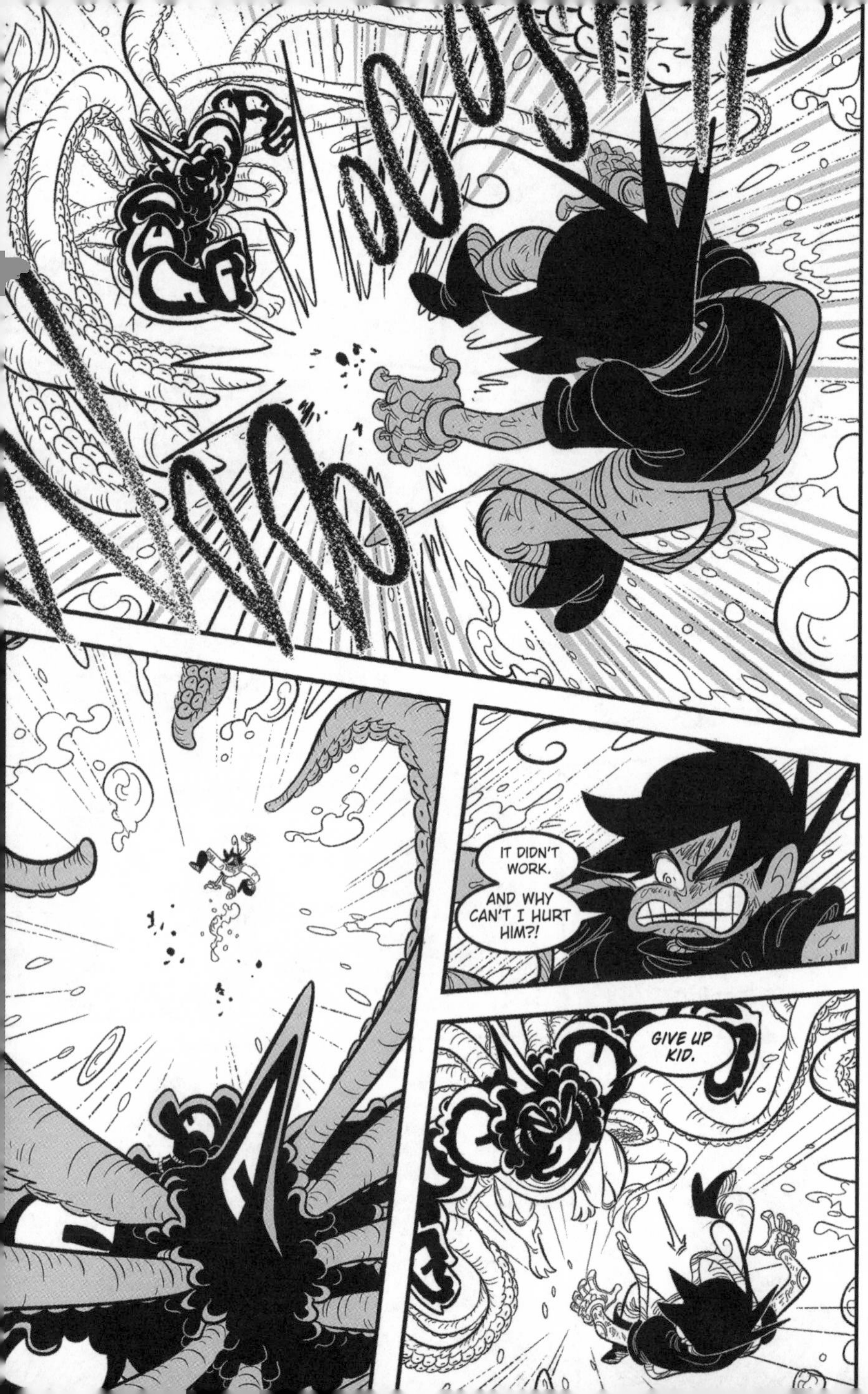
IT DIDN'T WORK.
AND WHY CAN'T I HURT HIM?!
GIVE UP KID.

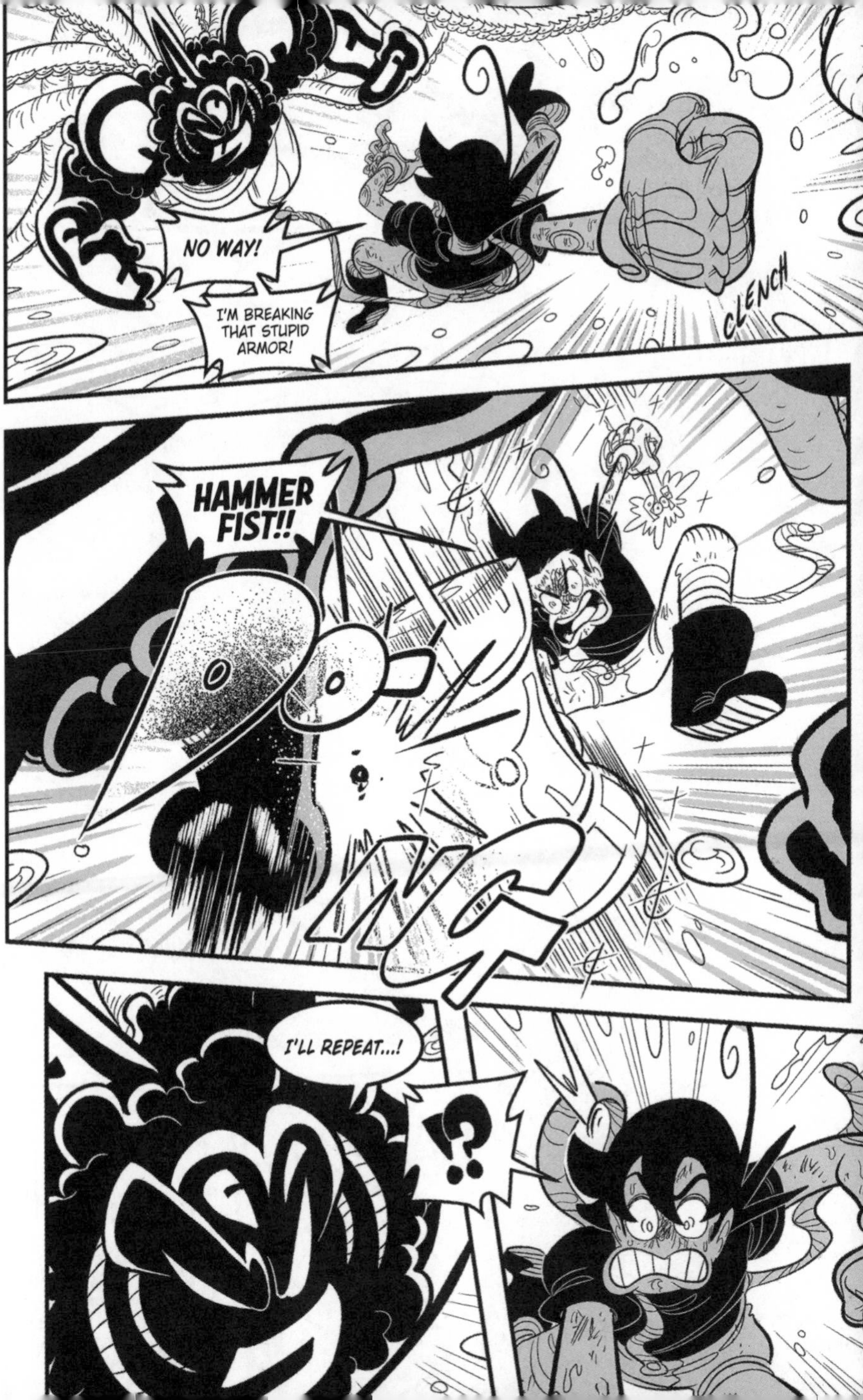
NO WAY!
I'M BREAKING THAT STUPID ARMOR!
CLENCH
HAMMER FIST!!
POP
I'LL REPEAT...!
!?

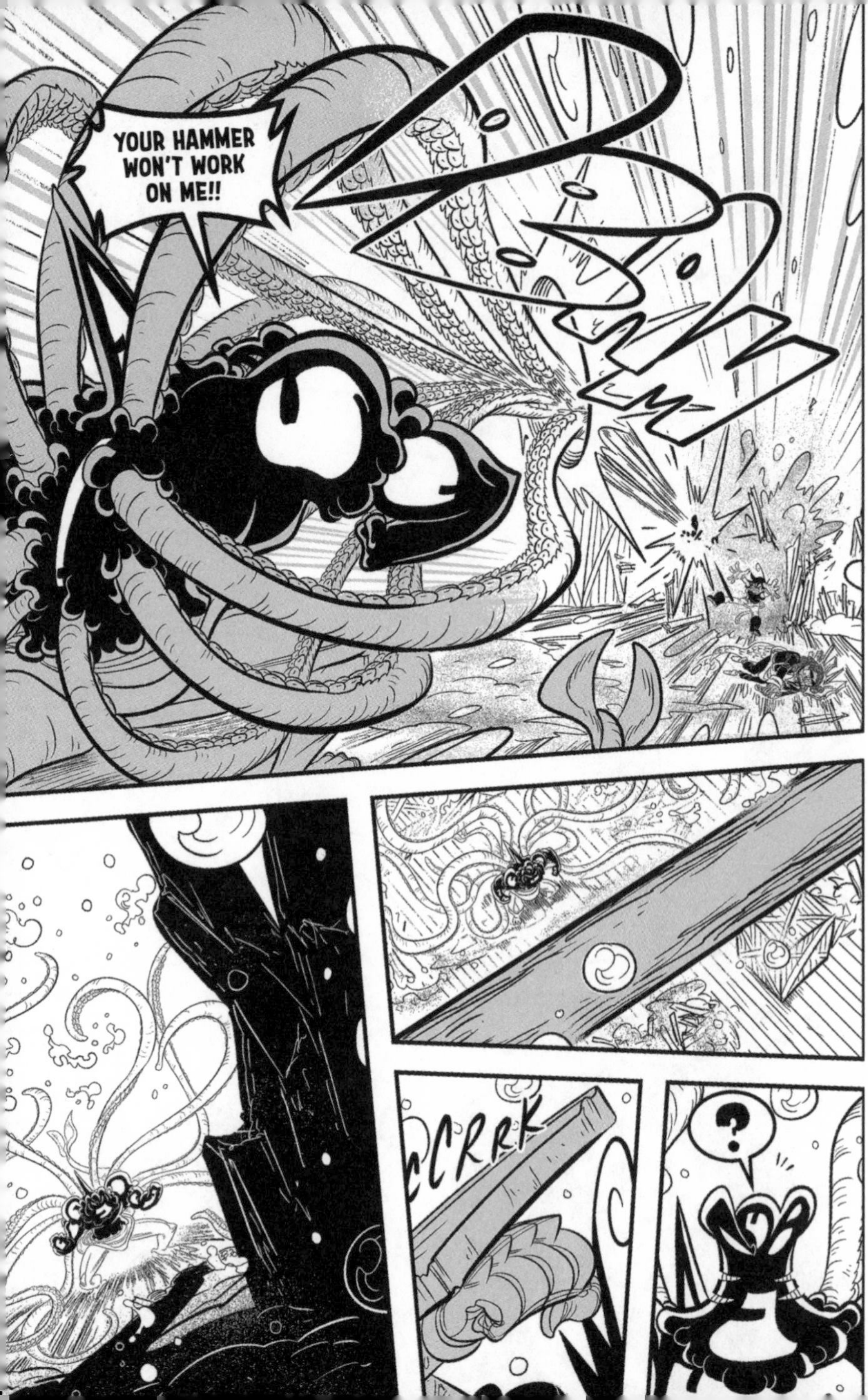
YOUR HAMMER WON'T WORK ON ME!!
CCRRK
?

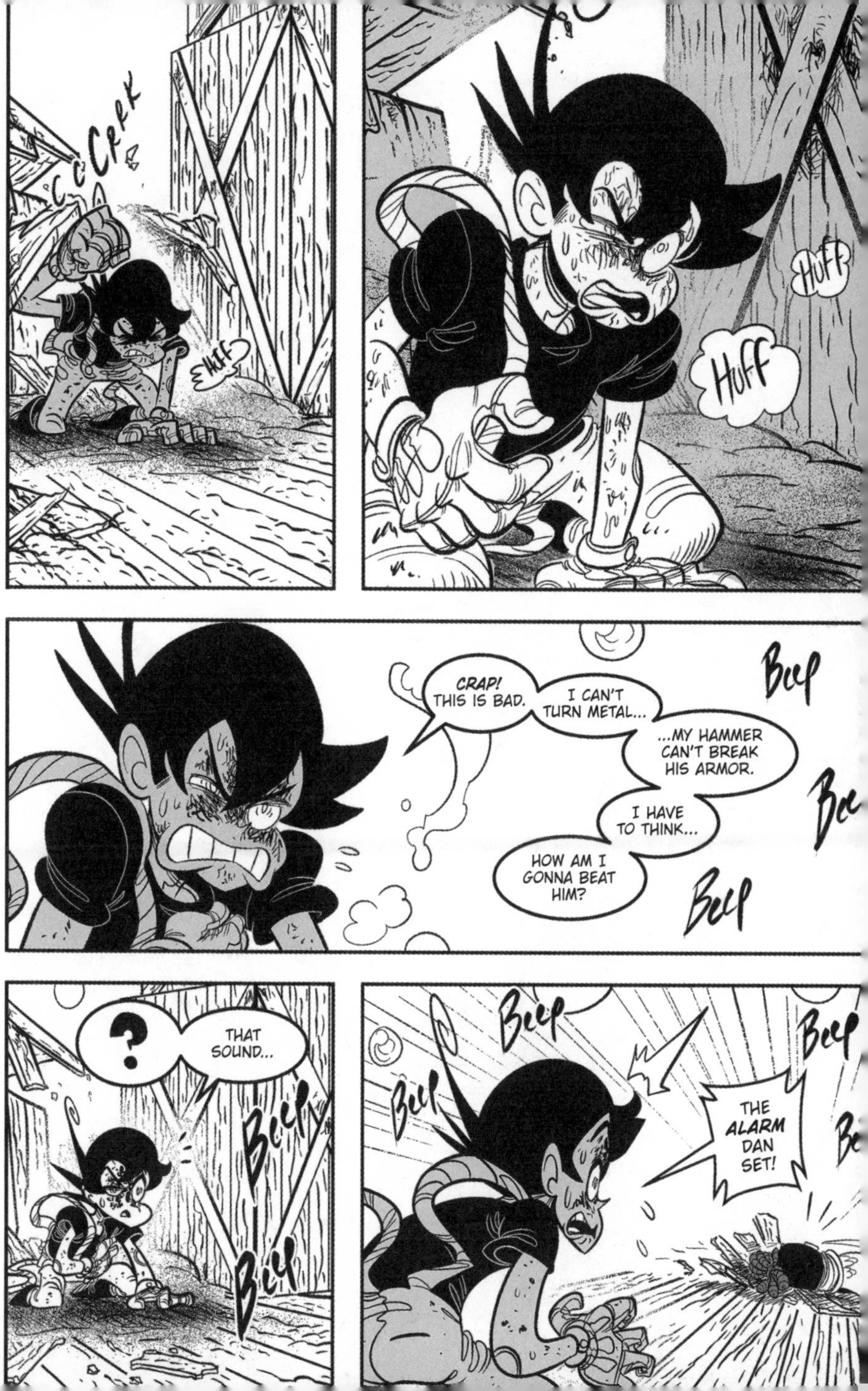
CCCRRK
HUFF
HUFF
HUFF
CRAP! THIS IS BAD.
I CAN'T TURN METAL...
...MY HAMMER CAN'T BREAK HIS ARMOR.
I HAVE TO THINK...
HOW AM I GONNA BEAT HIM?
Beep
Beep
?
THAT SOUND...
Beep
Beep
Beep
Beep
Beep
THE ALARM DAN SET!

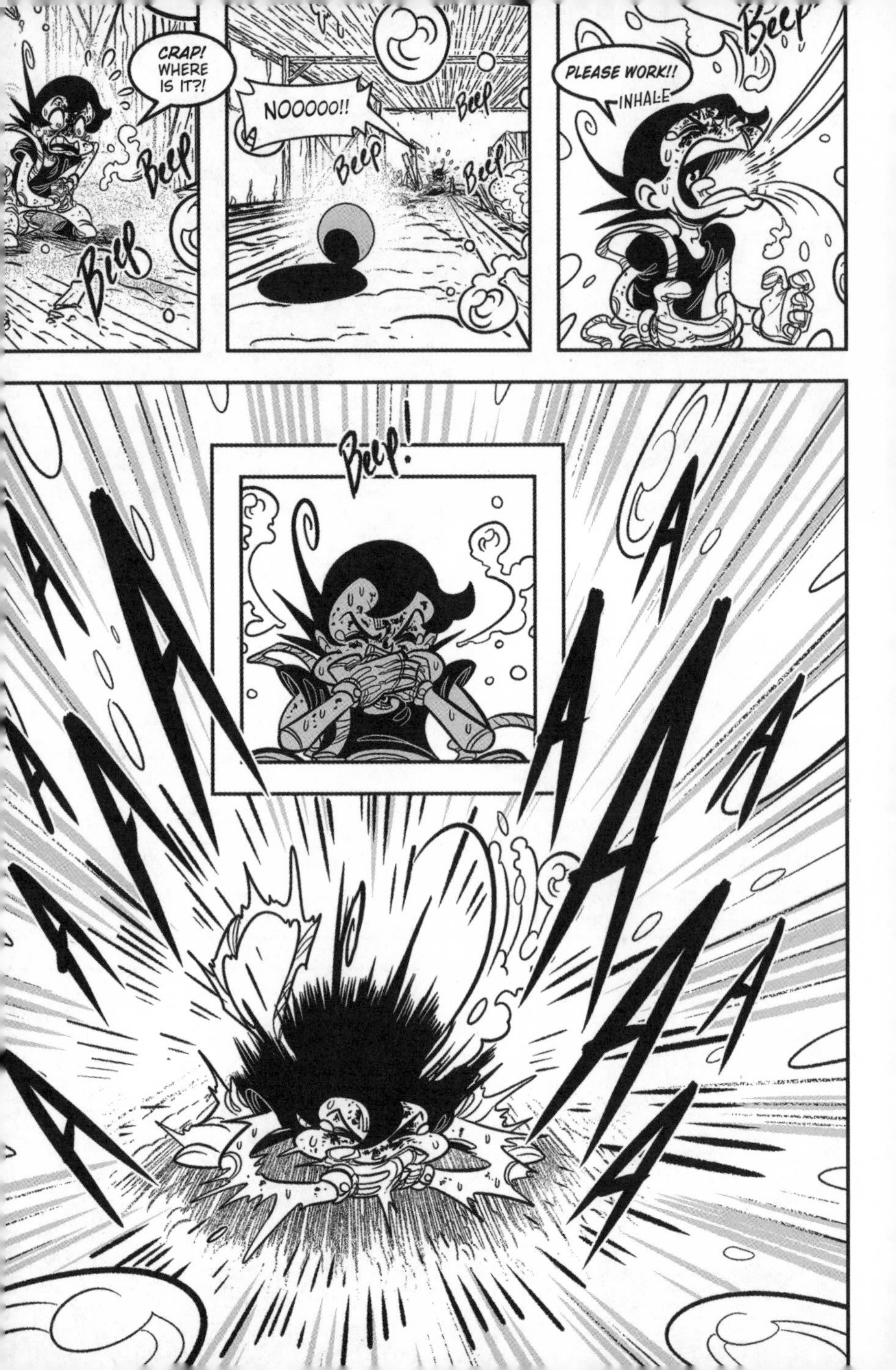
CRAP! WHERE IS IT?!
Beep
Beep
NOOOOO!!
Beep
Beep
Beep
PLEASE WORK!!
INHALE
Beep
Beep!
AAAAAAAAAAAAAAAA

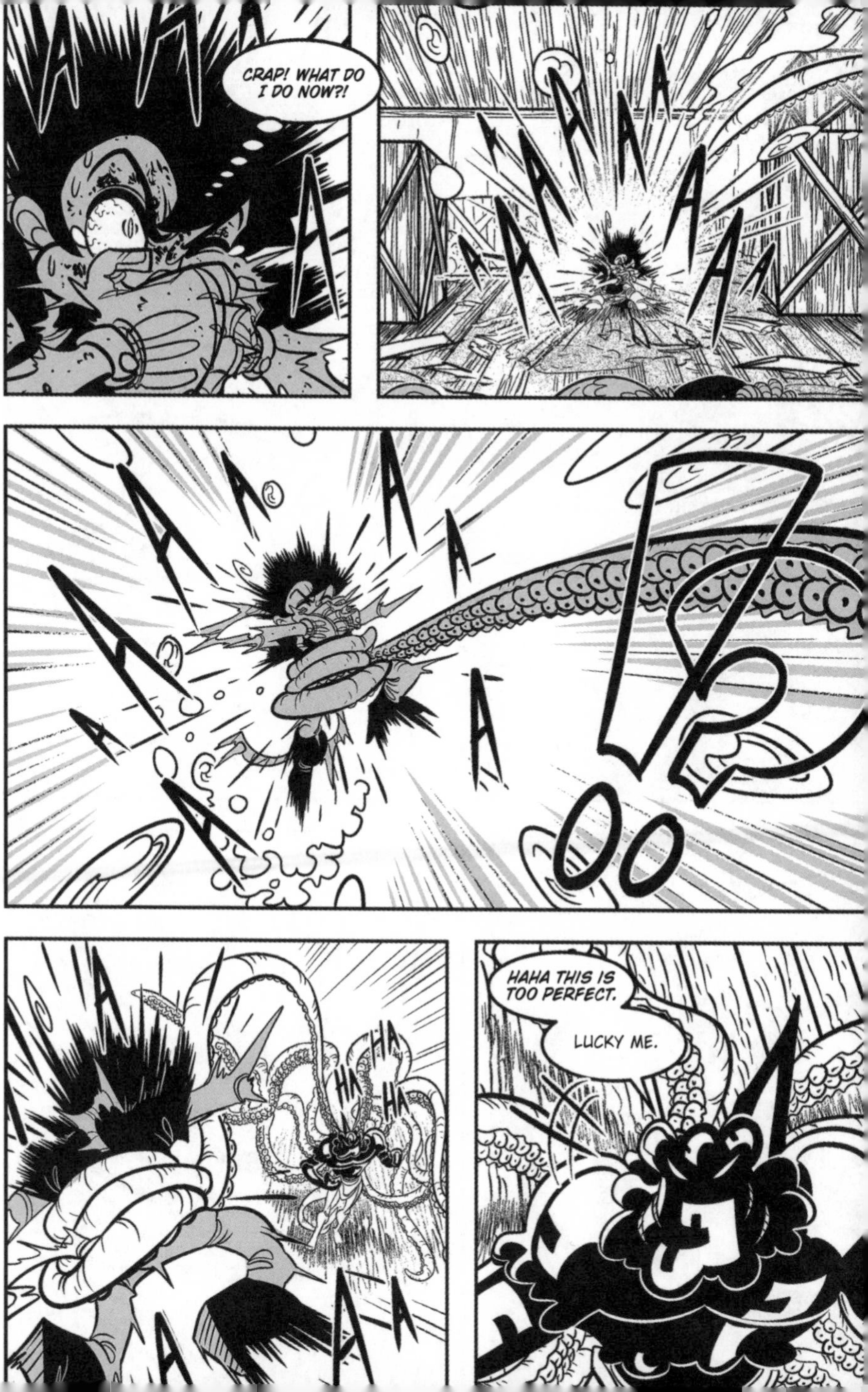
CRAP! WHAT DO I DO NOW?!
HA HA HA HA
HAHA THIS IS TOO PERFECT.
LUCKY ME.

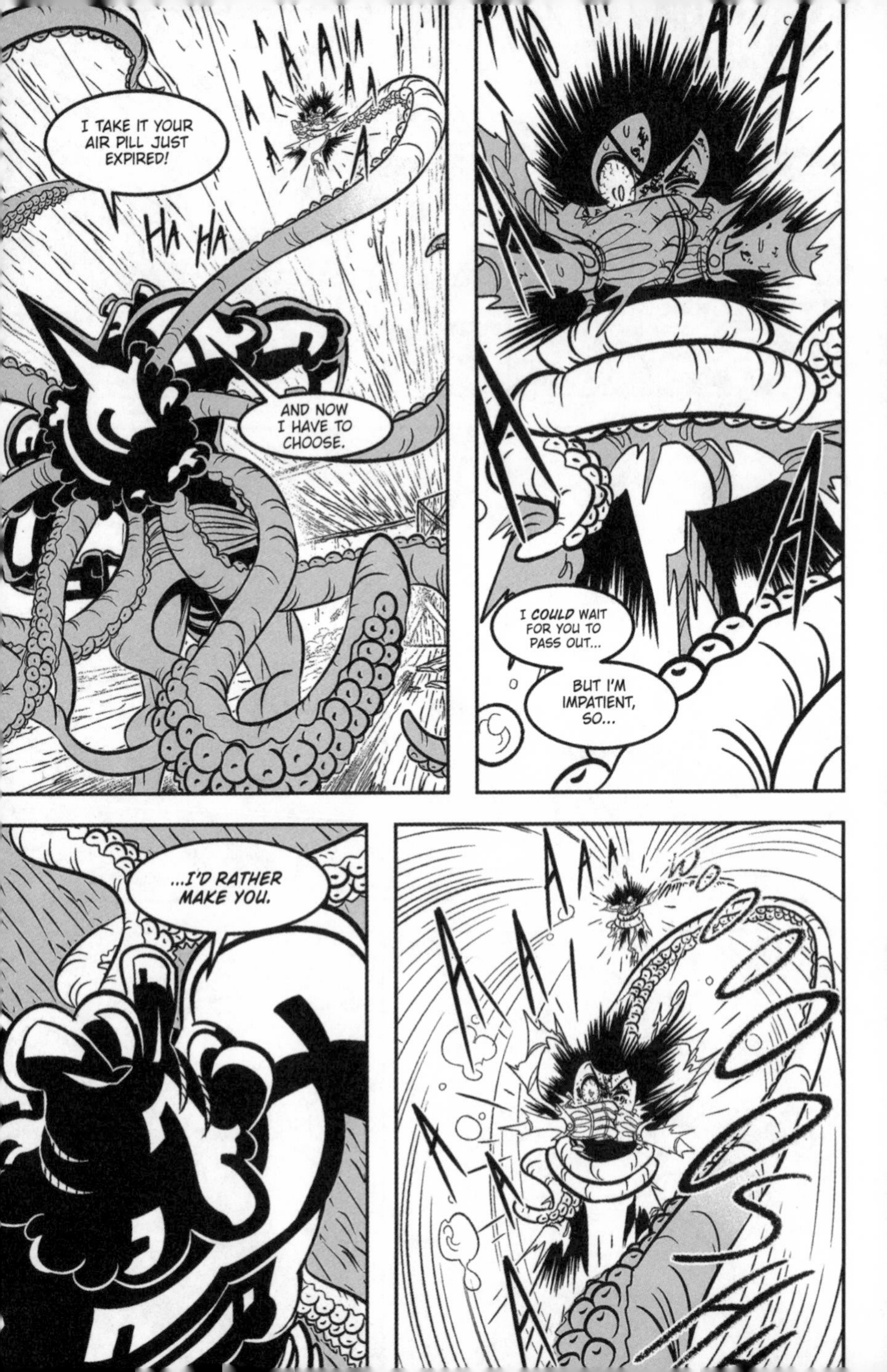
I TAKE IT YOUR AIR PILL JUST EXPIRED!
HA HA
AND NOW I HAVE TO CHOOSE.
I *COULD* WAIT FOR YOU TO PASS OUT...
BUT I'M IMPATIENT, SO...
...I'D RATHER MAKE YOU.

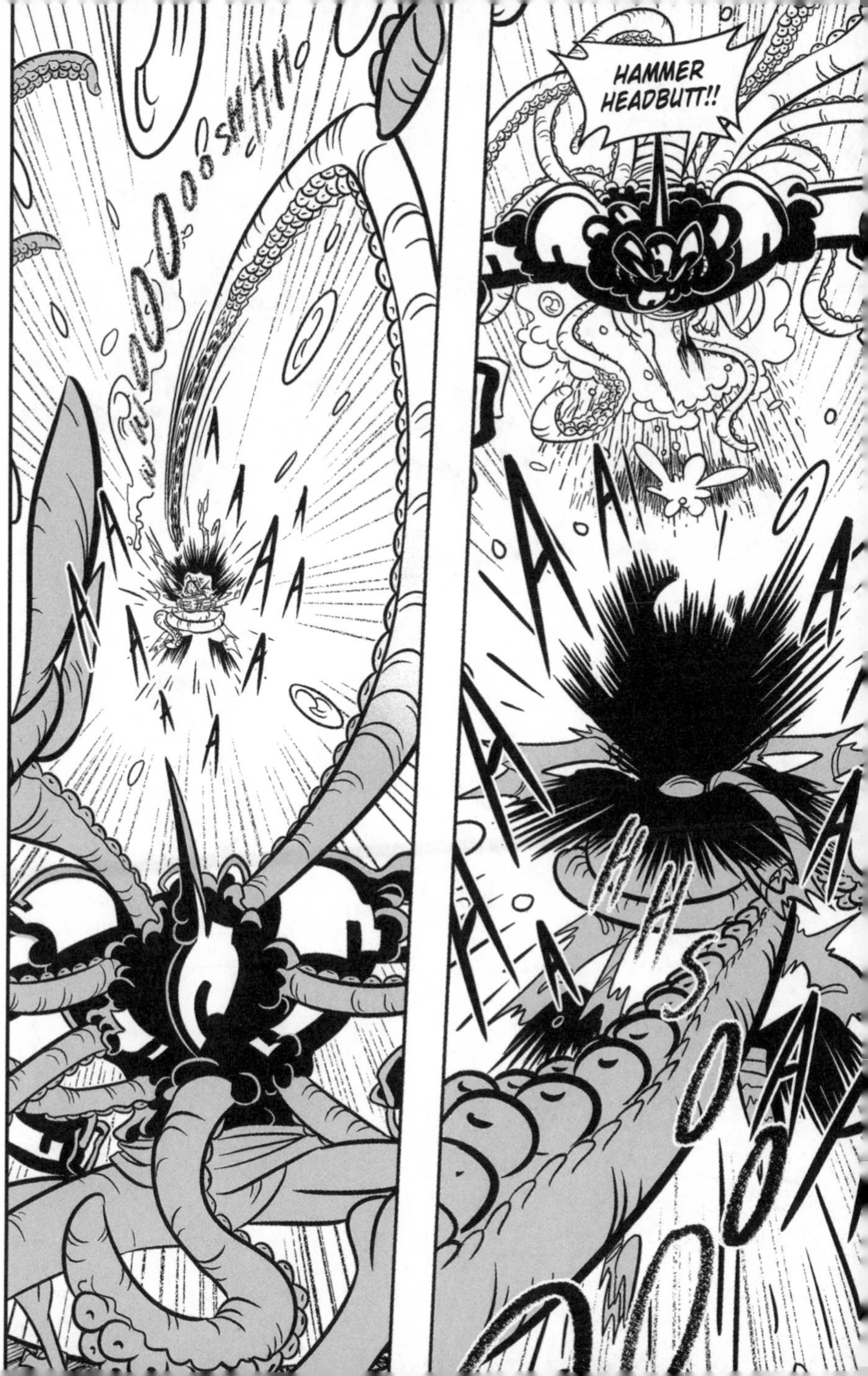
HAMMER HEADBUTT!!

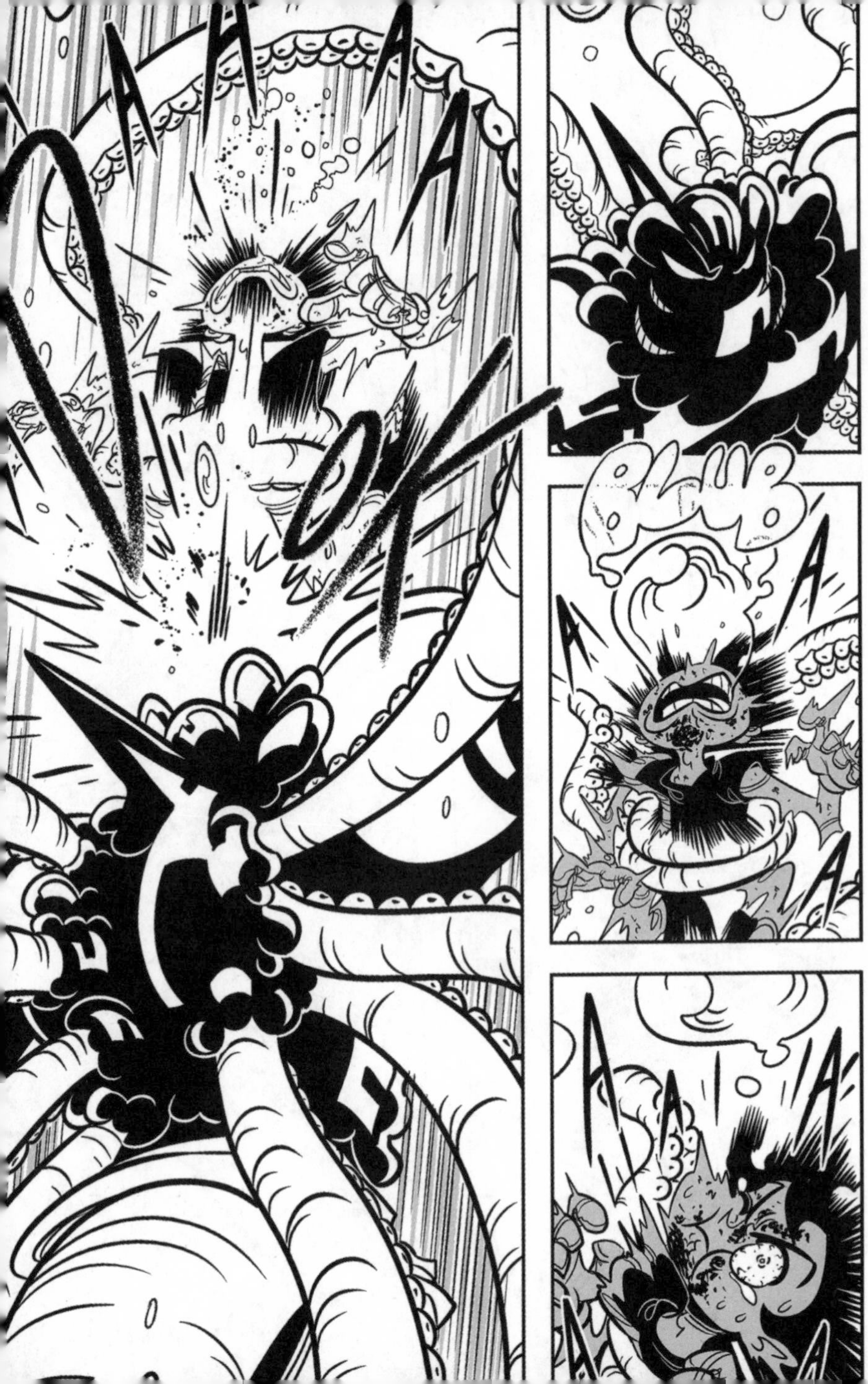

AAAAAA
DOK
GLUB

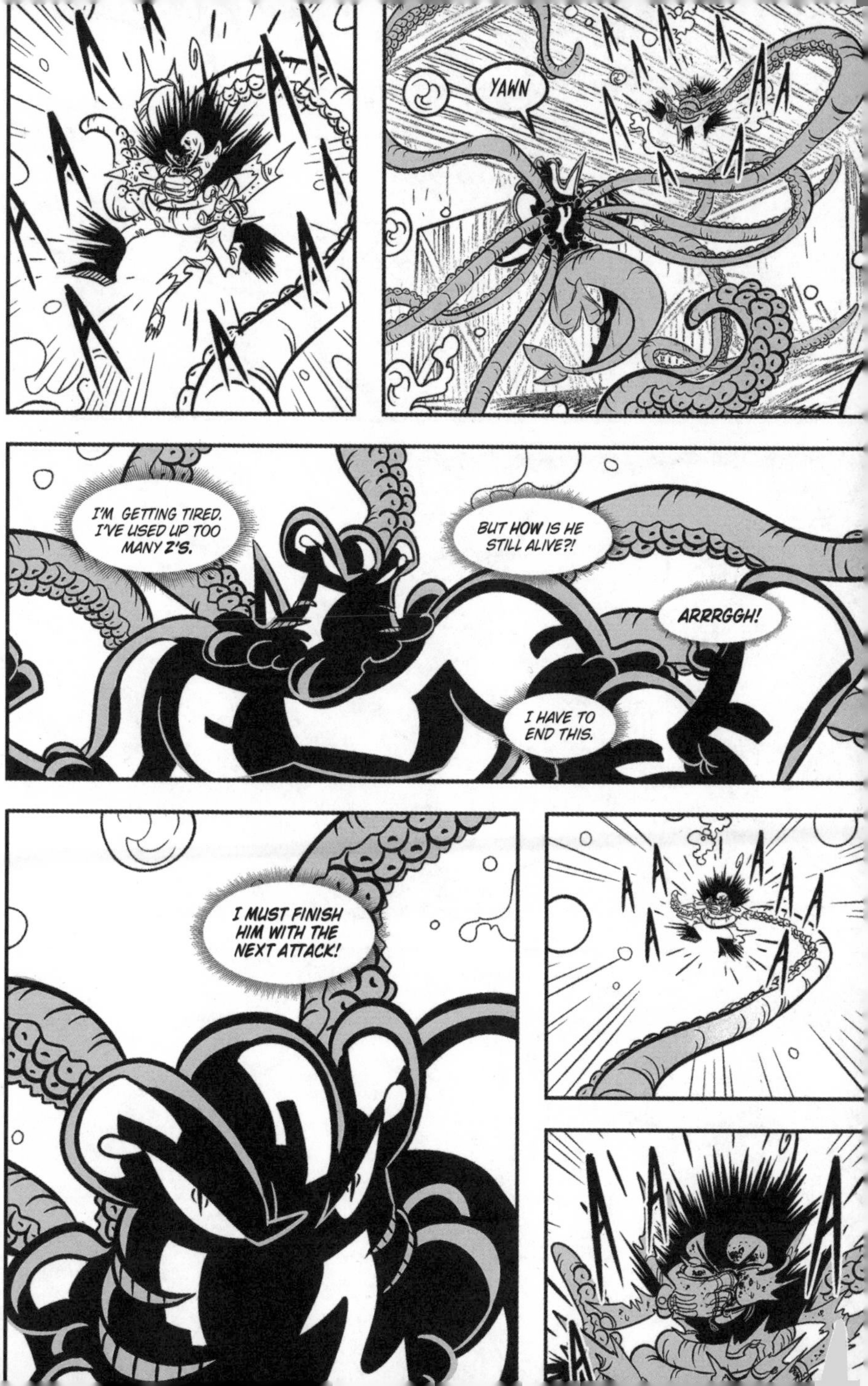
YAWN
I'M GETTING TIRED. I'VE USED UP TOO MANY Z'S.
BUT HOW IS HE STILL ALIVE?!
ARRRGGH!
I HAVE TO END THIS.
I MUST FINISH HIM WITH THE NEXT ATTACK!

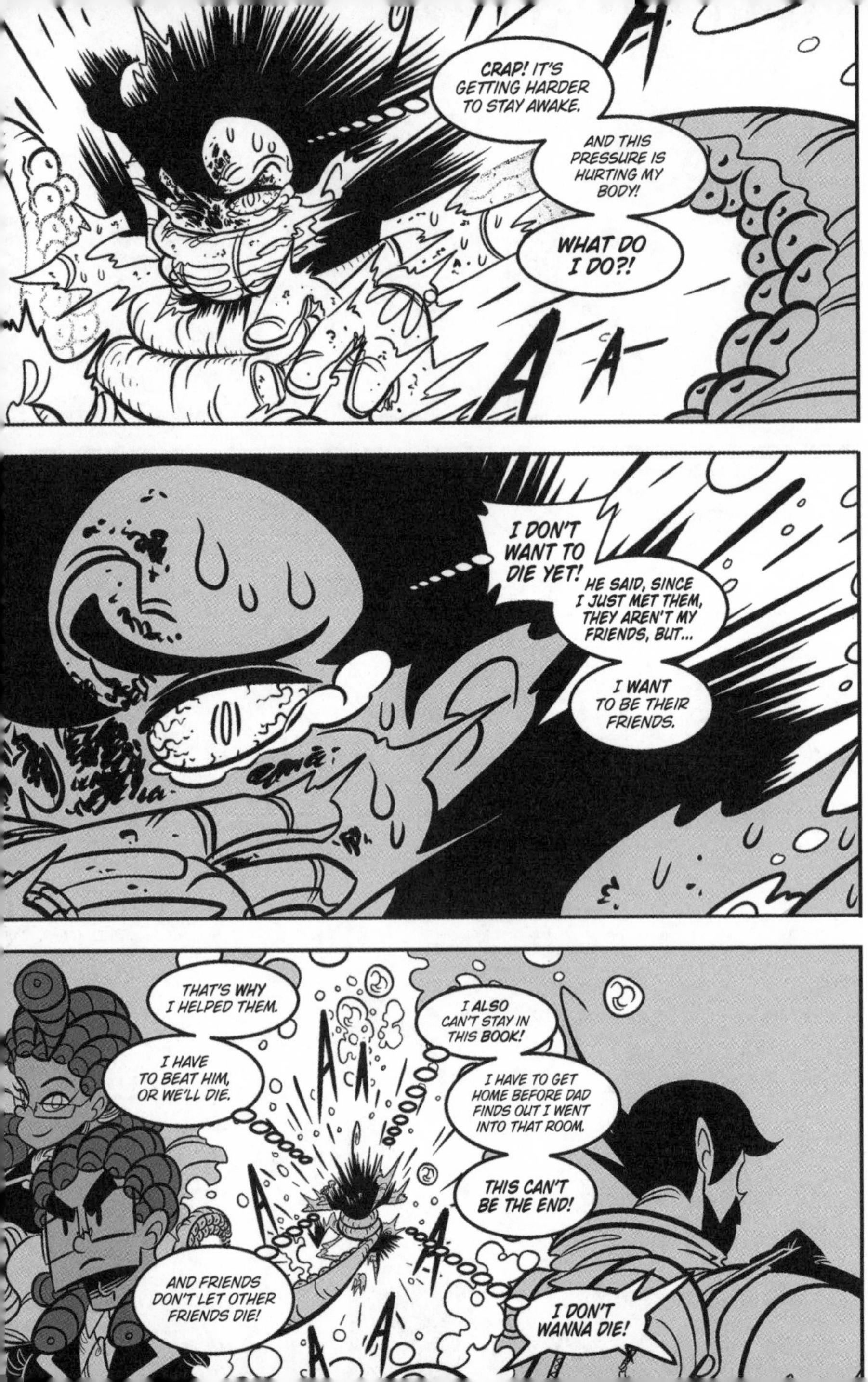
CRAP! IT'S GETTING HARDER TO STAY AWAKE.
AND THIS PRESSURE IS HURTING MY BODY!
WHAT DO I DO?!
I DON'T WANT TO DIE YET!
HE SAID, SINCE I JUST MET THEM, THEY AREN'T MY FRIENDS, BUT...
I WANT TO BE THEIR FRIENDS.
THAT'S WHY I HELPED THEM.
I HAVE TO BEAT HIM, OR WE'LL DIE.
AND FRIENDS DON'T LET OTHER FRIENDS DIE!
I ALSO CAN'T STAY IN THIS BOOK!
I HAVE TO GET HOME BEFORE DAD FINDS OUT I WENT INTO THAT ROOM.
THIS CAN'T BE THE END!
I DON'T WANNA DIE!

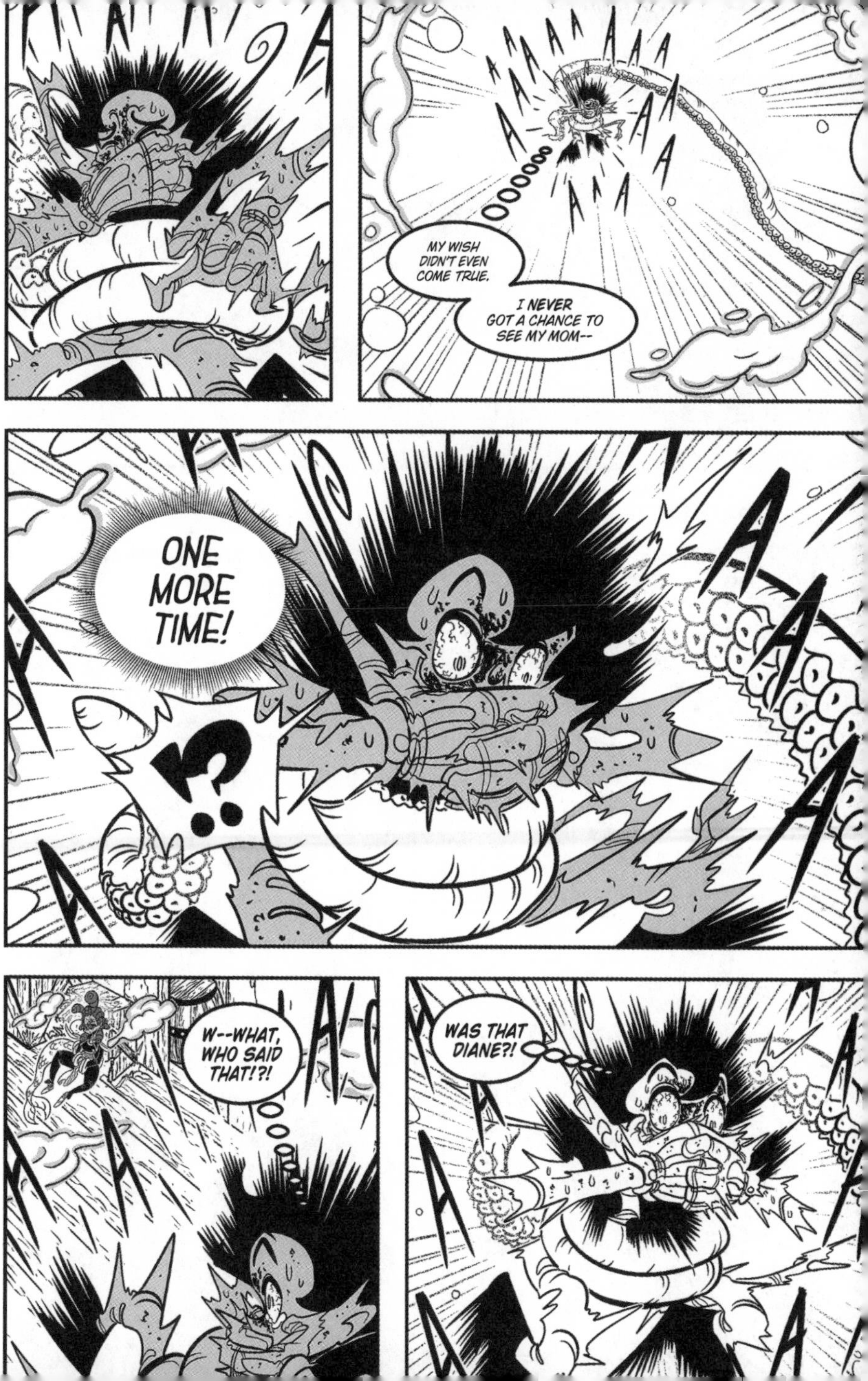
MY WISH DIDN'T EVEN COME TRUE.
I NEVER GOT A CHANCE TO SEE MY MOM--
ONE MORE TIME!
!?
W--WHAT, WHO SAID THAT!?!
WAS THAT DIANE?!

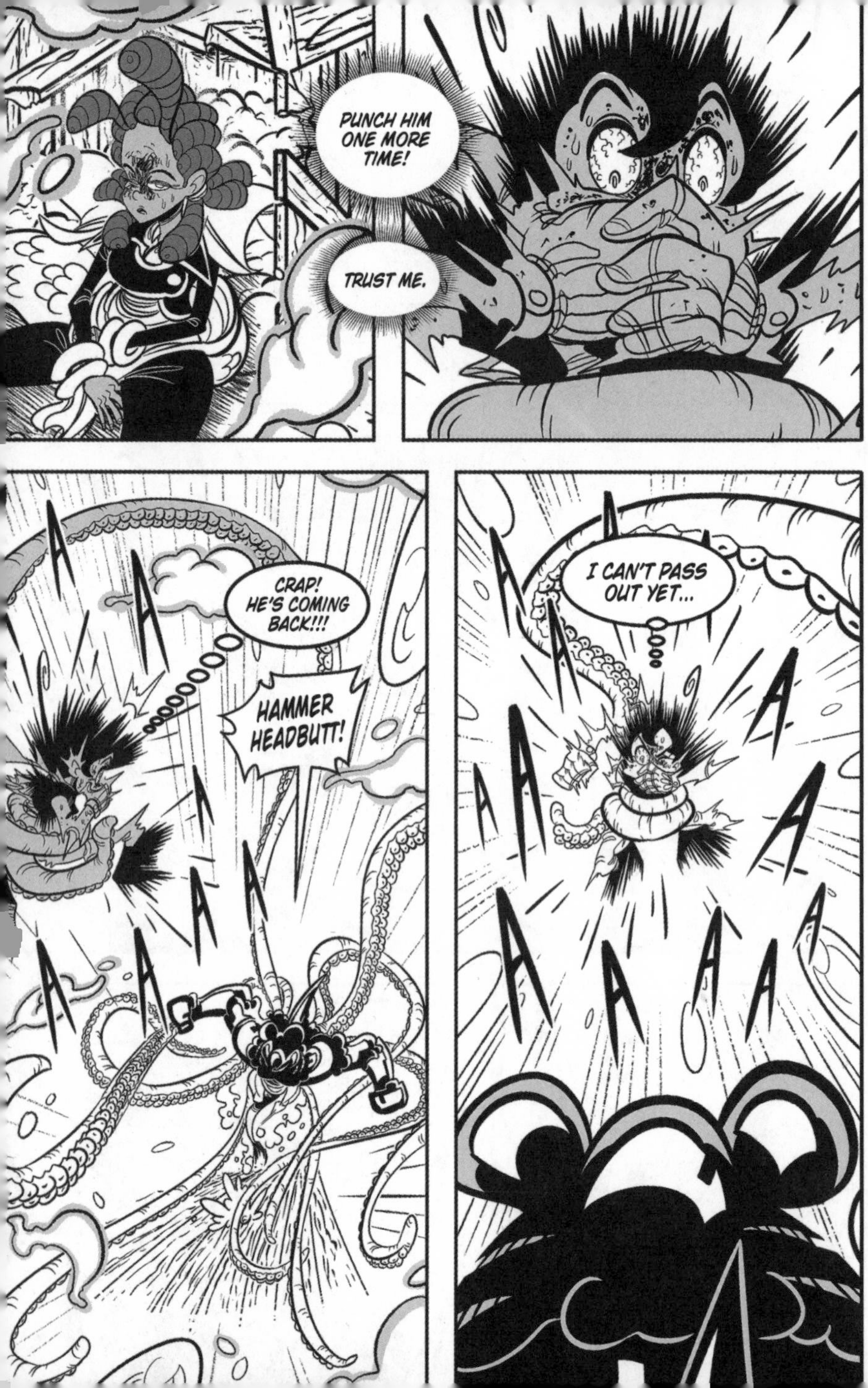
PUNCH HIM ONE MORE TIME!
TRUST ME.
CRAP! HE'S COMING BACK!!!
HAMMER HEADBUTT!
I CAN'T PASS OUT YET...

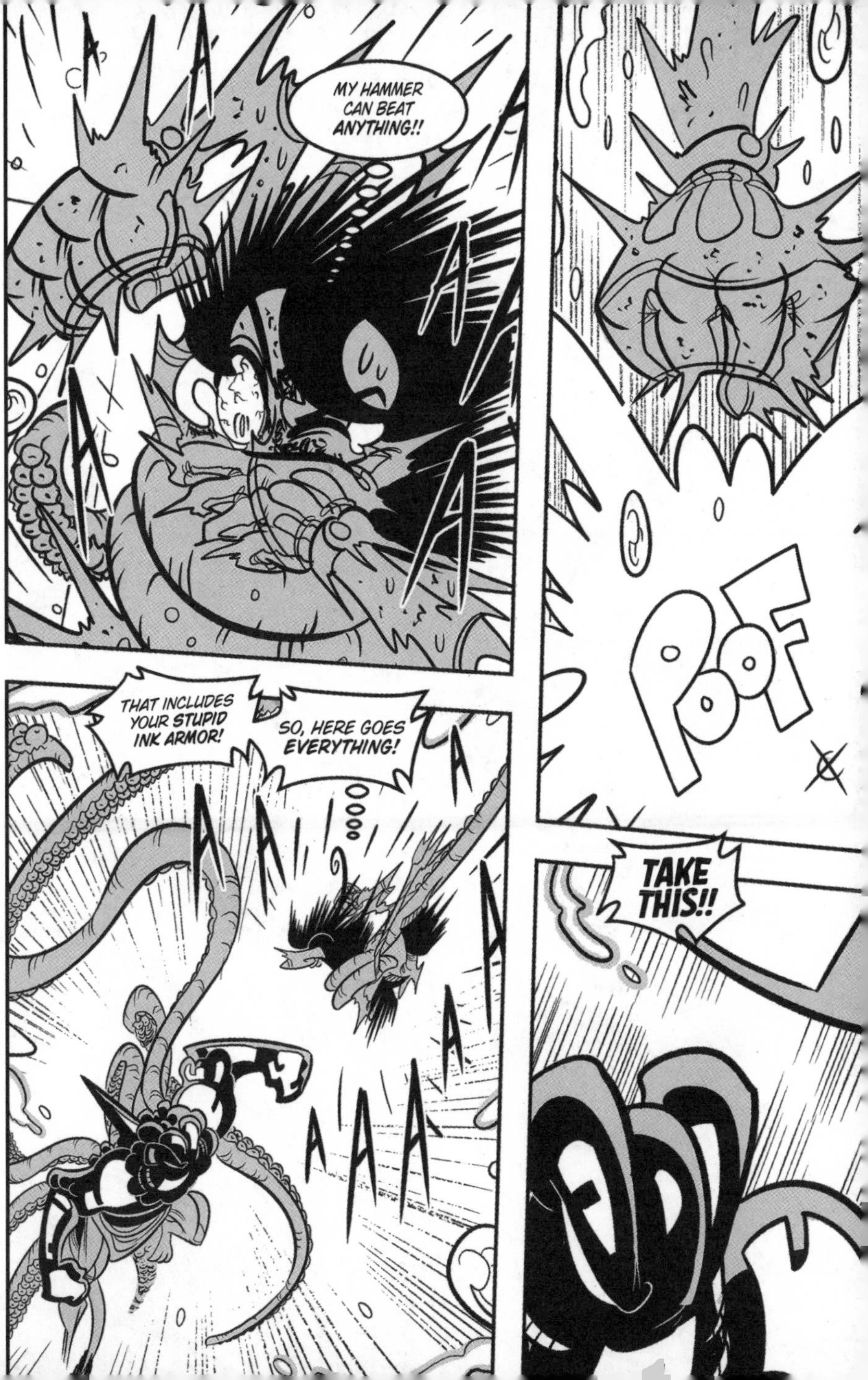
MY HAMMER CAN BEAT ANYTHING!!
POOF
THAT INCLUDES YOUR STUPID INK ARMOR!
SO, HERE GOES EVERYTHING!
TAKE THIS!!

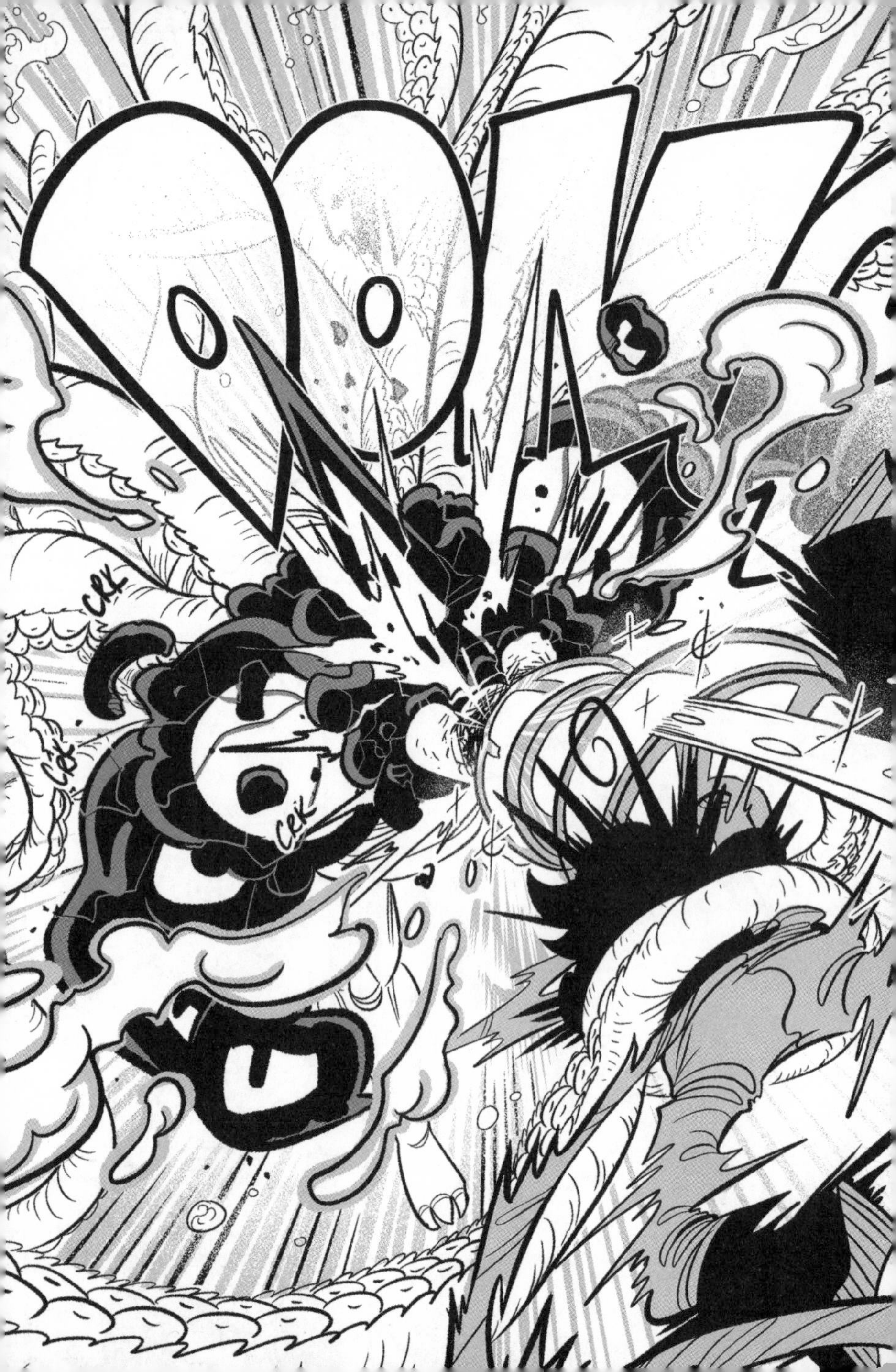
CRK
CRK
CRK

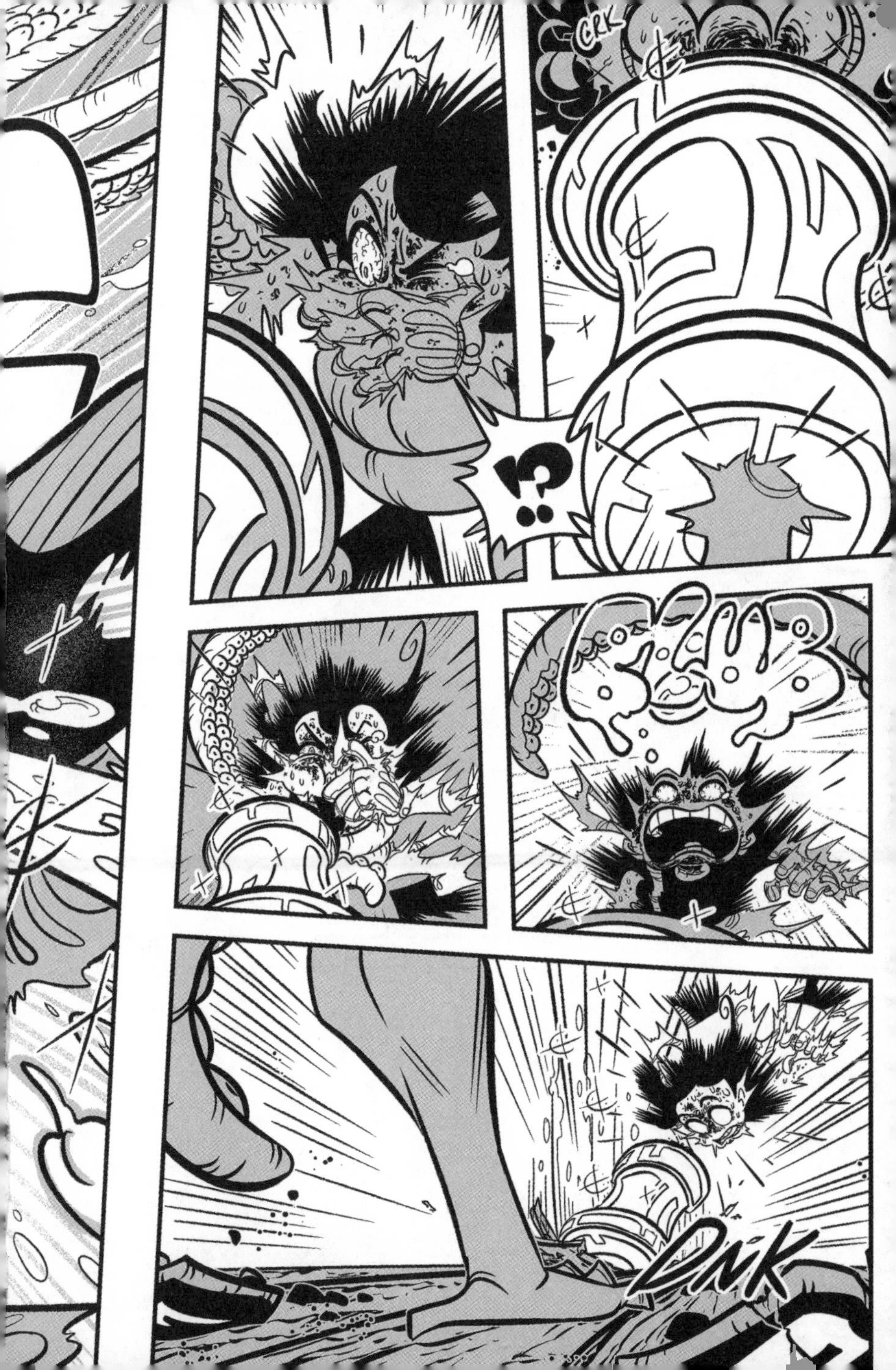

CRK
!?
DINK

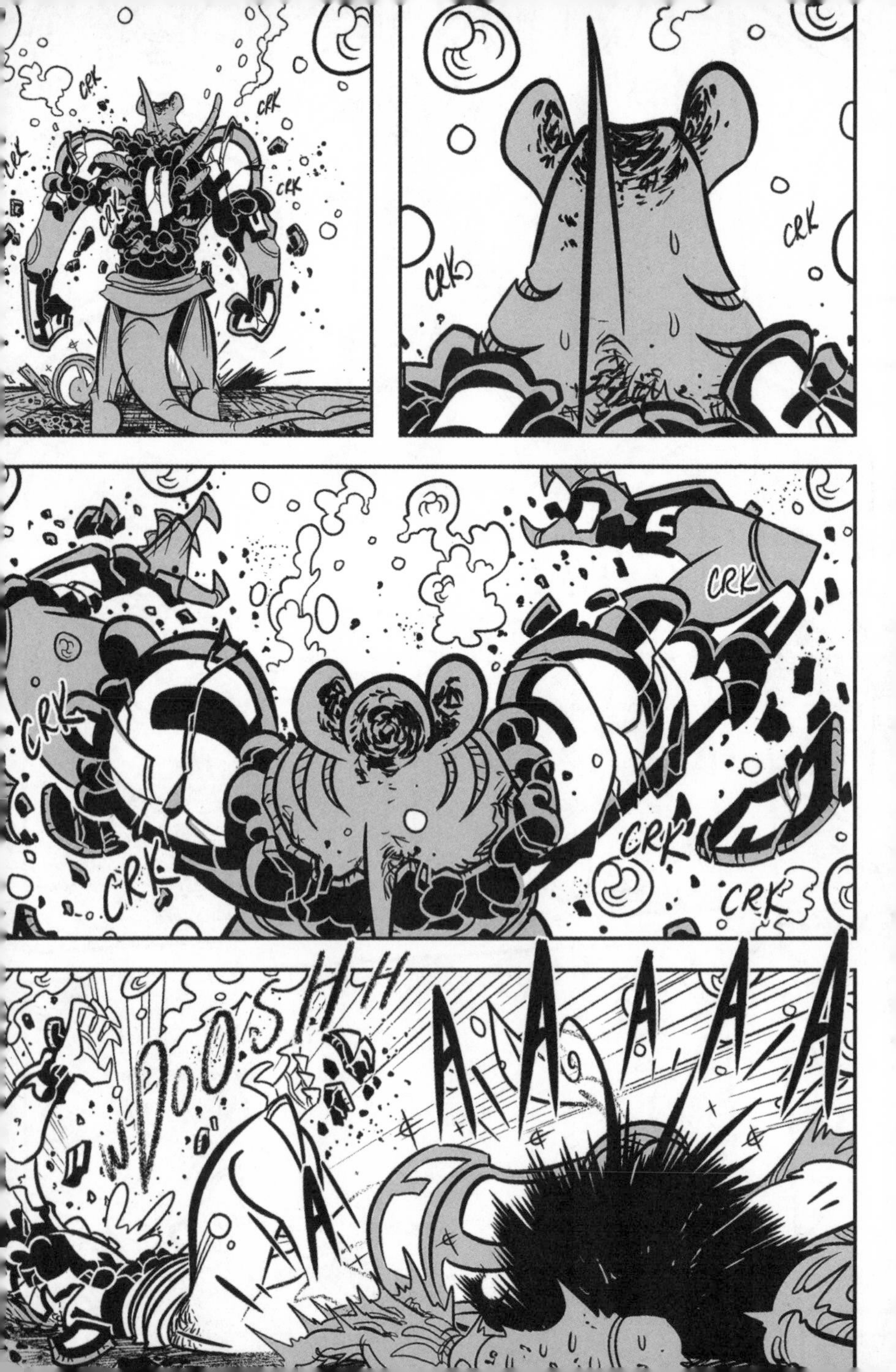
CRK
CRK
CRK
CRK
CRK
CRK
CRK
CRK
CRK
CRK
CRK
CRK
CRK
WHOOOSHHH
AAAAAA

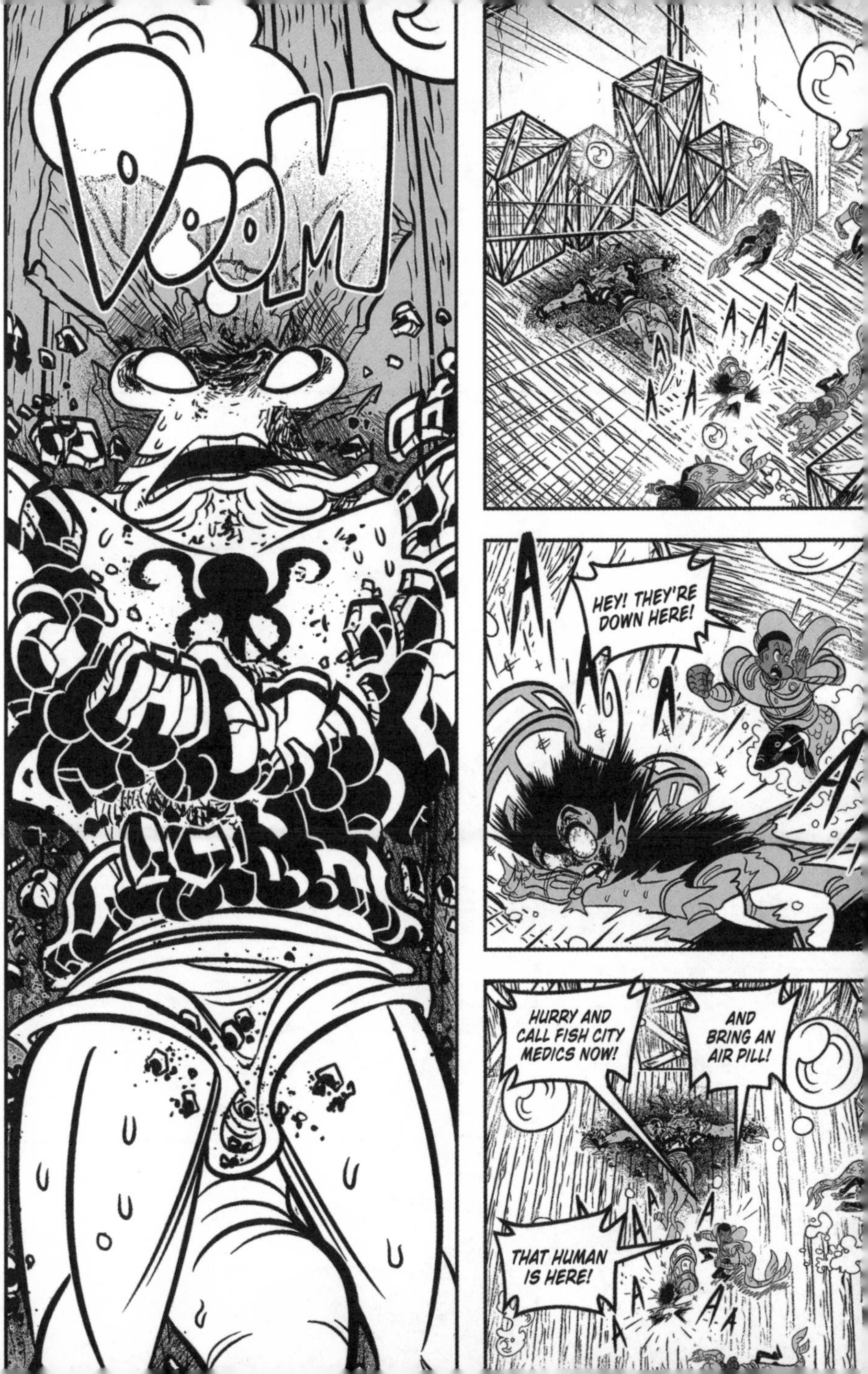
DOOM
HEY! THEY'RE DOWN HERE!
HURRY AND CALL FISH CITY MEDICS NOW!
AND BRING AN AIR PILL!
THAT HUMAN IS HERE!

HAMMER

CHAPTER 13: KINGDOM MAPS

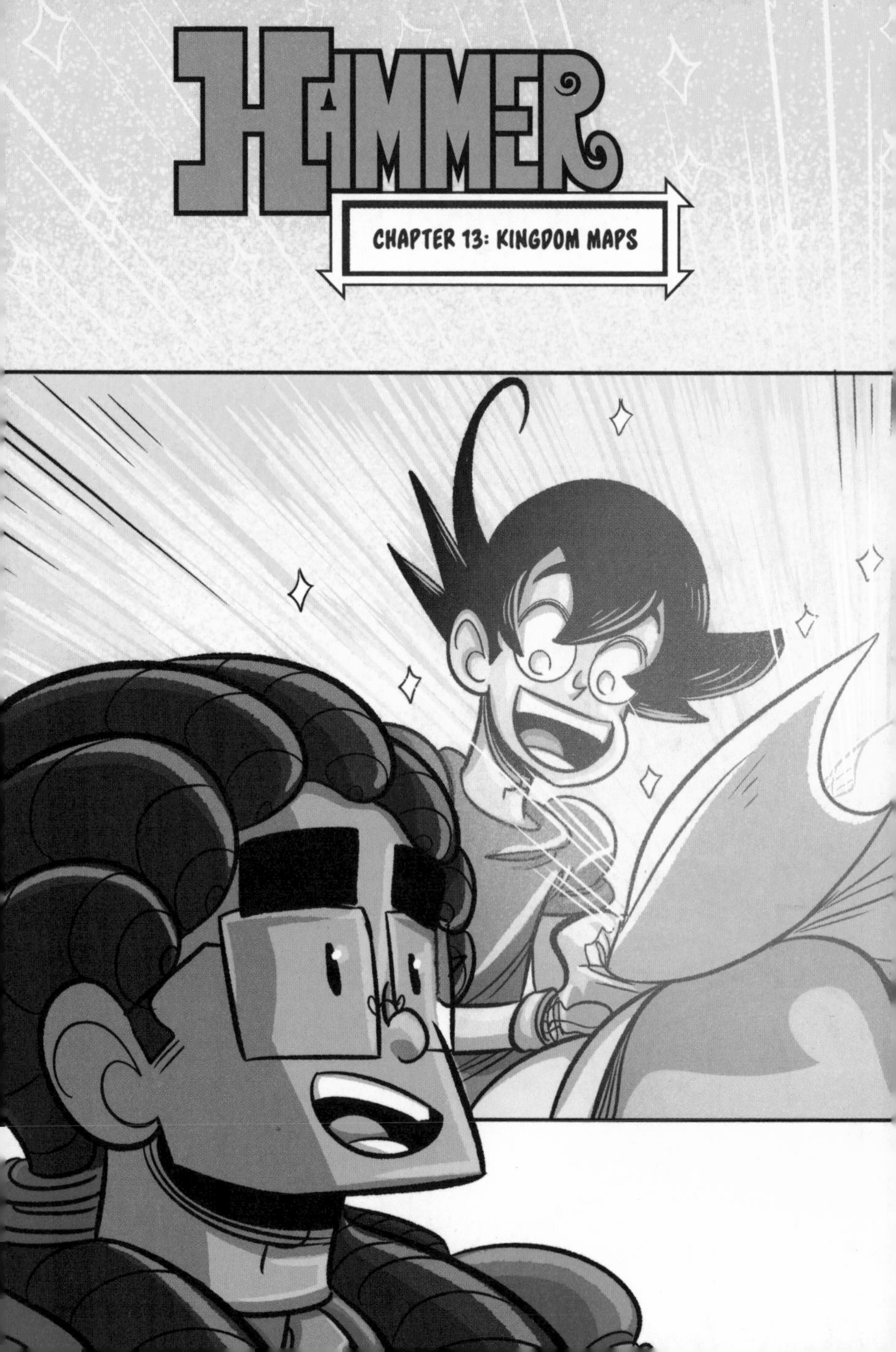

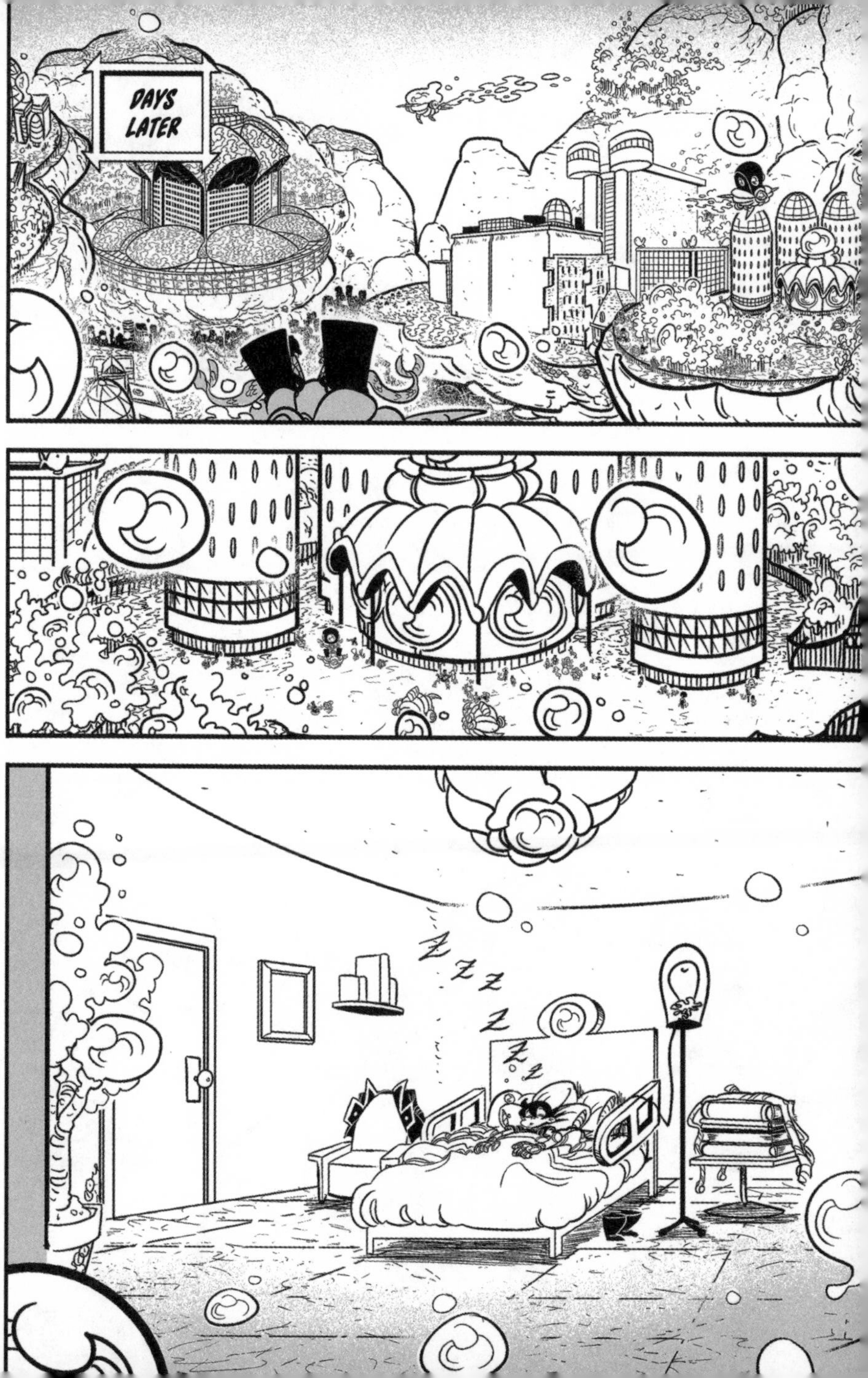
DAYS LATER
Z Z Z
Z
Z z

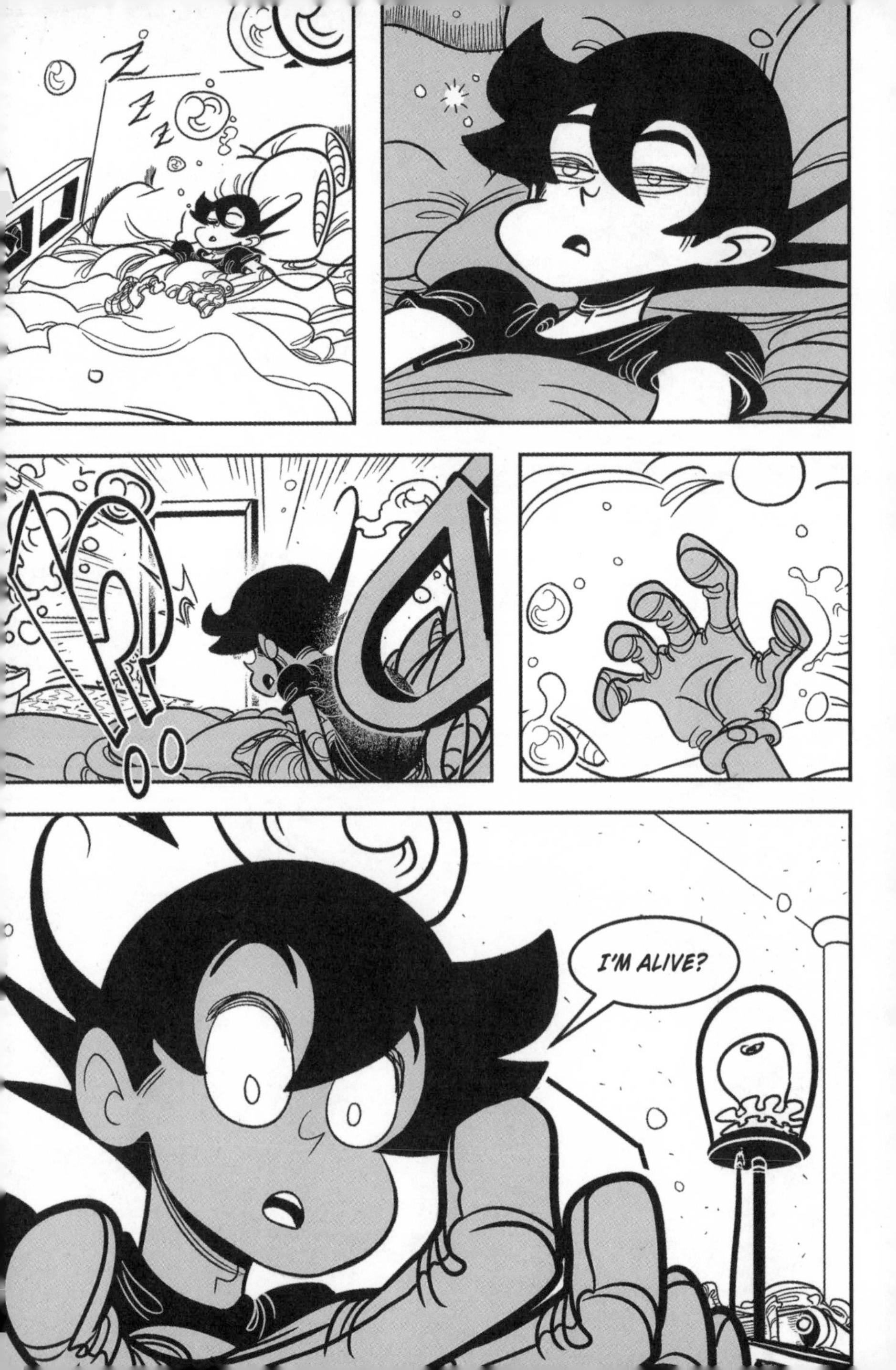
I'M ALIVE?

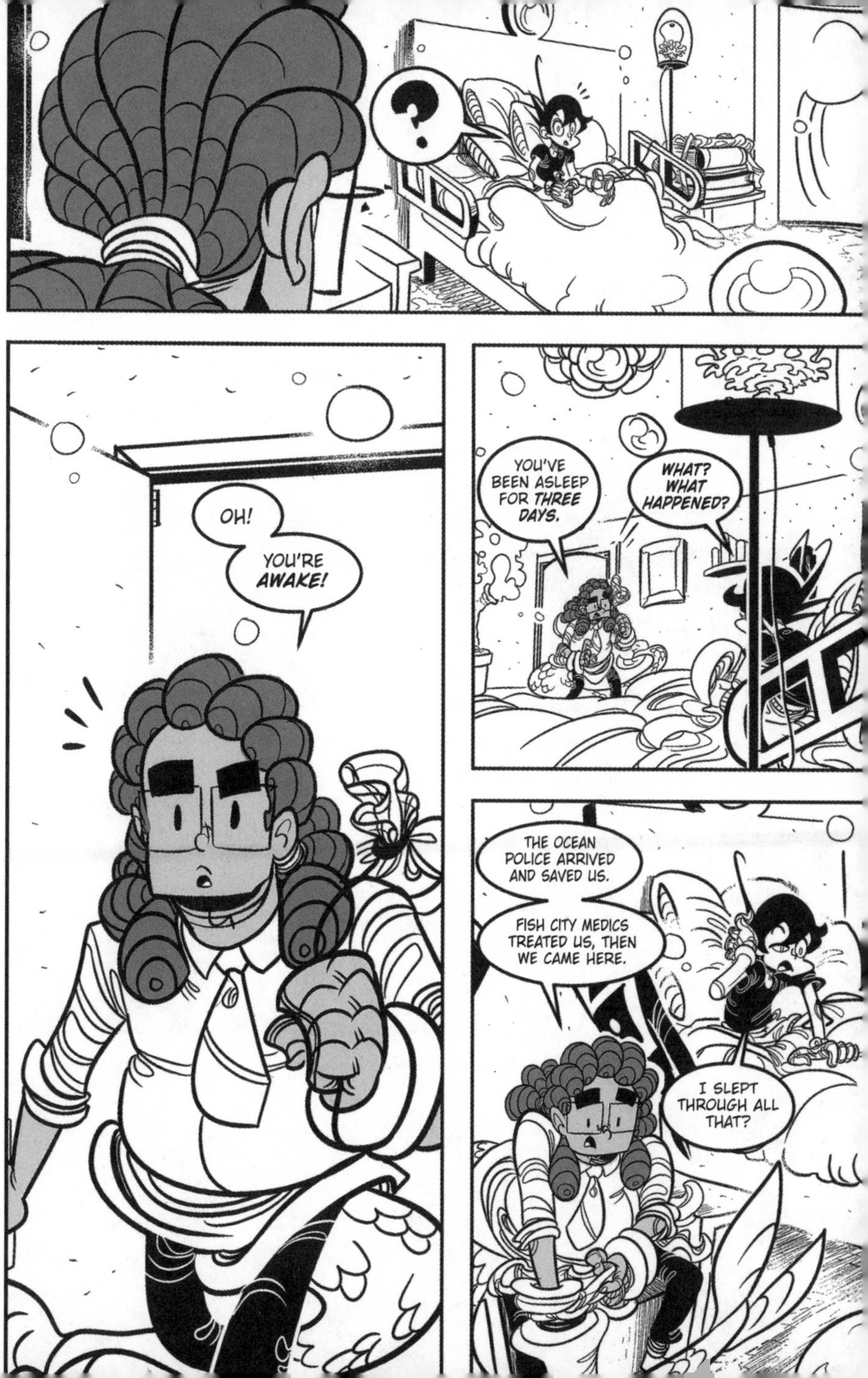
?
OH!
YOU'RE AWAKE!
YOU'VE BEEN ASLEEP FOR THREE DAYS.
WHAT? WHAT HAPPENED?
THE OCEAN POLICE ARRIVED AND SAVED US.
FISH CITY MEDICS TREATED US, THEN WE CAME HERE.
I SLEPT THROUGH ALL THAT?

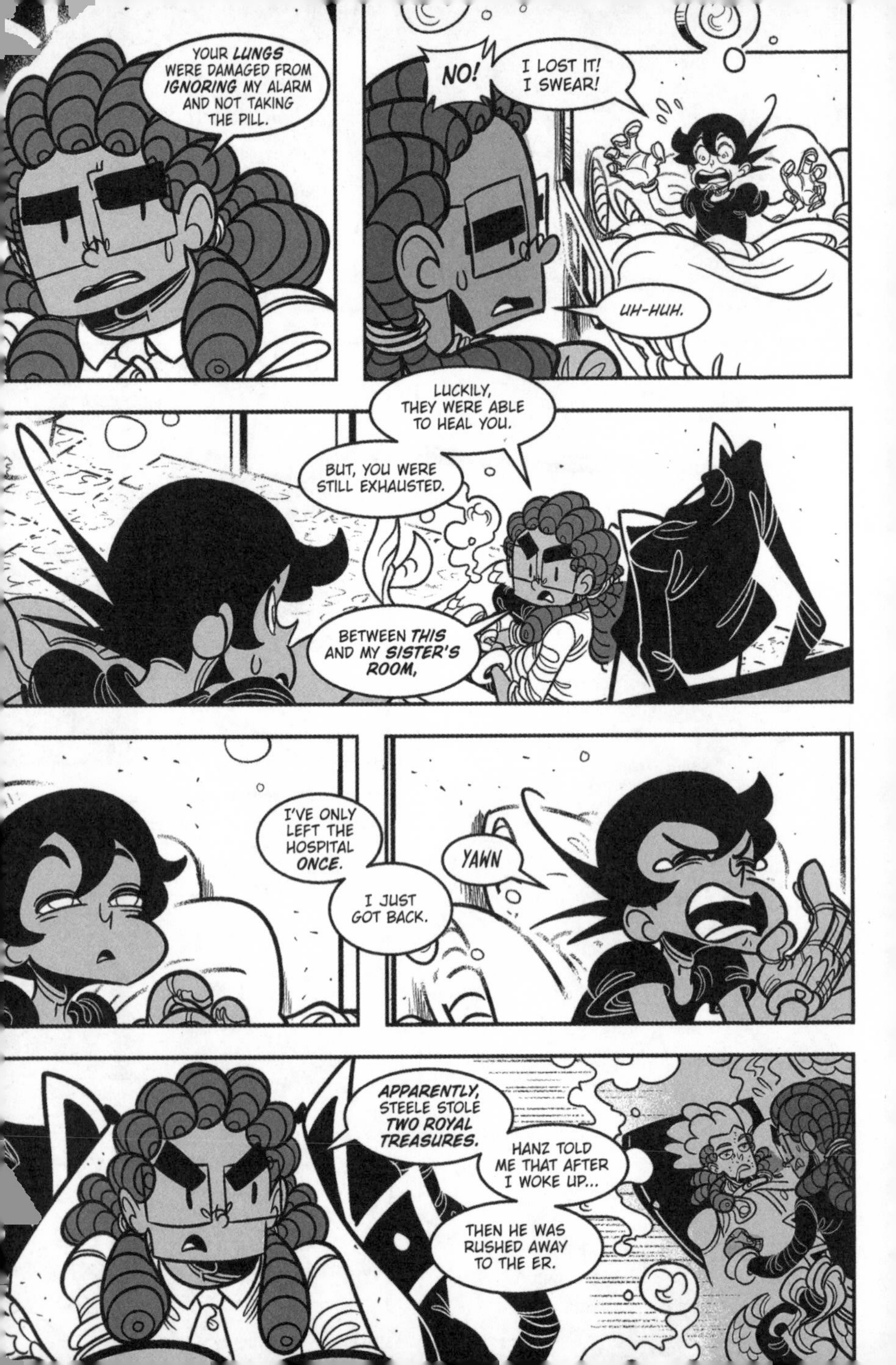
YOUR LUNGS WERE DAMAGED FROM IGNORING MY ALARM AND NOT TAKING THE PILL.
NO!
I LOST IT! I SWEAR!
UH-HUH.
LUCKILY, THEY WERE ABLE TO HEAL YOU.
BUT, YOU WERE STILL EXHAUSTED.
BETWEEN THIS AND MY SISTER'S ROOM,
I'VE ONLY LEFT THE HOSPITAL ONCE.
I JUST GOT BACK.
YAWN
APPARENTLY, STEELE STOLE TWO ROYAL TREASURES.
HANZ TOLD ME THAT AFTER I WOKE UP...
THEN HE WAS RUSHED AWAY TO THE ER.

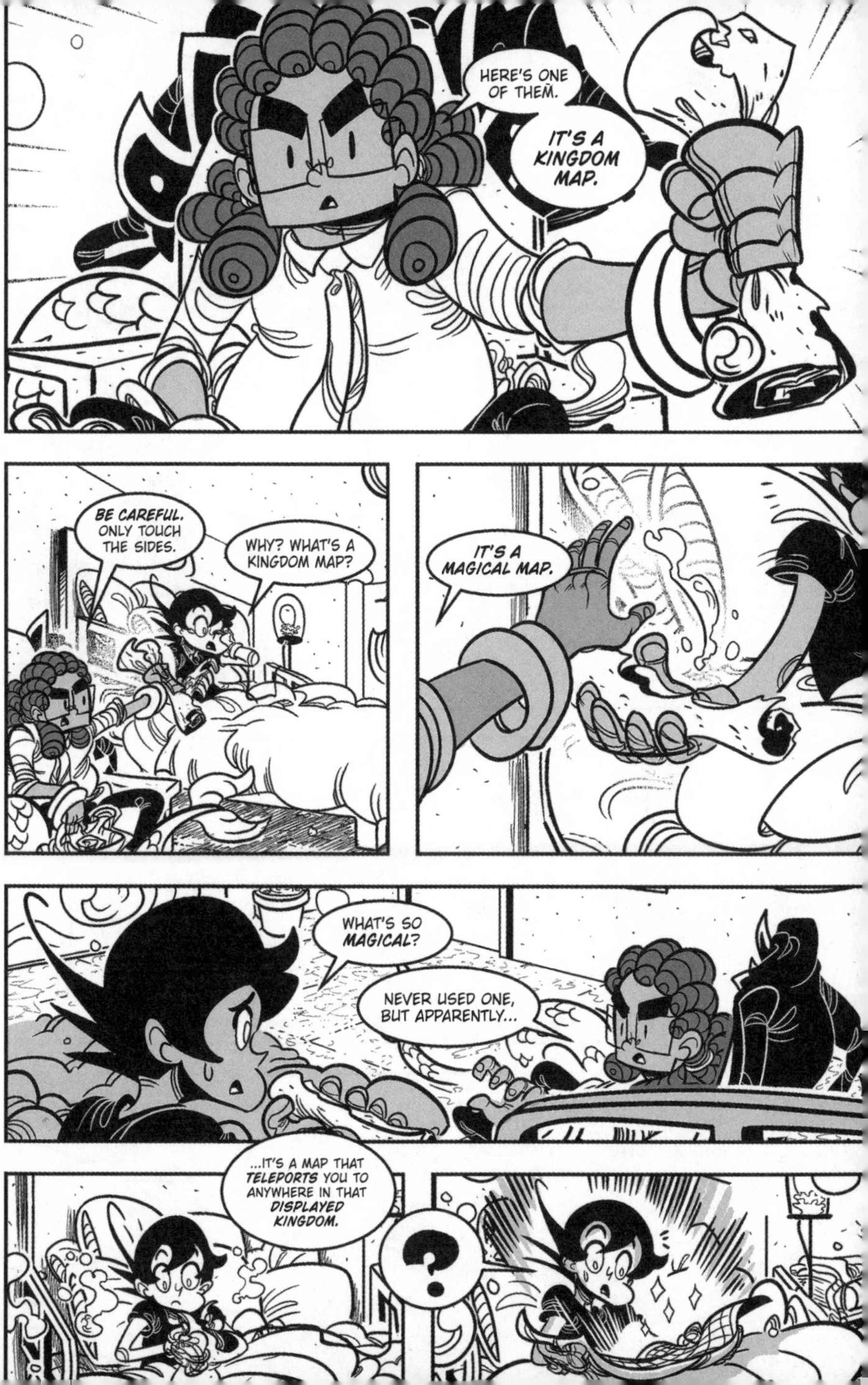
HERE'S ONE OF THEM.
IT'S A KINGDOM MAP.
BE CAREFUL. ONLY TOUCH THE SIDES.
WHY? WHAT'S A KINGDOM MAP?
IT'S A MAGICAL MAP.
WHAT'S SO MAGICAL?
NEVER USED ONE, BUT APPARENTLY...
...IT'S A MAP THAT TELEPORTS YOU TO ANYWHERE IN THAT DISPLAYED KINGDOM.
?

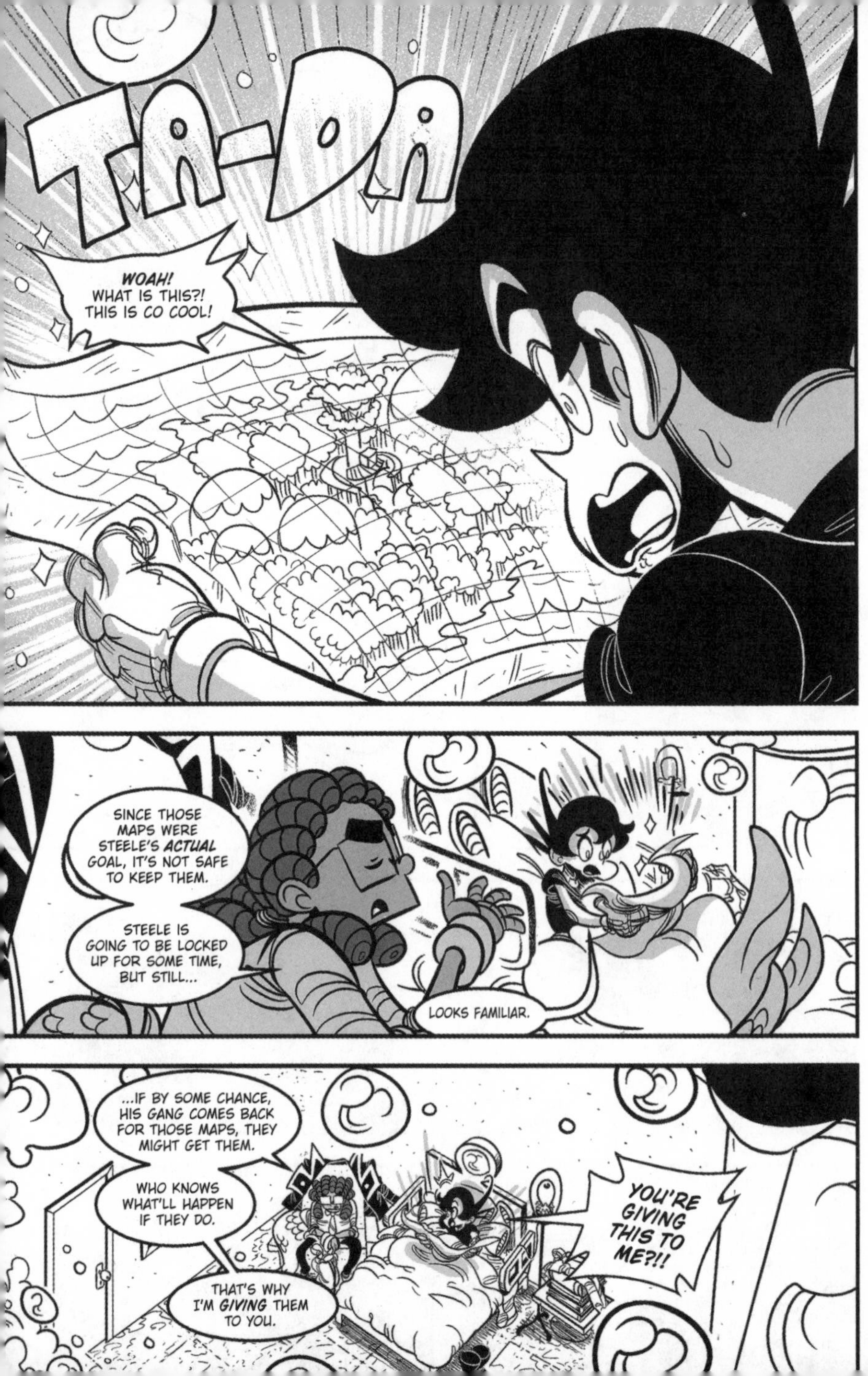
TA-DA
WOAH! WHAT IS THIS?! THIS IS CO COOL!
SINCE THOSE MAPS WERE STEELE'S ACTUAL GOAL, IT'S NOT SAFE TO KEEP THEM.
STEELE IS GOING TO BE LOCKED UP FOR SOME TIME, BUT STILL...
LOOKS FAMILIAR.
...IF BY SOME CHANCE, HIS GANG COMES BACK FOR THOSE MAPS, THEY MIGHT GET THEM.
WHO KNOWS WHAT'LL HAPPEN IF THEY DO.
THAT'S WHY I'M GIVING THEM TO YOU.
YOU'RE GIVING THIS TO ME?!!

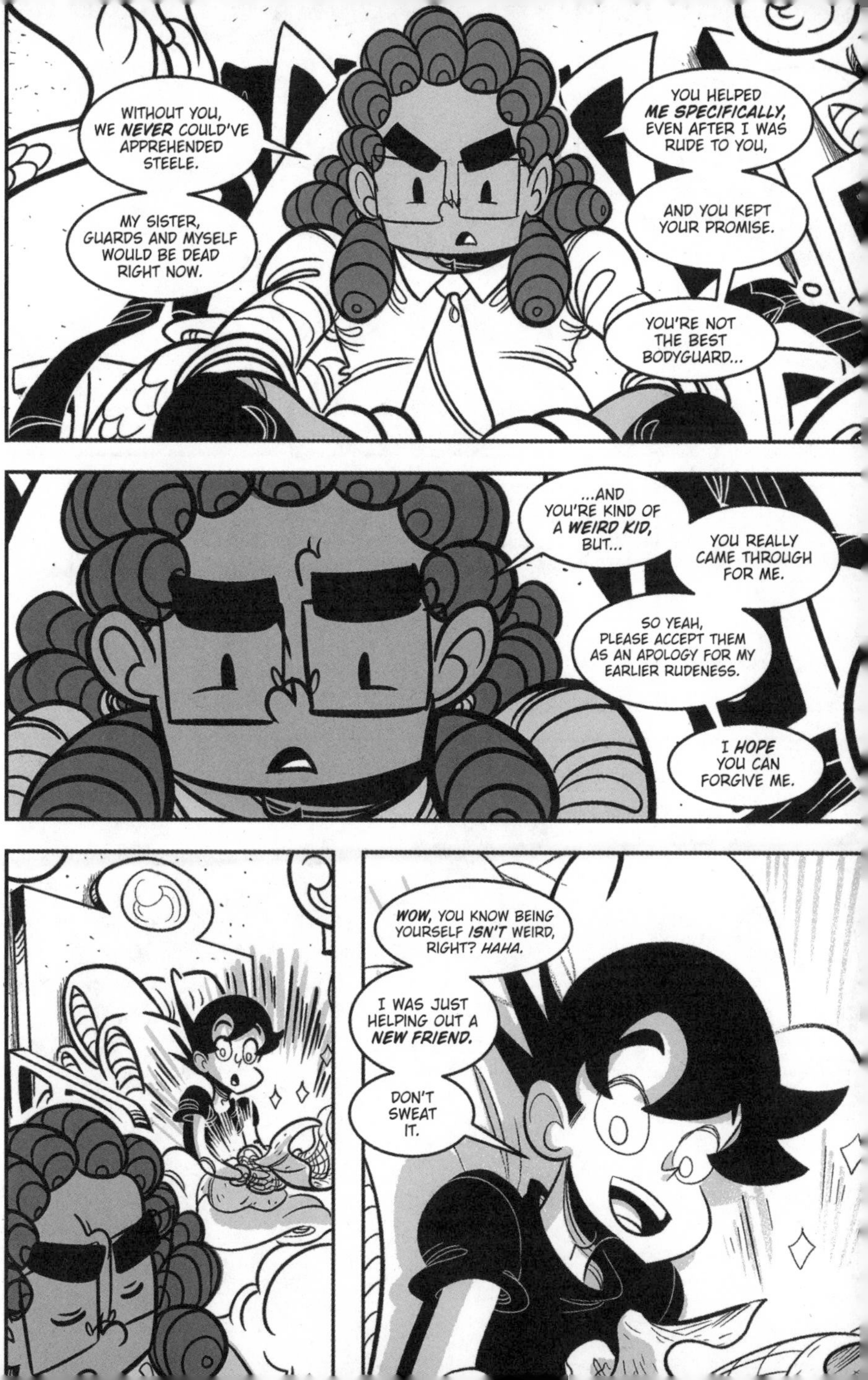
WITHOUT YOU, WE **NEVER** COULD'VE APPREHENDED STEELE.
MY SISTER, GUARDS AND MYSELF WOULD BE DEAD RIGHT NOW.
YOU HELPED **ME SPECIFICALLY,** EVEN AFTER I WAS RUDE TO YOU,
AND YOU KEPT YOUR PROMISE.
YOU'RE NOT THE BEST BODYGUARD...
...AND YOU'RE KIND OF A **WEIRD KID,** BUT...
YOU REALLY CAME THROUGH FOR ME.
SO YEAH, PLEASE ACCEPT THEM AS AN APOLOGY FOR MY EARLIER RUDENESS.
I **HOPE** YOU CAN FORGIVE ME.
WOW, YOU KNOW BEING YOURSELF **ISN'T** WEIRD, RIGHT? **HAHA.**
I WAS JUST HELPING OUT A **NEW FRIEND.**
DON'T SWEAT IT.

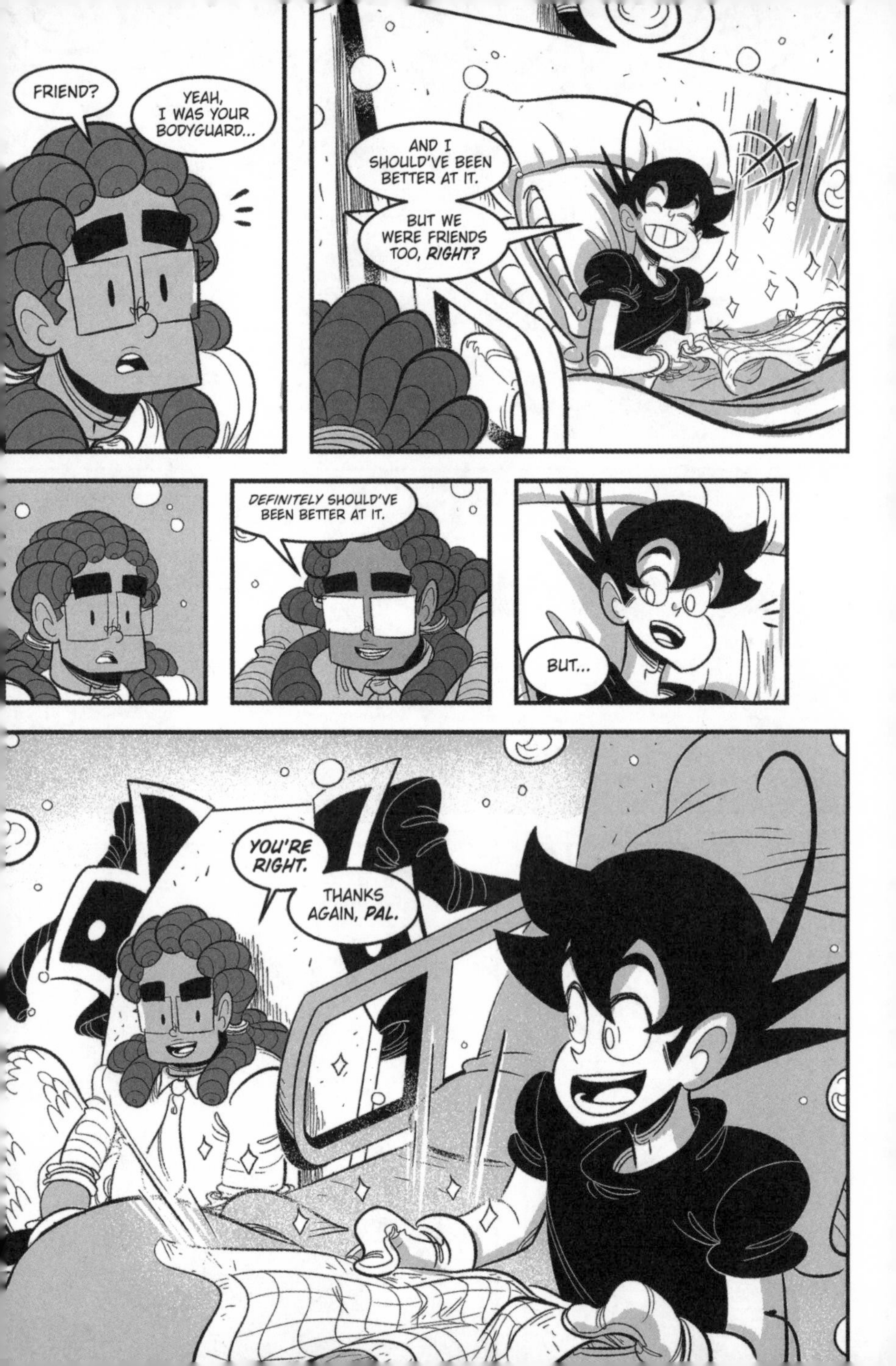
FRIEND?
YEAH, I WAS YOUR BODYGUARD...
AND I SHOULD'VE BEEN BETTER AT IT.
BUT WE WERE FRIENDS TOO, *RIGHT?*
DEFINITELY SHOULD'VE BEEN BETTER AT IT.
BUT...
YOU'RE RIGHT.
THANKS AGAIN, *PAL.*

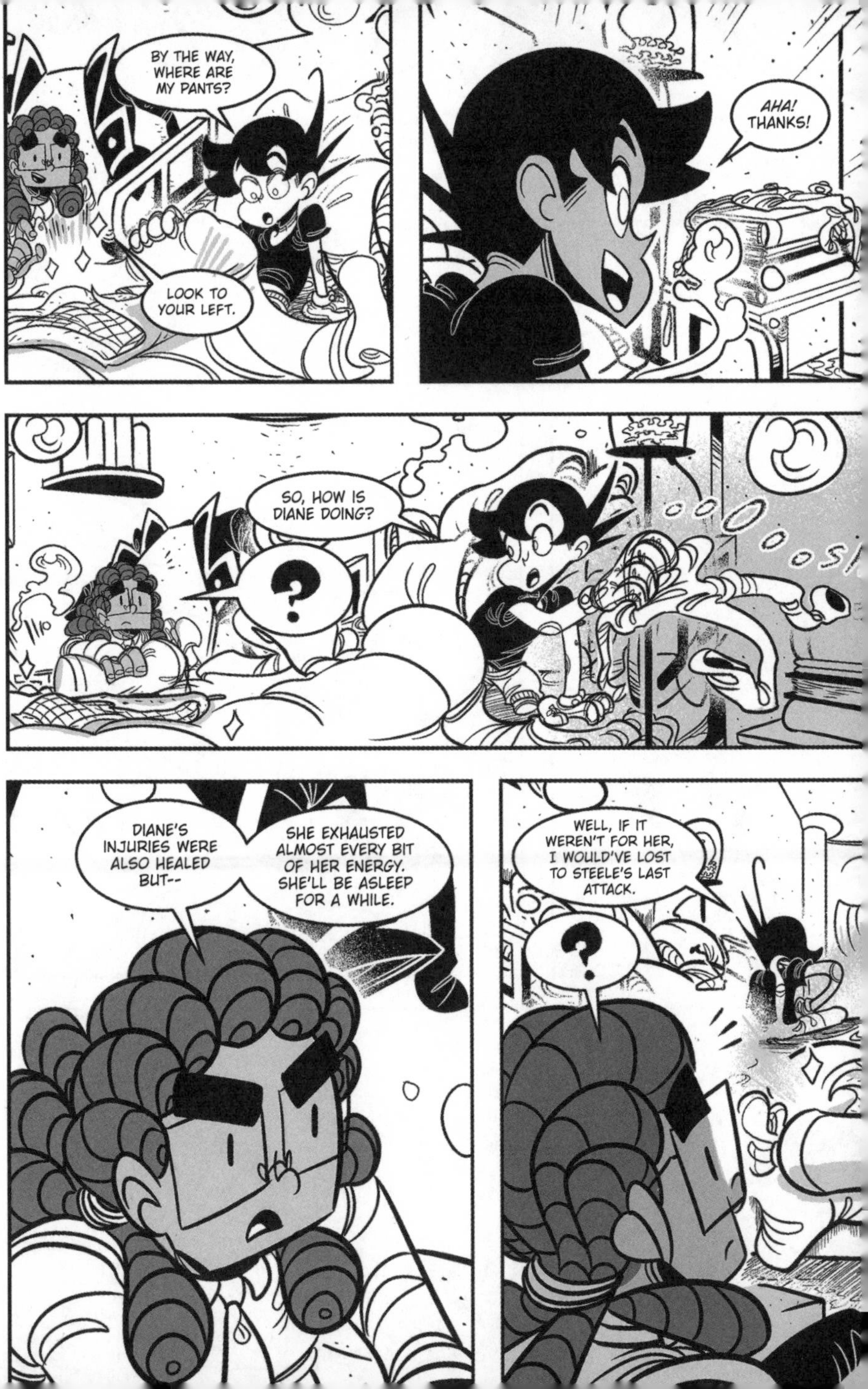
BY THE WAY, WHERE ARE MY PANTS?
LOOK TO YOUR LEFT.
AHA! THANKS!
SO, HOW IS DIANE DOING?
?
OOOOOOSH
DIANE'S INJURIES WERE ALSO HEALED BUT--
SHE EXHAUSTED ALMOST EVERY BIT OF HER ENERGY. SHE'LL BE ASLEEP FOR A WHILE.
WELL, IF IT WEREN'T FOR HER, I WOULD'VE LOST TO STEELE'S LAST ATTACK.
?

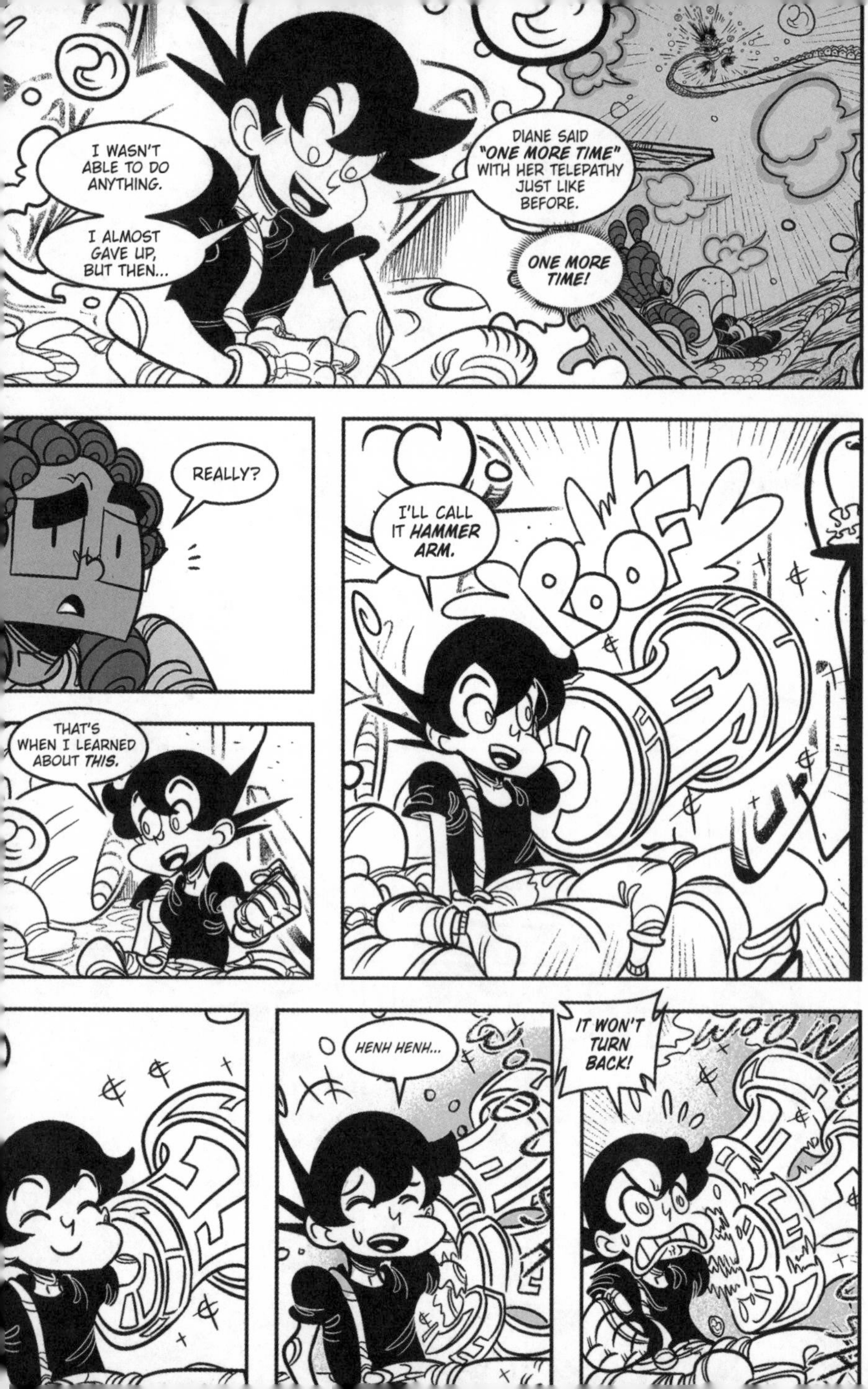
I WASN'T ABLE TO DO ANYTHING.
I ALMOST GAVE UP, BUT THEN...
DIANE SAID "ONE MORE TIME" WITH HER TELEPATHY JUST LIKE BEFORE.
ONE MORE TIME!
REALLY?
THAT'S WHEN I LEARNED ABOUT THIS.
I'LL CALL IT HAMMER ARM.
POOF
HENH HENH...
IT WON'T TURN BACK!
WOOM

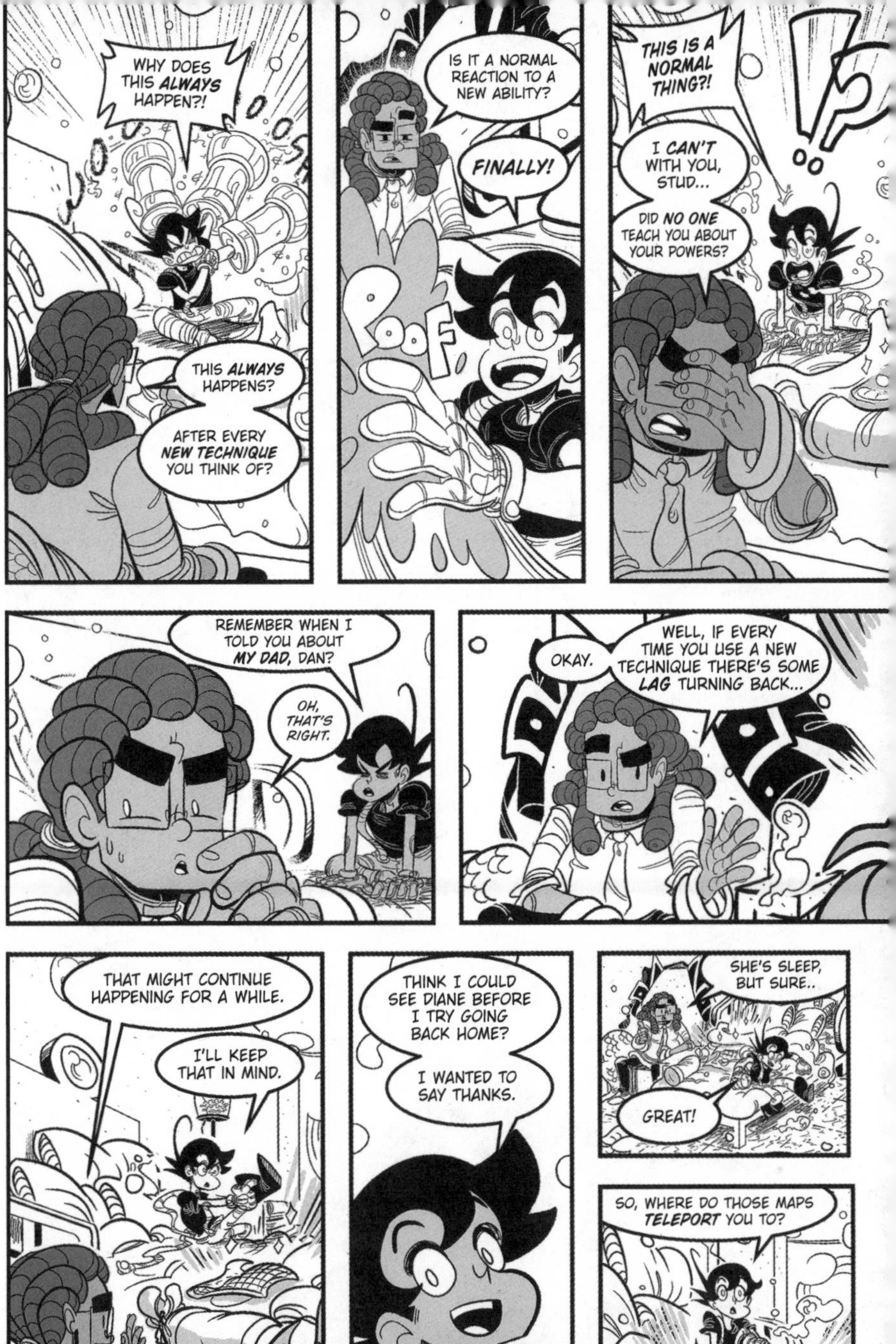
WHY DOES THIS ALWAYS HAPPEN?!
THIS ALWAYS HAPPENS?
AFTER EVERY NEW TECHNIQUE YOU THINK OF?
IS IT A NORMAL REACTION TO A NEW ABILITY?
FINALLY!
POOF
THIS IS A NORMAL THING?!
!?
I CAN'T WITH YOU, STUD...
DID NO ONE TEACH YOU ABOUT YOUR POWERS?
REMEMBER WHEN I TOLD YOU ABOUT MY DAD, DAN?
OH, THAT'S RIGHT.
OKAY.
WELL, IF EVERY TIME YOU USE A NEW TECHNIQUE THERE'S SOME LAG TURNING BACK...
THAT MIGHT CONTINUE HAPPENING FOR A WHILE.
I'LL KEEP THAT IN MIND.
THINK I COULD SEE DIANE BEFORE I TRY GOING BACK HOME?
I WANTED TO SAY THANKS.
SHE'S SLEEP, BUT SURE..
GREAT!
SO, WHERE DO THOSE MAPS TELEPORT YOU TO?

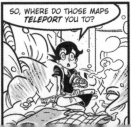

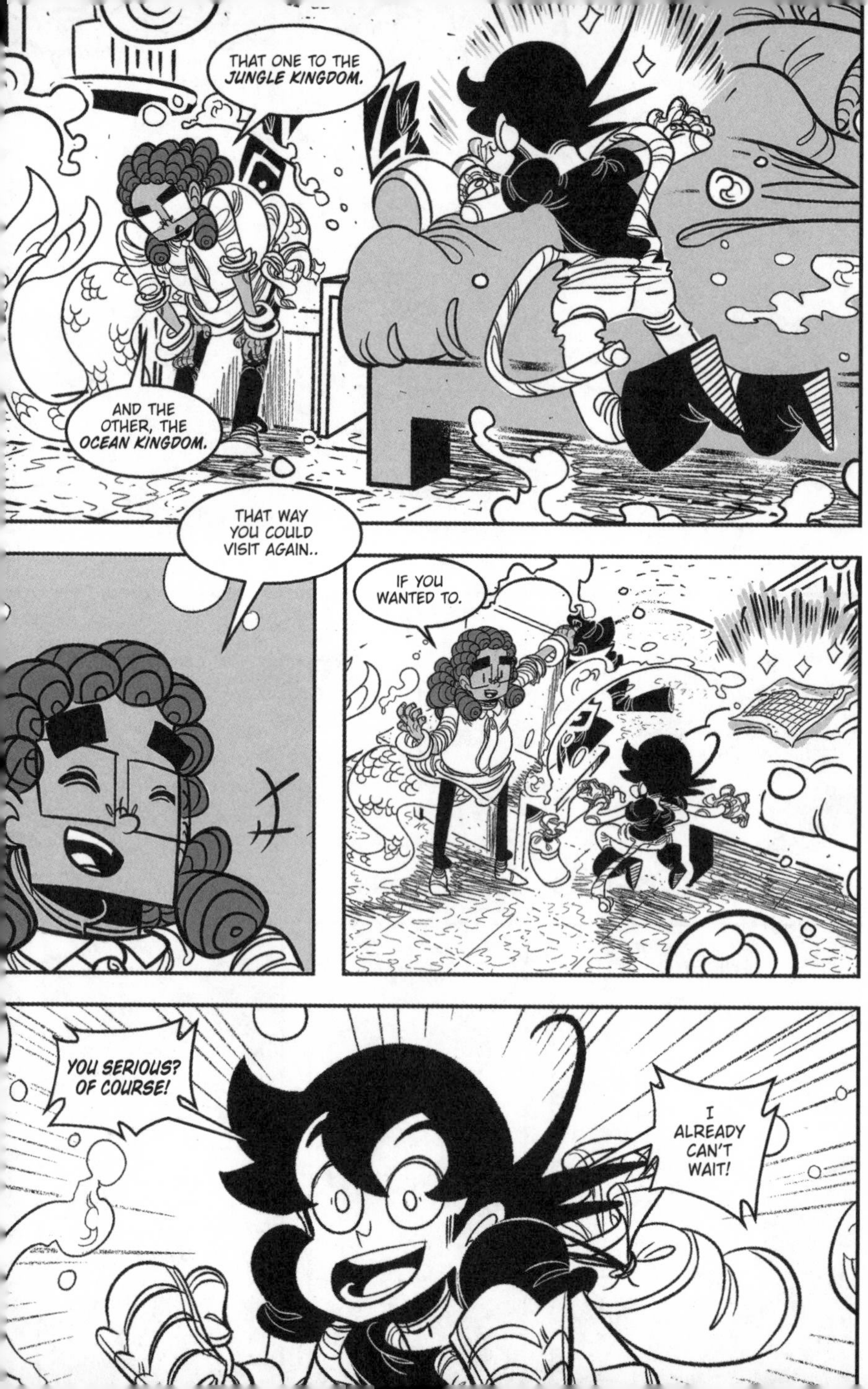
THAT ONE TO THE *JUNGLE KINGDOM.*
AND THE OTHER, THE *OCEAN KINGDOM.*
THAT WAY YOU COULD VISIT AGAIN..
IF YOU WANTED TO.
YOU SERIOUS? OF COURSE!
I ALREADY CAN'T WAIT!

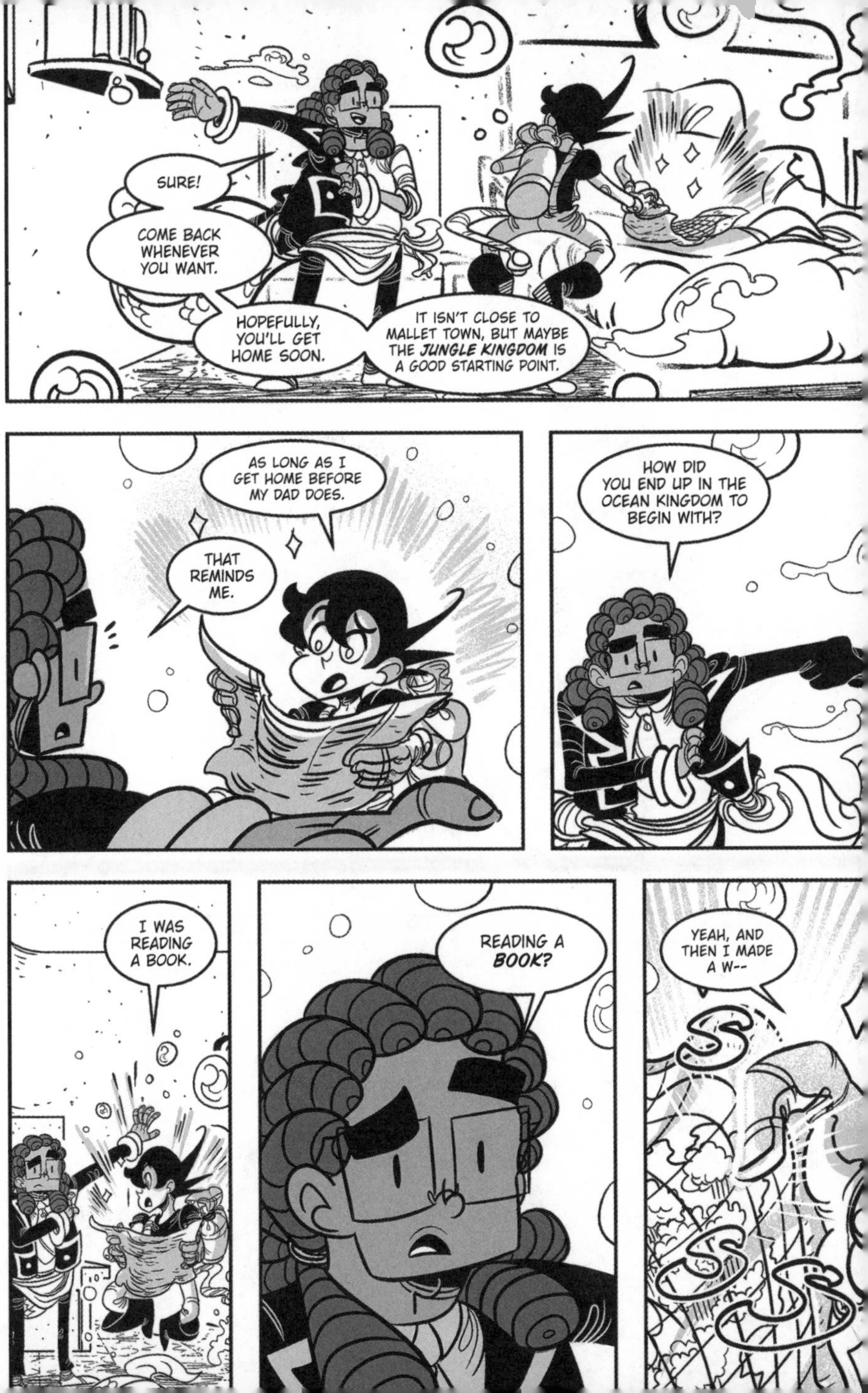
SURE!
COME BACK WHENEVER YOU WANT.
HOPEFULLY, YOU'LL GET HOME SOON.
IT ISN'T CLOSE TO MALLET TOWN, BUT MAYBE THE *JUNGLE KINGDOM* IS A GOOD STARTING POINT.
AS LONG AS I GET HOME BEFORE MY DAD DOES.
THAT REMINDS ME.
HOW DID YOU END UP IN THE OCEAN KINGDOM TO BEGIN WITH?
I WAS READING A BOOK.
READING A *BOOK?*
YEAH, AND THEN I MADE A W--

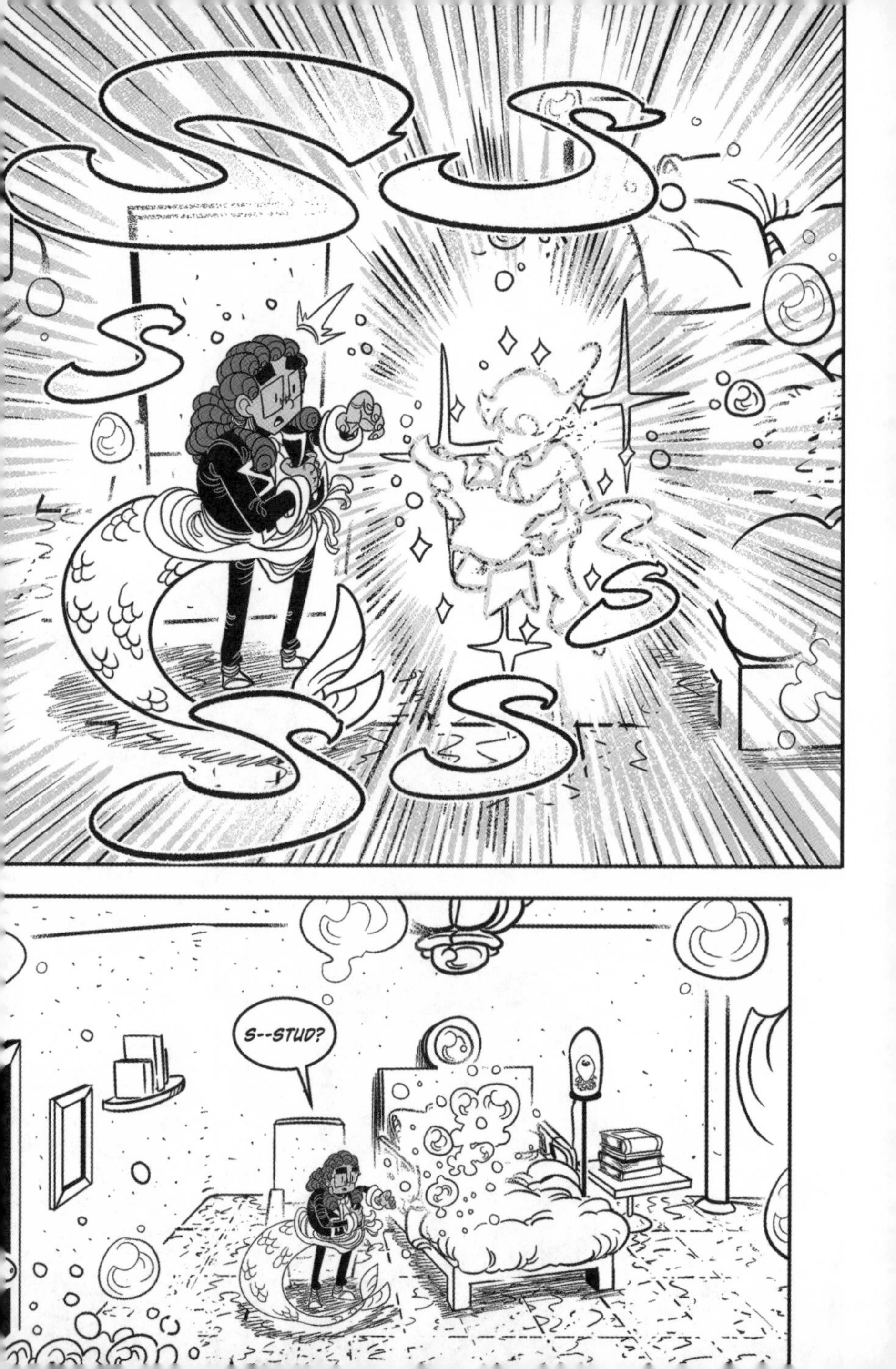
SSSSSS
S--STUD?

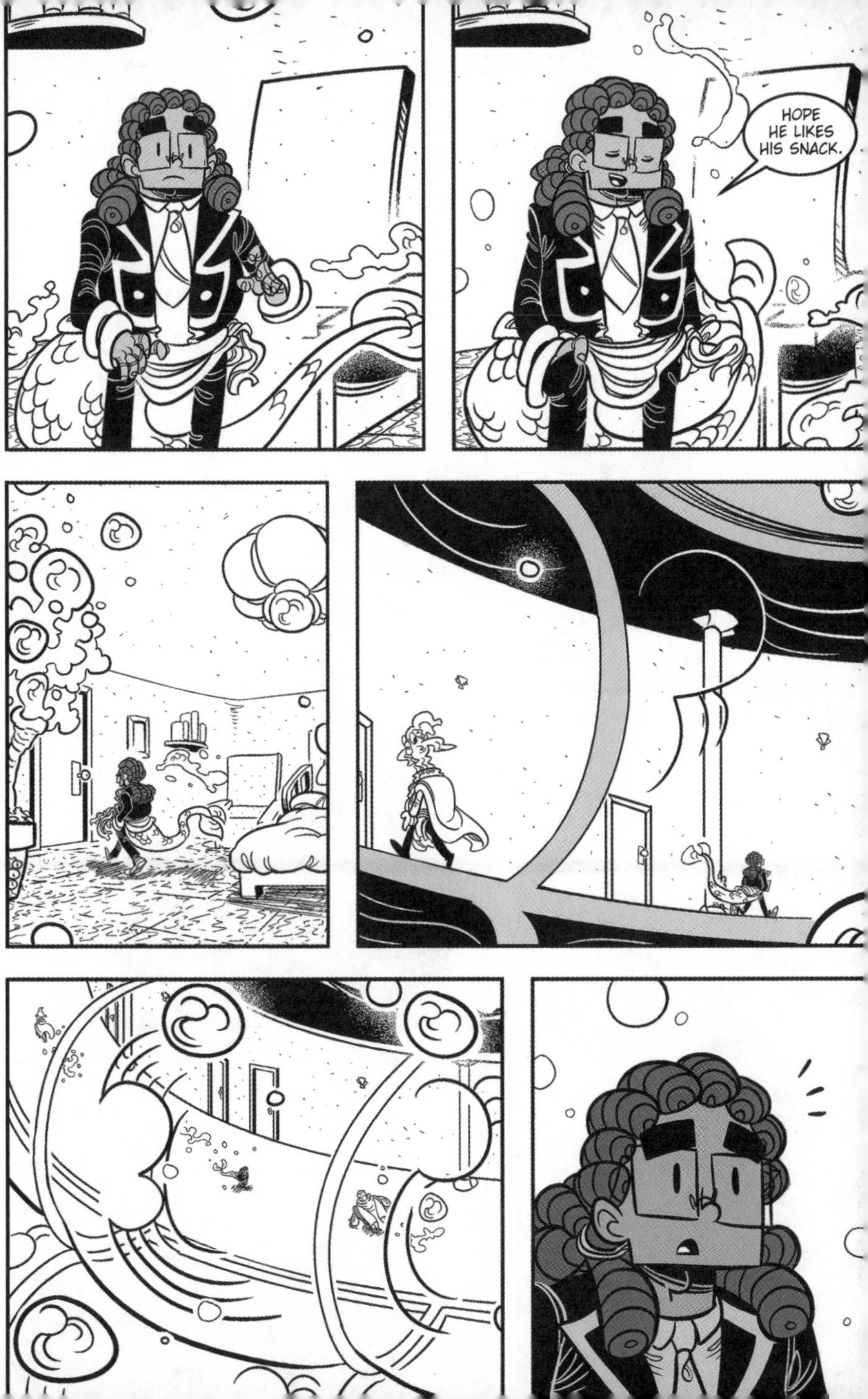
HOPE HE LIKES HIS SNACK.

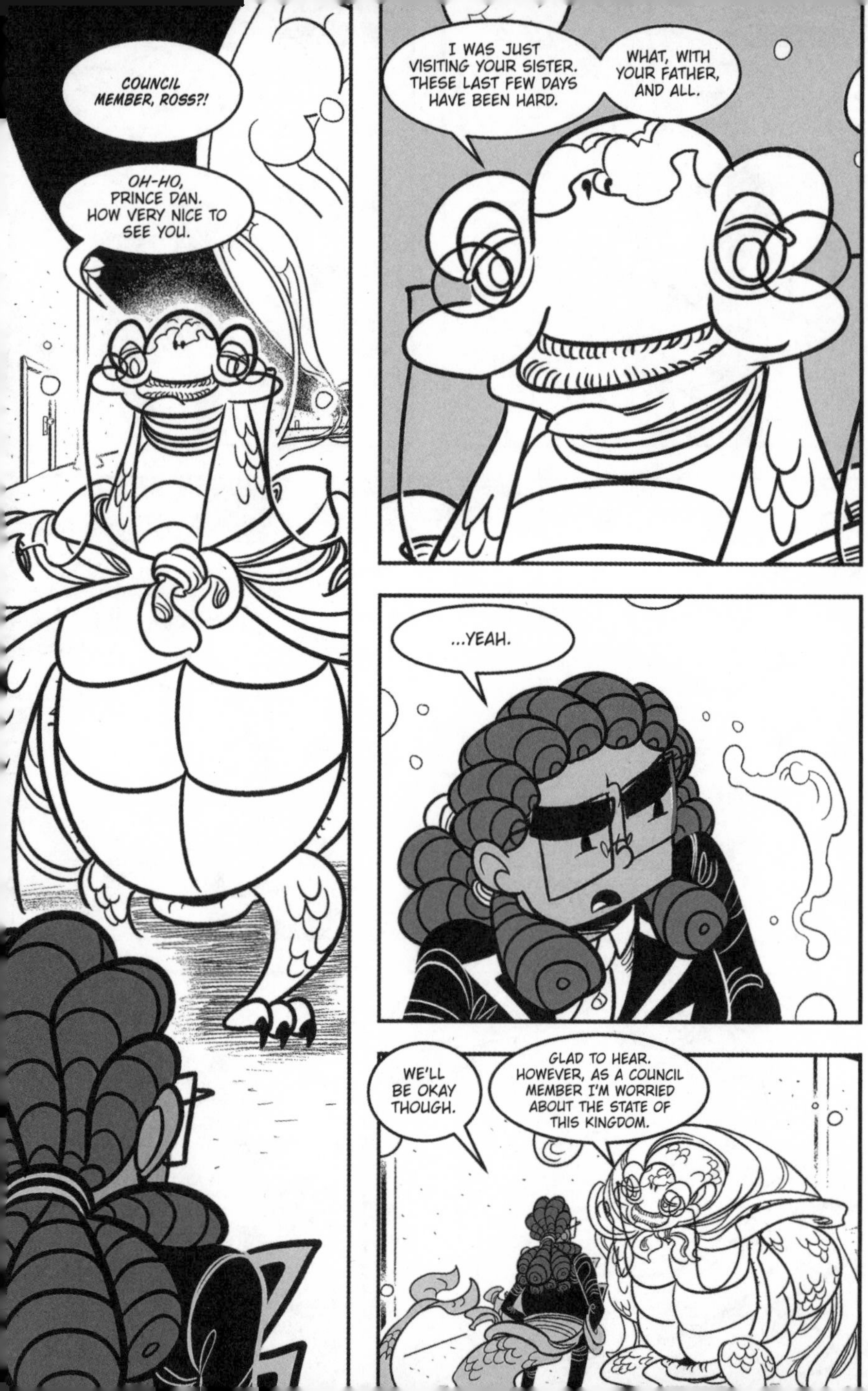
COUNCIL MEMBER, ROSS?!
OH-HO, PRINCE DAN. HOW VERY NICE TO SEE YOU.
I WAS JUST VISITING YOUR SISTER. THESE LAST FEW DAYS HAVE BEEN HARD.
WHAT, WITH YOUR FATHER, AND ALL.
...YEAH.
WE'LL BE OKAY THOUGH.
GLAD TO HEAR. HOWEVER, AS A COUNCIL MEMBER I'M WORRIED ABOUT THE STATE OF THIS KINGDOM.

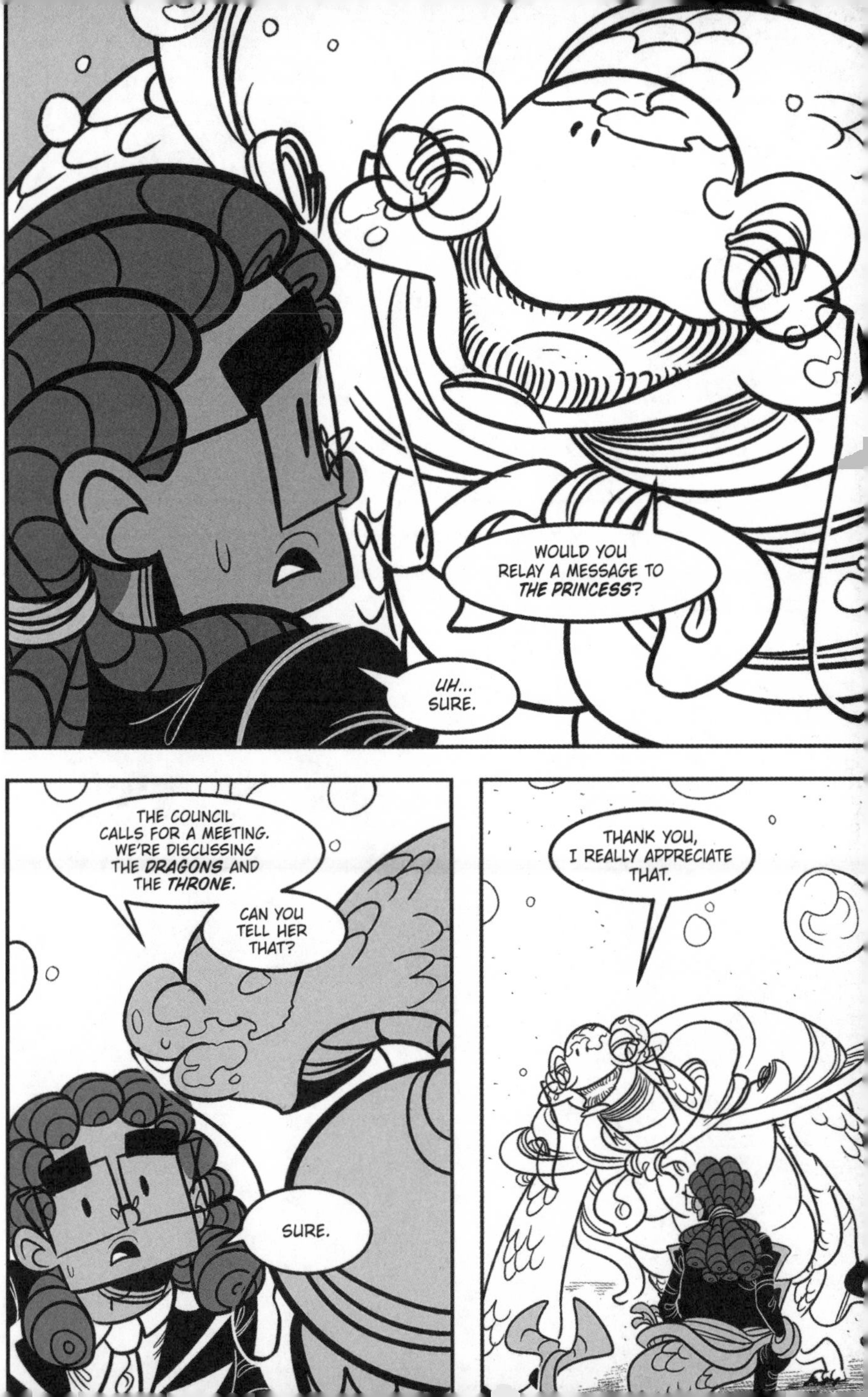
WOULD YOU RELAY A MESSAGE TO *THE PRINCESS*?
UH... SURE.
THE COUNCIL CALLS FOR A MEETING. WE'RE DISCUSSING THE *DRAGONS* AND THE *THRONE*.
CAN YOU TELL HER THAT?
SURE.
THANK YOU, I REALLY APPRECIATE THAT.

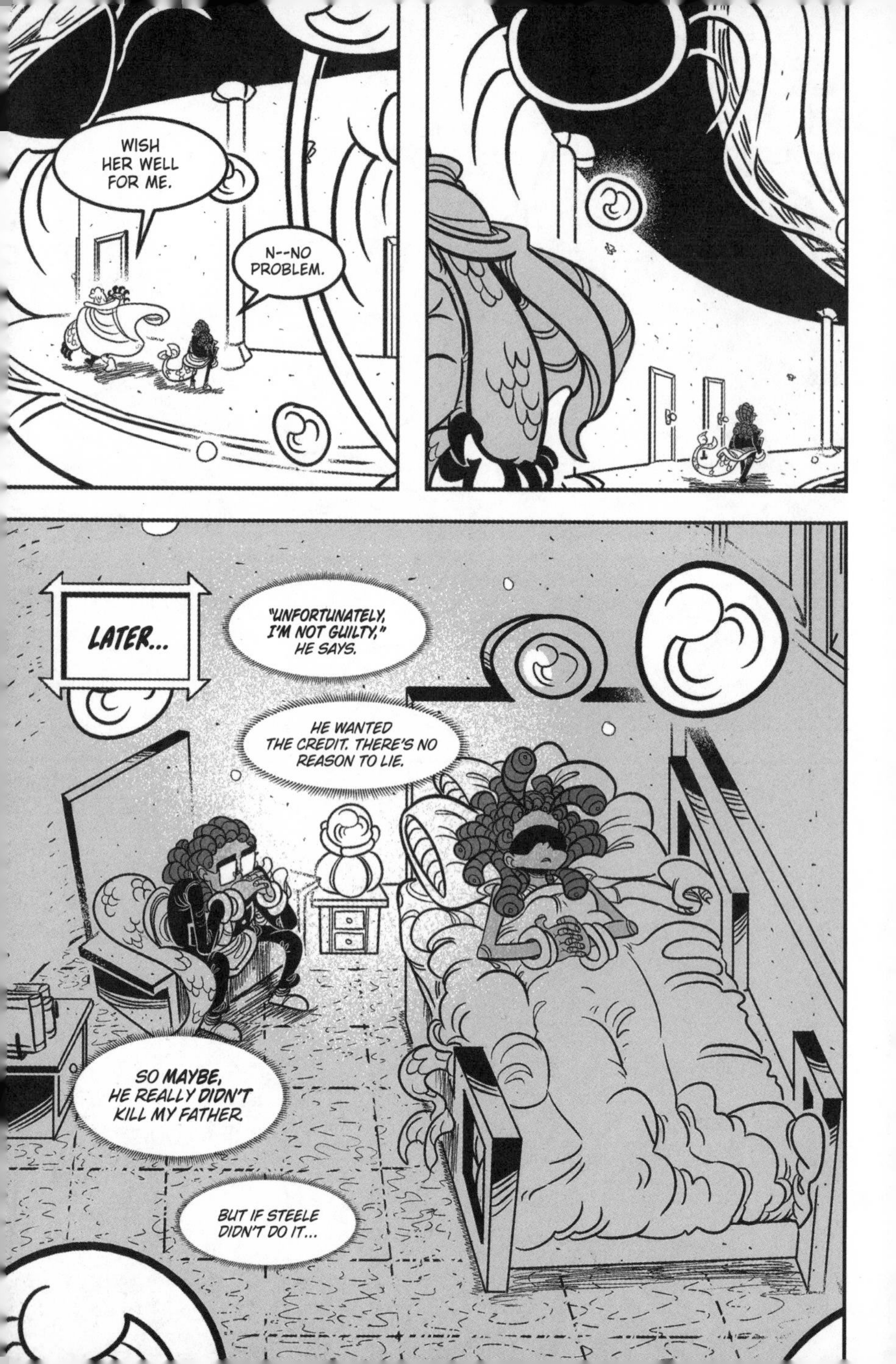
WISH HER WELL FOR ME.
N--NO PROBLEM.
LATER...
"UNFORTUNATELY, I'M NOT GUILTY," HE SAYS.
HE WANTED THE CREDIT. THERE'S NO REASON TO LIE.
SO MAYBE, HE REALLY DIDN'T KILL MY FATHER.
BUT IF STEELE DIDN'T DO IT...

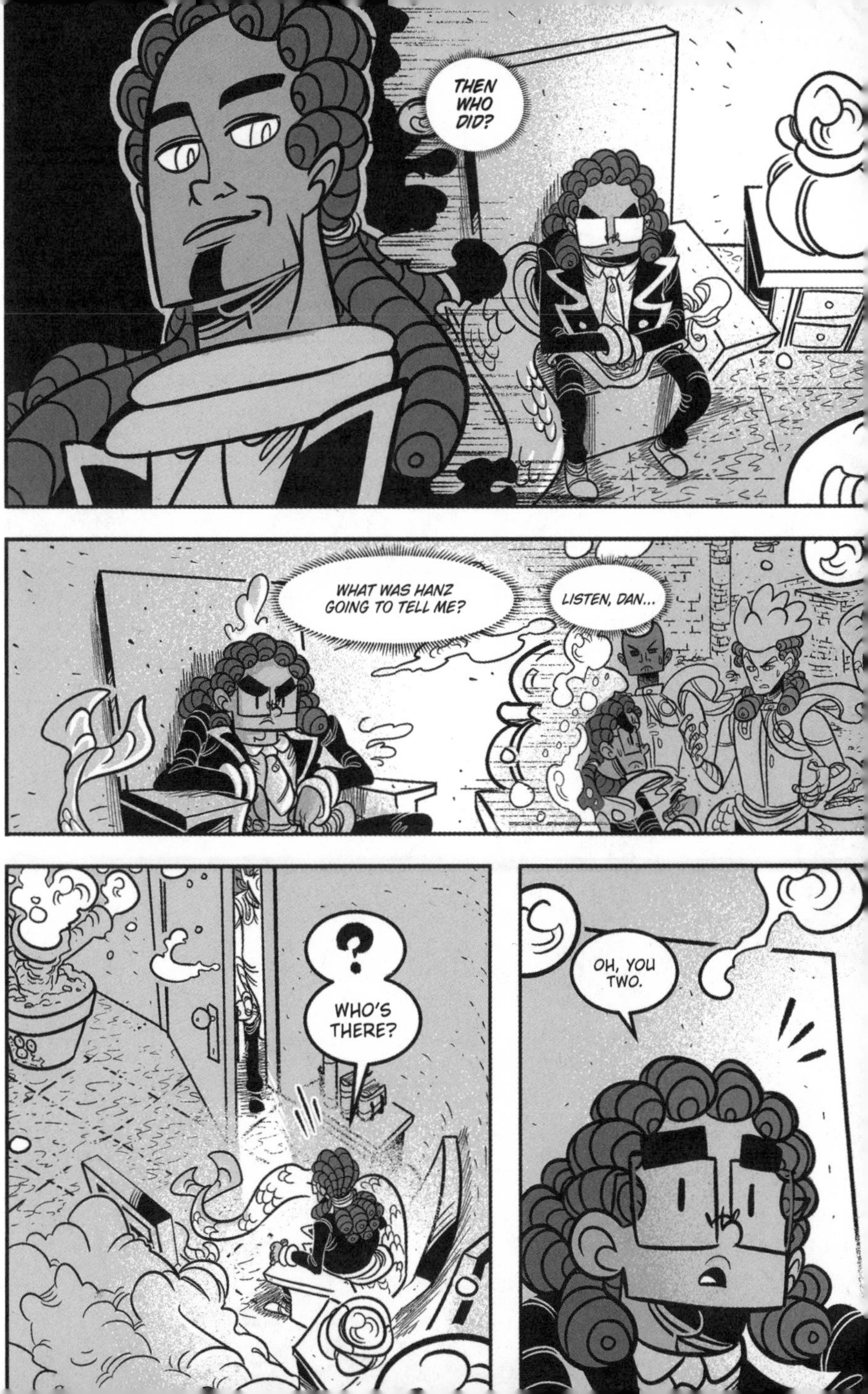
THEN WHO DID?
WHAT WAS HANZ GOING TO TELL ME?
LISTEN, DAN...
?
WHO'S THERE?
OH, YOU TWO.

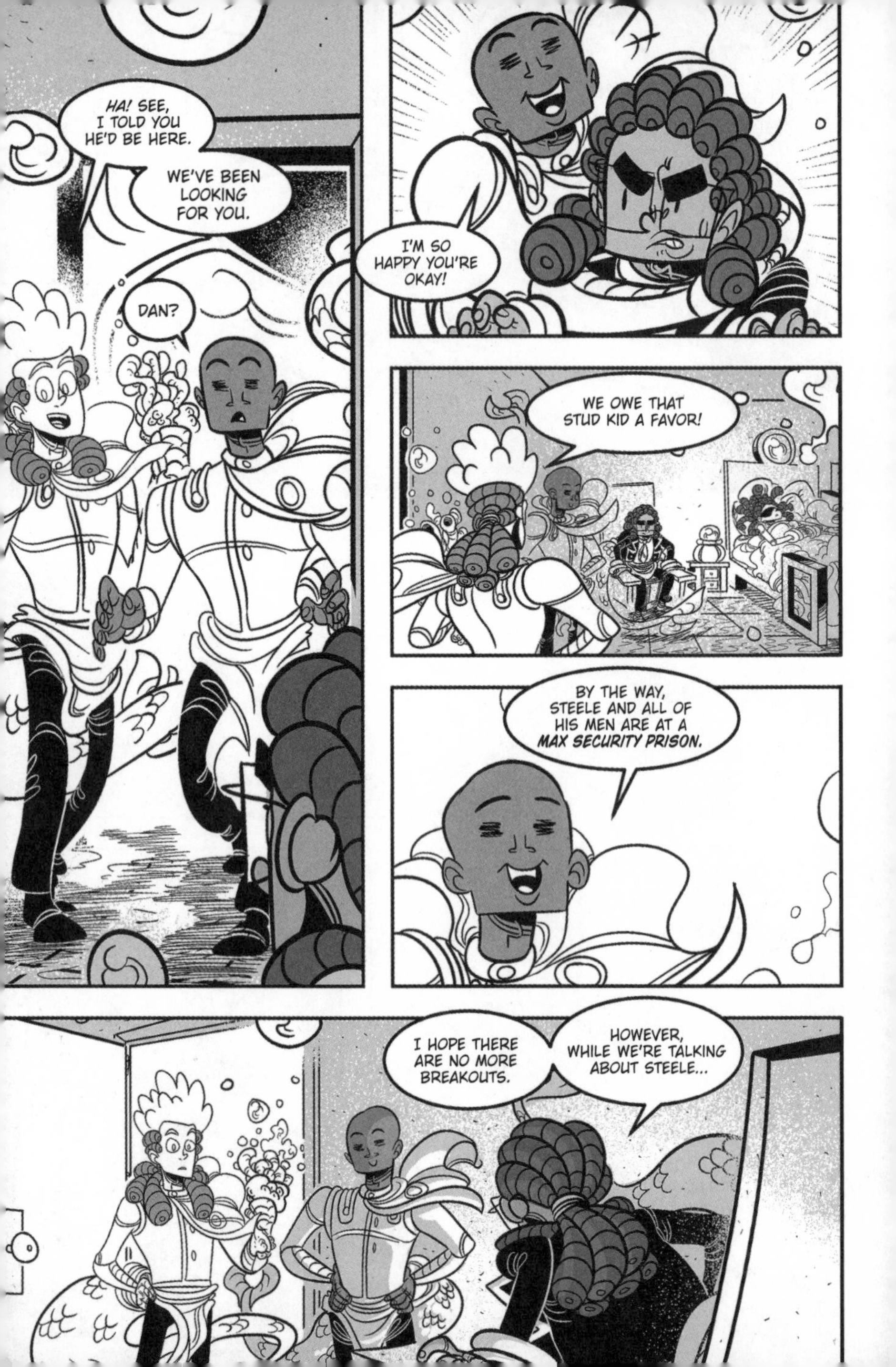
HA! SEE, I TOLD YOU HE'D BE HERE.
WE'VE BEEN LOOKING FOR YOU.
DAN?
I'M SO HAPPY YOU'RE OKAY!
WE OWE THAT STUD KID A FAVOR!
BY THE WAY, STEELE AND ALL OF HIS MEN ARE AT A MAX SECURITY PRISON.
I HOPE THERE ARE NO MORE BREAKOUTS.
HOWEVER, WHILE WE'RE TALKING ABOUT STEELE...

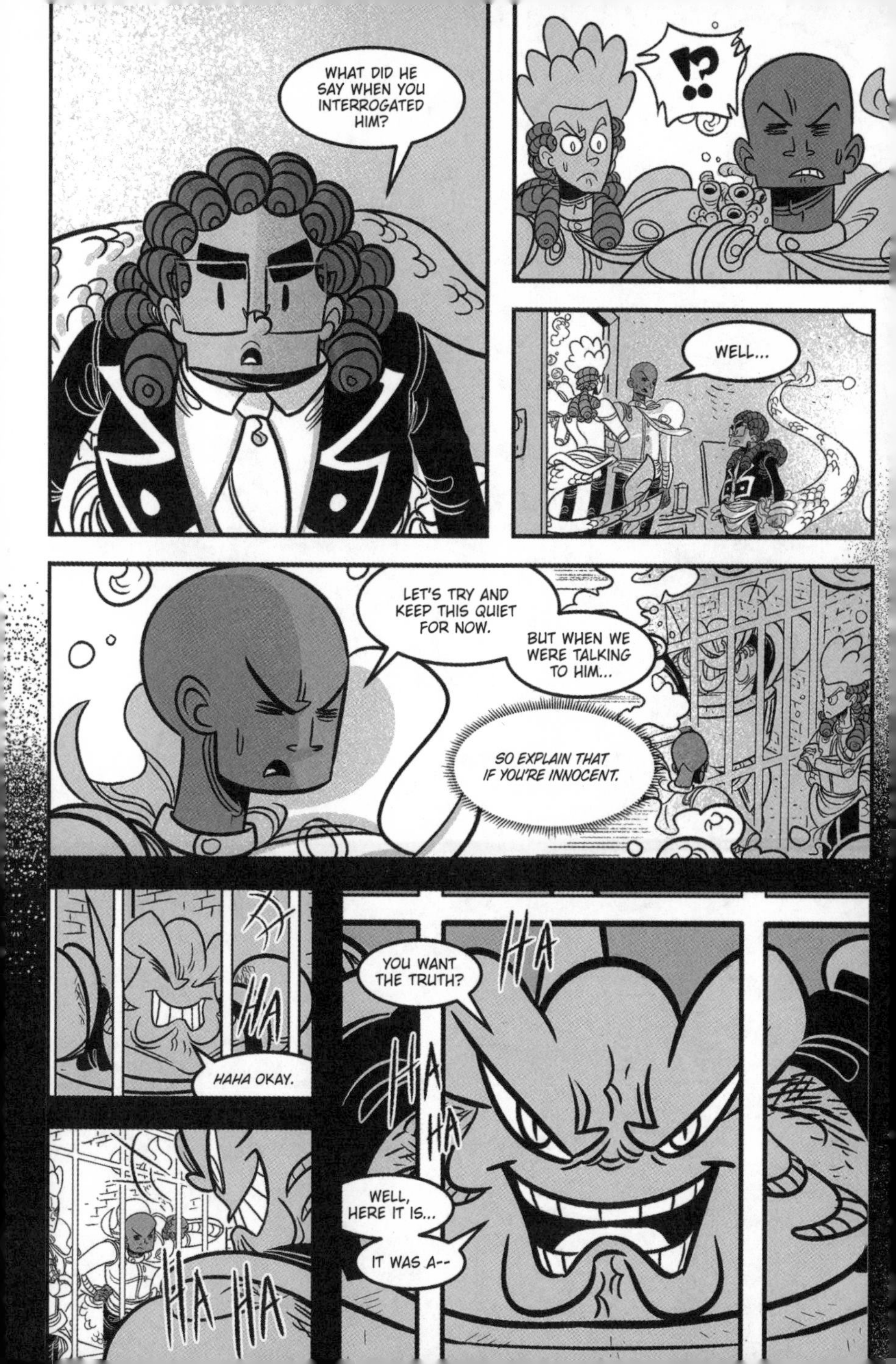

WHAT DID HE SAY WHEN YOU INTERROGATED HIM?
!?
WELL...
LET'S TRY AND KEEP THIS QUIET FOR NOW.
BUT WHEN WE WERE TALKING TO HIM...
SO EXPLAIN THAT IF YOU'RE INNOCENT.
HA
HAHA OKAY.
HA HA
HA
YOU WANT THE TRUTH?
HA
HA
WELL, HERE IT IS...
IT WAS A--

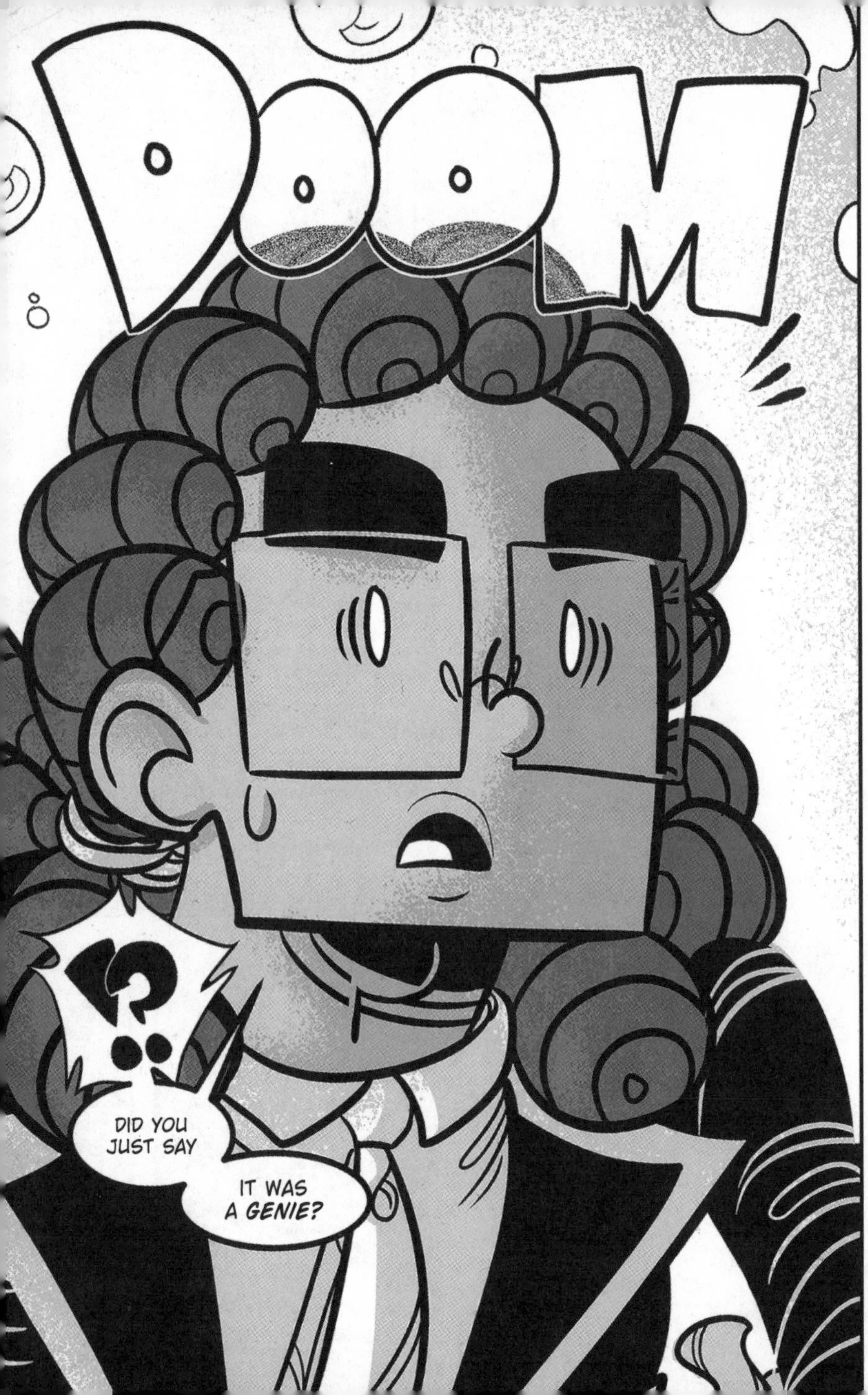
DOOOM!
?!
DID YOU JUST SAY
IT WAS A GENIE?

HAMMER

END OF VOLUME 2

ABOUT THE AUTHOR

JEYODIN

Born in New Orleans, Louisiana, manga artist **JeyOdin**
attended Savannah College of Art and Design in 2010,
where he majored in sequential art. In addition to
Saturday AM, many top publishers have published
this prolific artist, including Antarctic Press,
USA Today, and Oni Press.

ACKNOWLEDGMENTS

FINALLY, THE CONCLUSION TO THE OCEAN
KINGDOM ARC IS IN YOUR HANDS.

THIS STORY FIRST POPPED INTO MY HEAD
AROUND A DECADE AGO WHEN I WAS
DAYDREAMING AT MY CUSTOMER SERVICE JOB.

I'M GLAD TO SEE IT'S FINALLY PUBLISHED
AROUND THE WORLD! PRETTY SURREAL
MOMENT FOR ME.

THIS DREAM WOULD'VE NEVER COME TRUE IF I
HADN'T MET MY AMAZING, SUPPORTIVE WIFE,
SO THANK YOU BABY! ;3

LASTLY, I WANT TO THANK YOU ALL FOR YOUR
CONTINUED SUPPORT.

I CAN'T WAIT TO SHOW YOU MORE OF THAT
EPIC DAYDREAM!

—JeyOdin

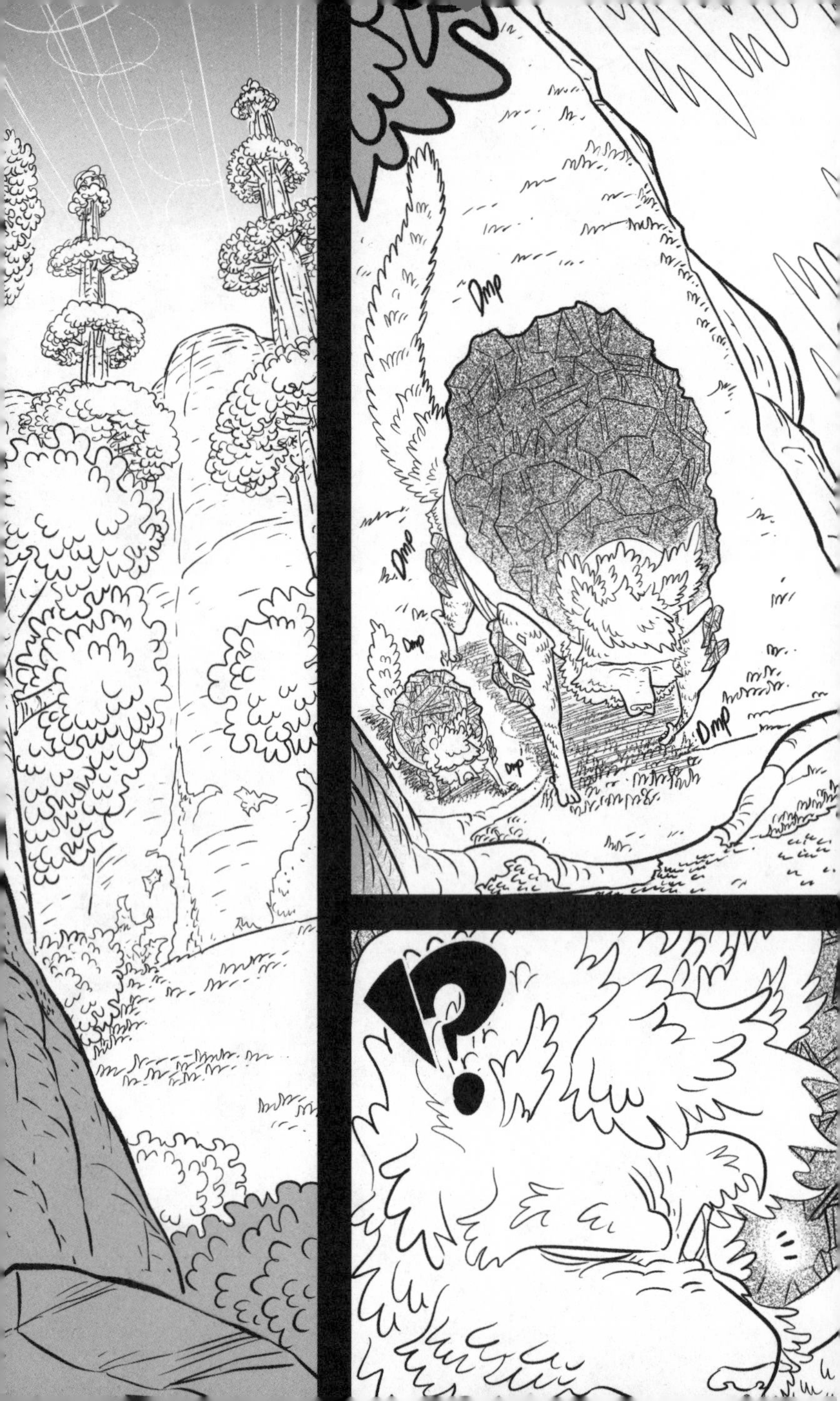
Dmp
Dmp
Dmp
Dmp
Dmp
!?

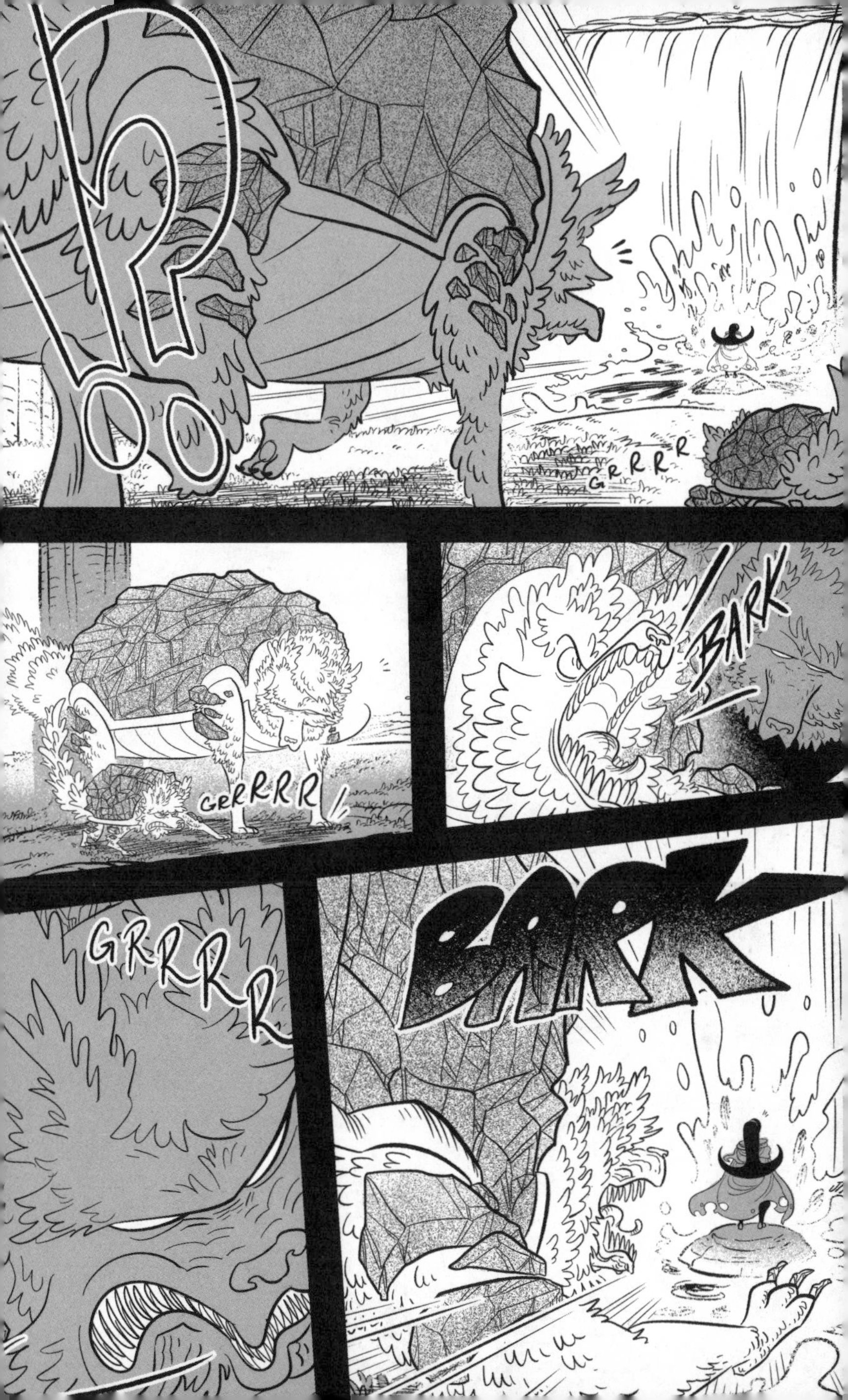
!?
GRRRR
GRRRRR
BARK
GRRRRR
BARK

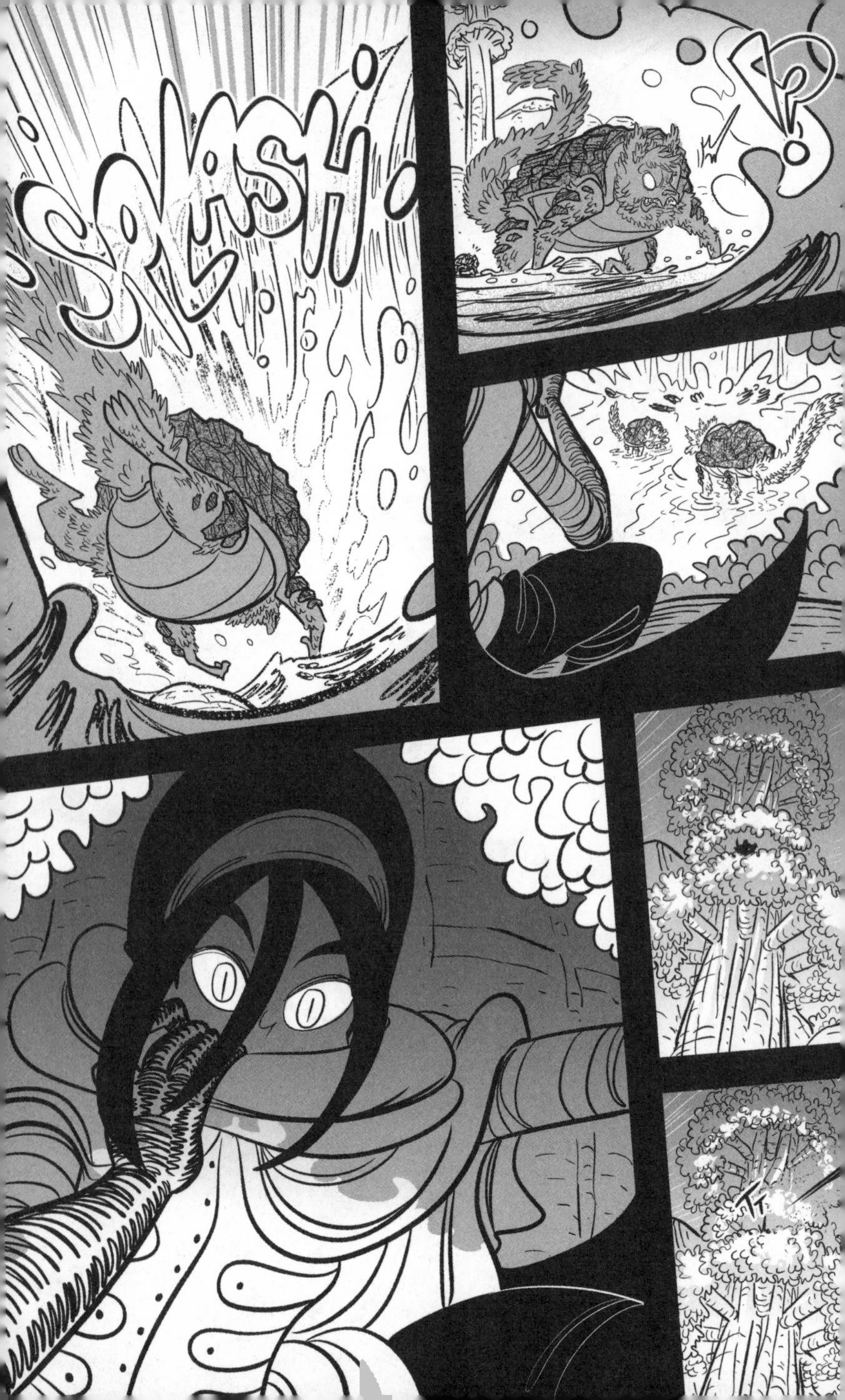
SPLASH!
!?

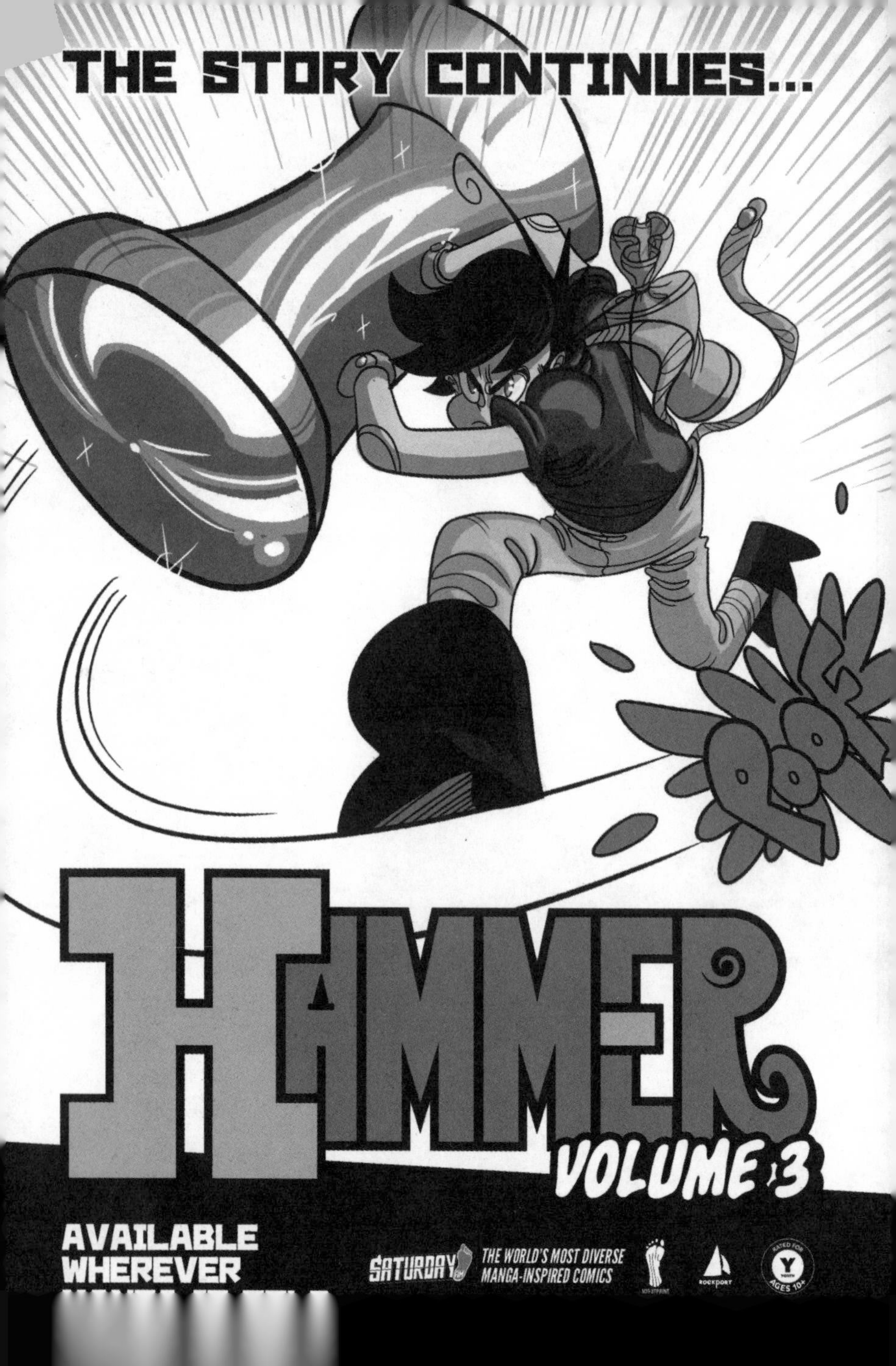
THE STORY CONTINUES...
HAMMER
VOLUME 3
AVAILABLE
WHEREVER
SATURDAY
THE WORLD'S MOST DIVERSE
MANGA-INSPIRED COMICS
ROCKPORT
RATED FOR
AGES 10+

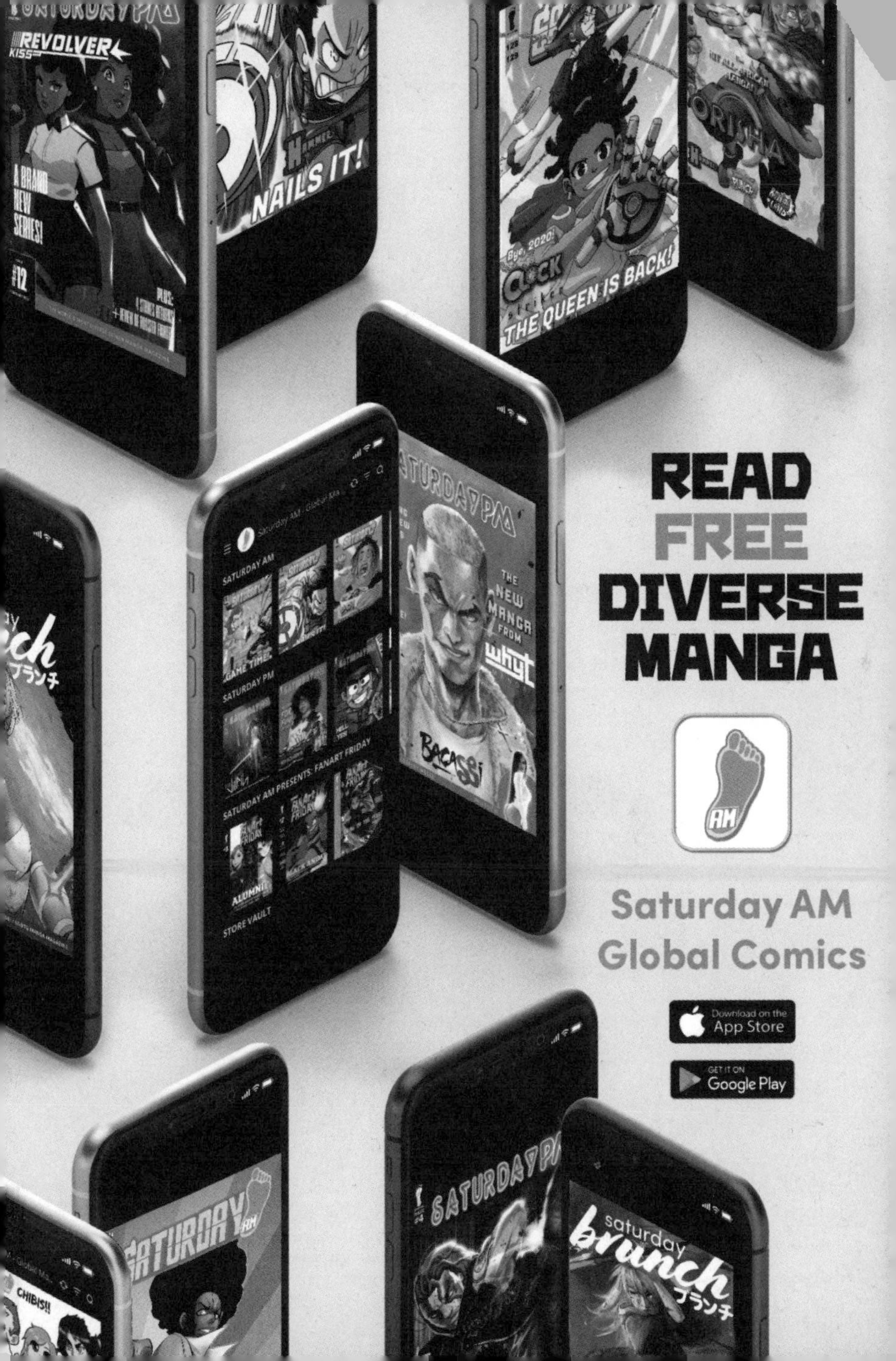
READ
FREE
DIVERSE
MANGA
Saturday AM
Global Comics
Download on the App Store
GET IT ON Google Play

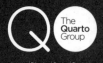

Brimming with creative inspiration, how-to projects, and useful information to enrich your everyday life, quarto.com is a favorite destination for those pursuing their interests and passions.

First published in 2023 by Rockport Publishers,
an imprint of The Quarto Group,
100 Cummings Center, Suite 265-D, Beverly, MA 01915, USA.
T (978) 282-9590 F (978) 283-2742 Quarto.com

10 9 8 7 6 5 4 3 2 1

ISBN: 978-0-7603-7692-8
Digital edition published in 2023
eISBN: 978-0-7603-8178-6

Library of Congress Cataloging-in-Publication Data is available.

Art and story by: Jonathan Mullins
Lettering: Evan Hayden and Mitch Proctor
Book Design: Mitch Proctor
Editors: Frederick L. Jones, Peter Doney and Austin Harvey

Printed in USA

RATED FOR Y YOUTH AGES 10+

Hammer, Volume 2 is rated Y for Youth and is recommended for ages 10 and up. It contains mild profanity and some violent action scenes.